DISCOURSES
on
Architecture

DISCOURSES

on

Architecture

Translated from the French of
EUGÈNE EMMANUEL VIOLLET-LE-DUC
By
BENJAMIN BUCKNALL
Architect

*Illustrated By Thirty-Seven Steel Engravings
And Two Hundred Woodcuts*

Vol. II

GROVE PRESS, INC.   NEW YORK

First American Edition Published 1889
By Ticknor And Company, Boston

Grove Press Edition Published 1959

LIBRARY OF CONGRESS CATALOG CARD NUMBER: 59-6254

Grove Press Books and Evergreen Books
are published by Barney Rosset at Grove Press, Inc.
64 University Place   New York 3, N.Y.

Foreign Distributors:
In Great Britain: John Calder Ltd., 17 Sackville St., London, W. 1
In Canada: McClelland & Stewart Ltd., 25 Hollinger Road, Toronto 16

MANUFACTURED IN THE UNITED STATES OF AMERICA

TABLE OF CONTENTS.

LIST OF PLATES.

LIST OF PLATES.

LECTURE XI.

MASONRY.

IN the times of Classical Antiquity, as also during the Middle Ages, there was perhaps no product of human intelligence which more clearly indicated the social condition and aptitudes of a people than their method of building. Nothing but the confusion of ideas existing in modern times, and a long succession of false teaching, could have brought about the chaotic state of things and the inconsistencies presented by our buildings of the present day. It is none the less certain that from this transitional phase there will be evolved architectural methods proper to our age and social condition. It should be the endeavour of all earnest and impartial persons to put an end to this chaos.

If we will consent to regard the works of the past as belonging to the past,—as steps by which we must pass if we would attain to the knowledge of what is appropriate to our own social condition; if we proceed by way of analysis, and not by that of unreflecting imitation; if amid the accumulated remains of former ages we search for methods that are applicable, and if we know how to determine in what respects they are applicable; in short, if, abandoning effete doctrinal traditions, we rely on our own observation, we shall have opened the way and shall ourselves be able to pursue it.

Subjected to Roman domination, and having almost become Romans,—at least as regards a considerable part of the territory that now constitutes France,—we adopted the Roman methods of building. Restored to independence, and invaded by populations whose genius was of an order quite different from that of the Romans, we wavered for several centuries indeterminately between very diverse modes of building. At the end of the eleventh century and the beginning of the twelfth, we went to the East for models, and succeeded in producing a kind of Romano-Greek Renaissance, which was not devoid of merit, but which, like all other art revivals, could not run a long career. At the close of the twelfth century we observe a very energetic artistic movement, originating with ourselves, and which very soon developed a fruitful germ. That age was wanting in all that we now possess; it had not our wealth of means, our variety of materials, our iron and manufactures. This remarkable movement, based on a true perception of the requirements of modern society, took a wrong direction. Occurring six centuries too soon, it exhausted itself in futile operations with a stubborn or inadequate material; so that, in consequence of our mobile disposition, we came to regard it as a mistake, and sought an art at second-hand,—a mixture of various traditions,—to produce from it what we call the Renaissance Architecture. Form was then the leading consideration; principles were no longer regarded, and structural system there was none. Then supervened that colourless period which began in the seventeenth century and ended in chaos.

This is, in brief, the history of Architecture among us, considered solely from the structural point of view,—that is to say, in reference to the judicious employment of material. And that is not Architecture which does not regard the material in prescribing a mode of building and the form which results from it; and we could not cite a single classic Greek or Roman edifice that is not erected in accordance with this principle.

What then are the materials which the architect has had at his disposal at all times, and which he has now at command? Earth massed and moulded, pise, unburned, and, subsequently, burned brick; then in lieu of primitive forms of pise, concretes or agglomerations of gravel, made with the help of mortar; stone, —granite, marble, basalt, limestone, etc.; wood and metals. Nothing appears at first easier than to make use of these materials; but when we have to build something other than a mud cabin or a hut of branches,—when we have to employ these materials simultaneously, to give each its appropriate form and place, and so as not to make a too lavish or too niggardly use of them, to have a thorough acquaintance with their nature and duration, and to secure for them those conditions which will be most favourable to their preservation,—difficulties present themselves on every side.

In fact, a material that is good in one set of conditions is bad in another; this kind of material will destroy that; one kind is unfitted for such or such a function. Wood enclosed,— excluded from the air,—decays; iron let into stone-work oxidises, decomposes, and bursts the stone; certain limes produce salts in quantity which destroy the stone they are intended to unite. Experience gradually makes the builders acquainted with innumerable phenomena which occur in every structure; and it is evident that the more complicated the structure is,—that is, the more varied are its component materials,—the more numerous these phenomena become. While the Egyptians, in erecting a temple with blocks of limestone, placed in juxta-position, had but few observations to make on the effects displayed in their structure, the architect who builds a house in Paris, in which stone, brick, mortar, wood, wrought and cast iron, lead, zinc, slate, and plaster are simultaneously employed, must necessarily accumulate a considerable number of practical observations. It is singular that there should be a desire to imitate with this considerable variety of materials edifices that were built with one only. This shows a want of rational reflection on which I need not dwell. And what is perhaps still more strange is the attempt to imitate with inferior materials constructions resulting from the use of massive materials: for example, to erect columns built up with thin courses and to surmount them with jointed lintels, so as to simulate monoliths; or, reversing the operation, to construct, with solid blocks of stone, buildings whose appearance would indicate masses of rubble-work covered with stone facings.

We shall devote this lecture to the examination of questions of construction relating solely to worked stone and walling. There are only three general principles that are applicable to structures of jointed stone and walling: 1*st*, The principle of simple stability in the superposition of materials resulting in vertical pressures; 2*d*, The principle of agglomeration producing concrete masses and originating with hypogæa (underground structures); 3*d*, The principle of equilibrium obtained by forces acting in contrary directions. The Egyptians and the Greeks employed scarcely any other structure than that of jointed stone-work in accordance with the first principle; the Romans adopted the second, and the Western nations, from the twelfth to the sixteenth century, the third. If, as occasionally happens, two of these principles were simultaneously applied, the union is always apparent; and a bastard product is the result, which, considered from the point of view of art, never has the frank expression which we like to find in every architectural work.

In fact, all architecture proceeds from structure, and the first condition at which it should aim is to make the outward form accord with that structure. If therefore it is faithful to the principles just laid down, and at the same time adopts two of them, it will betray its diversity of origin and transgress the first law, which is unity. If, while adopting two, or even three, principles of structure, it seeks unity of form, it will be untrue to two of those principles at least, if not to all three. It must be acknowledged that it is the art of contravening these principles which has for a long while been taught us, when we have been taught anything.

The Asiatic nations employed simultaneously the system of concrete masonry and that of stability obtained by superposition. Against masses of unburnt or burnt bricks, or even earth, they put facings of stone, as if to enclose these slightly consistent cores in cases. In India (for example), in China, and in the kingdom of Siam, they adopted rubble or brick masonry, united by mortar and covered with stuccos. We find the same principle of structure in Mexico; and the Pyramids of Egypt themselves are piles of enormous stones united by mortar, against which were placed regular courses, which again were originally coated with painted stucco covering their projecting angles. It would therefore appear that in times the most remote the art of masonry employed mortar as a necessary agent. But how was it that, from a very high antiquity, the East, whence all the arts are derived, proceeded in masonry by the method of agglomeration, in preference to the principle which appears the simplest and most natural—that of superposition?

The great Aryan white race, which in the earliest times spread from the northern plateaux of India over the lower and warmer lands, does not appear to have adopted any kind of structure other than timber-framing; since wherever we find traces of that race, the wooden structure prevails. Having invaded Turanian races which occupied the Indian continent, and which appear to have been settled from the remotest times in the extreme East and beyond the Caspian Sea westward, those white races were soon led to adopt the modes of building employed by the conquered races : and it must be observed that the yellow races have a special aptitude for earth-work, and consequently for masonry-work proceeding by agglomeration. Facts oblige us to conclude that the different races which constitute mankind are endowed with diverse aptitudes. Some, whose home is found on elevated plateaux covered with forests, take timber as the material suitable for erecting their houses and temples. Others, settled amid immense marshy plains, build with mud and reeds. Others again, such as the black races who occupied Upper Egypt, and who are now thrust back into Sennar, excavated their dwellings on the slopes of calcareous hills. From the first invasions of white among yellow races, there must frequently have resulted in the buildings erected a strange mixture of traditions imported by the conquerors with the customs that had taken root among the conquered. This explains the singular character of the most ancient Indian buildings, where we see forms derived from timber-work rendered by means of rubble masonry coated with stucco, or even hewn in the tufa or the rock. This explains why in Egypt buildings constructed of large superposed stones reproduce a structure whose origin is certainly due to buildings of mud and reeds. Without further enlarging on these origins, we will only remark that in the ancient East there does not exist a principle of masonry building, but rather a mingling of very various methods. To us of the West, who make a point of investigating the rationale of everything, these buildings appear to have no applicable principle, methodically pursued and fruitful in deductions. The Greeks were the first to reduce this chaos to order. Disregarding the methods of building employed by the Assyrians or by the Medes,—abandoning the imitation of timber-work in stone practised by certain nations of Asia Minor, they frankly and without any compromise adopted the first of the principles we expressed above,—that of simple stability obtained by the superposition of shaped materials. To bring to light a very simple principle amid a confusion of principles, and to have the courage to apply it uncompromisingly, is a proof of very special genius, such as is but rarely met with in the history of man. In accomplishing this the Greeks showed with what exceptional aptitudes they were endowed; they rendered an immense service to the West, teaching it to employ reasoning in matters of art. In a word, Architecture became an art in their hands, whereas throughout the whole East it was only a craft more or less skilfully practised. Sustained by this example, we shall not cease to repeat that there is no art without the intervention of reasoning. The Greeks were the first to establish and apply this law; if we lose sight of it we take a step downwards, and from being artists as the Greeks made us we fall back into the condition of slaves working for capricious masters.

We can well understand how and why the Greeks could not adopt the principle of masonry erected with the aid of mortar,—of adhesive matter. For the execution of pise or even of rubble-work only labourers are needed. The Greeks had conceived too lofty an idea of architecture to be willing to develop its glories by the aid of such rude means; and we see that much later on,—in the Greco-Roman districts of Syria, near Antioch and Aleppo,—the humblest buildings are erected with that hewn stone-work which excludes rubble masonry and the employment of gangs of labourers everywhere organised by the Romans. Moreover, while it is possible to produce a false appearance by means of constructions following the system of agglomeration, it is difficult to do so when we only employ the method of hewn stone-work without mortar. The laws of statics do not permit it. In this latter case every stone must have a determinate function.

When the Grēeks had to erect a *cella* behind a portico, for example, they formed a kind of frame-work of stone which they filled in with blocks, cut parallel only on the two exposed faces fitted by means of a bevel so as to avoid as much as possible the labour of squaring the stones. Certain limestones and marbles fracture in rhombohedrons rather than in parallelopipeds; by

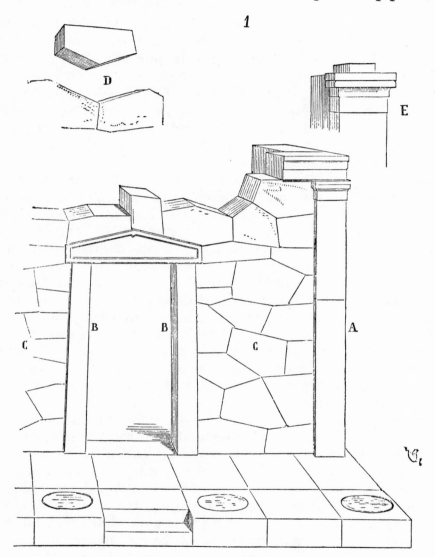

FIG. 1.—Early Greek Masonry.

this means they were enabled to utilise much material which they must have rejected if they had wished to make walling of level courses.

Figure 1 will explain what we are describing. The plan of the *cella* having been marked out, and the foundations laid, the corner antæ A were set up; then the door jambs B, care being taken to slightly incline the latter towards each other, so as thereby to diminish the bearing of the lintel, and to give the weights a direction tending to the middle of the wall. The intervening spaces C were then filled in by means of blocks selected so as to obviate the trouble of squaring them. In fact this method of stone-work, called Cyclopean, seldom presents more than one angle to be fitted: taking this angle with a bevel, a stone was sought for, which offered a projecting angle corresponding with the interior angle measured with the bevel, as shown in the detail D. This irregular masonry was maintained by the antæ and by the jambs of the door; especially as the jointed stones of these antæ and jambs frequently had tenons which fitted into mortices sunk in the incumbent blocks as shown in detail E. This construction, as compared with that of the buildings of Nineveh, *e.g.*, shows an advance, or rather the intervention of a course of reasoning which is absent in the Assyrian buildings: for the latter present only masses of unburnt brickwork cased with slabs of alabaster or limestone, as a sort of decorative wainscoting. In primitive Greek architecture the masonry assumes a function; it lives, so to speak, and ceases to be an inert mass. But in their buildings of early date, the Greeks plainly showed whence they derived the method of construction; they erected in stone, by a process of reasoning, buildings such as were originally made of timber; their merit however was the not having imitated in calcareous materials forms borrowed from timber-work, as did the Lycians and most of the peoples who inhabited the coasts of Asia Minor. When the methods of quarrying were improved, the Greeks ceased to employ what is called the Cyclopean order of construction in their masonry; they built in courses, but their genius never led them to become wallers. They were stone-fitters, that is to say, jointers and superposers of stone. The idea of the concretion,—the agglomeration of materials,—was evidently repugnant to them; since we see that very late, even in the fourth and fifth centuries of our era, they could not make up their minds to adopt that mode of building, and that even at this late date they appeared to prefer the lintel to the jointed arch.

It must, moreover, be fully admitted that there is in jointed masonry of the simplest and most natural kind a powerful charm to which the Western races are sensible as if by instinct. To employ large materials appropriately, to shape them according to their function, laying them so as to render the structure stable in appearance, must be reckoned as constituting, since the Greek period, an essential part of the art of building; and, in this respect the architects of the twelfth century, *e.g.*, were nearer to true art than we now are. We shall soon see why.

It is not necessary here to offer to our readers that which they can find everywhere,—the structure of a Greek temple, for instance. Besides, nothing is more simple: blocks as large as could be procured for the columns; architraves in one piece, or composed of two blocks placed side by side, bearing from one column to another, and for the walls, materials of inferior dimensions; square stones forming the two faces—outer and inner. Upon the architraves, lintels in one piece across the width of the portico; upon these lintels, slabs, or in some cases, where stones of sufficient length and strength were wanting, wood. A frieze composed of a series of uprights, with slabs between, and on the uprights, the cornice. A sparing use of large blocks where they were not necessary, and beds and joints invariably coinciding with the members of the architecture. If this displays no great skill, at any rate reason and the eye are satisfied by a structure in perfect harmony with the form.

This method does not admit of any tie resulting from agglutination; sometimes we find a few cramps or dovetails of bronze, or even of wood: stability is secured by superposition, and weight acting vertically on vertical supports.

The Romans, who took whatever came to hand, and recognised every practical principle, did not disdain the Greek system; but they employed it simultaneously with a process of building which was absolutely contrary to it. They employed the concrete system—that of agglomeration obtained by mortars. Forming thick masses composed of pebbles, rough stones, brick or rubble-work united by lime and sand, they sometimes cased these cores with facings of jointed stones, close fitting, without mortar, according to the system in use among the Greeks: or, on the other hand, against concrete walls or masses they set up columns with their entablatures, according to the Greek principle; but the Romans never laid jointed stones in mortar: in making use of the two very different systems, they would seem to have respected them both, and not to have allowed them to be confounded. This fact is remarkable, and tends to give their masonry an altogether special aspect. So little did they confound these two principles, that we even observe them following the purest Greek method in their stone-jointed structure; for example, not continuing the beds of wall-courses into jambs: forming these of monolithic blocks; making antæ and columns of single stones; not bonding the stones of a very thick arch, but forming it of several concentric arches;[1] and extradossing their arch-stones. In a word, the jointed stone structure of the

[1] At the Pont du Gard and the Amphitheatre of Arles, for instance.

Romans is frankly Greek, conforming to the Greek method; which, however, does not hinder them from simultaneously adopting an altogether different method,—that of the concrete structure. It is in this respect that we should imitate the Romans; and this is what we fail to do, both in our domestic and public buildings.

The Romans, with their practical good sense, had clearly perceived that the two systems of building which they adopted might aid each other, but only on the condition of not being mingled. They had perceived that a granite column is incapable of sinking or depression; that such a support placed against a mass of rubble-work must necessarily give rigidity to the mass on the side against which it was placed, for the mass, inevitably contracting through the drying of the mortar, must sink a little, while the column preserved its full height. In many cases this was an expedient useful to the builder. In surrounding the Coliseum with a casing of jointed stone-work, the Roman builder felt that this enormous interior mass of brick and rubble was stayed at its circumference by an absolutely firm and rigid belt incapable of settling, breaking, or cracking. It was a buttressing. While the Greeks erected only small edifices, the Romans built enormous ones, and their mixed method was perfectly adapted to their requirements; since, by always placing on the exterior, or under the arches, in the interior, jointed stone-work without mortar, they made their masonry stay itself, as every rigid resistance tended to throw the pressure towards the centres, and that which was in harmony with good construction was at the same time an adornment.

What cannot be too strongly insisted on is the economy observed by the Romans in their buildings. Thoroughness in the execution is always evident, but never excess of strength. Relying, and with reason, on the excellence of their mortar, they gave their walls and piers the thickness that was necessary, and carefully levelled the rubble-work at various heights, in order to avoid unequal settlement, and to enable the mortar to harden equally. It is an error to suppose that the Romans erected walls of great thickness when they had only to support inconsiderable weights acting vertically; in such cases, on the contrary, it is often surprising to observe how slight was the thickness of the walls compared with their height.[1] In their great vaulted buildings, such as the Pantheon at Rome and the halls of the Thermæ, the section of the piers is rather slight than strong relatively to the weight they carry. It is true that these piers were gene-

[1] In the Basilicas with timber roofs, for instance. Among Gallo-Roman buildings, see the tower of Vésone, the square building at Autun, situated outside the town on the other side of the river, and known as the *Temple of Janus.*

rally stayed by monoliths of marble or granite, and that, owing to the method employed by the builders, they formed but one single perfectly homogeneous block. Moreover, always regarding the faces as a casing—a crust,—whether erected of stone, brick, or rough range work,—they took the precaution to bond this casing at intervals, and the interior filling of rubble-work, either by through courses of brick or by flat-bedded stones.

Thus Roman masonry always consisted of a series of casings enclosing a perfectly solid and homogeneous filling. When they erected a pier (fig. 2) the builders formed faces, either of brick or of chopped stones (the courses A being levelling courses covering the entire surface). Between these faces and these levelling

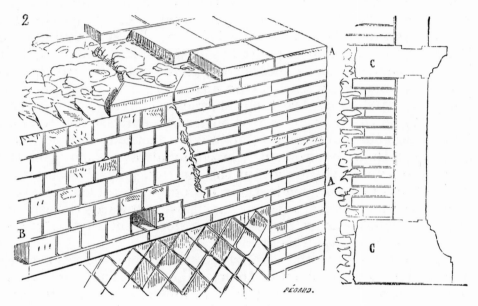

Fig. 2.—Roman Masonry.

courses they filled in with coarse concrete, leaving above each levelling course at intervals putlog-holes B to accommodate the scaffolding. If they wished to case these faces of chopped stone or brick with stone or marble slabs, they built string-courses C into the masonry, and the slabs were grooved into the horizontal projections of these string-courses.

We have here true mason-work perfectly adapted to the buildings they erected, and easy of execution. It must not be forgotten that their mortar was excellent.

Can these methods, on which it appears useless to dwell, since they are known to everybody, be applied in our days? Can we make any use of them? I think so : not however by imitating them without criticism, but by proceeding as the

Romans would have done had they possessed our materials and means of execution.

Employing simultaneously the principle of rubble building and that of jointed stone-work, the Romans, without ever confounding these two systems—as I remarked above,—employed them in conformity with their properties, always placing the less resisting structure inside and the more rigid outside. Moreover, in good Roman work the stone or marble envelope takes the form of a superposition of architectural members, not as a mere casing where the forms do not coincide with the jointing. It was only at a very late period that the Romans ceased to preserve this perfect correspondence between the form and the jointing; and we see that in countries where Greek art maintained its influence—in Syria, for instance,—the jointing and the form continued to correspond. We may observe the same fact in the West, during a considerable part of our mediæval period. But we must not forget that the constructive art cannot and should not establish as laws methods which are not in harmony with the usages of the times; on the contrary, it is the usages of the times that should originate the system of construction suitable to them.

The Greeks were divided into small communities who could indulge in those refinements of execution which we admire in their works. The Romans had the whole known world at their command; they had slaves in prodigious numbers, they made their soldiers work, and did not scruple to resort to requisitions. The Middle Ages employed forced labour, and in certain cases, labour paid for at a low price; but, on the other hand, they had but inefficient means for procuring and transporting materials, and indifferent machinery. Such is not the state of things in our days. Materials are easily procurable from every quarter, exactly where we want them, while labour is expensive and time valuable. It would be reasonable therefore to try to build in accordance with these novel conditions, rather than to think of imitating the Greeks, the Romans, the builders of the Middle Ages, or the imitators who lived in the time of Louis XIV. In French architecture down to the Renaissance there was a perfectly logical advance,—as logical as had been that of the Greeks or that of the Romans. In the twelfth century,—that period so brilliant for the arts, for architecture, sculpture, and painting,—France was divided politically into numberless lordships; roads were few, and the means of transport were inconsiderable; it was difficult to go to a distance to procure and load heavy materials; payments were made in kind, and forced labour was the custom. Masonry was constructed with small materials, easily transported and lifted,—capable, for the most part, of being carried on the shoulders,—and with these resources great buildings were erected. But the architecture was adapted to a structure of small stones rather than to one of jointed blocks. It was a compromise between the Roman rubble-work structure and the structure of jointed stone. Great projections necessitating the use of large stones were avoided. In a word, the architecture readily subjected itself to the means at command. A little later on, towards the end of the twelfth century, political unity was realised, the great towns obtained their franchises, and building appliances became abundant. Materials of large dimensions were procured, transported, worked, and raised. It was no longer abbots or secular nobles, confined within their narrow domains, and having at their disposal an inconsiderable staff of workmen, who were the builders, but populous and wealthy cities. Machines were improved, guilds were formed, and the workmen were paid good wages in money. Workmanship was improved, but there was an endeavour to economise it; materials were plentiful and well selected; but their cost was recognised, and they were not uselessly lavished; every stone was roughly shaped in the quarry and dressed before it was laid. Materials of large dimensions were used only where they were necessary. In every other case stones of inconsiderable size were constantly employed. With the fourteenth century arose the vast civic buildings, well planned and simple, and in which we see manifested a spirit of method sometimes carried to excess. It was the age of regulations; building reflected its spirit; it was uniform, consistent, and subject to strict surveillance: the building-staff was a government in which every one had his appointed function. It was the age of *pattern stones;* the courses were regulated and had consequently been ordered a long time beforehand. The architecture of the period took its tone from this *quasi*-administrative regularity, and became hard and monotonous. But at no time was there a more thorough knowledge of the nature of materials and their special properties. During no period were the quarries worked with more order and method. Moreover, a strict economy was observed in the employment of the stone. The fifteenth century built well, employed freestone by preference, as being easier to work and to quarry in large pieces; accordingly, the architectural features began to be less rigorously in accord with the jointing, but they certainly did not contravene it. The Renaissance almost lost sight of structure, virtually disregarding it; all modes were indifferent: there ceased to be selection as regards the quality; there was no longer any understanding between the architect and the mason. The architect gave the form; the mason interpreted it in his setting out to the best of his judgment, or as far as the materials at his command allowed.

There were exceptions, however. Philibert Delorme, for instance, paid great regard to the structure; but he also complained of the ignorance of his brethren in this matter.[1]

At the present day we have retrograded still further, if possible, than the architects of the Renaissance; while our shortcomings are less excusable than theirs, for they at any rate were carried away by the impulse of a fashion whose power was too strong for them to resist. We proceed wilfully—we are perfectly cognisant of the methods employed by the ancient builders,—we do not sin through ignorance. We bring into our building-yards, on monstrous waggons, enormous stones sometimes cubing four or five yards. Do we proceed to take advantage of these splendid materials; will our architecture be in accordance with their strength? No: we set to work to cut in them meagre pilasters, thin architraves, narrow string-courses, so that in the building the stone will appear to consist of four or five pieces. We go so far as to work in it thin courses,—yes, thin courses,—with grooved joints, to imitate an architecture built with materials of less considerable cube. We saw these enormous blocks into pieces to form jointed lintels resting on iron bars. We erect masses of stone-work, jointed without any regard to the form the building will assume; and when the whole is thus piled up, a host of stone-cutters will come and dress down the rough rock to the shape which it shall have pleased the architect to adopt. Beds and joints will cross the sculpture or the mouldings—no matter: for some years to come plaster-of-Paris tinted with ochre will mask these blunders. Thus it is that, though aided by extensive knowledge, and having at command the numerous and powerful appliances afforded by modern civilisation and industry, it has come to pass that we are no longer able to give to our buildings the character, the expression, which we have always admired in the works of our predecessors, who were less favoured in every respect than ourselves. But our predecessors made great use of their reasoning faculty, while we dare not have recourse to it, for fear of seeing our efforts regarded by a few coteries who base their influence on the indifference of the enlightened public to matters of this kind, as an attempt at emancipation.

We may therefore consider these two points as settled: that we have at our command materials and machinery formerly unknown; that our requirements are more various, and—which is especially to be considered—more extensive than were those

---

[1] One instance among a thousand will give an idea how little structure was considered by the architects of the Renaissance. The columns of the decorative porticos of the court of the château d'Ecouen each consist of two pieces of stone placed side by side on end, so that each column is formed of two half-columns. This would be enough to make an architect of classic times or of the Middle Ages turn pale.

of the Classic period, or even the Middle Ages; that as our materials are greater in quantity, and the means of transporting and working them are more efficient, we should take this abundance and these appliances into account; and that as our requirements are different or more complex, we should conform to these novel conditions. If we add to these fundamental laws of art those reasons for economy which are more imperative now than they were in former times, we shall be able to advance on sure ground. We do not live in times when a monarch could compel whole populations to raise a pyramid such as that of Cheops; we are scarcely willing even to allow of the resources of the State, that is, the public revenue, being used to satisfy the taste or caprice of a Sovereign, unless some material or moral advantage is to be secured thereby for all; and, proceeding from general considerations to details, we are approaching a period when it will no longer be permitted to adopt in public buildings forms which are not the exact expression of the requirements of the case.

Now not only do I believe that the rigorous observance of these conditions is not opposed to an artistic expression, but I am convinced that this alone can produce it.

In order to be able to apply these principles the architect needs only complete liberty, and no one can give him this liberty if he does not know how to acquire it. Let him study what has been done, and make use of that study by rationally applying it, by always making what has been acquired his point of departure for a resolute adoption of the methods rendered necessary by the new conditions; let him regard or adopt any architectural form of the past merely as an expression of a still existing, or a no longer existing necessity, as the case may be; let him consider it as an instructive study, not as an imperative, traditional, invariable model; then, in place of those strange compilations of forms capriciously borrowed from all quarters, and which constitute what is now denominated architecture, he will be able to originate an art,—an art of which he will be the master, and which will be the reflex of our civilisation.

All discussion on these points resolves itself into this: Is it the *letter* or the *spirit* that you should follow when anterior arts are in question? If it is the *letter*, let us copy the Greeks, the Romans, the works of the Renaissance, or the Middle Ages, without distinction, for these various forms of art offer us admirable productions; but if it is the *spirit*, the case is completely altered; the question is then no longer that of adopting a form, but of ascertaining whether the conditions now existing are such that you ought to adopt that form: for if the conditions are different, the form, which was a rational one simply because it resulted from a rigorous attention to a special condition, has no further reason for its existence, and should be abandoned. That we should reason like Aristotle is most commendable; but that we should adopt all his ideas is quite another thing. Now this distinction, which modern thinkers so wisely make between the method of reasoning adopted by the ancients and their ideas, discoveries, or hypotheses in the fields of philosophy and science,—why should we not make it in the domain of art? or without going so far for a parallel, though we read the works of Descartes, do we think it possible to regard all his theories as true, as infallible? While we employ his method, is it not in many cases with a view to argue against and contradict him? Why then in art should we use materials as they might have been used in the seventeenth century? and what meaning have the *architectural features* or forms which were adopted in those days for us? What do they express? To what modern requirement or taste do they correspond? And if it should come to be shown that these *architectural features* did not correspond with the social exigencies of the times,—that they were only an unintelligent imitation of a previous art, what should we think of this imitation at second-hand in modern times? If we purpose imitation, we should at least revert to original sources.

Let us then examine (for we must enter on the consideration of practical questions) what are the methods of building which our materials suggest to us, when masonry is in question, and what are the forms dictated by these methods. Thanks to the appliances for quarrying which we possess in the present day, and to our railways, we can obtain for our buildings stone of very various kinds.[1] The question is how to employ them according to their particular nature. The stones most commonly employed for building are the limestones; but there is a considerable number of materials that might be used besides them,—such for instance as the granites, the schists, the sandstones, and lavas.

Moreover, the limestones, even the best and hardest, are nearly all decomposed by saltpetre; or at any rate absorb the moisture of the ground or the air to such a degree as to destroy the wood-work or the painting applied in the interiors. It would therefore, in many cases, be advantageous to employ a method greatly in vogue among the Romans—a method of which we have previously spoken, and which consists of rubble and brick-work, or rubble-work only, cased with large stones. It is, in

---

[1] In no country in Europe are materials suitable for building more abundant than in France. The Jurassic limestones are met with over a great part of the land. We may add to these rocks, which are generally a good building material, the alluvial limestones, the chalks, the granites, the lavas, the marbles, schists, and sandstones.

fact, scarcely comprehensible why,—in the construction of great buildings, for instance,—walls or piers of a yard and a half to two yards in thickness should be built of solid blocks of stone, when the weights are not such as to justify this lavish use of materials. The method of casing would have the advantage of permitting the use of materials relatively expensive, of various colours and very durable, such as certain compact limestones, marbles, lavas, or schists.

If instead of placing columns or pilasters on the outside of buildings as a mere ornament, we justified that decoration by making it contribute to the strength of the building, reason and taste would not be offended by it, and the outlay would at least produce a positive result. Since we very seldom leave the stone apparent in the interiors of our public or private buildings, since—with the exception now and then of a vestibule or stair-case—we think it necessary to line it with plastering, wainscoting, or painting,—why make the faces of these interiors of block stone when we give these walls so considerable a thickness, that the blocks do not form parpings or through stones? I freely admit that necessity may oblige us to form the fronts of houses whose walls do not exceed half a yard in thickness, of solid stone; but what sense is there in placing inside faces of block stone where we give a yard or more of thickness to the walls? Why not in this case adopt the sensible method of the Romans, which consisted in forming ashlar casings only with a few bonders, backed by rubble-work, much better fitted than block-stone for receiving plastering, painting, or wainscoting?

Making use therefore of the methods left us by our predecessors, so far as they are applicable in our times, and profiting by the experience acquired, we proceed to consider in their order the resources which the mason builder now has at command, combining under the same denomination the structure of jointed stone and the concrete structure according to the custom in use.

FOUNDATIONS.

From the very nature of the ground on which the Greeks erected their buildings, they but rarely had occasion to make considerable foundations. They preferred to build on the rock, and their foundations are in truth merely basements, that is to say, masses of stone-work laid close-jointed without mortar. When in particular cases they were compelled to go deep down for a hard bottom, they built their foundations of dry stone in courses sometimes cramped together with iron, and raised on this carefully executed foundation their plinth courses. The slight weight moreover of their buildings, which were generally small, rendered foundations of great strength unnecessary. The Romans, on the contrary, who erected a great number of colossal buildings, which from their concrete structure did not accommodate themselves to any movement or settlement, were obliged to employ in their foundations means for producing strength exceeding any that have been adopted since. The Romans always went down to solid ground, however deep it might be; and having reached it they filled in wide excavations with coarse concrete made of stones, gravel, and excellent mortar; and on this artificial rock they erected their buildings. During the Middle Ages both very good and very bad foundations were made; it was a question of expense. There are no finer foundations than those of the cathedrals of Paris, Amiens, and Reims; there are none worse than those of the cathedrals of Troyes, Séez, and Châlons-sur-Marne.

When the foundations of the Middle Ages are well made, we find them always cased with a facing of stone accurately dressed and laid, enclosing a coarse concrete thrown in according to the Roman method.

In laying the foundations of an edifice two essential conditions have to be observed: perfect stability must be secured, because our buildings are large, and the means employed must be subject to conditions of economy. It is therefore important to ascertain the methods which may satisfy these requirements. Our towns are no longer built on plateaux and elevated sites; on the contrary, they are situated on the banks of rivers, and frequently rise even from marshes. In these cases solid ground cannot always be met with, but shifted soils, mud, recent alluvial deposits, and compressible ground. The ingenuity of the architect must then compensate for that which nature has refused him.

All virgin soils, those, viz., which present a natural stratification, are incompressible,—with some special exceptions, to which we shall presently refer. Foundations may be laid on sand or clay and on marl, with equal or even greater security than on rock or tufa: for the deposits of sand, clay, or marl are homogeneous, settled, and without interstices; while it sometimes happens that rocks enclose unsuspected hollows, and fracture or slip beneath a heavy weight. But the virgin soil is often found at such great depths that it would be enormously expensive to lay it bare by excavating the made earth which covers it. In this case, during the Middle Ages and down to our own times, piles were driven into this shifted earth as far as they would go; on the heads of the piles was bedded a floor of framed oak, and on this floor were laid the first courses of the masonry. This system had two disadvantages: it was very costly, and if the piles were not all equally driven in quite as far as was possible, unequal settlements were occasioned, and consequently dislocations in the building. Since the beginning of the present century we have employed for the bottom layers of foundations *concrete;*[1] that is, a mixture of mortar made with hydraulic lime and pebbles of equal size. Well-made concrete possesses the advantage of forming a united, homogeneous, and incompressible mass, which hardens with time until it forms a veritable rock on which a tool can make no impression. If therefore on soft compressible ground we lay a sufficiently thick bed of concrete, we obtain a homogeneous foundation, which is not easily broken, and which forms a kind of imperishable floor upon which the walling can be raised. Of course the under layer of concrete should have a thickness proportionate to the weight it has to sustain. But it has the advantage of distributing isolated weights over a large surface, and consequently of diminishing the probabilities of unequal settlements. There is no ground so bad (provided it does not consist of very recently shifted earth) as not to have undergone compression of itself by the soaking in of rain and by its own weight. Consequently it always affords over a wide area a surface adapted to sustain a given weight. All that has to be done therefore is to distribute the pressures over a surface which shall compensate by its extent for what it wants in density. Here the experience and consideration of the architect are necessary.

We must remember that moist ground is much less compressible than ground of a powdery nature. If therefore over mud that is impregnated with moisture we lay a platform of concrete, a yard in thickness, for instance, we shall be able safely to erect on this platform a stone building twenty yards high, consisting of isolated piers and walls. Perhaps a settling, a sinking, will occur, but it will take place uniformly and without occasioning dislocations in the building. Certain altered clays, which when dried in the air are light, and have no more consistence than peat, when in their natural place beneath the ground, when impregnated with moisture, will not suffer compression under enormous weights, provided a platform of concrete which will have the effect of a raft on a thick bed of liquid mud is interposed between that weight and the clays in question. We must therefore ascertain whether these soft beds are not dried up for a time, and whether their degree of moisture remains always the same. We have seen old buildings, in which no settlement had previously occurred, dislocated when the ground on which they rested was drained. A danger to be apprehended is that the pulpy ground may squeeze out under the pressure of

---

[1] Concrete is of Roman origin. The Romans used concrete not only for making foundations, but also for vaulting, and for entire walls behind facings of chopped stone or brick.

the platform of concrete; when, *e.g.*, hollows are formed around buildings, such as large sewers, or even when the surrounding ground is not kept very compact by a well-maintained system of embankments, or by other neighbouring buildings. To obviate this danger of the squeezing out of soft ground under the pressure of a platform of concrete, it is well to form below the edge of the platform an extra thickness of concrete, forming an under rim, as shown in section by figure 3; this rim A will hinder the mud from slipping beneath the weight. Another precaution which in this case should always be taken, is, before putting down the concrete, to spread over the muddy ground a layer of good sand or gravel a few inches in thickness. This layer of sand gives consistence to the soft clay, and is especially useful in

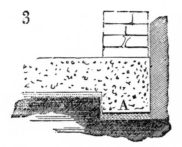

Fig. 3.—Foundation on Soft Clay.

preventing the concrete from being decomposed before it has thoroughly set.

Although the formation of a platform of concrete may not cost so much as a general system of piles, it nevertheless necessitates a considerable outlay. In cases where the expense must be restricted within very narrow limits, a method which often succeeds, and which we recommend as advantageous, is that of making—not beneath the foundation of the perimeter of the building, but outside that perimeter, at the bottom of the excavation—a wall half a yard in thickness and in height, of masonry built with mortar made with hydraulic lime, and filling in the whole interior area, that is the surface which the building would occupy, with good sand, well rammed and wetted, as shown in the section, figure 4. On this artificial ground may then be built the foundation-walls. Settlement occurs, but it occurs equally. Of course this method can only be resorted to when the buildings are not excessively heavy.

Again, it may happen that in excavating a foundation, you will find the bed of an old stream, or of a trench that has been filled up, and that thus by the side of an excellent bottom,—a soil of tufa, for instance,—you have a vacuity, a void space of more or less extent. When the vacuity is not too wide, it is sufficient to cut a slope in the sides of the tufa, excavate the made earth to a convex shape, and fill in the space A (fig. 5) with concrete, without troubling to find the bottom of the made earth B. You then obtain a kind of concrete arch, to which you give a thickness proportioned to the weight it will have to carry. It will be understood that I do not here purpose to lay down absolute rules, but to point out methods, of whose efficiency the architect must be the judge according to circumstances; for as the cases vary, so must the means. The architect, in consequence of deficient elementary knowledge, is too often inclined, in difficulties of this sort, to rely on the opinion of builders, whose interest it naturally is not to lessen the expenditure, and who, fearing to compromise themselves, are inclined to adopt the means they consider safe, however costly they may be. Concrete is of immense service in foundation-walls, if we duly consider its properties and observe the nature of the ground we have to deal with. We have seen

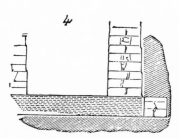

FIG. 4.—Foundation on Soft Clay.

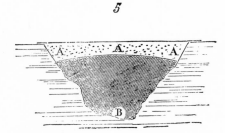

FIG. 5.—Foundation on partly-made Ground.

buildings of no inconsiderable weight erected, whose foundations were laid on a very treacherous soil mingled with vegetable débris, by sinking at intervals in this alluvium conical holes, which were filled with good sand, and covering the whole with a layer of concrete, twelve or eighteen inches thick, without the occurrence of the slightest settlement; so that, excepting turf-bog, there is scarcely any ground which we should now regard as absolutely unsafe, and in which piles would be necessary to sustain a building of considerable weight.

Clays afford a foundation that is excellent and incompressible, if they are prevented from slipping or being squeezed out. This is easy on plane and homogeneous ground; but if the clays are on the slope of a hill, there is great danger of the weight causing them to slip or be squeezed out on their slanting bed. The most careful precautions are then indispensable to prevent springs or even rain-water from moistening these clays, and thus occasioning their slipping. In front of the foundations therefore we must form culvert drains perfectly water-tight on the side next the buildings, and terminating at a considerable distance

from the plateau on which they stand. For example, let A
(fig. 6) be a building situated on a slope B C formed of clay. The
line *a b* marks the foundation-level. It will be necessary to form
outside, along the whole length of wall G, a culvert drain D
perforated with slits on the side *g*, water-tight on the side *h*,
and having its channel *i* a little lower than the first course
of the foundations. Naturally, this culvert will have a rather
rapid fall, and will discharge the water it collects at a distance

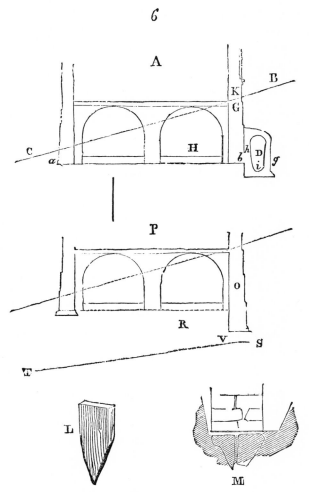

Fig. 6.—Foundations on Clayey Slopes.

from the building. This culvert will also be an excellent means
of preventing damp in the cellars H of the building, and the consequent formation of saltpetre on the basement courses K. When
for economical reasons we are unable to make a culvert drain, it
will at least be necessary to carry down the foundations of the
back wall lower than those of the front wall, as shown in the
section P, and to coat the wall outside with cement down to its

foot. The whole of the clay ground R will then be rendered permanently dry, and the water, compelled to pass at S T, will leave above it a mass of clay sufficiently compact and thick not to be pressed out under the weight of the foundations towards the lower side, and to offer resistance to the slipping of the under layer of clay V.

When the ground consists of pure clay, that is of very fat slippery matter, it will be well to drive in with a *beetle* (all the above described precautions being taken) under the walls, and before laying the concrete or beginning the walling, pieces of schist or flat hard stones edgewise, as shown at M, or even small oak piles flat and pointed, from eighteen inches to two feet in length. On these clayey grounds it is always desirable to give

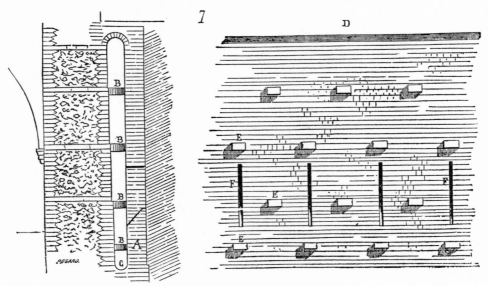

Fig. 7.—Roman method of Building against a Bank.

a considerable width of footing to the lower part of the foundation-walls.

The Romans adopted numerous precautions to render the underground chambers perfectly dry and healthy. To obtain this result they employed various methods. If a room was against solid ground, they built outside a retaining-wall (A, fig. 7), separated by a hollow from the main wall, to which it was tied at intervals by bricks or stones, B; they left slits in the retaining-wall, and formed at the bottom C an inclined channel to throw off on the outside the soakings percolating through the slits. If we make a longitudinal section through the isolating space, the retaining-wall then shows as in the diagram, D E being the tie-stones or bricks and F the slits. These brick or stone ties were intended to hinder the retaining-wall from giving beneath the pressure of the bank. The Romans were sometimes content (fig. 7 *bis*) to parget the wall on the side of the bank with a good coat of mortar with a footing at bottom к. The soakings flowing along this damp-proof coating could not penetrate into the masonry. In building our cellar walls we nearly always neglect to put an exterior coating. As foundation-walls are not smooth-faced, but present numerous rugosities, the water in-

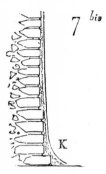

Fig. 7 *bis*.—Roman method of Building against a Bank.

variably penetrates them at last. Having discovered the mischief, we seek to cure it by damp-proof cementing applied inside; but this means cannot in any degree hinder the walls from being saturated with moisture, which ultimately throws out saltpetre and detaches the cement. The mediæval builders employed an excellent method for preventing the wet from

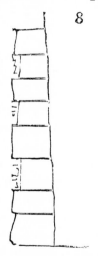

Fig. 8.—Mediæval Foundation Walls.

penetrating through the underground walls: they faced these walls outside with fine deep courses, and as carefully as those above ground (fig. 8). The soakings produced by the adjacent earth finding nothing to arrest them on these facings, glided over them, and did not penetrate into the masonry. Certain kinds of stone are, however, so absorbent that even when placed in the open air, above the foundations, they soon draw up the moisture of the ground, and gradually raise it to a considerable height. Such are the sandstones, certain rocks of the basins of the Aisne and the Oise, of Burgundy and Upper Champagne. There is only one means of preventing this result of capillary attraction, which is to put between the upper surface of the foundations and the first course above ground a layer of impermeable substance, such as asphalte, slabs of schist, or even mill-board well tarred. Thin slates were often used during the Middle Ages to obviate this capillary effect, which is so fatal to the durability of buildings at the level of the ground ; for we shall observe that courses of sandstone, for example, laid immediately on the foundation, and forming basements, absorb a quantity of water sufficiently considerable to effect the disintegration of the first courses of freestone which surmount them, and the more rapidly since certain of these sandstones contain salts in abundance. In great buildings standing by themselves,—mansions, *e.g.*,—too many precautions cannot be taken to insure the dryness of walls just above the ground, by draining, by cementing the outer surfaces of foundations, or, lastly, by the interposition of a damp course.

Masonry in Elevation.

In cases where we have both weatherstone and freestone, it is of great consequence to the architect that each should occupy its proper place.

And this is not merely a question of good construction, but also of economy. Of course the basements should always be built of weatherstone ; first, because it is better able to bear weight and resist injuries than freestone ; second, because it is less pervious and less liable to give out saltpetre. But above the basements there are some kinds of weatherstone which do not so well resist atmospheric effects as freestone ; or, again, it may even happen that weatherstone has a destructive influence on the freestone it ought to protect. This phenomenon may be remarked in many of our public edifices. Vergelé[1] used on buildings for the projecting features—bold string-courses and cornices—has endured for centuries in the open air ; but laid beneath a slab of weatherstone, the vergelé has been rapidly decomposed. Vergelé in the open air and exposed to the rain wears away in course of time, but is not disintegrated ; it is gradually reduced, but does not scale or perish in dust. The reason is, that stone of this kind, being very porous, dries as quickly as it imbibes moisture. In its case the rain-water never remains

---

[1] A freestone found in the neighbourhood of Paris.

long enough in its contexture to decompose it, whether through the action of frost or the development of salts. But if the projecting stones in question are covered by a slab of hard stone, even of a very close-grained nature, the latter invariably produces the effect of a filter, and so causes the moisture gradually to penetrate into the underlying freestone, which, not being able to dry, develops salts or perishes by frost. The following (fig. 9) is what takes place. Let A be a cornice of vergelé covered by a tabling of weatherstone B C. The moisture communicated from the hard stone to the soft by percolation cannot be evaporated by the air: it develops salts in the interior of the layer, which eventually crystallise on the under surface at G; and signs of decay are soon visible beneath the drip,—first, by an efflorescence, then by scaling, and lastly by decided exfoliation. The same cornice not covered with hard stone would be weathered, worn by the rain, but not decomposed. In such cases, metal is greatly preferable to hard stone, inasmuch as it is impervious

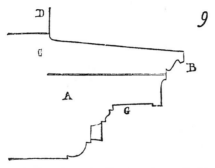

FIG. 9 —Danger of covering Freestone by Weatherstone.

to moisture. The same phenomenon occurs beneath gutters of hard stone laid on the thickness of a wall. These gutters will be durable if the stone is good, but the underlying outer courses will soon present symptoms of decay. Special care must therefore be taken in making use of weatherstone as a protection to freestone. The section of mouldings greatly influences the preservation of stone-work, and those should always be adopted which tend to throw off the rain-water quickly. On this account the mouldings now usually employed, and which are considered imitations of the classic, are very bad, inasmuch as they nearly always present surfaces opposed to the rain, and consequently obstacles to its rapid discharge, while they cause splashings, very injurious to the surfaces which surmount these horizontal obstacles: for (fig. 9) the rain which beats on the surface B C splashes in fine drops along the surface C D, impregnates it with moisture and causes its decay. As a general rule, soft and porous stone should either be placed so as to be entirely protected from moisture, or isolated so that it may be readily dried by the air : the placing of hard over soft stones hastens the decay of the latter, especially if those hard stones, though excellent in quality, are very hygrometric, like the Chérance stone and sand-stones, limestones of Burgundy known as Anstrude, Mance, and Ravières stone.   We need not go far to find cornices made not long ago of Saint-Leu stone, and covered with slabs of Chérance, which are already perishing.[1]   If it is possible by not adhering exactly to mouldings recognised as *classic*, to avoid the decay which manifests itself beneath horizontal surfaces, it is of essential importance to secure the preservation of weatherstone gutter-courses.   In such cases it is advisable either to carry these gutters on corbels that leave their under-beds exposed to the air, or to contrive between that under-bed and the underlying surface of freestone a hollow space with ventilation at intervals, as shown in figure 10.   The mediæval builders, who so frequently

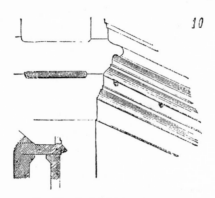

Fig. 10.—Isolated Stone Gutters.

placed gutters or exterior passages at the mid-height of their buildings, were always careful to isolate these courses underneath by supporting them either on corbels or on double walls, as, *e.g.*, in the upper galleries of churches (see A, fig. 10).

The Romans, by always erecting their dressed masonry close-jointed, without mortar, keeping it, so to speak, independent of the backing, insured the preservation of the faces.   This was all the more necessary as they used hydraulic lime, which develops salts in abundance, and since the presence of mortar in the beds and joints induces the decay of the edges of the stone.   This decay shows itself round the stone next the mortar by an efflor-escence, subsequently by exfoliation, to such a degree that in the course of a century this (fig. 11) is what takes place.   The mortar beds A endure, the surfaces of the stone are preserved at B, and the parts C are deeply decayed.   This phenomenon may be observed in many of the mediæval buildings, which were

[1] Notably at the palace of the Conseil d'État, in Paris.

erected, as we know, with thick mortar joints between each course. But the mediæval buildings are nearly always erected with small courses; mortar consequently plays an important part in their construction. This cannot be the case with our modern stone buildings, which are erected with large blocks, and which should therefore be constructed in the Roman method. It may be remarked that the difficulty involved in close-jointed masonry has been greatly exaggerated. It is not necessary, as some writers tell us, to rub the beds of stone one against the other to obtain a perfect junction. Besides, admitting that the ancients used this method for the beds, how could they have applied it to the joints? But the vertical joints of the ancient buildings are as accurately fitted as the beds. It is sufficient to dress these beds and joints very truly to the straight edge, and to set the stones with the lewis. By examining attentively the

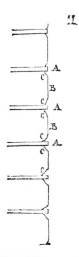

Fig. 11.—Disintegration of Stone caused by Mortar Joints.

beds and joints of the massive order of Roman masonry, the dressing-marks made by a tool similar to the toothed chisel can be plainly distinguished : but while in many Roman buildings the faces are roughly dressed, or sometimes even simply scabbled, the beds and joints are invariably dressed with perfect accuracy. This may be observed even in buildings of late date. The stability of the massive Roman masonry is, in fact, entirely due to the close fitting of the beds and joints. Not satisfied with this means alone, the Romans thought it necessary also to connect the courses by dowels or dovetail keys of metal, iron, or bronze, in order to prevent their giving. All the stone or marble buildings of ancient Rome show at the corners of the beds of each of the stones, sinkings intended to receive metal dowels. During the Middle Ages many of these dowels were extracted : that is why we see in the walls of these buildings a number of holes made with the mallet and chisel to get out the metal. These dowels were usually of the form presented in figure 12, the part A being let into the upper bed of the lower course and the part B into the under bed of the upper course (see the detail c). In marble masonry these dowels were often of bronze, in stone masonry (Travertine) they were ordinarily of iron. Their utility is however questionable, since the walls from which they have been abstracted have remained none the less firm.

The Roman buildings were pretty solidly based. The rubble-work of which they consisted was sufficiently compact and homogeneous, and the masonry in blocks of sufficient size, to render it unnecessary that they should be tied or cramped; accordingly the lavish use of dowels scarcely appears in any but the splendid edifices of ancient Rome, and is uncommon in other

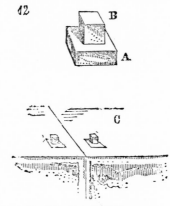

Fig. 12.—Dowelled Masonry.

countries. Still the Romans sometimes thought it advantageous to cramp together the stones of a course with dovetails of iron or bronze run with lead. This was in fact necessary in certain hydraulic works, and to secure friezes or cornices above porticos. We have even found such dovetails in wood.[1] But of chain-ties, properly so called, there are no vestiges. During the Middle Ages, that is to say, dating from the end of the twelfth century, iron cramps leaded in were frequently used to tie together the stones of a course; these cramps thus formed veritable chain-ties at various heights. In reference to these a remarkable fact may be noted. When the iron is in contact with the stone only, whether run with lead or not, it rusts but little, consequently does not swell, and occasions no cracks in the stone; but if there is mortar next the iron, that is, if above these cramps which connect the stones of a course there are thick beds of mortar, the cramps, whether surrounded by lead or not, must very

[1] In the substructions of the Arch of Saintes.

quickly swell and burst the stones. The oxidation is still more rapid if the beds are filled with plaster of Paris.

The Romans, therefore, when they employed metal in certain cases to strengthen masonry, since they laid their stone without mortar, had not the effect of oxidation to fear, whereas, in our mediæval edifices and in those we are now erecting, the presence of metal in the masonry is a serious danger, since we invariably interpose beds of mortar or plaster-of-Paris between the stones. But we shall revert later on to the employment of iron in masonry.

Not regarding elasticity as one of the conditions of structure, the Romans proceeded in a logical manner by laying the courses with close joints, or by filling in between facings of brick or chopped stones with masses of concrete walling.

On the other hand, considering elasticity one of the conditions of structure, the mediæval builders did not proceed less logically in laying the courses of their buildings on thick beds of mortar. It is in fact natural to adopt one or other of these methods. If we imitate the Roman style of architecture let us build like the Romans; if, on the other hand, we build like our predecessors of the Middle Ages, viz., by making use of mortar in the dressed work, let us abstain from adopting the Roman style of architecture, which cannot adapt itself to that method. If we do not require the structure to possess a certain degree of elasticity, let us build after the Roman method, which gives an absolutely inert stability; but if we are compelled by our requirements to secure elasticity to a certain extent in our buildings, let us not seek to imitate (and imperfectly) the appearance of Roman structure. In a word, let us make our methods of building harmonise with the architectural forms we profess to adopt, or, if our methods of building are satisfactory, let us not seek to reproduce architectural forms that are at variance with those methods. We have on the whole too flattering an opinion of our methods of building as regards masonry. We really build poorly, expensively, and without due consideration of the nature of the materials. If rents and dislocations do not show themselves in our public buildings, it is because we make use of twice as much materials as would be absolutely necessary; but it is clear that this extravagance is costly. As regards economy and the judicious use of materials, our private houses are very much better built than our public edifices. We often make an intelligent use of cast or wrought iron and of stone or brick in our domestic buildings, while a few steps off we see in our public buildings enormous masses of stone accumulated out of all reason, metal being never employed except for floors, tie-bars, and roofs. Yet it is not to be doubted that if the Romans had had at their command cast-iron of large dimensions they would have used it. The mediæval builders would have been glad to possess that material, for they did their best to find a substitute for it by using very tough stone placed on end, when heavy masses had to be erected on slight supports. It is strange that our architects, possessed of materials so various, so novel, and at the same time already so well tested, and having at hand illustrations of all styles of architecture, from those of ancient times to those of most recent date, should consider themselves obliged, amid such fruitful elements, always, when the erection of a public building is in question, to keep to the system of construction employed during the seventeenth century, when, if people wrote in a very good style, they built very badly. Even if we do not use cast-iron for supports, have we not now tough stones whose quality is equal to that of the most compact marbles? Why not make due use of these materials, by giving them the slender forms which their strength admits of? Why—and I come back to this important point—put solid blocks of stone when rubble-filling would suffice? Why is it that the laureates of the Academy, on their return from Rome or Greece, do not bring with them, when they come to build in France, any of the excellent methods of building employed by the Romans, but still adhere to the routine of the seventeenth-century builders, who were much less skilful than their predecessors? Why laud so highly the arts of classic Rome, and yearly send youthful architects to draw inspiration from the buildings it has left us, if the study of those buildings is to end in nothing more than counterfeiting an architecture whose rationale we do not investigate, and if in our study of those vast and beautiful edifices we do not fix upon that which is their essential part, the structure, with a view to its application, as far as it is applicable, to our own requirements and social conditions? It is long since there has ever been an attempt to explain these contradictions; but stones continue to be piled up as irrationally as ever, and while novel materials abound they have led to no change in the methods of building. Machines are being improved, and enormous blocks of stone are easily lifted with their aid to great heights, but apparently with a view to cut them up into architectural members adapted for stones of small dimensions such as those which were lifted with sheers. We might make good use of these fine materials—as the ancients never failed to do. On the contrary, we make a point of putting them out of sight beneath a mass of details and mouldings, which make our largest edifices look like cabinet work-boxes or rubble-work coated with stucco. Amid this collection of mouldings, square returns, pilasters, architraves, meagre archivolts, string-courses, and lavish carvings, we look for one of the enormous stones we saw being hoisted to vast heights, and we perceive only small surfaces—forms cut in every direction; those prodigious blocks have disappeared. Why then not build, as they built in the sixteenth century, with small materials?

To give a clearer notion of the illogicality that seems to prevail in our more pretentious architectural works, I will here call attention to a fact which will show to what the neglect of intelligent consideration in the employment of materials has led us. At the beginning of the seventeenth century we made considerable use of a combination of brick and stone; and the method was rational. Stone served for the corners of buildings, —for vertical ties; that is for the parts which had to support the heaviest weights, for window-cases and string-courses,—the first to facilitate the fixing of the windows, the second to level up and tie the walls horizontally; in such case the brick was merely an exterior casing for rubble-work, since it had been found that in our climate outside plastering on rubble-work was not durable. This mode of building was very good, very sensible and economical; moreover, it plainly indicated to the eye the method employed. Now it happened that a short time ago the taste for this kind of buildings revived, and with a view to simulate their appearance we have seen wall piers erected of solid stone, to let in . . . marble? . . . bronze? . . . No! brick. This is much the same as if we embroidered a satin dress with cotton or worsted. If our descendants build more rationally than we do, they will some day be much astonished to discover block stone behind these brick casings, whose proper use was to conceal rough-walling and replace plastering, and will be inclined to conclude that in our times brick was a costly and highly-valued material.

It would seem as if we regarded block stone as a natural production of which we cannot be too lavish, so great is the abundance; and yet we see quarries exhausted after some years' working. There is no longer any stone fit to build with in the plain of Montrouge and Bagneux, which for many centuries supplied Paris with materials. Some of the best quarries in the basins of the Oise and Aisne are exhausted. We are now compelled to seek weatherstones in Burgundy, in the Jura, and the Haute-Saone; and here too it is the quarry proprietors who come to offer their materials to the architects. It does not occur to the latter to visit our Departments, and to gather information for themselves in each locality respecting the stone most suitable for building. Why do we not employ in Paris the lavas of Auvergne, which offer so many advantages; the sandstones of the Vosges, incomparable in quality when well selected; the

schists of Anjou or Autun, which would be so serviceable in very
thin courses to prevent the effects of capillary attraction ; the
granites of the Vosges and of the Morvan, which would enable
us to make very strong and slender monoliths ? Why, in cases
where in our great buildings we think it desirable to use lintels,
do we always adhere to the plan of arch-jointing and supporting with iron, and not employ for the purpose single stones such as
those with which the quarries of Chauvigny in Poitou, those of
Anstrude in Burgundy, and others besides, would supply us ?
If expense is the objection, would it not be easy to economise in
the useless masses of block stone now employed by using block
material only where necessary, and then selecting it for the
purpose ? The Romans were great builders ; but with what
care did they choose their materials ! how intelligently did they
employ them as regards their qualities, and without ever wasting
them ! How is it that, possessing, as we do in France, building
stone in the greatest variety, of the greatest excellence, and
having to a much greater extent than the Romans the means of
quick and easy transport, we are inferior to them in this important respect ? And again I say, let not expense be made a
pretext, for—I repeat it—we are wasting vast sums in our public
buildings by a ridiculously lavish use of block stone, as if we had
not, like the Romans, excellent limes, gravel, imperishable rubble-
stone and brick !

In fact we have to begin again as regards the art of masonry ;
we must forget all the methods in use during the last three
centuries, and inaugurate fresh ones based on the experience
gained by the ancients and the mediæval builders, with due consideration of the abundant resources which our own times have
contributed. But to obtain this result certain conditions must
be fulfilled. Architects should be asked to consider the structure at least as much as the appearance, and not follow the
routine methods in vogue with most contractors ; to be so well
assured of the goodness and soundness of methods they adopt
as to be able to insure their adoption and appreciation by those
who carry out their work—for happily, among ourselves, every
clearly explained method is immediately accepted by our craftsmen ; to mark out their stone jointing for themselves as did
the masters of the Middle Ages, who are most frequently dis-
paraged by the very persons who are incapable of imitating
them ; to be acquainted with the materials, and to see about
them themselves ; to consult their reason rather than their port-
folios, and to consider that in architecture a wise economy is a
proof of knowledge and taste. Uselessly to consume means
which would be well employed in satisfying absolute requirements is certainly not a proof of good sense or of correct taste.

In every specimen of mason-work each piece taken separately in the case of dressed stone, or each section in concrete works, should clearly indicate its function. We ought to be able to analyse a building, as we take a puzzle to pieces, so that the place and function of each of the parts cannot be mistaken. The ancients have given us examples of such work; and when we find the ruins of one of their buildings it is owing to the observance of this principle that we can unmistakably restore it. The great builders of the Middle Ages were more rigorous, if not than the Greeks, at least more so than the Romans, in the application of this method of building. With them each piece of dressed stone is an indispensable member, complete in itself,—a kind of organ which, subjected to analysis, finds its exact place and function in the whole. We can imagine the interest which works of masonry thus conceived must possess, not merely for him who designs but also for those who execute them and those who see them. Each stone having a distinct function, the combination which directs their assemblage testifies to an intellectual labour which leaves an indelible trace on the building, and dictates a well-marked and characteristic form; the workman is conscious of being engaged in a labour whose use he comprehends, and he has the spur of emulation and a feeling of satisfaction; the passer-by who contemplates the finished work recognises it as the result of a comprehensive inspiration, with a view to producing a certain effect; there is unity in the whole, because there is an exact and necessary correlation between all the parts. No one will assert that unity is the work of chance. Unity is the combined product of parts. Every organic body is a unity because its various organs are combined in view of one harmonious purpose; and it should be the same with the *ensemble* of an architectural design. If we remove an architectural member from the structure of a Greek temple we endanger its stability; if we take a stone from a mediæval edifice we compromise its durability. We cannot say as much of the buildings erected in the present day. Does it therefore follow that we must adhere to the principles of construction adopted by the Greeks or by the builders of the Middle Ages? Certainly not: but we may proceed as they did and profit by what they accomplished.

Taking for granted that an architect needs but an inconsiderable stock-in-trade, and that the practice of his art is a very easy thing, certain connoisseurs have since the epoch of the Renaissance invaded his domain, and have taken upon themselves to declaim authoritatively about *orders*, *proportions*, and *symmetry*; and have formulated opinions, citing passages from Vitruvius and Palladio, proceeding to inspect architectural monuments as one might the pictures in an album, and thereupon setting up for arbiters of taste in matters of art. At the present day, thanks to the inadequacy of our educational appliances, these connoisseurs have almost taken the place of masters; they have applied their critical dogmas to principles, traditions, and practical means; and have soon come to regard their caprices as a measure of progress. This one rules that roofs must be concealed; a second regards a building as serving no purpose but to look at, and insists on symmetrical arrangements; a third declares that the buttresses in use during the Middle Ages and in Roman times to counter-thrust the vaulting are only an admission of weakness in the construction,—that modern ingenuity ought to substitute novel contrivances for these apparently inert masses. If you question these self-sufficient connoisseurs as to the means they would themselves propose, they invariably reply that with the help of a working mason or some English gardener, they have built a château or a mansion, substantial and convenient, where everything is wonderfully contrived—a very fairy palace. Six months afterwards you are sent for as an architect to strengthen flooring, to tie cracking walls, rebuild flues, underpin foundations, replace decayed roof-timbers and dilapidated roofing in this paragon of a mansion. Has the lesson been profitable? No. A fortnight afterwards the connoisseur whose blunders you have had to correct,—a man of "influence,"—will offer a hundred criticisms on a design submitted to his inspection : there he would like a vaulted ceiling where you have put a wooden one ; here, it is your walls that are too thick ; there, he finds buttresses that scarcely please him ; elsewhere, openings or solid parts are indispensable, and so on.

Have we been provided by an earnest, extensive, and critical course of teaching, with the means of opposing these caprices of the architectural dilettante, on whom, in many cases, our professional success or failure is dependent? By no means. Against these impertinent attacks we have generally no other weapon than such as routine furnishes. While the evil has been continually increasing, it is not of recent origin, for Philibert Delorme called attention to it in energetic language, and since his time some enlightened minds have made a stand against the despotism of the false in regard to building. It is instructive to read what was said in 1702 by a writer who took a deep interest in architecture, and who studied buildings in a spirit of impartial criticism very unusual at that date. In his *Mémoires critiques d'architecture*, Frémin, treasurer of France,[1] *à propos* of the construction of several of the Paris churches, thus expresses himself :—" You

---

[1] *Mém. crit. d'archit. contenans l'idée de la vraye et de la fausse architecture* (Paris, 1702), Lettre VI.

will see in the carrying out of the Church of Notre Dame and that of the Sainte Chapelle, two edifices built in accordance with the object, the subject, and the place ; while in Sainte-Eustache and Saint-Sulpice you will see two buildings in whose construction neither reason, nor judgment, nor prudence has been exercised.

" In Notre Dame, the architect who originated the design first conceived his general idea, and then entering upon each of the considerations which were required to promote the object, he reflected on them; he thought that this church, which, as regarded the requirements of the time when he lived, need not be very spacious, because Paris was then very restricted and small, would, however, require to become so at some future time, if the hopes entertained should be fulfilled ; that it must therefore be made extensive : he considered that as it was designed for a cathedral, it should have spaces and arrangements altogether peculiar, because there is a difference between a church of this kind and a mere parochial one. He thought that if he limited his ideas to the mere extent of his site he would not give so much space as it was desirable to provide to contain a greater number of men ; he conceived that a church where chanting is almost incessant should be of a construction that would shut in and prevent the dissipation of the sound ; he knew that all the arrangements for the mass were such as to enable it to be seen, and that accordingly, far from concealing or obscuring the view by columns, it was necessary to aid and favour it. What then did the architect do ? In view of future requirements he made a spacious interior and doubled the accommodation by galleries. With a view to promote the effect of harmony, which becomes more full and melodious when it is reverberated, he lowered the vaulting of the aisles; with a view to give more light, by lowering the vaulting, he enlarged the vast windows, and thereby facilitated its entrance. That the Sacrifice might be plainly seen, he reduced the pillars to a moderate thickness, and made them round, so as not to impede the view by angles, as is the case when the pillars are square. This architect, knowing that the weight of a vault which is buttressed by counter-thrusts never bears vertically on the pillars, because there is never equality of action in the weight of the vault and the action which that weight produces when it tends outwards,—he makes those of moderate size which support the double vault of the aisles, and those which support the great vaults a little larger : he at the same time gives suitable dimensions to both. Here we see an intelligent consideration of the object and of the subject, and a clever adaptation to the site. This may be called good architecture. This man builds two towers ; he is aware that with the form which he gives

them their superstructure only needs supporting by good angles—
he raises them on piers which, forming double entrances to the
aisles of the church, appear to have no more than the necessary
thickness ; so that, without perceiving their size in relation to
the interval which divides them, he accords them a proportion
which pleases the eye : thus, in everything, intelligence and good
sense are manifest." After criticising, not without reason, the
Church of Sainte-Eustache, and concluding that its architect was
only "a very bad mason," Frémin passes on to Saint-Sulpice.
"This," says he, "is another variety of false architecture, but
which, taken in connection with the former, proves that the
accumulation or assemblage of stones does not constitute building, for it is astonishing to see *to what an extent our architects*
distrust themselves ; if, as at the Church of the Petits Pères, they
do not accumulate *whole quarries* to support a little pedestal,
they tremble lest this work should fall as soon as it leaves their
hands ; so great and so general is this prejudice, that the
moment you propose to construct some piece of delicate work, you
find yourself beset and cried down by a host of masons. I say,
then, that Saint-Sulpice presents another kind of false construction ; first in the general conception, secondly in the carrying
out of the conception. As to the general conception, we cannot
say what it is ; if the architraves stuck up against the vaults had
been omitted, the building would have had scarcely any attractions ; the cornices that crown the pilasters of the lower vaults
are features whose purpose cannot be defined . . . ; the pilasters
attached to the square masses supporting the arches are needless;
a pillar nine feet square is ridiculous in a church, both on account
of its shape, since its corners obstruct the view, and of its thickness, as it takes up too much space and ground, and consequently
occupies the room required by the congregation. . . . Looking at
the pilaster against the pillars, I fancy to myself a very strong
and upright man, against whose body a post was placed to support
his chin. I will not take the trouble to go through all the
blunders of this edifice. I am offended every time I enter it."
While preferring the construction of the Church of Notre Dame
to that of Saint-Sulpice, Frémin was none the less a lover of
progress, and in all his letters he continually inveighs against
routine, which in his days was already tending to tyrannise over
building methods. But we must enter upon a closer consideration of our subject, and come to the application of principles. I
allow that in certain cases we must try to do without abutments,
whatever their form, and whether plainly expressed or disguised
under the appearance of engaged columns. But if we erect
vaultings of masonry above a hall, it is absolutely necessary to
support their thrust, if we would not see the vertical walls give

FIG. 13.—Example of Vaulting without Buttresses.

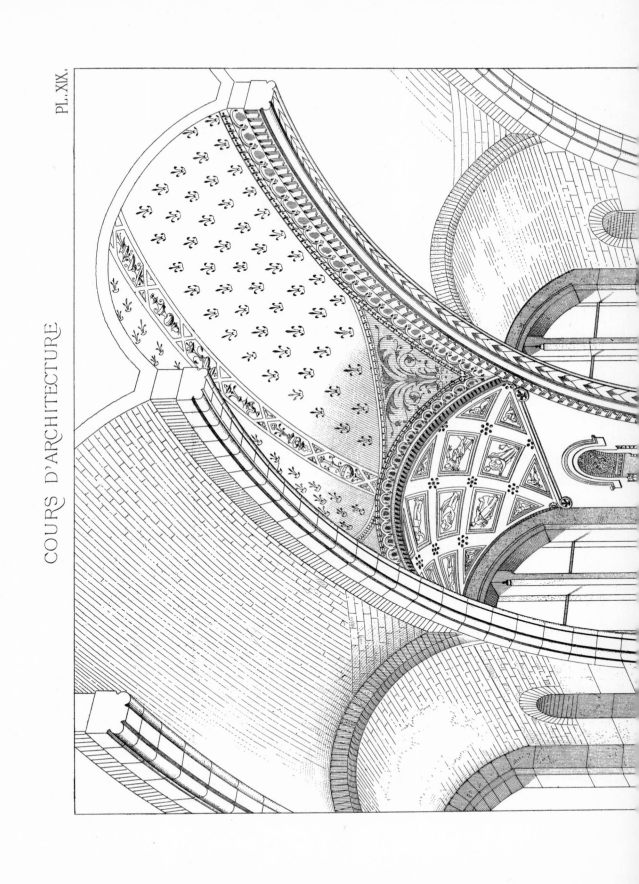

MAÇONNERIE.

E. Viollet-le-Duc del.

Ch. Sauvageot sculp.

A. Morel et Cie éditeurs

Imp. Lemercier. Paris

out and the vaulting fall in. Let us then try to find by what means we might vault with masonry an interior of 65 feet in the clear, on walls 4 feet 6 inches thick at their widest parts, and without those external buttresses which some regard as marks of weakness. Let figure 13 be the transverse section of this hall; we shall build with hard stone the basement A B, divided into bays of 20 feet from centre to centre. It will even be easy for us to reduce the thickness of the wall between the supports to 2 feet 3 inches. On corbels C we shall place brackets of cast-iron D, held by iron straps and keys E, on the exterior. On these brackets we shall lay bed-stones F, their ends being built into the wall; then the springers supporting the arches G, shown frontways at H. On these arches we shall form a gallery, K. Setting cast-iron columns I slightly in advance of the spandrel faces of the arches G, and from the spreading capitals of these columns to the pier I, we place two stone lintels M, the second forming the springers of the great transverse arches N. We shall be able to perforate the cheek above these lintels, as seen at O. From one to another of these transverse arches we shall turn the barrel-arches P and the annular vaults Q. To enclose the hall, a wall of a foot and a half to two feet pierced with wide openings above the gallery will suffice. If we form a roof consisting of plate-iron principals R, bringing their weight to bear a little outside the upright of the cast-iron columns, this weight will partly neutralise the resultant pressure of the transverse arches. Suppose the barrel-arches P turned in brick, and the annular vaults Q in pottery, we shall have a resultant pressure which will be directed almost entirely on the cast-iron column: and, taking into account imperfection of workmanship and accidental effects, this resultant will in no case fall beyond the point A. Here, then, we unite the conditions of stability and space by the combination adopted; we avoid buttresses and a useless bulk of material entailing additional expense.

I wish it to be understood that I do not here profess to offer an architectural model, but simply to suggest a method of procedure for meeting special requirements by reverting to the principles previously explained with the aid of the experience acquired by our predecessors and the appliances which our own age affords us. If, for instance, we build the basement of heavy and durable stone; if, for the lintels M only, we select very tough materials, all the rest of the building might be of freestone, or of solid or hollow brick. The barrel-arches P and the annular vaults Q could be built, the first with very slight wooden centring resting in the cheeks, the second with curves made to shift on the transverse arches. Only for the great transverse arches would framed centres be required, and by leaving out corbels at s as rests for the ends of the tie-beams of the centres, a prop would suffice for their support in the middle. The engraving, Plate XIX., gives an interior perspective of the bays of this hall, and an idea of its general appearance. It is evident that this kind of architecture would lend itself to painted decoration, whether partial, leaving visible the dressed stone-work, or complete. It would appear that it can only be by sharpening the intelligence of architects that the art could be directed to the production of works appropriate to the times, and consequently novel in aspect and economical in structure. To effect this, a rational, intelligent—I might even say scientific—construction should serve as the starting-point; and the ancients should be consulted only that we may not fall short of that which they produced, and that we may profit by their efforts.

The brick-maker's art has been greatly improved in recent times, why then should we not avail ourselves in our public buildings of the means it affords? why employ stone when we might with greater economy make use of a material which offers so many advantages—facility in transport and lifting, lightness, perfect adhesion to plastering and stuccos, dryness and unlimited durability?

Why in our palaces and mansions should we forego the use of glazed terra-cotta,—always keeping in our exteriors to stone facings, which are cold and cheerless of aspect, especially in our climate? By the judicious use of faience or even of painted stucco in the sheltered parts, we could effect a saving in stone sufficient to compensate for the extra cost occasioned by these coatings. The architects of the Renaissance, in Italy, and even in France, did not hesitate to employ such appliances, which are at once decorative and economical; they respected stone sufficiently to prevent them from lavishing it uselessly. I am quite aware that it is easier to design a front on paper without taking account of these various means, and to leave to a clever stone-cutter the task of reproducing the design in the material he has at command, *i.e.* block stone. But is it not incumbent on the artist himself to designate the use of the various materials,— to select them,—to avoid profusion and useless expenditure? Even when building only with block stone, a thoughtful arrangement of the beds and joints can effect a considerable economy in the quantity of the material employed and in the labour. Every one knows that blocks of freestone—those most frequently employed for building—come out of the quarry of various heights in bed; some three or four feet in bed, others not more than a foot and a half, or even less. What course is therefore adopted now in architects' offices? A drawing—an outward form—is designed before ascertaining the heights in bed of the stone

COURS D'ARCHIT.^{RE}

MAÇONNERIE.

E. Viollet-le-Duc del.

C. Sauvageot sculp.

A. Morel et Cie éditeurs.

Imp. Lemercier, Paris.

that will be employed.   This outward form decided upon—this representation drawn—the question comes as to the kind of stone that should be employed in building the edifice; then this design is divided horizontally by joint lines almost arbitrarily, so as not to be too much at variance with the architectural features adopted (it is the most scrupulous architects who proceed thus).   But when the work comes to be executed, very few stones correspond exactly to the heights of the courses marked in the design; blocks too high in bed have to be lowered, and blocks too low cast aside.   All this evidently costs money. It would seem much more rational to proceed as did the ancients who are commended to us as models, and as did the mediæval builders whose methods are rejected,—viz., before drawing the design, to ascertain the materials with which it can be rendered. Everybody would be benefited thereby, and architecture would lose nothing; on the contrary, it would gain by such a course; since the variety in height and quality of the materials would produce a variety in effect.   We have at command limestones —those of the Jura and of certain beds in Burgundy, for instance—that might with impunity be set on edge: why not make use of them in that way? why build with courses sawn at great expense of labour architectural members that could be formed in one piece?

It would therefore be desirable for the architect, before proceeding in the erection of a building, to ascertain the qualities and heights of stone the quarries will afford him; and it must be remarked that in this matter he should not rely for information on the builders, who are too much inclined to follow customary methods—to do to-day as they did yesterday,—but should take the trouble to visit the quarries and get an idea of their various beds.   That done, it would be well for him, in designing his building, to subordinate the various features of his design to the heights of the stone that will be brought to the ground.   These are elementary principles, which should be taught in schools of architecture, when we really have such in France.

I will support these last observations by an example, without reference, be it understood, to any particular style of architecture,—for our concern here is not with architectural forms, but structural methods.   We have, Plate XX., a palace front to build of masonry, consisting of a basement, a vaulted ground-floor, and a first story with attics.   We wish to have a gallery or wide balcony on the first floor.   We build the basement with a thick casing of large weatherstones, the backing of the masonry being of rubble-work.   On the front of this basement we erect monolithic pillars, the building behind being, with the exception of the first course, raised with rubble and brick.   On these pillars we put lintels of hard stone, relieved on the wall side by corbels. On these lintels we build arches of *banc royal*. As this kind of stone furnishes blocks of large dimensions, we take advantage of it to get very high springers ; next we form the arches of stones extradossed and of moderate thickness—since they support no weight—but of considerable width between the beds. We fill in the spandrels between the arches with walling, but set back so as to facilitate the placing of faience tiles. On the wall levelled up to the top of the arches we lay the cornice course of hard stone, forming a balcony. The first story will be raised only on the rubble-work part of the substructure. The piers between the windows will consist of a first course of weatherstone to counteract the effect of the splashing of the rain on the balcony ; then courses of *vergelé* or *banc royal*[1] according to the height of the blocks. On these piers we shall set equal-sized springers, only over the reveals, and arches also occupying only the thickness of the reveals and the rebates ; the remainder will be built of rubble or brick-work. Mouldings of glazed terra-cotta will surround the springers and the extradossed arches, and will receive faience tiles covering the rough walling ; we shall likewise level up with a layer of glazed terra-cotta, on which will rest the stone corbels that support this cornice receiving the lead gutters. The spaces between the corbels will be filled in with walling covered by faience tiles. Then will come the eaves-wall carrying the roof and the dormer-windows, whose stone construction is shown in our engraving. As the ground-floor arcade forms abutment we shall be able to vault this story with concrete or hollow bricks. The walling behind this arcade could be coated with painted stucco, since it is perfectly sheltered. Thus, inside, we shall have hewn stone only in the piers of the first story, *i.e.* in the part which should be wainscoted. All the rest being rough walling, will allow of being coated with stucco or plaster, and permit the application of painting, which never endures well on stone. Supposing the building to be constructed entirely of hewn stone, we should find no other advantage but that of increasing the expense and preventing the use of those means of external coloured decoration we have been pointing out ; and we should have interiors less healthy and less fitted to receive painting.

We have at command a material invaluable as an auxiliary in building, especially in masonry,—iron, cast and wrought. The ancients hardly ever made use of iron in their masonry, except for cramps or dowels, that is to say, in very small pieces. The great mediæval builders themselves, although they had some presentiment of the advantages offered by the employment of

---

[1] Freestones from the neighbourhood of Paris.—*Tr.*

iron, and used it intelligently, had not this material at command
in considerable dimensions. Having, however, adopted the system
of elastic masonry, iron was of essential service to them in many
cases. In our day it is no longer possible to overlook this most
efficient element of construction, which modern manufacture supplies us with at small cost, and in dimensions formerly unknown.
It is desirable therefore to consider how we may make our means
of construction such as to enable us to avail ourselves of the use
of these novel materials. But while iron is a useful appliance in
certain cases, it must not be forgotten that in connection with
masonry it is also a very active disintegrating agent. By oxidation, iron not only swells and bursts the firmest and toughest
materials, but it also loses its properties; from tough it becomes
brittle, and passes from a metallic state to that of an ore. It is
therefore necessary to place the iron under such conditions that
its oxidation shall be only superficial, if we would not have this
metal destroy, within a century or less, the masonry of which it
furnishes the sinews, and lose all its useful properties. These
disadvantages are not a matter of much concern in private
dwellings,—in houses whose duration is on the average of comparatively limited extent; but they become a serious consideration in public edifices, built to last for centuries. I have already
mentioned that wrought or rolled iron, placed inside masonry
where lime or plaster-of-Paris play an important part, very soon
completely perishes, and by its irresistible expansion bursts the
hardest stones. If the iron is detached, if it is merely in contact
with stones that are but slightly porous, it takes a glaze, and
oxidises only at the surface. Its expansion is then inappreciable.
This phenomenon may be remarked in old stanchions, whose let-
in parts are entirely eaten away by rust, while the parts exposed
to the air have preserved their original appearance. We have
seen built-in iron cramps a yard from the outer surface of the
masonry totally destroyed and reduced to the state of carbonate
of iron; while in the same building, dowels of column shafts
only six inches in diameter had preserved their metallic character.
Hence the deeper iron is bedded in the masonry, the more it
tends to corrode. When there was no other means of tying
except by cramps let into a course, the danger here pointed out
could not be provided against: but now that we can tie with
iron bars fifteen or twenty feet long, or even more, it is perfectly
easy to sink a free passage for them in which they will no longer
be in immediate contact with the masonry. An interval of two
or three eighths of an inch is then sufficient to prevent the effects
of complete oxidation. In all buildings intended to last, the
iron employed in ties should be regarded as straps whose ends
alone should be firmly secured, and for the claws or holdfasts

painting must be regarded as a very insufficient makeshift; they should be galvanised with zinc or copper, and be let in with resinous mastics. But it is always preferable to place the hold-fasts outside, exposed to the air; and there is no reason for objecting to this method, while if desired they may be made a decorative feature. No sufficient reason can be given for our present plan of adopting longitudinal and transverse ties in constructions built after the Roman manner; that is, having walls of a thickness sufficient to present any dislocation. The advantage of employing iron as sinews in masonry is that it enables us to adopt a very slight system of structure, kept in equilibrium by ties: a proof of its efficiency being presented by our street houses, whose walls, only 1 foot 8 inches in thickness, are raised to a height of sixty feet or upwards, support roofs and floors, and yet are perfectly stable when well built. Why should we exhibit less ingenuity in our public than in our private buildings? and why, while increasing the means of strength, and moreover taking every precaution requisite to assure their duration, do we not in the construction of our public buildings largely and usefully employ the resources with which modern industry furnishes us? Always enslaved by the so-called *majestic* style in vogue at the end of the seventeenth century, we cannot bring ourselves to construct buildings answering to the conditions which reason, economy, and the material resources of our time would demand, but sacrifice all the advantages thus offered to considerations of ordonnance which are in fact regarded as important only by the Académie des Beaux-Arts, and do not in the least interest the public which pays, and whose wonder is excited at the continual accumulation of enormous masses of stone, that frequently produce only a very poor result, both as regards the requirements and the effect. In construction we are as it were attempting to ride two horses,— the one which is advancing and the other obstinately holding back; and while in private undertakings every endeavour is being made to discover appliances of an unceasingly practical, economical, and truthful character, monumental art appears to take no heed of them, but to be desirous of maintaining methods which are no longer in harmony either with the requirements or the spirit of the age.

While wrought-iron is very useful in masonry when suitably employed, cast-iron may serve numerous purposes. Cast-iron notoriously possesses great rigidity; it is extremely durable, for it is less liable to decay than wrought-iron; and when exposed to the air, as in supports, and when complicated joints and causes of fracture are avoided, it may be regarded as unassailable by time. But it is evident that, in employing this material, forms of a suitable character should be given to it, and that it would be absurd to simulate in cast-iron, columns (*e.g.*) of a diameter proper to stone supports.   Hitherto we have not seen cast-iron supports for stone-work except in very small buildings.[1] Grand results might, nevertheless, be obtained by so employing it, on condition of adopting the equilibrated structure success-fully carried out in our country by the mediæval architects.   In fact, while iron serves scarcely any purpose in monumental masonry, such as we now conceive it, and which is based on the principle of massive and concrete structure, it would find a rational and useful function in equilibrated masonry, by employ-ing cast-iron for rigid supports or wrought-iron for ties.   With these appliances we might erect vaulting in masonry on very slender supports,—a thing hardly ever done.   Vaulting is fre-quently formed of mortar pugging on iron framework ; but this somewhat barbarous mixed method is expensive, and does not seem to be very durable ; for, when iron has to be used simul-taneously with masonry, it can only be on the condition of allow-ing these two materials to be independent of each other.   More-over, iron is liable to variations according to temperature ; in warm weather it stretches, in cold it contracts ; when buried in the pugging, it occasions in the latter, which is an inelastic mass, con-tinual movements, and causes cracks.   If, on the contrary, with iron employed under conditions of liberty, we adopted a system of masonry vaulting having a certain degree of elasticity, there would be no fear of dislocations.   Vaults carried on extradossed arches, independent of the filling—such, for instance, as those adopted during part of the Middle Ages,—have the advantage of yielding to considerable movement without dislocation and without losing any of their strength.   This system of vaulting permits every kind of combination, and may be used for covering the largest spaces ; why, then, not adopt it ?   What resources would it not supply us with, using iron for supports and as a means of bracing oblique thrusts ?

Observe that we only erect buildings that are entirely of iron, such as the *halles centrales* of Paris, and some great railway stations, and simultaneously with these buildings, which though well designed are after all only sheds, we build citadels of stone —but as regards the mixed method, consisting in a simultaneous employment of masonry and iron in the same building, it has hitherto been attempted only in a timid way, and, it must be confessed, with unsatisfactory results.   At the same time, it must be admitted that a building erected entirely of masonry, that is, with slight stone or brick-work vaulting, and walls of

[1] Buildings thus designed, of small dimensions, the products of our younger architects, might however be cited.

sufficient thickness to serve as a protection against damp or extreme heat, affords, in many cases, advantages which nothing can compensate. But is there nothing intermediate between a vaulted block of stone, like the Madeleine, and a railway station? Are we condemned to have for our public buildings only hypogæa or sheds? and for our palaces is there no medium between casinos of trumpery iron-work, lath, and plaster, and Versailles or the Louvre? Observe again, that in times when meetings are becoming so large that no hall is capacious enough to hold them, we have not succeeded in building a single hall in our public buildings or palaces of really grand proportions, in which a crowd may at ease, breathe comfortably, and come in and go out freely; so that, in fact, we are still compelled to have recourse to the great buildings of the Middle Ages when we have to find room for a multitude. Our concert-rooms are narrow and low, and are encumbered with obstructive architectural features. They are badly lighted by day, and the artificial light makes them stifling. With our wealth and efficient resources we obtain mean results, as if we no longer had the ability to cover vast spaces otherwise than with slight iron and deal construction. Masonry has grown so timid that it no longer ventures to cover spaces twenty or thirty yards broad by means of veritable vaulting. It is in our time incapable of doing more than heaping stones one on the other, and if it does not pile them in great masses, the wall threatens to fall even before it is finished, and it has to be stayed. The truth is that the art of building is no longer taught among us; not merely is there no instruction proportioned to our resources and requirements, but there is absolutely none. The architect finds himself engaged in building before he has gained the slightest acquaintance with practical construction: if he acquires experience, it is at his own or his client's expense, and every architect is obliged to pursue a course of study *in anima vili*. In domestic buildings clever and experienced builders usually make up for the lack of practical knowledge, and these constructions being very similar, provided the architect has some little tact, observation, and intelligence, he soon makes himself acquainted with the methods in vogue. But in public buildings it is otherwise. There it is necessary for the architect to take the initiative; he must know thoroughly what he desires to do and how he wishes to do it; at every step he encounters a difficulty. Feeling the weight of this responsibility, he inclines towards the methods in previous use; in case of doubt he prefers to err on the side of excess of strength: not daring to adopt bold measures, which, in his case, would be acts of temerity, he hides his inexperience behind what he deems rules of art, but which are often only those of routine. It must be remembered, moreover, that in any case bold measures are only permissible to those who have acquired a thorough knowledge of their subject: the contempt which, since the seventeenth century, architects have professed for the practical knowledge possessed by the great builders who lived before that period, and their altogether superficial manner of studying the works of Classical Antiquity, have gradually contracted the domain in which they are able to move. Without determinate methods, voluntarily ignorant of the pliant and fertile principles of the building art during the Middle Ages, and imbued with prejudices, they have ceased to be the real masters of the work. They have ceased to aim at anything more than the reproduction of forms which are becoming more and more debased, because they are not renewing their vitality by being referred to the true principles of construction: and if things continue thus a little longer, architects will be reduced to the condition of mere decorative designers.

It is chiefly in the art of masonry that the architect has to regain that directing influence which he has lost, and those practical habits of procedure which alone are fertile in results. The manner in which he arranges the worked stone in masonry is either productive of a considerable saving or of useless expense. It would seem to be the province of the architect himself to settle the dimensions of the materials for the mason-builder, whereas this is habitually left to the builders. And these have no interest in saving expense, whether of material or labour. Very few builders ever trouble themselves about these questions. According to the mode of measuring work generally adopted in France, but more particularly in Paris, the dressed work is paid for, not according to the actual quantity, but according to that contained by the block before the sinkings; moreover, the sinking, which represents the stone cut away, is charged for as extra labour. It is therefore to the interest of the mason-builder to increase the occasion for sinkings. It is the architect's business to avoid them, if he has any concern to build economically; it is for him, therefore, to mark the jointing, and to give the dimensions of the materials to the mason-builder. But if this is to be the case, must not the architecture adopted—the form —lend itself to such economy? Here we have already the elements of a reform in the art of building in stone. We shall have occasion to return to the question of economy and of wise direction of the works.

The rapid and easy escape of the rain-water is one of those problems which must be encountered in every building, and which is generally resolved in a very imperfect manner. The *mode majestueux* does not take heed of these necessities; yet it rains in France, and it would be in every case worthy of consideration how to provide the simplest means of preserving buildings from the inconveniences thence resulting. The Greeks, who erected scarcely any but buildings of small dimensions, and covered with roofs of double slopes, got rid of the rain-water by issues in the gutter crowning the cornice drip : the inconsiderable height of their buildings obviated the necessity of down-spouts ; the water fell from the open mouths of the gutter direct on the ground. The Romans, who erected very large buildings, often covered by very complicated roofs, adopted vertical pipes passing down through the walls into drains. Their style of architecture favoured the employment of this system, the concrete masonry, very thick in certain parts, and consisting of excellent rubble-work, being quite impervious. When they adopted a mode of building analogous to that of the Greeks, as in the temples and basilicas, they threw off the rain-water from the gutters on to the ground by gargoyles. The great builders of the Middle Ages could not think of perforating the very narrow walls of their buildings with down-pipes ; they therefore adopted an opposite system ; they led off the rain-water from the gutters by open channels down to the parts nearest the ground. There they adopted the gargoyles—no longer short, like those used by the ancients, but projecting, so as to throw off the falling water as far from the walls as possible. In many cases they even employed down-pipes of metal (lead) so as to obviate the splashing of the rain-water against the lower parts of the building. But they always thought of the means of discharge, and arranged their buildings with a view to it. Far from confining the water, they conducted it outside, and with characteristic genius made the appliances for satisfying this requirement decorative features. In Gothic edifices the carrying off of the rain-water determines certain arrangements which dictate the exterior of the structure. Except in rare cases, these means for the escape of the water are apparent, easy to inspect, to keep in repair, and even to replace ; they take the shortest way, and, passing over the surfaces, they cannot endanger the durability of the structure itself. In the present day municipal regulations prohibit the discharge of water by gargoyles into the street. It must be carried down to the ground, and even beneath it into drains. This is certainly a necessary prohibition, but our public buildings ought to be so contrived that the escape of the rain-water may not take place, so to speak, clandestinely. To carry down as an after-thought cast-iron pipes against fronts, through string-courses and cornices, is a barbarous procedure, and one that denotes a complete absence of forethought on the part of the builder ; to carry them down through the thickness of the masonry is very dangerous, and sooner or later causes dilapidations which cannot be perceived until all the mischief possible is done. How, in fact, can we be aware of the bursting of a pipe caused by frost or settlement, if this pipe is completely buried in the masonry? It is only when the wall is saturated with moisture that the cause of the mischief can be ascertained, and it is then too late to obviate it. If the building is sufficiently massive to allow of spacious vertical shafts being left in the thickness of the walls, adapted to receive down-pipes which could be easily inspected and replaced at need, all difficulty would be obviated, and we could dispense with external down-pipes on the fronts; but such cases are rare, and there are but few, even among public buildings, where the room could be thus afforded. In most cases, therefore, the rain-water pipes must be put on the outside. Then why not frankly prepare a place for them? Why afterwards cut through cornices, string-courses, and plinths to make a place for these pipes, which then present the appearance of an after-thought and break all the lines of a design which was not arranged to receive them?

The extent to which the absence of forethought on the part of architects is carried is incredible to those who have not observed it. For instance, in a public building erected not long ago, the gutters pass through the attics, and form in each room, under the windows, a little trough covered with a board, and where water may be drawn any rainy day; and the down-pipes carried through the thickness of the walls, pour torrents of water into the rooms during a thaw; and all this for the sake of not interfering with the lines of a certain classical form of architecture. Generally, when we thoroughly examine these monumental façades, which seem to be built solely for show, we discover much poverty beneath this useless luxury of stone. Those who live behind their costly walls are soon made aware of it. Here you have gutters passing under your feet; there down-pipes which periodically flood you, and deafen you with their rush of water on rainy days. Elsewhere you have windows which cannot be reached without a ladder; rooms all but absolutely dark, or receiving their light near the floor; corridors which are never ventilated, and where you must light lamps in the middle of the day; enormous windows for small rooms; embrasures which hinder any direct light; accommodation narrow and insufficient side by side with considerable spaces wasted,—disproportionate arrangements which seem in fact contrived to satisfy the needs of beings of a different race; perpetual sacrifices to external show—to monumental exigencies as costly as they are useless. Having these strange abuses of a mis-directed art constantly in view, it is especially desirable to cling to true principles of construction, and to endeavour to practise them with more rigorous scrupulosity than ever.

There is another cause of expense in our monumental buildings, about which our architects do not concern themselves,— viz., scaffolding. A somewhat careful examination of the largest edifices erected by the Romans will show us how careful were the ancient builders to adopt the least expensive plans of scaffolding. Whether they employed concrete walling cased with brick or chopped stone, or built with hewn stone, they always left putlog-holes in the walls, and contrived projections to receive the scaffold timbers. These holes were stopped at the dressing down with stucco and other coverings, and the projections were cut off. Thus the scaffolding necessary for the use of the masons and the placing of materials was raised at the same time as the building, and was kept up by it. Our largest mediæval buildings were thus erected : there may still be seen, on the front of the Cathedral of Paris, for instance, the putlog-holes which served to hold very slight scaffolding, whatever its height might be. Besides these holes, which it is so easy to stop on cleaning down, projections may be contrived for receiving struts or plates. The excess of stone thus required is nothing compared with the cost occasioned by a scaffolding right from the bottom, independent of the building,—a kind of temporary wooden structure erected in front of the permanent one of stone. There is no façade, however high or wide, which cannot be erected with a few hoisting stages and slight scaffoldings fastened to the building itself, and rising with it. Even if trolly ways are employed for moving materials, these might be easily formed on bridges connecting the hoisting stages by very economical means, such as inverted iron tie-bar trusses, without having recourse to those veritable monuments in wood which are profitable only to the timber-dealers. What we say here respecting scaffoldings is still more applicable to centering. The Romans in making their great vaultings scarcely employed any but unpropped centres— that is to say, only supported by projections left on the springers. Again, these centres were used only for the arches ; the soffits were turned on lagging very simply contrived.

The mediæval vaulting was likewise turned by very inexpensive means, and with the use of a small amount of timber. We shall have occasion to speak of these methods of scaffolding and centering when we come to treat of timber-work. But here we confine ourselves to showing that the architect, by being the real director of the works, and by having a practical acquaintance with all the branches of industry he employs, may largely obviate expense and obtain a much more satisfactory result than he now does. The enormous cost of our public buildings,—a cost out of proportion with the results,—proves this point in particular— that the architects do not sufficiently consider the practical side of their art,—that they habitually put themselves at the mercy of the builders, who have of course no interest in economising material or labour. But where, in fact, should architects have become acquainted with these practical means, as hitherto they have not been taught them in the only architectural school that exists in France? And who is to be blamed if, when they come to practise their art, they bring with them, as their only stock-in-trade, many prejudices, a very insufficient quota of knowledge, and sketches capriciously made, without criticism or selection.

LECTURE XII.

THE CONSTRUCTION OF BUILDINGS.

MASONRY (*continued*).

METHODS OF EXECUTION—SIMULTANEOUS EMPLOYMENT OF STONE,
BRICK, AND IRON—ECONOMY IN THE OUTLAY.

No country in Europe offers so great a variety of materials adapted for building as France. From granite to tufa, nearly every natural substance that can be employed in masonry is to be found. Hence it might be supposed that each geological zone would possess a method of building appropriate to the material furnished by the soil, and therefore characteristic architectural forms. Such is, however, by no means the case; the buildings erected at Limoges—a granite country—resemble, in every respect, those which are built at Tours, where tufa prevails. Designs centralised in Paris, at the " Conseil des Bâtiments" Civils, are forwarded to the prefectures without any comment on the more or less judicious employment of the local materials. These are details not thought worth consideration. In Paris, thirty years ago, no stone was used except that of the plain of Montrouge and the Oise basin. The Jura and Burgundy now supply us with calcareous materials of considerable strength, in large blocks, and which may, with impunity, be set edge-bedded. We obtain sound tough limestones of excellent quality from Poitou, sandstones from the Vosges, and " vergelés " from the Oise. Have we taken advantage of these novel importations to give our architecture forms in harmony with the special qualities of these materials? No! We have been content to substitute the weatherstones of Burgundy for the " roche " de Bagneux, while retaining the same forms and the same methods of construction. The cost of building is increased, and that is the only result. If, perchance, a few monoliths have been used in lieu of superposed courses, they have been regarded as a decoration—a feature of luxury; there has been no endeavour to turn these novel elements to account, whether to realise a saving in the expense, to obtain new effects, or useful results.

There are nevertheless remaining numerous edifices of Classic and Mediæval times, in which the nature of the materials employed afforded the architects both decorative and useful elements. To obtain similar results nothing more is required than to contravene certain usages in vogue among the contractors who profit by them, and who have no difficulty in maintaining them in opposition to architects little prepared by the education they have received for these contentions with the building trades.

The improvements in machinery, and in the rapidity of execution, should also have modified the system of construction, and have lessened instead of increased the expense of building; yet never comparatively has building been so expensive as it is now.

The relative values of material and labour have considerably changed since the beginning of this century: it would be wise to take these changes into account. The more extensive and powerful appliances for extracting them, and the greater facility of transport, enable us to obtain materials in greater abundance and in better condition for use; on the other hand, the price of labour has been constantly increasing. It is in the working therefore that economy should begin, and hence it is advisable to employ materials as far as possible in the form in which we receive them, subjecting them only to inconsiderable transformations. When blocks of weatherstone, cubing upwards of two yards, can be sent to the building without augmentation of the price per foot, to divide such blocks into four with the sand-saw adds considerably to the price. Admitting that the addition to the cost does not appear in the schedule of prices, it is none the less certain that it must really have been taken into account, and that as things now are—whether the architect endeavours to economise the working or whether he does not— there is no economy in the cost of material. Thus vicious methods occasion indifference on the part of the architects. Finding no advantage in opposing them, they submit, and despite all the efforts of the constructor, mason's work remains exorbitantly expensive. The fact is, that architects do not regulate the schedule of prices according to the nature of the work to be done, but are obliged to accept the schedule fixed by persons who are not practically familiar with construction; and hence their desire for reform, supposing they display any, is checked by customary rules to which they must yield. We find ourselves here in a vicious circle, so to speak. If architects were generally capable and skilful builders, they would draw up reasonable schedules of prices, and effect a considerable saving; for they would make the prices conform to the methods they adopted; if the schedules of prices were more in accordance with the various methods of building, architects would find an opportunity of effecting a saving that is out of the question under present circumstances. Intent, however, on continuing forms of art which are in harmony neither with our materials nor our present methods of using them, architects have failed to acquire the authority and experience which alone would enable them to influence the estimates. It would even appear that the opinion of the master of the works in these matters is daily becoming of less weight; and if things continue thus, the architect will cease to be anything but a designer,—an arranger of outward forms, having no direct influence in the carrying out of the work. The evil would not be so serious if architectural art did not lose by this compromise; but we must not deceive ourselves; architecture ceases to be an art when the design and the execution are separated.

It must be acknowledged that the strangest misconceptions on the subject have taken possession of the public. It is generally imagined that to get a beautiful and substantial building, it is sufficient to procure designs from an architect of repute, and to allow his drawings to be carried out with the aid of any mason that may chance to be picked up. Some administrative bodies have even attempted to systematise this procedure; the consequences of such a course are deplorable, not only from an artistic, but from an economical point of view.

If, therefore, the artists of the present day do not wish to see the architect's profession sink into insignificance, and, which is much worse, their art itself annihilated, they must absolutely set themselves to hinder these tendencies. How can they do so? By becoming skilful builders, ready to profit by all the resources afforded by our social condition, by seeking methods that shall be right, judicious, and economical, and by departing to some extent from the injurious modes of procedure which prevail in all our building-yards, in favour of new ones dictated by reason; as also by preserving that independence of character without which the artist is only a valet of more or less ability, paid to conform to the caprices of his master.

Previous ages have had their several systems of construction; our age alone possesses railways, steam-engines, and appliances of superior force and strength. For what reason then do we adhere to the method of building in vogue during the last century, especially in the case of masonry? Classical Antiquity and the Middle Ages, which certainly did not possess our material appliances, were bolder in conception than we are,—more inventive. How is it that we do not take our starting-point from the level which our predecessors had already reached? How is it that we are less subtle, less ingenious? Why reject methods, which, developed with the help of the powerful appliances we possess, might produce novel features, and effect a considerable economy in our manner of building? Is it not high time we left to the hinderers of progress those puerile disputes respecting the comparative worth of the methods employed by the architects of Classical Antiquity, of the Middle Ages, of the Renaissance, and of Modern times, to profit by all those inventions, and to adopt the various principles suggested to us, without exclusion or prejudice, though with the aid of close and critical examination? If we establish the superiority of the Parthenon to the Cathedral of Rheims, or of the Cathedral of Rheims to the Parthenon, it will little advance us as architects intrusted with the building of our century, if in these two conceptions we fail to discover elements applicable to our own times; or if, imbued with exclusive prejudices, we reject the principles adopted in either of these edifices, with a view to please this or that coterie, in which the public has scarcely any interest, and whose influence will be forgotten a quarter of a century hence.

The study of the systems adopted by the builders of former times is undoubtedly the right means of learning to build ourselves, but something more must be obtained from this study than insipid copies. Thus, *e.g.* we perceive that in the principle of Mediæval vaulting there are elements which are admirable, inasmuch as they admit of great freedom in execution, and an extreme lightness combined with elasticity. Does it then follow that if we would make use of the novel materials with which our manufactures supply us, such as cast or rolled iron, we should content ourselves with substituting arches of cast or plate iron for arches of stone? No; we may adopt the principle, but while adopting it, since the material is changed, we should change the form. In the previous Lecture we showed how, by the moderate employment of cast-iron, we may vault with masonry a very wide hall without having recourse to buttresses. We must develop the applications that can be made of these novel materials, and show how, while preserving the excellent principles adopted by the old builders, we should be led to modify the features of the structure. It is not necessary here to repeat what we have already often said respecting the conditions of masonry structure; we take it for granted that our readers understand that in point of general principle there are but two systems of structure,—passive, inert structure, and equilibrated structure. More than ever we are being led to the adoption of the latter only, both on account of the nature of the materials used, and from reasons of economy, which are becoming increasingly imperative. The architects of the Middle Ages opened for us the path we should follow; clearly one of progress, whatever may be said, and we should pursue it.

As a first example, here, figure 1, is an arrangement fre-

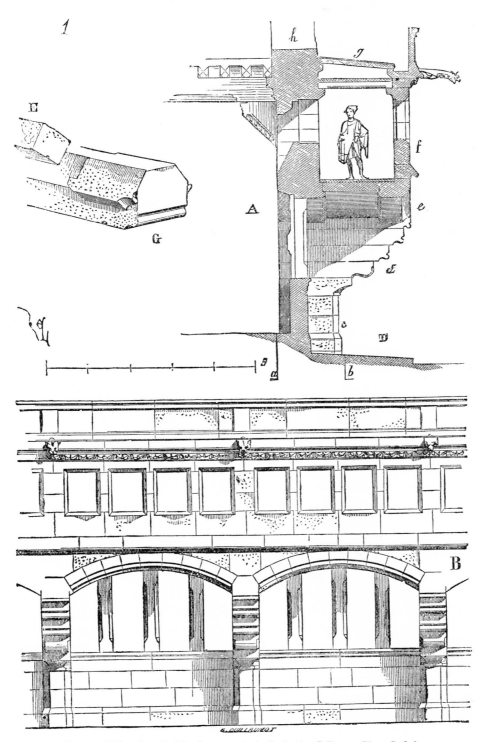

FIG. 1.—Mediæval method for the support of a Projecting Gallery on Stone Corbels.

quently adopted in the civil edifices of the Middle Ages, and which presents certain advantages. In those times, buildings were seldom erected of double thickness; each block of building contained only a single apartment (in its width), but passages were often contrived at half-story height, which afforded easy communication without the necessity of passing length-wise through the chief apartments. These passages were placed in form of "entresol," so as not to obstruct the light, and by means of a few steps to form an approach at the same time either to the room on the ground-floor or to those on the first-floor. As shown in figure 1, these passages were carried by vaults placed on corbelling (see section A). By this arrangement the foundations had only the thickness a, b. Buttresses c supported the corbelling d, on which rested the arches e, receiving a thin wall of stone, f. In exterior elevation, this construction presented the appearance B. The vaults carried on this series of corbelling afforded a shelter D at the ground-floor level, on the exterior most useful in a palace court. This was undeniably a piece of construction which presented advantages, which was easy of execution, and which only demanded a little care in selecting the large stones that constituted the corbelling d. The outer arches rested on the springers shown in detail at G, which also received the barrel vaults E thinner than the outer arches, since they had only a paved floor to carry. The passage was ceiled by joists and covered by stone slabs standing clear and serving as a terrace for the upper hall. The weight of the wall h counterbalanced the overhanging of the corbel courses a.

Supposing that a similar arrangement were required now, and that we sought to adhere entirely to the principles of this structure,—should we rest satisfied with exactly reproducing the design in figure 1? Certainly not; the employment of cast-iron enables us to dispense with the corbelling in courses of hard stone which is expensive and severe in appearance. We shall effect a saving in expense and shall obtain a building that will present greater security, will be less weighty, and will allow a better circulation of air about the ground-floor. Thus, figure 2 (see section A), the novel system adopted will enable us to diminish the projection of the buttresses c, and consequently to make a saving in the foundations. In lieu of the four corbel courses of hard stone, we shall have a cast-iron column or strut d, set at an angle of 45°, and whose capital, furnished like the base B with a dowel, will support the stone springer D, shown in detail at D'. The overhanging of this column and of its springer will be kept up by the double tie-bar T, which will be keyed either at e or in the thickness of the pier. The springer L will rest on the pier furnished with a corbel G; its breaking will be hindered by the two bars T serving the purpose of lintels. Above

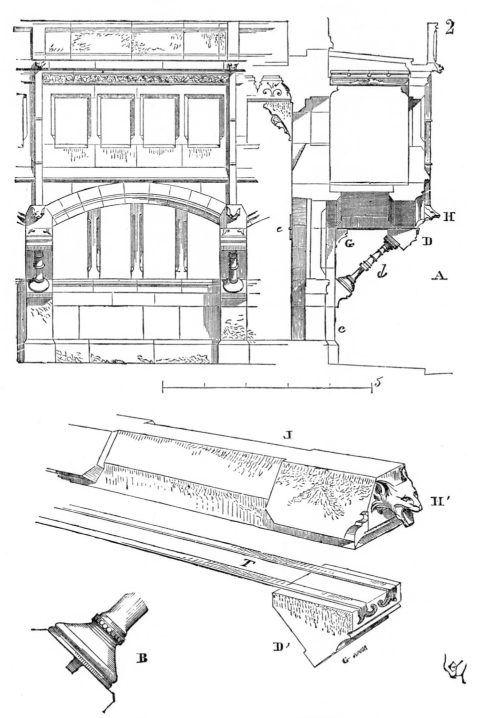

Fig. 2 —Method for supporting a Projecting Gallery on Iron Struts.

the springer we might proceed as in figure 1. Many improvements however could be made on the original structure. Instead of throwing off the water from the terrace by gargoyles, it will be conducted by pipes to the issues H (fig. 2), contrived at the ends of the springers L, and shown in detail at H'. Falling thus nearer the ground, it will not be likely to splash the walls. The ceiling of the gallery might be made by means of double T-iron, on the flanges of which might be laid slabs of glazed terracotta protected by a coat of plastering on the upper side, etc.

This example is sufficient to show how we may turn to account principles adopted in mediæval masonry, while profiting by the resources of our own times. If we study with attention and without prejudices the principles applied in the masonry work of the thirteenth and fourteenth centuries, we shall soon perceive that the structure consists only of independent members, each fulfilling a determinate function. We no longer have, as in Roman architecture, concrete and homogeneous masses, but rather a kind of organism whose every part has not only its purpose, but also an immediate action, sometimes even an active one, as, *e.g.* the flying buttresses and the vaulting arches. The latter, as already mentioned, are simply permanent centres, possessing a certain elasticity, such as curves of iron would have. It is plain, however, that had the mediæval builders possessed cast or rolled iron of considerable dimensions, they would not have employed such a material as they employed, stone. That would have necessitated joinings of too complicated a character, and useless work ; they would on the contrary have sought contrivances more in harmony with the nature of metal. It is likewise evident, however, that they would not have failed to take advantage of the principles of elasticity which they were already applying to buildings of stone, and that they would have rendered the different members of their structure still more independent.

Hitherto cast or rolled iron has been employed in large buildings only as an accessory. Where edifices have been erected in which metal plays the principal part, as in the *Halles Centrales* of Paris,—in these buildings masonry ceases to take any but an exceptional part, serving no other purpose than that of partition walls. What has nowhere been attempted with intelligence is the simultaneous employment of metal and masonry. Nevertheless it is this which in many cases architects should endeavour to accomplish. We cannot always erect either railway stations, markets, or other immense buildings entirely of masonry, such buildings being very heavy in appearance, very costly, and not presenting sufficiently ample interior accommodation. A structure in masonry, regarded as an envelope protecting from cold or heat, offers advantages which nothing could replace. The problem to be solved for providing great edifices destined to accommodate large assemblages would therefore be this :—To obtain a shell entirely of masonry, walls and vaulting, while diminishing the quantity of material and avoiding obstructive supports by the use of iron; to improve on the system of equilibrium adopted by the mediæval architects, by means of iron, but with due regard to the qualities of that material, and avoiding the too close connection of the masonry with the metal; as the latter becomes not only a cause of destruction to the stone, but perishes itself very quickly when not left free. Some few attempts have been made in this direction, but timidly,—for instance by merely substituting columns of cast iron for stone pillars. Iron, however, is destined to play a more important part in our buildings; it should certainly furnish very strong and slender supports, but it should also enable us to adopt vaulting at once novel in plan, light, strong and elastic, and bold constructions forbidden to the mason, such as overhanging projections, corbellings, oblique supports, etc. Is it not evident, for example, that while retaining the system of vaulting employed during the Middle Ages, the thrust of that vaulting might be resisted by the means represented in figure 3 ? The use of rigid shafts or cast-iron columns as oblique supports, is a means of which our builders have not yet thought, I hardly know why, for this system is fruitful in deductions. It somewhat contravenes the principles of Greek and even Roman architecture; but if we would invent that *architecture of our own times* which is so loudly called for, we must certainly seek it no longer by mingling all the styles of the past, but by relying on novel principles of structure. An architecture is *created* only by a rigorously inflexible compliance with modern requirements, while the knowledge already acquired is made use of, or at least not disregarded.

Here there is a means of counterthrusting vaulting of masonry built according to the mediæval method. We know that this vaulting had the advantage (to say nothing of its lightness) of directing all the weights and thrusts on known points, and in lines of inclination that are easily ascertained. It is clear that if the resultant of the pressures takes the direction $a\ b$, the cast-iron column c, placed in the prolongation of that line, will counterthrust the vaulting. By placing a second column d, at an inclination similar to that of the column e, and bracing the apex e of the triangle by means of a tie-bar, the thrust resisted by the column c will be directed to f. Thus on piers and walls only five feet thick at the base of the edifice we shall support and counterthrust vaulting of masonry whose key-stones are at a height of fifty feet, and whose span is forty feet. Nothing will be easier than to make use of the tie-bar to support a floor, to build a low wall of masonry on the coupling shoes *e*, and to put a lean-to roof *g* on these walls, and thus obtain a passage of communication *h*, or small upper gallery. Structures of this kind necessarily demand a certain thoroughness of execution. Thus the walls must be well founded and built; their superincumbent weight should be sufficient to insure great firmness in the building from *i* to *k*. The springers of the arches should be formed above the abutment of the column *c*, in the manner shown at *l*, so as to well shore the vaulting. The coupling shoes *e*, of cast-iron, should be contrived as shown in this diagram A; the surface *m* being intended to receive the base of the column

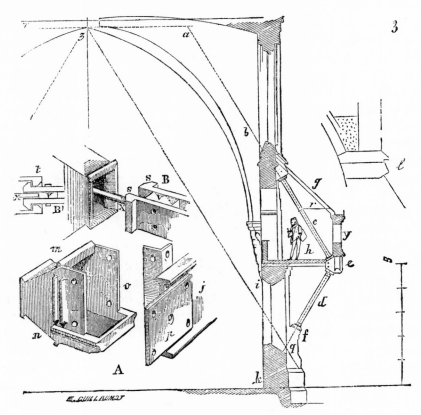

Fig. 3.—Novel method of resisting the thrust of Vaulting.

c, and the surface *n* the capital of the column *d*. Two bars of double ⊤-iron, or plate-iron with angle-pieces riveted on, will fasten, the outer ones at *o*, and the inner ones into grooves projecting from the sides of the shoe. The coupling plate *p* of the outer bars will be drilled to receive the ends of the tie-bars, which for greater security (for the strength of the work will depend on their firm hold) will be double, as seen at B and B′, and furnished with claws *s* at their extremity, which will enter into a jaw indicated at *t*. A key through which passes the bolt *x* will force the tie-bars to remain in their notching. The bolt will pass through the plate p, and will be terminated by a screw-nut. On the bars of double ⊤-iron, or on the iron plates with the riveted angle-irons, we shall be able to build the low enclosing wall of masonry y. The thrust of the lean-to will be met by the ties r. Tie-bars placed above the vaulting at u at the base of the roof will complete the trapeziums a e q z, which will rest on solid masonry at their angle q.

This *organism* is undoubtedly less simple than was that which consisted of a series of massive stone buttresses intended to counterthrust the vaulting. It is however less expensive, as this combination of iron stays cannot cost so much as the buttresses with their foundations : besides, less space is taken up.

In the terrestrial economy the tendency is always towards increased complexity; the organism of a man is more complex than that of a batrachian. Our social condition is much less simple than was that of the Greeks in the time of Pisistratus, or of the Romans of the Augustan age. Our clothes consist of twenty or thirty parts instead of three or four, as did those of the ancients, and the scientific outfit of a learned Greek would not fill a quarter of the brain of a Bachelor of Arts of the present day. It is therefore somewhat childish to tell us now-a-days that we ought to build like the Greeks. In every phase of civilisation all its phenomena are linked together, and if architecture has reached a very difficult and dangerous crisis, it is because we have not sufficiently thought of making it follow the intellectual and material movement of our age. While endeavouring, if we will, to perpetuate or to modify the architectural forms adopted in past times, and adopting them more or less successfully to present requirements, it will be desirable to consider how we may make the utmost possible and the most rational use of that which our age and knowledge supplies us with. The study of the past is obligatory, in fact indispensable, but on the condition of deducing therefrom principles rather than forms.

Substituting a shaft of cast-iron for a column of granite or marble is all very well, but it must be acknowledged that this cannot be regarded as an innovation,—the adoption of a new principle. Replacing a lintel of stone or wood by an iron joist is all very well in its way. It is not however, any more than the former, the result of a great intellectual effort. But substituting oblique for vertical resistance is a principle which, if not absolutely novel—since the mediæval architects had already adopted it,—may assume a very high degree of importance and lead to novel contrivances, now that the introduction of iron into buildings enables us to attempt undertakings of which former ages had only a vague presentiment. During the last twenty years we have seen engineers making a quite novel application of iron employed as a building material. From the *Pont des Arts* to the tubular bridges there is in fact an immense step, but neither engineers nor architects have as yet succeeded in combining in a really satisfactory manner masonry with iron construction; and yet there are many cases in which the system of masonry building could not be superseded. It is scarcely possible to obtain a building satisfactory as regards the health of the inmates, warm in winter and cool in summer, unaffected by variations of temperature, constructed of iron alone. Masonry walls and vaulting will always present advantages superior to those obtained by any other method. We must therefore be content in most instances to continue to employ masonry. Can it then be combined with iron construction? Certainly it can; but under the condition that these two methods of building shall each preserve its characteristics, that they shall not be combined to their mutual injury. Cast or wrought iron, moreover, is liable to variations which must always be taken into account; it must therefore be allowed a certain liberty of movement, it must not be embedded in the masonry, and must retain its independent function.

Moreover, while as a support cast-iron presents a rigidity greatly superior to that of any of the materials constituting masonry, it has not their stability. These vertical supports therefore can only be kept up by very strong stays. This greatly complicates the work, augments the weight, and consequently the expense. If rigid cast-iron supports were so contrived as mutually to stay each other, we should thereby get rid of a whole mass of secondary parts.

Let us suppose that we have to build—as is often done in the provinces—a large assembly-hall over a covered market-place. If we raise this hall in mason-work on rows of cast-iron columns in order to gain space and secure more air and light in the market, these supports must be tolerably numerous, and must be connected at their upper part by powerful stays, so as to hinder the superstructure from toppling over, and we shall have a rather inconvenient row of columns along the side of the street. If, on the contrary, we adopt a plan analogous to that shown in the section, figure 4, it is evident that the hexagon whose half is drawn at $a\ b\ c$ presents a stable figure, and that even the addition of the triangle $b\ d\ c$ in nowise lessens this stability while the line $c\ e$ remains unbroken.

With this elementary figure as our basis we may support the great hall over our market-place as shown by the drawing A. On stone blocks f, solidly bedded, placed at distances determined by the width of the bays, we set cast-iron columns inclined at an angle of 60°. The capitals of these columns are held by the transverse wrought-iron girders which carry the joists of T-iron, from one to another of which we turn barrel arches of brick. From the ends of the girders *g* may be suspended stirrups for the support of cast-iron shoes, to receive the springers of stone arches *h*, on which we shall build the walls of the hall, likewise of masonry. Brackets of cast-iron *i*, in two parts, secured by the tie-rods *j*, and whose thrust at foot will be counteracted by the triangles *o p q*, *o s q*, will sustain the longitudinal barrel vaults *k*, which will in their turn support the main upper vaulting. One

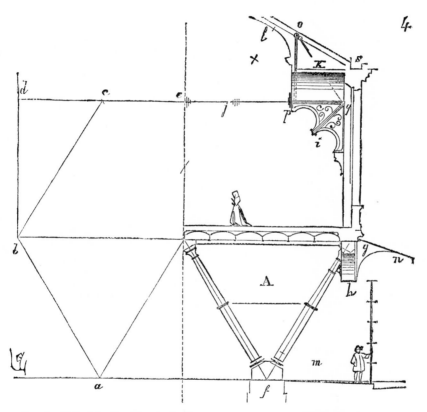

FIG. 4.—Method for the support of a Masonry Structure on obliquely set Iron Columns.

essential condition will be to bed the blocks *f*, not on separate foundations, but on solid transverse walls; for it is important that the feet of the columns *f, g, a, b*, should not be able to lessen their distance apart under the pressure and thereby raise the columns of the inner triangle.

As staircases will certainly be required, and anterooms, and means for heating the upper hall, the general plan will be that represented in figure 5, and these two end buildings will hinder any movement of the lower bays in a longitudinal direction. The spaces *m* towards the street (see figure 4) sheltered

E. Viollet-le-Duc del.

A. MOREL - Editeur.

Cl. Sauvageot, sc.

Imp. Lemercier, Paris

by the incumbent arches will be very convenient for the buyers and for placing the stalls; moreover there is nothing to prevent the fixing of awnings at *n.*

It will be understood that it is not my purpose here to offer specimens of architectural style. That is not the question now; my purpose is simply to suggest to our younger professional brethren the proper method for proceeding in the search for novel elements of structure. I should be happy to select examples for illustration from existing buildings constructed on a really original plan. As there are none, and as I am anxious to make myself clearly understood, in regard to the object towards which our endeavours might be directed, I am, much to my

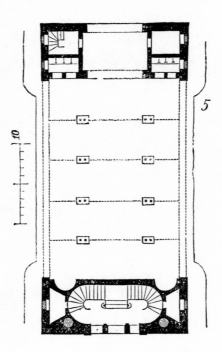

FIG. 5.—Plan of Building supported on obliquely set Iron Columns.

regret, compelled to give the result of my own reflections. I am aware that the forms which originate in the rational employment of the means of construction afforded by our age are not altogether classical,—that they depart somewhat from certain valued traditions; but if we honestly desire to inaugurate the era of a new architecture, in harmony with modern materials, appliances, requirements, and tendencies in the direction of a reasonable economy, we must make up our minds to give up to some extent traditionary Greek or Roman notions, or those of the *Grand Siècle,* when people built badly.

The constructors of locomotive engines did not take it into

their heads to copy a stage-coach team. Moreover we must consider that Art is not riveted to certain forms, but that, like human thought, it can incessantly clothe itself in new ones. Again, buildings are not made to be seen in geometrical elevations ; possibly the effect of that whose plan and section we have just given would not be entirely devoid of character. Plate XXI. will enable us to judge of this. All that is contemplated is merely a hall above a sheltered place. The question is how to provide this requirement in the simplest and most substantial manner.

Let it be well understood, once for all, that architecture cannot array itself in new forms unless it seeks them in the rigorous applications of novel methods of construction ; that casing cast-iron columns with cylinders of brick or coatings of stucco, or building iron supports into masonry, for example, is not the result either of calculation or of an effort of imagination, but merely a disguising of the actual construction ; no disguise of the means employed can lead to new forms. When the lay architects of the thirteenth century invented a system of structure different from any that had been previously used, they did not give to their architecture the forms adopted by the Roman or the Romanesque architects ; they gave a frank expression to that structure and thus succeeded in originating new forms possessing a characteristic physiognomy. Let us endeavour to proceed thus logically ; let us frankly adopt the appliances afforded us by our own times, and apply them without the intervention of traditions which have lost their vitality ; only thus shall we be able to originate an architecture. If iron is destined to play an important part in our buildings, let us study its properties, and frankly utilise them, with that sound judgment which the true artists of every age have brought to bear upon their works.

It is strange that we should have almost entirely abandoned masonry vaulting of wide area. We vault the lower story of a building by groining or doming in narrow bays, and on piers near together, and made with jointed stone-work,—which is very expensive,—or with brick ; but when wide spaces have to be covered, our ingenuity is generally limited to setting up an iron framework consisting of curves, braces, intermediate ribs and ties, the whole of which is afterwards pugged with pottery or hollow bricks. Besides being expensive, this kind of construction involves the enclosing of the iron—a material which readily oxidises and is affected by variations of temperature—in concrete masonry which the least movement must crack, and which has the effect of hastening the oxidation of the metal. Thus imbedded in the pugging it is impossible to ascertain the condition of the fastenings and bolts, and thereby to prevent mishap. In dwelling-houses pugged floors of this description may be all very well, as the habitations in a great city are not intended to last for many centuries, but in edifices which should endure as long as a city, this kind of structure consisting of iron and pugging conjointly leads to disastrous consequences. The skill of the builder is displayed not merely in assuring himself of the excellence of the materials and the methods he employs, but also in so contriving that the various parts of the structure may always be got at, examined, and repaired when required. The iron-work and timber framing should as far as possible remain visible, for these materials are perishable, and liable to changes in their properties. But we see edifices built, whose costly walls of solid hewn stone will defy the effects of time, while these walls enclose vaulting and floors whose duration is very problematical, so much so indeed that our successors, who will probably have been obliged to reconstruct or repair these parts of the structure several times, will scarcely comprehend the union of such unprecedented extravagance with such an absence of precaution. It would seem as if our architects were ashamed to employ iron; they conceal it as far as possible beneath plastering and pugging, which give it the appearance of a masonry structure. Some, we must do them the justice to remark, have ventured to show iron girders beneath the floors, and to decorate and dignify them; but when vaulting is in question, the iron is merely a concealed framework, an incased carcass. Iron is made to serve as an appliance for obviating the outward thrust of masonry vaulting, not by means that are frank and apparent, but by contrivances which are carefully concealed, and which, as is the case with all appliances of the kind, are wanting in efficiency.

We are familiar with the simple and natural methods by which the mediæval architects of our own country counterthrusted their vaulting,—namely, by buttresses and even flying buttresses, that is by exterior resistance, inert or acting obliquely. In Italy, architects adopted a more simple contrivance; they placed horizontal iron tie-bars above the springing of the arches at the line of thrust. In point of fact, the thrust of vaulting must be resisted either by abutments or by ties, to obviate the spread. How is it that while in France we object to the appearance of interior ties beneath our masonry vaulting, our sight is not offended by the presence of those which are so profusely employed in Italian buildings? I shall not attempt to explain this inconsistency; I merely remark that the architects who sketch the Italian buildings of the Middle Ages and the Renaissance suppress these iron ties in the edifices built in imitation of them, which leads one to suppose that they regard them as offensive on this side of the Alps; why, then, should they have no objection to them on the other side ? I will add that the ties across the springing of the Italian vaulting make no pretension whatever to be a decorative feature ; they are simply iron bars. It is fortunate, however, that it has not occurred to the Italian clergy to have these bars cut away in their churches, as our French curés have done with the tie-beams of all the timber ceilings ; for had they done so, many an edifice which now excites the admiration of travellers would have fallen.

Nevertheless the proper function of iron in masonry vaulting is that of a tie, whenever we wish to avoid having recourse to the expensive contrivance of buttresses and abutments. The principle being resolutely adopted, we should avail ourselves of all the advantages it affords, with rather more intelligence than was shown by the architects of the Italian Renaissance, who, while adhering to the Roman system of structure, or adopting that of the French mediæval vaulting, were content to brace the thrust by means of iron bars ; for this is merely a makeshift, it is not a novel system of structure.

The use of iron allows of feats of construction from which we seem to shrink back. It would appear that we have only an imperfect confidence in the properties of this material. We employ it only as a means of producing additional security, *i.e.* with reservations, so that instead of lessening it often serves only to increase the expense. Vaulting built according to the mediæval method, with iron ribs in place of stone ones, is neither sensible, nor good, nor cheap ; it cannot be regarded as an intelligent use of iron in view of its properties. We may thereby somewhat diminish the thrusts, but we scarcely benefit by the advantages which a structure of mingled iron and masonry is capable of affording. As we just now observed, the erection of an iron framework in the form of a barrel or groined vaulting, and imbedding this structure in plaster of Paris or hollow brickwork, is a contravention of true construction,—placing in close contact two materials of opposite nature ; it is shutting up the wolf in the sheepfold. Provision should be made for the contraction of the iron and for its changes, and it should only be used under conditions favourable to the development of its properties. When, therefore, we would build masonry vaulting on iron, the latter should retain its liberty of movement and be able to expand without rending the concrete envelope which it supports. The fastenings should remain visible—clearly seen—so that, should any part give way, it may be promptly repaired. If we propose to use iron conjointly with masonry, we must give up the traditional methods of Roman structure. We have no longer to contemplate erecting buildings based on inert immoveable masses, but to

provide for elasticity and equilibrium. The distribution of
active forces must replace an agglomeration of passive forces.
For the attainment of these results, the study of the structure
of the French mediæval buildings can be of great service, for
the architects of that period had already substituted the laws of
equilibration and elasticity for those of Roman structure; but it
does not follow that we should imitate the forms which they
employed—forms which are admirable where masonry only is
used, but which are unmeaning where iron and masonry are
similtaneously employed. Had the mediæval architects possessed
the products of our metal manufactures, they would assuredly,
in virtue of their logical and subtle intelligence, have adopted
other forms. They would, *e.g.* have endeavoured to reduce the
great height of their vaulting—a height which was occasioned
by the mode of structure adopted, much rather than by æsthetic

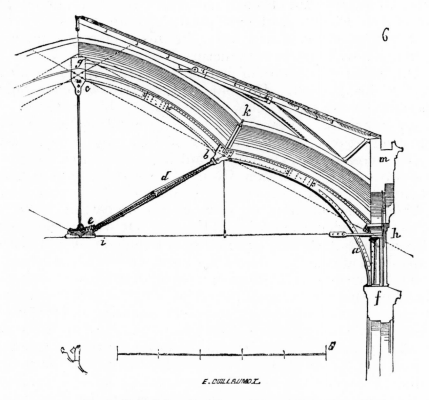

FIG. 6.—Method of combined Iron and Masonry Vaulting.

considerations—a height which often involved difficulty, and was
an occasion of expense.

It is possible by means of iron, employed as sinews and
tendons, to construct vaulting of little rise and great span.
Figure 6 shows a method for obtaining this result.

Suppose an interior of 50 feet in width. Dividing it into

bays of 14 or 15 feet, and placing at each division arch-ribs *a b c* formed of plate and angle-iron, and fitting at *a* into cast-iron uprights; bolting coupling plates at the elbow *b*, bearing on cast-iron struts *d*; footing these struts into boxes *e*, firmly suspended from the strengthened junctions *g*; and maintaining the heads *h* of the cast-iron uprights in place by the ties *h i*, we shall obtain firm and substantial ribs, whose intermediate spaces may be arched with annular vaulting carried by the trusses. As the cast-iron supports simply rest on the top of the wall at *f*, the expansion, through the form given to the barrel arching,

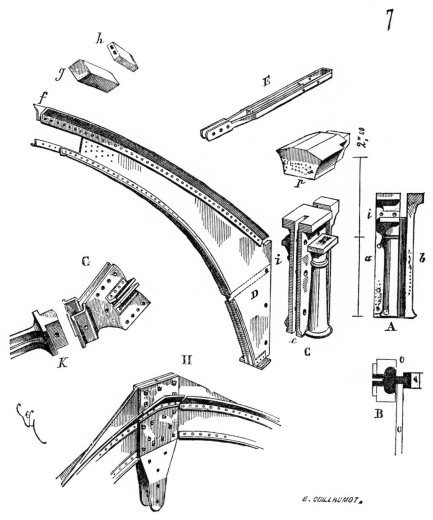

Fig. 7.—Details of Iron Vaulting Truss.

will only be able to occasion ruptures at *k*. But if at *k*, from one truss to another, we have fixed a rib of plate- and angle-iron inclined in the direction of the meeting of the two segments of barrel arching, the rupture caused by the expansion of the iron, will take place at this point of junction, and will do no harm, since the junction will be supported by the double flanges of the angle-iron bracing. On the capitals *h* of the cast-iron supports we shall be able to build the arches, spandrils, and cornices of masonry *m*.

A few details, figure 7, will be necessary to explain the construction of the iron truss supporting the annular masonry vaulting. At A is drawn the side elevation, and at B the section through *a b* of the cast-iron uprights. At C the perspective view of these supports. The plate-iron curves D fit into the grooves *e* of the uprights, the curves are strengthened at their extrados with angle-irons *f*, which receive the stones *g* on whose beds rest the bricks *h*, forming the annular vaulting. At E is drawn the clip in two parts of the tie-rods passing at *i*. At G the coupling-plates marked *b* in figure 6, with the end *k* of one of the cast-iron struts. At H the coupling-plates marked *g* in figure 6. At *o* would be placed the window casements.

On the cast-iron uprights would rest the stone springers *p* of the arches forming wall-ribs, and reveal for the glazed casements. A perspective view, figure 8, will complete the illustration of this structure.

Is it possible to give these iron trusses an architecturally decorative appearance? I think so; but this cannot be done by giving them forms appropriate to masonry. With our present appliances for iron structure, a decorative effect cannot be obtained except at considerable cost, for our manufactories do not supply us with the elements required for producing it. But the reason why our manufactories fail to supply them is that we have hitherto given iron only an accessory or concealed function in our great buildings, because we have not seriously considered how to make the best use of the material by giving it forms appropriate to its nature.[1] Further on, when we come to treat more especially of the employment of iron, we shall endeavour to show how this material may be rendered ornamental, or rather what are the decorative forms appropriate to it. When we look at the structural iron-work employed in buildings twenty years ago, and compare the complicated, weak, heavy and consequently expensive girders of that time with those constructed within the last few years, it is impossible not to recognise a marked advance. Is it the architects of repute who have been the promoters of

---

[1] Routine is a goddess still powerful among us. In our metal manufactories she receives a veritable worship; and should Free Trade effect no other result than that of gradually suppressing this worship, it will have done good service. We have known large manufactories refuse to make iron rolled to a novel section, because cylinders would have to be constructed, though the order amounted to more than a hundred tons weight. If one of these manufacturers was willing to execute the order, as he was aware that others had been applied to in vain, he demanded so high a price that the saving which iron of the new pattern could have effected was rendered impossible.

this progress? Unfortunately, no! It is to our engineers that
it is due; but since their architectural education is very limited,
they have employed iron merely in view of practical utility without regard for artistic form; and we architects, who ought to
have been able to afford them aid when form was in question,
have on the contrary done our utmost to hinder the adoption

FIG. 8.—Perspective View of combined Iron and Masonry Vaulting.

of these novel appliances; or, if we have adopted them, it has
been merely as a mechanical means, which—I repeat it—we
have been careful to conceal beneath certain forms hallowed by
tradition. Hence it has been concluded, not without reason,
that architects are not sufficiently *scientific* and that engineers
are not sufficiently *artistic*. And yet in view of our present

requirements and our novel appliances it is more than ever necessary that the builder should be both artist and savant if we would obtain original artistic forms, or, more correctly, artistic forms in harmony with the requirements of our age. If we take a fair and unprejudiced view of things we cannot shut our eyes to the fact that the professions of the architect and the civil engineer tend to merge one into the other as was formerly the case. If it is the instinct of self-preservation that has caused architects of late to resist what they regard as the encroachment of the engineer on their domain, or to set themselves against the methods adopted by the latter, this instinct has badly served them, and if it rules, will have no other result than gradually contracting the architect's field and limiting him to the function of decorative designer. A little reflection will show us that the interests of the two professions will be best saved by their union, for in point of fact the name is of little consequence : it is the thing which is essential, and art is that thing. Whether the engineer acquires a little of our knowledge and love for artistic form—so far as that love is rational and is something more than mere sentiment,—or whether the architect enters upon the scientific studies and adopts the practical methods of the engineer,—whether both thus succeed in uniting their faculties, knowledge, and appliances, and thereby realise an art truly characteristic of our times, the result cannot fail to be advantageous to the public and creditable to the age. Some endeavours in this direction, it may be observed, have not been unsuccessful, and the city of Paris may well congratulate itself on having engaged one of its most distinguished architects to carry out, in the building of the *Halles Centrales*, the idea and general design of an engineer. If among the numerous buildings erected of late years this better than any other fulfils the conditions of the programme, and if it is approved both by the public and by professional artists, is it not to the concurrence of two orders of intellect that such a result is due ? What danger therefore, or what disadvantage to art would ensue if the architect or the engineer combined in himself those two elements which are now separated ? What could the architect reasonably hope for, from the maintenance of certain absolute dogmas respecting art which are at variance with what our times demand ? Or what advantage could the engineer expect to gain by ignoring the liberal studies of art and confining himself more and more within the limits of formulas ? Whether fifty years hence the engineer calls himself an architect or the architect an engineer,—as the two professions must inevitably merge into one another,—I cannot but think that the rivalry or distinction which is sought to be kept up between these two branches of art, which are destined in the nature of things to coalesce, will appear somewhat puerile. Some years ago, a member of our profession,—I forget who,—felt convinced that he inflicted a fatal blow on that of the engineer by the discovery that its name was derived from the word *engineor* (maker of engines). Against this plebeian origin, it may be remarked, might have been set that of our craft, which is scarcely more dignified.

But let us leave for a while these fears and rivalries, which are regarded with little interest by the public, and complete our task—borrowing as occasion may require some of the appliances adopted by the engineer, and endeavouring to reconcile them with the art of architectural construction, continuing the consideration of the ways in which modern appliances may be allied with the ancient tradition of masonry. For among us architects of the nineteenth century—and this cannot be too often repeated,—originality can result only from the adoption of appliances hitherto unused with forms previously invented, though without contravening those appliances. So far our age has not been hard to please in this respect, since we have seen the substitution of novel materials, without change of shape, dignified with the title of originality. It is not for us to condemn these attempts—though they remain barren of results—because they have on the whole tended to draw the attention of the public and of architects to the consideration of these new materials, and have reduced those among the latter who were not too much the slaves of routine to seek for something out of the common way. But this seeking has been hitherto rather superficial. On the one hand sufficient regard has not been paid to the essential principles of construction, and on the other hand courage has been wanting to break with forms which are consecrated and dogmatically prescribed. Much has been said about progress, but in point of fact it has been persistently regarded as the upsetting of all that we had been accustomed to respect. Classical architects have continued to produce pseudo-Roman architecture, loading it with iron ; thenceforth considering themselves bold and progressive enough to have the right of accusing *Gothic* architects of the desire to make art retrograde. On the other hand, Gothic architects have regarded their opponents as rather more retrograde than themselves,—an accusation which might pass for true, since Gothic came after Roman art.

But if the latter (I refer to the so-called Gothic architects) manifested *progress* in their conceptions, the general result amounted, as I said above, to nothing more than the substitution of iron supports or arch-ribs for the stone piers and arches of the Middle Ages. But there is no more progress in this than there is progress in keeping up the architraves of quasi-Roman entablatures with iron bars. Had the Romans, who were sensible people, possessed iron of large dimensions such as we can procure, they would have adopted original forms in place of those derived from the Greeks. The Romans were too practical not to have taken advantage of these appliances. Similarly the great builders of the Middle Ages who so clearly adapted their conceptions to the materials they possessed, would have lost no time in giving forms to their architecture suited to these novel materials. The conditions in which we architects of the nineteenth century find ourselves are different; preceding ages have bequeathed to us two or three distinct styles of art, without reckoning their derivatives. It is not in our power to ignore them; there they are present before us; and it is a strange and even absurd fancy of our times to endeavour to obliterate one of those forms of architectural art, and to declare it non-existent. This mode of proceeding has an unfortunate resemblance to that attributed to the Père Loriquet in making Louis XVIII. the successor of Louis XVII. It may be perfectly reasonable to prefer the architecture of Rome and Greece to that of the Middle Ages; but if we would advance according to the logical order of progress we must accept the results of the efforts to improve made by successive generations of builders. Progress is nothing other than the superposition of efforts to improve, made with the fresh elements originating at certain periods. Nature, whose methods are certainly well deserving of attention, has not proceeded otherwise. She neither forgets nor suppresses any portion of her past, but adds and improves. From the polypus up to man she advances without interruption. What would be said of the naturalist who should suppress an entire order of organised beings and link the monkey with the birds under the pretext that mammalia of a lower order do not merit attention? or who should maintain that the reptile is a more perfect creature than the cat, because a severer injury may be inflicted on the former than on the latter without causing its death?

Because you might remove a pillar from a Roman concrete structure without endangering the building, whereas you could not remove a single stone from the arch of a flying buttress of a Gothic nave without insuring its ruin, it does not follow that in order of structure the Gothic building is not an advance on the Roman. The inference is rather, that in the former edifice each member is necessary—indispensable, because the structure is more perfect. Man, who is considered the most perfect of organised beings, is far more susceptible to injury than most of the mammalia, and his limbs when cut off will not grow again like those of a cray-fish. Extreme sensitiveness and delicacy of organism are therefore among the conditions of progress in the order of creation ; and it is the same with that secondary creation which is produced by man, and which is called building. The greater the ingenuity displayed by man in subjugating inert matter,—the more capable he becomes of bending it to his necessities,—the more the organs—if I may so term them—of this creation must be essential, delicate, and consequently fragile. Calculation, new principles of equilibrium, of counterpoise, of inverse action and neutralising forces,—all then take the place of inert mass, stable in itself.

For the passive stability of the Greek buildings and the concrete structure of the Romans, the great builders of the Middle Ages substituted equilibration,—a more delicate law affording more extensive, varied, and unrestricted results. Those builders had advanced on the Greek and Roman systems of structure. With our materials and the employment in our buildings of metal of large dimensions we may advance beyond the mediæval builders ; but this cannot be effected by ignoring what they did, or by following them step by step, but by starting from the point which they had reached, and mounting still higher the ladder of progress. Let who will call the principles here enunciated exclusive doctrines, the accusation will, I am convinced, recoil on those who make it, for they cannot retard the advance of real progress, and this will ultimately be acknowledged.

Let us therefore continue our endeavours ; however imperfect they may be, they will none the less show what a field is open for the art of building in the present day, and prove that architecture will assume an original form only when it shall frankly adapt itself to the really novel and rational appliances afforded by our times.

There are some who continue to assert that Greek architecture, being essentially beautiful, lends itself to every requirement. To show the falseness of this opinion, it will suffice to request them to construct vaulting with the structural system of the Greeks, who did not erect any. It is true that in the view of many amateurs, and even some artists, the essence of Greek architecture consists in the use of a few bits of ornament or a few mouldings. These blind adherents of Greek culture seriously believe that they are following the arts of the age of Pericles, when on a house-front five stories high they have copied a jamb moulding or a cornice from Attica. Without enlarging on these puerilities, we are compelled to admit that the Greeks did not consider it worth while to vault their buildings, and that to imitate them in this respect would be rather a step backwards —that the Romans built concrete vaulting, and that the mediæval builders erected a great deal of vaulting on an elastic system which has its advantages. These are facts against which neither regrets nor admiration can prevail. But Roman vaulting required abutments as well as that of the Middle Ages. We have shown how the thrust of vaulting may be supported by iron. The matter which concerns us to analyse still more attentively is the applications that can be made of iron in vaulting buildings, and to consider whether it is not possible without the aid of tie-bars to counteract the thrust of an arch by a combination of iron construction with masonry.

Let figure 9 represent an arch of 30 feet in span; A is a band

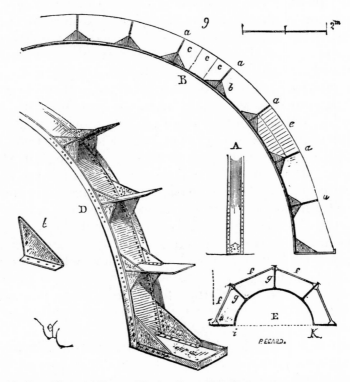

FIG. 9. –Combination of Iron and Masonry Construction.—Method of counteracting the thrust of an Arch.

of plate-iron 15 inches wide, bent to a semicircle, on which are fastened spurs, also of plate-iron a, 2 feet 3 inches long, by means of brackets b, as shown in the drawing B. Two angle-irons, riveted to the curved band, serve to secure the flanges and to stiffen the work. If, between these spurs, we place voussoirs of stone c, or even of brick e, the arch cannot give way. The perspective drawing D illustrates the system of this iron construction. For example, suppose E an arch of plate-iron, to which are fixed spurs g secured by stiff braces f; it would not be possible for the two points i, k, to spread, since any action tending to spread those points would only have the effect of thrusting the braces more closely against each other. Now the arch B, partly of iron and partly of masonry, is subject to the same law. Any spreading action results in a greater squeezing together of the voussoirs, and as the iron band presents a continuous surface, the joints cannot open at the intrados; these joints, therefore, being unable to open the arch, cannot give way.

A giving way could only occur through the stretching of every portion of the arch passing from the curve to a straight line under considerable pressure, so as to make the band of the intrados polygonal instead of circular. But it will be observed that the curve between each spur is hardly apparent, and that, moreover, it is stiffened by the angle iron and the brackets. It would, therefore, require a much greater pressure than that exerted by ordinary vaulting to produce that stretching of each section of the circle.

An experimental model of this construction may be constructed at small expense with hoop-iron or even with zinc, and by fitting little blocks of wood between the spurs it will be easy to prove its strength.[1] An arch thus constructed costs more than an arch of stone or brick, but besides the saving in the quantity of those materials (for an arch of that span might be safely turned with voussoirs only 16 inches thick), it is in the abutments that the real saving would be effected.

By adopting this system, we might construct transverse vaulting ribs to carry groined vaultings of brick or rubble work, such as the Roman vaulting, on piers of very small section. Here then would be an advance as regards economy of construction, and the surface occupied by the solid parts on the ground. Now, while in our towns materials are expensive, space is restricted; the builder should therefore do his best to economise both.

It will be evident that the conditions under which iron is thus employed will be favourable to its durability; for though the iron spurs are imbedded between the stone or brick voussoirs, their function is merely passive, and depends on the simple pressure exerted on them by the voussoirs. The band of the intrados, the angle-iron and its brackets, which constitute the chief strength of the system, are exposed to the air, at least on one face. Besides, the stone or brick voussoirs, being under cover and beneath the vaulting, cannot give out moisture or salts in sufficient quantity to affect the duration of the iron. But here we have only the adaptation of iron to an ancient system of structure. These arches have, like the Roman and mediæval arches, the disadvantage previously pointed out; they

[1] An arch 3 feet in span at the intrados, 3 inches by 2 inches in section, formed of zinc without brackets, and with twelve spurs simply soldered in, with plaster of Paris voussoirs, bore a weight at the key of 20 lbs. without giving way.

COURS D'ARCHITECTURE

MAÇONNERIE

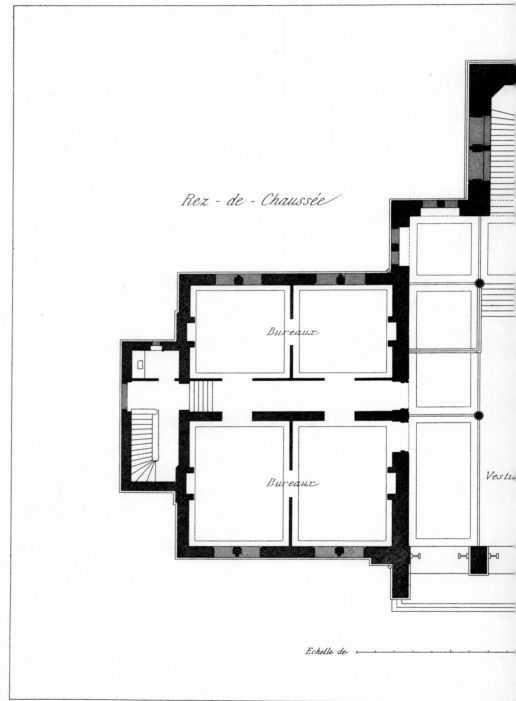

Rez - de - Chaussée

Bureaux

Bureaux

Vestu

Echelle de

E. Viollet - Le - Duc del.

HÔTEL

Emp

A. MOREL — Editeur

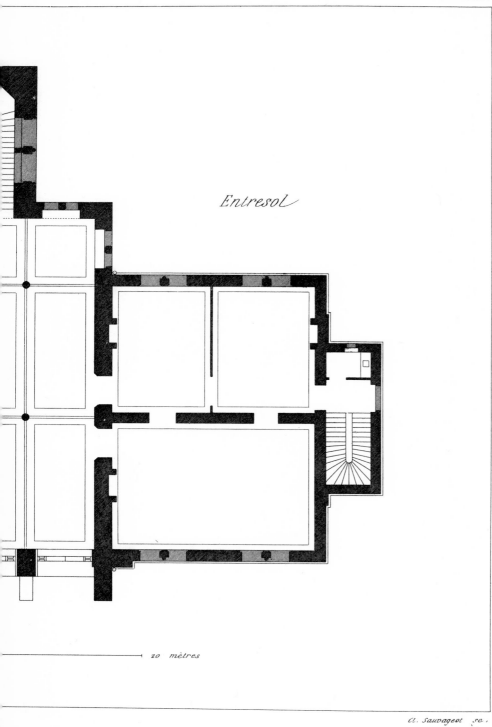

Entresol

20 mètres

a. Sauvageot sc.

ILLE

Imp. Lemercier et Cⁱᵉ Paris

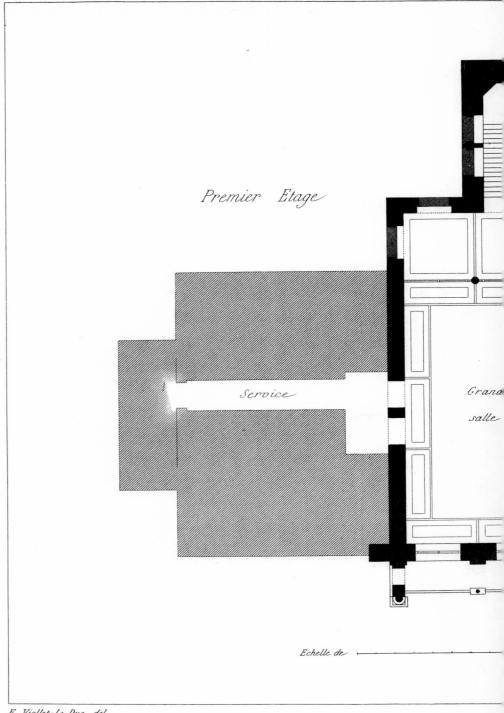

Premier Etage

Service

Grand

salle

Echelle de

E. Viollet-Le-Duc del.

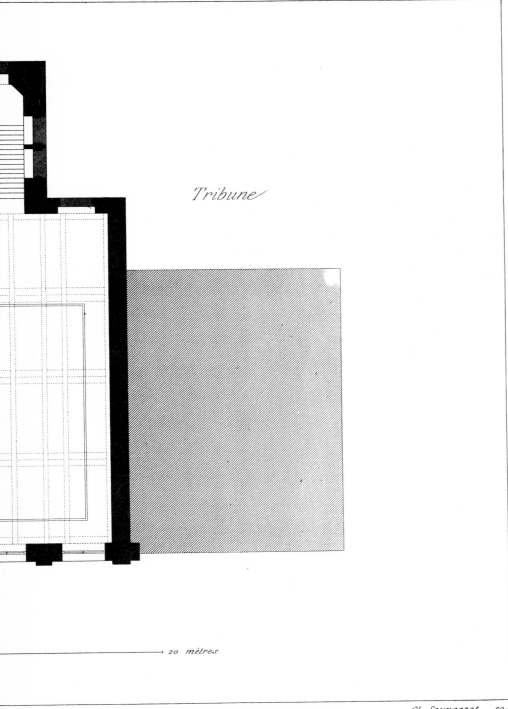

Tribune

20 *mètres*

Cl. Sauvageot sc.

VILLE

fer.

Imp. Lemercier et Cⁱᵉ Paris

are of great height and of considerable weight; the Roman groined vaulting demands expensive centering. When it is required to construct vaulting over a very wide space—60 or

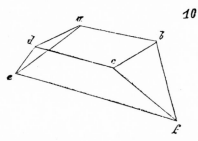

FIG. 10.—Combination of Iron and Masonry Construction.—Method of Vaulting.

70 feet for instance—without exerting any thrust, not needing any considerable amount of centering, not occupying a great height, allowing large openings for light at a lofty elevation above

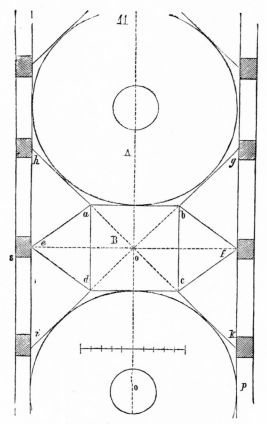

FIG. 11.—Plan of Vaulting.

the floor, more architectural than the vaulting given in figures 6, 7, and 8, and in which iron is employed merely as supports and ties—economically, therefore,—we shall have to resort to contrivances differing from those adopted by the Romans or the mediæval builders.

Let *a b c d*, figure 10, be a frame with four struts, *a e, d e, b f, c f*, and a tie *e f*. It is evident that if the framework consisting of these pieces be weighted at the points *a b c d*, no giving way will be possible. It is on the principle illustrated by this diagram that the system of vaulting we are about to work out depends.

Let figure 11 represent part of the plan of a hall 65 feet wide in the clear, and consisting of a series of bays. If at *a b c d* we set up a framework designed in accordance with figure 10, the lines *a e, d e, b f, c f*, will give the horizontal projection of the supporting struts, the lines connecting the points *a b c d* that of the frame, and the line *e f* that of the tie. If we turn arches corresponding with the lines *a h, a d, d i, b g, b c, c k, a b, d c*, we shall have a cluster of arches on which we shall be able to erect the round dome A, a square dome over the rectangular space B, and barrel vaults over the trapeziums *h a d i, g b c k*. We shall be able to support the entire system on walls of six feet in thickness, pierced by windows and without buttresses.

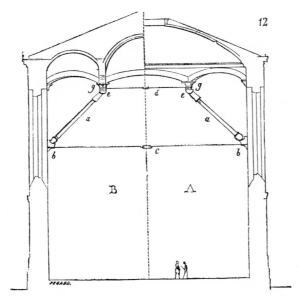

FIG. 12.—Combined Iron and Masonry Construction.—Section of Vaulting.

The section, figure 12, through *o p* at A and through *o s* at B, explains this system; but it will be still better explained by the perspective view of the interior, Plate XXII. The supporting struts or slanting columns *a* (see section, figure 12), are of cast-iron, resting at *b* in shoes likewise of cast-iron connected by a tie-rod *c*. The feet of these supporting struts are spheroidal, and fit into two cups sunk in each shoe. The tops of these struts have tenons fitting into spheroids *e* surmounted by dwarf shafts, which again tenon into the cast-iron capitals *g*, each of which carries the springer of three arches. The dwarf shafts are connected by the ties *d*, which, with the arches above them, form the sides of the frame that supports the square dome and part of the cupola. Thus these four arches with their tie-rods cannot exert any thrust. Only the arches *a h, d i, b g, c k* (see the plan, figure 11), could exert a thrust on the side walls; but if, above these arches, we put a band of iron around the dome, the thrust, which is already very oblique, will be counteracted.

The perspective view, Plate XXII., shows that the side walls may be perforated with large windows rising to the springing level of the vaulting system. This vaulting cannot push out the walls unless the tie-rods *c* (see section) break. But the pull on these rods is not so considerable as might be supposed, as soon as the structure is completed and has kept its place. When a building is substantially constructed and the vaulting is well made, the initial effort of thrust produced by the latter is very trifling, and a slight obstacle suffices to arrest its development. Supposing the arches and their springers to be of stone, and the vaulting of hollow bricks, each of the struts will at most have a weight of 15 tons to support. As a consequence of the obliquity of the strut a considerable part of the weight is divided vertically down the walls, the pull on the great lower iron brace will be reduced to an inconsiderable action, whose force may be ascertained, but which, allowing for the weight of the wall itself above the shoes, and its direct resistance, will produce an effective action on the braces equal to 5 or 6 tons,—a pull which need cause no apprehension. A structure of this kind would be very economical, for we see that only one pattern is required, either for the struts, the shoes, or the capitals.

On the scaffolding, which would serve for fixing the slanting columns, the centres (all alike) would be easily set up, and the vaulting, provided it is made in a particular way, may be turned without centering, or at least without lagging, as we shall explain presently.

This method of structure in iron and masonry fulfils the conditions which, in our opinion, should characterise such works. Thus the iron framework is visible, independent, and free to expand and contract, so that it cannot cause dislocation in the masonry, whether through oxidation or variation in temperature. The masonry, while concrete in parts, yet preserves a certain degree of elasticity, owing to the small arches which carry the whole. As the system of vaulting only takes up a very considerable height in proportion to the width of the interior, it allows of large windows comparatively elevated,—it requires a minimum of materials, and only thin walls, which (excepting the points of support) may be partly built of rubble stone;—in the iron-work, the use of bolts, which are liable to be injured or broken, is avoided, bolts being employed only for fastening the tie-rods to the braces or collars. Figure 13 represents in detail at A one of the cast-iron capitals, with its dwarf shaft and spheroidal base at B; at T the collar of the upper tie-rods; at C the head of the struts; at D the foot of the same, and at E the shoe, with the branches of the tie-rods F and of the keys G. It will thus be manifest that these fastenings are free to move, incapable of causing either ruptures or dislocations, and that they neither occasion trouble in fixing nor require fitting on the spot.

It is evident that in a construction of this kind everything should be prepared in advance. The various parts of the work can be executed in manufactories or special workshops, and be brought to the building ready fitted, so that they can be raised into place without further trouble.

A serious difficulty to be considered in building in the present day is that of yard space. Space has become so valuable in our populous towns that it would seem desirable to seek the requisite means for lessening as much as possible the area of these yards. For the masonry especially the custom of bringing to a building blocks of uncut stone, in which the stone-dresser has to find all the pieces required for the building, entails the inconvenience of accumulating an enormous quantity of stone in pure waste, as the quantity will be lessened in the working. Since the stone is charged for according to the number of cubic feet supplied, and the carriage according to weight, it is clear that as from each block of stone a fourth or fifth of its quantity is cut away before the fixing, so many useless cubic feet of stone have to be paid for as well as the cost of its carriage, which profits no one, and for which the builder has to be indemnified. This needless outlay paid to the builder at the works has gone to pay part of the dues entailed and part of the expense of carriage. The cost of the stone used therefore includes in addition to its actual value that of the waste and the carriage of the waste.

If the size and shape of the stones, especially in the case of large buildings, were completely specified by the architect when giving the plans to the builder, the latter might order a great part of his stone from the quarries cut to shape, and thus would not be obliged to rent and occupy such large yard-spaces. It would be a saving to him, and a proportionately less outlay would be incurred by the Government and individuals.

If in slight masonry work, such, *e.g.*, as vaulting, certain

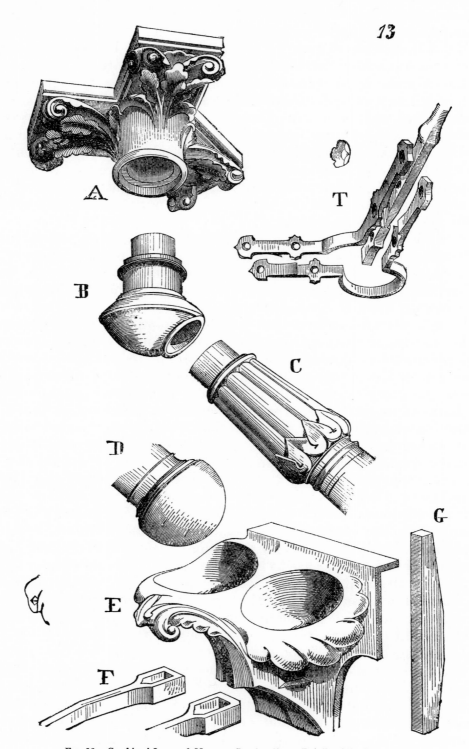

13

A

T

B

C

D

G

E

F

FIG. 13.—Combined Iron and Masonry Construction.—Details of the Iron-work.

methods were adopted which would obviate the necessity of having on the ground a stock of materials in the rough,—if the parts of these slight structures came from a manufactory ready to be fixed,—a still greater saving would be effected in the raising, the workmanship, and the time. Improvements in the art of building should be manifested in the saving of time, space, and labour, such as that expended in hoisting materials, only a part of which will enter into the structure. What is the use, for instance, of carrying up water to a height of 60 feet when a considerable part of the water may be used on the ground or in a workshop? What greater waste of labour could there be than is expended in tempering plaster or cement on the ground in troughs which have then to be carried by the mason's labourer to the top of the building? How much time and labour lost! how much occasion for detriment through damage, accident, and carelessness!

Let us then see how, in vaulting especially, some labour and preliminary operations now considered necessary might be avoided, with a consequent lessening of expense. Besides plaster of Paris, which, used inside, is an excellent material, we have cements and concrete moulded or agglomerated, with which large portions of vaulting may be prepared beforehand in work-shops to the required shape, under the best conditions, with every facility of control, so as to be easily raised and readily fixed, at a quite moderate cost. Our present method of vaulting requires a system of timber centering on which are laid boards representing the convex form of the vault. This preparatory wood-work, which will have subsequently to be taken away, involves considerable expense. The Romans employed the same method. On those wooden forms they turned brick arches whose interspaces they filled in with concrete rammed close, and thus they made vaulting of wide span. The great builders of the Middle Ages fixed up wood centres for the transverse and diagonal vaulting-ribs on which by means of moveable curves they built the soffits.[1] This latter method was a step in advance in lessening the quantity of timber-work required for vaulting on the Roman plan. But we are not bound to adhere to these methods; we should only retain what is advantageous in them, and seek for better ones, if possible. Plate XXII. shows several forms of vaulting employed at the same time for covering an interior. On the scaffolding that will have served for fixing the cast-iron struts, we are obliged to place centres (all made to the same pattern) to receive the stone arches; but for the cupolas we can dispense with the complicated and cumber-

[1] See the explanation of this method in the *Dictionnaire raisonné de l'Architecture Française*, article CONSTRUCTION.

some timber-work usually set up for that form of vaulting at so much expense of time and money.

The Oriental builders have a very simple method for making spheroidal cupolas. They fix one end of a wooden rod to the centre of the spheroid, so that it can be moved round as a radius in every direction, and with this guide they successively lay in plaster the bricks which form the concavity. Each arch of bricks, or rather each horizontal section of the sphere, forms a ring which cannot give way, and the workmen are thus enabled to close in the vault. It stands to reason however that this plan can only be adopted for cupolas of inconsiderable radius, and that it must be tedious in execution. This method is nevertheless good in certain cases, and might be advantageously applied in an improved form, as for instance by employing several of these moveable rods attached at foot to an iron or even a wooden axle having as many grooves as there are rods. But for a dome of 65 feet in diameter at the base, and whose radius is 45 feet, like that represented in the section figure 12, the plan above described could not be used. By means however of a novel system of masonry the cost incurred by centering may be greatly reduced.

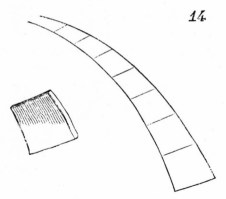

FIG. 14.—Method of vaulting a Dome.

Suppose a dome 65 feet in diameter at the base, whose circumference at the base will consequently be 195 feet; we divide this circumference into sixty parts, and making a templet of a slice of the dome thus divided, we cut this slice into a certain number of panels, as shown in the perspective drawing, fig. 14. Nothing can be easier, especially if we have several of these domes to cover in, than to have made in a workshop, moulded in plaster of Paris or pressed concrete, the requisite quantity of these panels. According to our figure, there would be only seven different patterns of panels; and if sixty be required for the lower zone a similar number will also be necessary for each (of the zones).

These panels, prepared in advance, even in winter, and sufficiently dried, may be raised into place like voussoirs and set with plaster of Paris or cement. Each zone as it is set, forms a concentric ring which cannot give way, and the next may be immediately superposed. It need not be added that the panels may be moulded into sunk compartments, so as to form an interior decoration.

The centering for a dome thus covered in by means of moulded panels will not need planking, as each panel presents a solid surface. All that is needed therefore is thirty centres or sixty half-centres under the ascending joints. For the fixing of these centres iron is very advantageous, since as that material retains its value it may be afterwards employed for other pur-

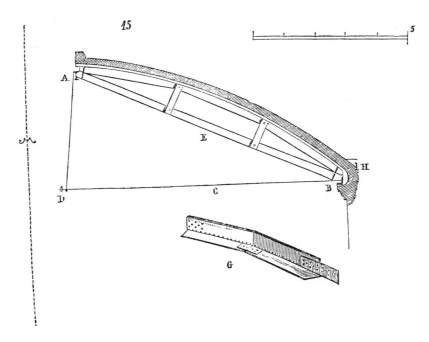

FIG. 15. —Method of centering for Vaulted Dome.

poses, or be exchanged when the work is completed. If therefore, fig. 15, we fix up a circle of T-iron or even cast-iron at A, and another circle of angle-iron at B; if as an extra precaution we tie this lower circle with fifteen tie-rods C, bolted to a ring D; then between the flanges of the upper circle and the flange of the lower circle it will suffice to fix sixty timber blades E, with wood curves and clips, which will stiffen them and serve for setting the panels; the ascending joints of the latter being over each of the centres. If instead of the lower circle we put a polygon of sixty sides of plate-iron, jointed at every second angle with rivet plates, as shown in detail G, we may dispense with the tie-rods.

Each panel will average only one and a half cubic feet, and will therefore weigh only, if in pressed concrete, about two cwt., or in dried plaster of Paris about one and a half cwt. Their number being 420, the total weight of the dome, 65 feet wide at the base and with a rise of 15 feet, would in pressed concrete be only 41 tons, and in plaster of Paris only 34 tons. The eight points of support of this dome would therefore have only a weight of four or five tons to support.

Any action of thrust may be easily obviated by a circlet of iron at H (see fig. 15). Still, these appliances do not constitute a novel system of structure. Here we have only iron supports in place of stone ones, and methods for executing ordinary forms of vaulting by means of economical expedients not in ordinary use. Iron does not enter into the structural principle of the vaulting, while its dimensions do not exceed those which are customary in our largest vaulted buildings. Nevertheless the necessity for still larger spaces than those afforded by any buildings of the past ages is becoming more and more manifest. Nowhere are our city halls sufficiently vast for the crowded meetings that sometimes gather in them. It has happened, for instance, that the places appropriated to popular concerts in Paris have not afforded room for half the persons who wished to get in. The *Palais de l'Industrie* and the railway terminuses are merely glazed sheds. They are not enclosed, comfortable buildings, capable of being warmed. These interiors cannot possess the resonance which is sometimes requisite. Draughts enter from every side, and the cooling surfaces are considerable. I repeat it therefore : buildings of masonry offer advantages which those constructed solely of iron and glass do not afford. If we examine the Roman buildings, which are in masonry, we see that the largest of them do not present interior spaces of very considerable dimensions.

For example, the great circular hall of the Baths of Antoninus Caracalla at Rome has a diameter of only 82 feet in the clear. The great cupola of St. Sophia at Constantinople measures but 100 feet, and that of St. Peter's at Rome only 30 feet more. Considering the mass of material employed to obtain these results, which even now appear prodigious, it will not be wondered at that we do not venture to attempt them, in view of the enormous expense they occasion.

If the use of iron in building does not enable us to exceed these dimensions at a decidedly less cost, then indeed we are inferior to our ancestors. In fact the great builders of the Middle Ages, like those of the Renaissance, were eminently men of subtle, active, and inventive intellect. I say inventive intellect, for that is the ruling characteristic of the works bequeathed to us by those old builders. It is apparent in the structure of our mediæval buildings, and only ceases to manifest itself when the material becomes inadequate. It is apparent in the attempts of the Renaissance; for, apart from the superficial imitation of classic forms which the architects of the latter period affected, they did not adhere to this imitation in the construction of their buildings and in the methods they employed. Without reference to the buildings of that epoch, we may find the proof of this fact in the written works of several of those architects, such as Albert Dürer, Serlio, Philibert de l'Orme, etc. On every page of their writings we find some original idea, or new adaptation; and as in the case of their predecessors, their ingenuity is circumscribed only by the inadequacy of their materials. Have we in the present day reached or even endeavoured to reach such a limit? I think not. In their great bridge-constructions our engineers have resolutely struck out a new path; but our architects have hitherto ventured no further than a timid adaptation of novel appliances to old forms. Sparing themselves the trouble of calculating, inventing, and contriving, under the pretext that such inventings, calculations, and contrivances are opposed to the formulas they have adopted, they prefer to exist on a past that is crumbling beneath their feet, and which will drag them along with it in its ultimate downfall. Amid a social condition in which everything is changing with surprising rapidity, they alone, as if they were the sacerdotal guardians of a sacred doctrine, set themselves in opposition to progress in their works; while the greater part even of the most capable exclude from their investigations a considerable section of those architectural monuments of the past which might lead to new discoveries.

And yet this regard for so-called system is after all nothing other than a mass of prejudices that have been maintained among us for barely two centuries. That public which is always complaining of the erection of buildings which suit neither its wants nor its wishes, which asks for originality, and asserts that it is being ruined by the erection of buildings whose purpose it cannot comprehend, sometimes prides itself on a false classic taste.

It is time however for our architects to think of the future; it is time we set ourselves to work to invent like our ancestors, and to regard what has been accomplished in the past as only a series of advances by which we should profit, and which we should analyse in order to advance still further; it is time to think of the paramount question of economy in building, if we would not soon see the public, weary of paying without obtaining anything that thoroughly satisfies its requirements, applying to persons who are indifferent to æsthetics, but who can construct and contrive in harmony with the spirit of the age.

We who are in mid career may not hope to become the originators of a new architecture, but we ought according to our ability to prepare the ground, and with the knowledge of all the ancient methods and the aid they can give us,—not of some only, to the exclusion of others,—seek new adaptations in harmony with the materials and the means we have at command. Progress always consists in passing from the known to the unknown, through successive transformations of methods. It is not by fits and starts that progress takes place, but by a series of transitions. Let us therefore conscientiously endeavour to prepare for these transitions, and so far from losing sight of the past let us rise above it by building upon it.

It is solely from this point of view that the examples given in the present Lecture should be regarded. I am not vain enough to think, or to wish it to be thought, that I have originated an entirely novel system of construction which would introduce a new style of architecture. I furnish my quota; my sole pretension is to point out methods enabling us to adopt the appliances with which our age supplies us. If every architect for his part does the same, while duly respecting classic and mediæval art, especially by analysing their remains, we shall witness the creation of that architecture of our time, whose advent the public calls for, but which our time will fail to give us if we continue to reproduce the arts of the past, without considering the conditions under which they were produced and the elements amid which they originated.

The series of examples given in this Lecture suggests the method which it would appear ought to be adopted in pursuance of these endeavours. We started with familiar contrivances, gradually modifying them, or rather applying new elements to them. We shall now attempt to enter more fully upon the employment of novel materials, and to deduce therefrom certain general forms of construction under novel conditions.

To obtain the largest space possible with the least amount of solid is certainly the problem that has had to be solved by every style of architecture, when it has been necessary to build for the public. The crowd did not enter the Greek temples; and, as I previously mentioned, the citizens of the small republics of Greece assembled only in unroofed enclosures. While the Romans were the first to construct buildings in which great numbers were able to assemble under cover, the mediæval builders, in working out a similar problem, endeavoured to reduce as much as possible the quantity of masonry. The materials which they possessed did not however permit them to exceed a certain limit, since these large buildings had to be vaulted. As they were not able to employ wrought- or cast-iron of considerable dimensions, it was only by contrivances of masonry,—a system of equilibrium of thrust and counterthrust,—that they succeeded in erecting spacious buildings such as our great cathedrals. But we possess those appliances which were wanting to them. Iron allows feats of construction hitherto unattempted, provided that material is employed with due regard to its nature. It is, I say once more, not the erection of market halls or railway stations that is in question, but covering in with masonry spaces that shall be amply lighted, and present those arrangements for salubrity and durability which our climate demands.

Solid bodies such as polyhedrons, consisting of plane surfaces, appear to suggest the elementary forms applicable to the structure of mingled iron and masonry where vaulting is in question. The nature of the metal and the forms in which it can be manufactured do not favour the construction of iron arches, whether by means of plates riveted, or of trapeziums of cast or wrought iron bolted together.

Thus fashioned, iron framing becomes expensive, and only answers the purpose to which it is applied by being made excessively strong, so as to prevent its bending or breaking. But if we regard plate-iron as a material specially adapted for resisting tension, if the masonry in conjunction with it be so combined as to prevent distortion of the iron-work, if we consider iron as easy to employ and connect in straight pieces ; and if of these separate

16

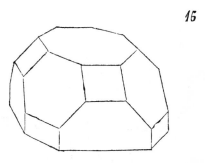

Fig. 16.—Iron and Masonry.—Vaulting of large Spaces.

pieces we form a kind of independent network, and on this network of girders we rest the vaulting in separate parts, we shall thus have contrived a system of iron framework consistent with the nature of the material, and a method for covering wide spaces by means of a series of distinct vaults. Let figure 16 represent a polyhedron capable of being inscribed within a hemisphere, and consisting of regular sides forming octagons, hexagons,

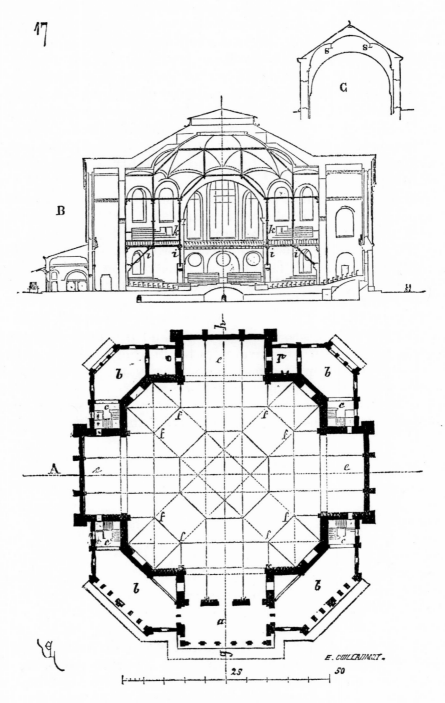

F<small>IG.</small> 17.—Iron and Masonry.—Vaulting of large Spaces.

and squares. It is evident that if we set up a framework of iron, in accordance with the lines of this figure, we shall obtain a perfectly strong network, and that we shall be able to cover the various parts of this network with portions of vaulting. Starting from this simple principle, let us suppose that we have to vault a large concert-hall—for example—capable of containing, inclusive of galleries, about 3000 persons. The plan A, figure 17, will meet these requirements. At *a* we shall have a vestibule for persons arriving on foot, at *b* vestibules for those coming in carriages, at *c* stairs leading up to the galleries. The hall, exclusive of the projections *e*, will have an interior width of 140 feet in both ways, and a superficial area of more than 6500 feet. At *f f f f f f f f* is drawn the plan of the polyhedron shown in figure 16, and at B is represented the section across *g h.*

The framework of the iron polyhedron will rest on eight cast-iron columns, which direct the weight on the oblique struts *i.* These struts will also support the galleries *k.* The walls of the four projections will sustain the thrust of the whole system,—thrusts which are, however, reduced to a very slight action. These projections will be vaulted (as shown in section C across *o p*) on plate girders *s*, so as not to exert any thrust against the gables. It will be remarked that every rectilineal member of the framework is of equal length—a length of about 28 feet for the polyhedron as well as the other parts of the vaulting. We shall consider the form of these members and their ornamentation when we come to treat more specially of smith's work.

The appearance of this structure is exhibited in figure 18. Owing to the strength afforded by the iron network, the portions of vaulting may be made of light material and be of slight thickness. We see that these portions of vaulting, in the spaces of the iron network, are divided with ribs which might be made either of terra-cotta or freestone, and that the intermediate spaces will be easily filled in either with pottery or with hollow bricks, flatways, or even with moulded material in sections, as previously described. The centering of these vaults could be fixed on the framework itself, which remains independent and visible below the vaults, and which only supports them at the points where the dividing ribs abut. The largest space to be vaulted is that of the central octagon, 68 feet in diameter, whose weight, however, is lessened by the circular opening at the top. The hexagonal spaces are only 50 feet from angle to angle, and their oblique position causes the weight of their vaults to be directed on the cast-iron columns. Fully to illustrate the execution of this system of construction would require an amount of detail

FIG. 18.— Iron and Masonry.—Vaulting of large Spaces.

for which we have not space here;[1] moreover, I have no idea of giving, in this example, anything more than one of the rational adaptations of the simultaneous employment of iron and masonry; —of simply indicating the direction our efforts should take if we would get out of the routine to which architecture is confined, and seriously adopt iron in our large buildings otherwise than as a mere makeshift or a dissimulated means of construction.

If we examine natural crystals, for instance, we shall find configurations the best adapted for vaulting of mingled iron and masonry. Most of the polyhedrons produced by crystallisation present arrangements of planes which not only enable us to use girder irons of large size for covering considerable spaces, but likewise shapes whose appearance will be very pleasing. When the employment of novel materials is in question, we must not overlook anything that might be suggestive; we must seek everywhere for guidance, but especially amid those principles of the natural creation with which we cannot make ourselves too familiar if we are to originate in our turn.

Suppose we had to erect an edifice of these dimensions, and that we covered in this enormous space by means of the structural method adopted by the Roman architects or even by those of the Middle Ages, we could easily estimate the area it would be necessary to give to the solid parts relatively to the voids, in order to sustain a vaulting of masonry exceeding by 50 feet the dome of St. Sophia at Constantinople. It is no exaggeration to say that such an area would be at least three times as great as that given in our plan. Would it be even possible to build a spheroidal vault of these dimensions of masonry on pendentives? It has never been attempted. "But," it will be objected, "what proofs can you furnish of the stability of the system indicated here? It is merely hypothetical; granting its ingenuity, you give us no experimental proof of its practicability." As it is not in my power to build a hall of these dimensions to prove the excellence of this system, I can only maintain it by reasoning.

First remark that the main vault,—that which replaces the masonry dome of a cupola on pendentives,—stands at a distance of 18 to 20 feet clear within the masonry supports; that the iron framework of this central vault consists of members all equal to each other, having similar junctions, and all forming, at the meeting of these members, a pyramid of like angles; that consequently, were there no fastenings, these members so abut together as not to allow of their pyramidal summits

---

[1] We shall have occasion to consider some of these details, especially as regards the joints, when we come to treat specially of heavy wrought work.

giving way; that these rectilineal members, surmounted by arches of masonry carrying the soffits of the vaults, are maintained rigid and cannot become distorted; that their expansion is unrestrained, since each mesh of the network is surmounted by a vault that is independent of its neighbour; that moreover the total weight of the vaults resting on the central polyhedron does not exceed 375 tons; for the developed surface of these vaults (of the central polyhedron only) is at most 1600 yards, and calculating the superficial yard of these vaults, including the ribs, at $4\frac{1}{2}$ cwt., we are rather above than under the actual weight. If to this we add the weight of the iron, about 43 tons 2 cwt., we have for the entire weight of the central polyhedron, iron and stone, 418 tons 2 cwt. Each of the eight columns therefore supports a weight of 52 tons $5\frac{1}{2}$ cwt., to which should be added a portion of the weight of the lateral vaulting, which will raise the weight on each column to at most 60 tons. It is easy enough to cast columns able to support the pressure. But these columns rest on struts leaning at an angle of 45°, which however are only 20 feet in length. The builder's chief consideration therefore should be directed to these oblique supports. Their thrust is to a great extent neutralised by the walls of the projections, and by the weight which bears on the interior summits of these walls. All that remains to be done, therefore, is to insure the strength of the braces which at their capitals hold the inclined columns in position. These braces will be of considerable strength, since they can be doubled or quadrupled in the height of the balustrade of the galleries. The central vaulting, firmly maintained by the horizontal stays placed between it and strongly abutting masonry, and by the lateral vaults, cannot give in any direction. The iron framework remains independent everywhere, and merely forms as it were the strings of bows in masonry. The joints may safely remain *slack* so as not to hinder the expansion, since the whole system of the framework consists in the combination of pieces, which, where there are no supports, always form the apex of a pyramid. Allowing for some movement in so extensive a structure it could not produce any mischief. The vaults, independent of one another, like the surfaces of the Gothic groined vaulting, are so constituted as to give with any movement without occasioning fractures or dislocations. If economy were a paramount consideration, it would be possible to confine the dressed stone-work to the angles of the perimeter; all the rest, and particularly the great spandrils of the four transepts, might be built of rubble-work, with relieving arches of stone or brick.

The quantity of dressed stone for the hall, exclusive of the accessory buildings, would be 135,800 cubic feet, and reckoning the cubic foot at 3s. we obtain a sum of . . . £20,370

 The quantity of brickwork would be 1960 cubic yards, which at 45s. per yard would amount to 4,410

 The quantity of rubble walling would be 36,650 cubic yards deducting for the openings, at 8s. per yard, ... 14,660

 The stone arches of the vaults would measure 3380 feet, which, at 12s. the lineal foot, would amount to 2,028

 The total superficial area of the vaulting soffits, including those of the galleries, would be 10,070 yards, at 8s. the superficial yard, centering included, ... 4,028

 The cost of scaffolding would be 3,200

 The weight of the iron-work would be 110 tons, at 42s. the cwt., ... 4,840

 The weight of ironwork in the outer roofing would be 75 tons, at 42s. the cwt., . . . 3,300

 The outer roof would measure 5680 yards, which, at an average price of 9s. per superficial yard, including lead gutters, would cost . . 2,546

 The iron-work for the windows would weigh 35 tons, at 42s. the cwt., ... 1,540

 The glazing would cost 1,400

 The plastering and dressing down, . . . 1,800

 The floors, including that of the galleries, . . 2,000

 Sundry works, such as fine blacksmith's work, ironmongery, joiner's work, and painting, . 3,000

 Add to these amounts the cost of the annexes, entrances, stairs, etc., ... 9,600

 That of the foundations, cellars, and heating, . 10,000

    Total, ... £88,722

 Adding for unforeseen extra works, commission and salaries, ten per cent. 8,872

The entire cost will be £97,594

 Now as the whole area is about 51,120 square feet, the cost would not reach £2 per superficial foot. Allowing that we have under-estimated the cost by one-third, and that the total outlay reached £150,000, the cost would still be considerably below that which a structure of such large proportions and monumental character usually requires.

Even supposing the walling of the hall and its accessories to be entirely built of dressed stone, the cost would not amount to £4 per superficial foot. Now we need not be reminded of what our large public buildings have cost in order to see the advantage to be derived, in point of economy and rapidity of execution, from employing simultaneously iron and masonry in our public buildings; especially when these buildings are intended to contain a large number of persons, and to afford them ample free spaces covered by vaulting, and therefore unaffected by atmospheric changes.

An element in the builder's art which now requires paramount consideration is that of economy. Architects as well as engineers are accused of unscrupulously exceeding their estimates. It is evident however that as the estimates are proportioned to the intended outlay, the excess of cost creates embarrassments and is a cause of continual annoyance. This matter is one of great difficulty, and requires careful examination.

Our directors of public works content themselves with determining lists of prices according to the nature of the work, and receiving tenders from contractors for work at these prices. But if the solid content, or the weight of the materials, or the workmanship, exceeds the estimates, the difference is due to the contractors, and in fact no one is responsible for the excess. The engineer or the architect may be blamed,—they may be accused of want of foresight, or experience,—but no further redress can be had, since the work really represents a value of which the Government alone has the advantage. If an architect or engineer should be required to pay the excess of the cost above the stipulations of the estimate, he might reply that a part of the building just completed belonged to him, since he had been at the cost of it. If the architect receives a commission of so much per cent. on the amount of the expenditure, he might, in case the estimates were unjustifiably exceeded, be reasonably mulcted of the commission upon the excess, since he might be suspected of having occasioned it with a view to increase his fees; but if, as is the case with the engineers and architects of Paris, and some of the Departments, these agents receive fixed salaries, they cannot incur any further responsibility than that determined by the *Code Civil*.

As salaried agents they are only employés under a board of directors, which is alone responsible; they are stewards commissioned to give orders for work and to furnish a statement of accounts; the directors have nothing to do but to pay, though, of course, they may find fault with their agents if they have exceeded the amount fixed by the Government estimates.

Under circumstances such as this, a board of directors can

only blame themselves if their employés or stewards do not conform to their views in point of order or economy, or have been weak enough to yield to the extravagant inclinations of contractors.

Some have thought that by lowering the status of the architect,—by making him more directly dependent on the board of directors,—reducing him to the position of a mere clerk,—the administration would be more at liberty to regulate its outlay and secure a better return for them.

Experience has shown this to be a mistake. The more the position of the architect has been lowered, the less control have the directors had over the outlay. By lowering the status of the intermediary agent, they have diminished the responsibility and therefore the safeguards against excess. If we would thoroughly remedy the evil not unreasonably complained of, we must investigate its causes. It is easy to lay the blame on the architect, who is labouring under the disadvantages of a bad system, and to consider him responsible for faults of which in many cases he is not the original cause. In many cases the prescribed amount of expenditure is insufficient for the requirements of the case ; and when the plans are drawn, the estimates are found to be too high and the architect is called upon to reduce them. He then finds himself in this dilemma : either he must cheapen the work until it fails to meet the requirements of good construction, or he is tempted to undercalculate the estimates. If he does not act thus he runs the risk of losing a perhaps long-hoped-for commission ; for there will not be wanting other architects who will profess their ability to carry out every requirement within the limits of the prescribed expenditure, and whose tempting assurances will be readily believed, although ultimately the estimates will be exceeded without the possibility of any material redress, since the architect is not personally responsible. Thus the scrupulous architect, who furnished trustworthy estimates, and refused to act the unworthy part to which he was impelled, is the sufferer by his honesty, without benefit to any one. Few determine to act thus heroically ; and if architects have been found thus scrupulous, it must be confessed that they have earned little thanks by their conscientiousness. At any rate there stands the building carried out by a rival architect, and, cost what it may, it must be paid for. Despite the assurances of this less scrupulous *confrère*, it has cost even more than if it had been left to the direction of the man of principle. The building has been erected, and the disappointment it has occasioned does not serve as a warning for future guidance ; at least such has been the case hitherto. We have seen, *e.g.* an amount specified for the erection of a building, for which architects were invited to compete. On examining the designs, no regard was paid to their conformity with that amount. The award has been made, the building has been erected, and the cost has been double or treble the sum prescribed; there may have been some complaint; but who was most deceived in the matter? Was it not the conscientious architect, who in conforming to the instructions, had foregone the attractive features which had gained the premium for his less conscientious, but evidently more astute or less practical rival?

But this is only one side of the question. The unparalleled and often extravagant costliness of our modern public buildings, and the lavish use of materials without good reason is an increasing evil; for, not liking to be surpassed by his rivals, the architect who is intrusted with a building is disposed to render his work more costly still, and to make a more lavish use of the most expensive materials. The builders eagerly encourage this tendency, chiefly from motives of interest, but also from pride. Are there many architects with sufficient resolution and good sense to resist temptation under such circumstances?—who in order to keep within the limits of their estimates, are willing to appear humble and commonplace before a public which scarcely sees anything in a building but a façade more or less ornamented with columns, pilasters and carving? And when the building is completed, does that public, which nevertheless has to pay for it, ask what it has cost,—whether the expense is proportionate to the practical value of the edifice,—whether if it had cost forty or fifty thousand pounds less it might not have been as useful or even as beautiful? Very few architects indeed could be found, who have been able to resist such considerations; and are they thanked for doing so? Have we not often heard their work criticised as plain and unimaginative?

A wealthy individual who builds a city mansion or country house for himself, may require what he pleases from the architect he selects; he may subject him to all his caprices, have a decoration or architectural feature altered ten times, if the fancy seizes him; he may adopt in turn the freaks of wife or friends, or of " people of taste," who are very lavish of advice, and are gratified at seeing the mark of their influence impressed on the building. The individual who pays out of his own pocket is quite at liberty to apply to a gardener or decorative painter to plan his building, if the architect is sufficiently in earnest in his profession to refuse to lend himself to all the ridiculous caprices of the employer.

But it is otherwise when public buildings are in question, constructed at the expense of the State, or by local taxation.

In this case the Government commissioner, even the architect, is responsible for the proper expenditure of these funds; and I do not consider that in this case the responsibility of the commissioner can altogether supersede that of the architect; for the latter is not ignorant of the source whence the funds are derived; his ambition as an architect must be subordinated to his duties as a citizen; he should therefore refuse to be a party to unnecessary expenditure, and set himself against mere caprices; his duty is to argue for, and urge the adoption of, what he considers right; in a word, to maintain his independence. I am aware that the Commissioners of Public Works are inclined to regard such independence of spirit as annoying, and would rather employ men who are more pliant; so as thereby to maintain the full prestige of their initiative; there are moreover many who are somewhat ambitious of personally directing public works, and who would wish to regard the architect as only a submissive foreman, so that they may be able to say: "*I* have erected this building; the artist has not perhaps exactly carried out my instructions; *I* changed this; *I* had that done." Few men placed in a position of command are proof against this singular *penchant* for being considered "something of an architect."

Louis the Fourteenth was quite possessed by it at times, though laden with all other honours; can we then expect a Commissioner of Public Works to be exempt from it? This indulgence of a somewhat childish vanity, aided by the weakness of architects, is, in short, disastrous to art and financially detrimental.

By duly considering the nature of his duties; by recovering somewhat of that independence of spirit which has been so assiduously stifled within him by his academical training; by getting rid of a host of prejudices and worn-out notions, and by earnestly devoting himself to the practice of his art; by learning to put his conceptions into a rational form, so as to be able, when required, to justify his views,—the architect will adopt the surest method of regaining the position which he is gradually losing, and of restoring his art to the position it ought to occupy.

In order therefore to restrict the cost of public works within more reasonable limits, it would seem desirable that competent boards of administration should make it a chief consideration to employ architects who are in all respects worthy of confidence, in point both of ability and character; and having found such, that they should abstain from interfering with the preparation of their designs and estimates, and the manner of carrying out the works; and that the architects who are intrusted with the erection of a building should be less anxious to produce an

"effect" on idle gazers than thoroughly to fulfil the requirements of the case, by the simplest and most economical means
appropriate to the object; and perhaps, by bringing to bear on
their work a more thorough knowledge of materials and of their
judicious employment. I allow that the public taste, accustomed as it has been to meretricious display, needs some degree
of correction; but if we do not perform our part, the public,
already weary of an unmeaning extravagance and lavish profusion, will ultimately insist on the erection of four plain walls in
rubble and stucco, which will give repose to the eye and not
empty the purse. And then the architects whose services are
so essential to the visible grandeur of a great State will be thrust
aside by a host of cheap builders, unscrupulous contractors, and
agents ready to undertake anything, and Architectural Art will
cease to exist among us, except as a memory of the past.

LECTURE XIII.

THE CONSTRUCTION OF BUILDINGS.

ORGANISATION OF BUILDING YARDS—PRESENT CONDITION OF THE ART OF
BUILDING—USE OF MODERN APPLIANCES.

OF late years much has been done to facilitate building operations; much however still remains to be accomplished
when architectural works are in question. Civil engineering
has promoted the adoption of practical appliances which greatly
influence the organisation of works. Railway works, embankments, and public buildings on a vast scale, which have become
so numerous of late, have compelled the managers of these works
to seek for economical and expeditious methods for excavation,
and for transporting, converting, hoisting, and fixing materials.
On their part, the manufacturers who supply elementary materials, such as limes, cements, bricks, and tiles, and iron to the
contractors, have been obliged to extend and simplify their
manufacture in order promptly to meet the increased demand,
and at prices which allow of their being largely used. The
novel machines adopted in engineering works have gradually
found their way into the building-yards superintended by architects. But it must be remarked that appliances which are serviceable on extensive areas,—spaces such as those which are
usually at the disposal of civil-engineering works,—railways,
bridges, and great public undertakings,—are not always suitable
for yards under the direction of architects, or for works of such
a nature as they have to superintend. These yards are confined
in space, or are at a considerable distance from the buildings,—in
fact, the builders have often no more room to move about in than
the space they are building in. In this case the only improved
machines that can be employed are those for hoisting, and some
small tramways laid on the ground or on the scaffolding.

In excavating and embanking the difficulty of employing

steam machinery is still greater for architects in towns; since in nineteen cases out of twenty these sinkings come to the verge of the street, and recourse must then be had to stages, shovelling, and to carts,—means for raising and transport which encumber the streets.   Evidently however these altogether primitive means might be improved upon.   Why, for instance, not employ the endless chain and buckets for raising the excavated earth and discharging it into the carts?   And why should not these vehicles —the old-fashioned carts—be improved upon and replaced by carriages to which might be hung boxes that could be discharged in all directions like the trucks employed in railway excavations? This method of transport would be less dangerous than carting. Carriages provided with wheels of large diameter would be less heavy to draw and less fatiguing for the shaft horse.   The tipping of the earth would never hazard the dragging of cart and horses down the embankment, as now sometimes happens.

All these questions are left to be settled by the contractors, and it is seldom that the architect troubles himself about them. As the contracts are seldom "general," but on the contrary are subdivided according to the nature of the work, each contractor acts merely within the precise limits of his department, and considers that he has no interest in adopting means advantageous to the common interest of the work.   The consequence is that in buildings of architectural pretension which require the concurrence of several trades, each adopts its own special means for raising or fixing the materials or work.   Hence time and strength are wasted.   The mason, who, of all the contractors, requires the most powerful machines and the most various means of fixing, is often compelled by his contract to allow the smith, for example, or the carpenter, to hoist pieces of iron or wood by means of the machine arranged for the masonry work, or again to leave the scaffolding which he had intended to serve for the cleaning down, until the carvers have finished their work; but these are measures of detail.

While steam, hydraulic, and gas lifting-machines already mark a considerable progress as compared with the old windlass, the means for shifting heavy materials on the spot do not appear to be more economical, sure, or expeditious than those formerly used.   Yet it would seem as if travelling cranes with moveable beams, to let down the stone where it is wanted, ought soon to replace the fixed hoist; in very large building works tramways are sometimes employed on the top of the scaffolding with trucks, so that by means of turntables stones may be moved to any point.   But these are appliances which are only adopted for very considerable works, and have not been employed in ordinary buildings.

It would seem as if in our day, when machinery and manufactures supply every want, town buildings ought to be erected without occasioning any inconvenience, without hindrance to traffic or annoyance to the neighbourhood, and with the precision which modern mechanical appliances insure. It is evident that very much still remains to be done if we would derive from these mechanical agencies all the advantages the public have the right to expect in the case of buildings that are not public works.

In many districts of France the architects are accustomed to have the stone sent from the quarry ready dressed. This plan offers certain advantages which are worth noting : only the required quantity and therefore only the required weight of stone has to be brought; it obviates the necessity of yards for the storage of stone previous to dressing; it prevents the sending of defective materials, since the dressing renders defects apparent, —cracks, soft beds, etc. It necessitates on the part of the architect a very careful study of the jointing and the setting out of "templets," since every piece ordered from the quarry must fit exactly into the place denoted for it in the drawing. We cannot ignore the fact that the material means of execution have their influence on the architecture; hence too many architects object to that plan as a constraint on design.

In districts where the practice obtains of having the stone worked in the quarry, the buildings often present a frank and simple structure which has a charm of its own independently of the more or less pleasing features of the architecture. It stands to reason that when templets have to be given, allowing the dressing of the stone at a distance from the building, it becomes necessary to simplify the sections as much as possible, to avoid the difficulties which would necessitate verbal explanations, waste of labour, and especially "there-abouts." The Greeks worked their stones at the quarry very nearly exactly fitting, and only needing a little cleaning off. The Romans did the same, as their ancient quarries show. During the Middle Ages this excellent method was constantly adopted, and every stone was completely worked before setting. It was in the sixteenth century that architects discontinued this method in certain provinces of France, and especially in Paris. Since that time the stone has been sent from the quarries in the rough, and the masons have had to select from the blocks those which were suitable for this or that part of the work. Hence have resulted considerable waste and lost labour on pieces discovered to be defective when the dressing was already far advanced, if not completed; hence the necessity for having large yards for storing, shifting, and shaping these blocks, and as a consequence the little trouble taken by the architect with the system of jointing. His chief concern being for a special style of architecture, which is not always in harmony with the nature of the materials to be used, he too often leaves to the mason the task of drawing the sections.

It is necessary to consider this important question more closely, in order that it may be duly appreciated. Thirty years ago at Paris, scarcely any material was used but the weather-stones of Montrouge and Arcueil, that is stone called "Bagneux," which is at most two feet in thickness of bed, lias stone only ten inches thick, and thin stone called "Moulin," for example, which is only twelve inches thick. In buildings erected by skilful men, even in the last century, these thicknesses were still considered; the architectural features and their horizontal lines were designed with reference to their height of bed. During the Middle Ages this principle was scrupulously regarded, as may be seen in the examples previously given. But for the last twenty years the ancient quarries being exhausted, it has been found necessary to import weather-stones from distant parts. The railways were completed just in time to facilitate these imports, so that we now get weather-stone from Burgundy and the Jura, and stone from Euville, Chauvigny, and the banks of the Rhône and the Saône. Now most of these durable lime-stones are three feet and upwards in thickness of bed; some even, such as those of Chauvigny, have no beds, and may be laid in any way. It would seem that such materials, as being finer than any hitherto used in these parts, ought to have produced changes in certain architectural features which had been adopted when only stone of much less thickness of bed could be procured. With rare exceptions this is not the case, and our architects have constantly adhered to the dimensions adopted by the builders of the last two centuries. We may see in our building-yards thick blocks being cut up into thin courses, with useless waste of labour, for the mere sake of conforming to traditional design,—the value of fine material being thereby depreciated,—and at great expense. Or again (which is worse), we see simulated on the large blocks in place, masonry in small blocks so that a single layer is made to appear as two or three. It might be supposed that an architect would be glad to have such magnificent materials, and would design his structure with a view to manifest their superior character : nothing of the kind ; he conceals it for the sake of adhering to a style of architecture in which the materials at command were of inferior dimensions. In one of the great cities of France—Lyons—which imports durable stone of extraordinary strength, and in blocks of enormous size, courses may be seen marked in monolithic jambs, and voussoirs marked in lintels of a single stone. It would not be more absurd to cut up a fine piece of cloth into little bits for the pleasure of sewing them together, or to represent pieces joined on a cloak cut from a wide breadth of stuff. Nevertheless it is to absurdities such as these that we are led through the dislike manifested by a certain school of architects for anything like reasoning, or rather the ridiculous fear lest reason should stifle inspiration. In no art is reason adverse to inspiration : on the contrary it is its necessary regulator, and most generally reason is a check only on caprice; true inspiration, in order to manifest itself, calls into action every faculty of intelligence, and far from dreading the light of reason, surrounds itself therewith as a rampart.

If, as may be expected, machines for the carriage and raising of materials are still further improved, and are more readily and frequently used, these materials will be delivered to us in the yards in larger blocks, if they are stone, and in pieces of greater weight and size, if they are iron. But even as things are now, our architecture has ceased to be in harmony with the appliances of the day; it endeavours to disguise these powerful resources instead of manifesting them; what then will be the state of things when these resources shall have become more considerable? Have we not in the judicious use of the appliances which our times afford us an element available for the renovation of art? When these appliances become more efficient, why do not architects take advantage of the augmentation in the quality or dimensions of the materials procurable? The only attempts that have been made in this direction of late years have been limited to the erection against façades of a few monolithic columns,—columns, moreover, which are merely an ornament,—which are "stuck on," and are not necessary to the stability of the buildings. How is it that these materials of exceptional dimensions or quality are not frankly utilised? From an æsthetic point of view what good reason can be urged against their use, not simply as a decoration, but as a necessary appliance for real and efficient support?

The fact is that there is an utter discordance between the practice of architecture and modern machinery; the novel means afforded to architects are a source of embarrassment to them, not the occasion of inventions and adaptations deduced from new principles. Not well knowing how to make use of means whose notoriety they do not venture to disregard, they only adopt them by way of superaddition—a sort of concession to that notoriety. Our modern architects are like *parvenus* who have come all at once into possession of a large fortune and do not know how to adjust their expenditure with that discretion which belongs only to accustomed opulence. We must not disguise from ourselves the fact that, in respect to the adoption of novel materials and machines, everything remains to be done in the domain of architecture; nothing has been seriously attempted. Only in the great yards of the civil engineer has anything been accomplished in this direction : but works of this kind which are little varied as regards the adaptation of materials, and are limited to the satisfaction of special requirements, cannot serve as precedents for the architect. And even if he takes these works for what they are or ought to be worth, he does not always adopt with frankness and determination the forms which the means employed would dictate. Even in civil engineering, bastard traditions hinder the invention of constructors.

In the previous Lecture, I entered on some questions relating to mixed iron and masonry construction, without any other purpose than that of offering to inquirers the elements of novel methods or novel applications of old methods—indicating the path which might be pursued. It would undoubtedly be more advantageous to give the readers of these Lectures some examples of modern architectural structures erected in accordance with these principles; but, unfortunately, such structures do not exist, and I am therefore compelled to suppose what they might be if the practical methods, which obtained at the various periods that were especially favourable to artistic activity, were adopted.

I would first call attention to the special characteristic of modern architecture, which is extensiveness. No previous civilisation has required the covering of such vast spaces. The largest buildings of antiquity are small compared with those which our requirements necessitate. Of course I am speaking here only of available dimensions; we cannot regard as vast buildings the pyramids of Memphis, for instance, or the Assyrian palaces divided into a multitude of cells, or even the Roman amphitheatres which were merely enclosures occasionally covered. Modern civilisation, which tends more and more towards democracy, which does not tolerate slavery or serfdom, or even privileged castes, erects buildings intended for all. The Middle Ages set the example in building their Cathedrals, and the programme laid down was admirably carried out. In the nineteenth century, in Europe as well as in America, in spite of the network of traditions by which we are encompassed, we must look upon all that is not made for the public—the entire public—as transient. Now the places which the public frequent for business or pleasure are never vast enough. This axiom of modern architecture is being constantly illustrated. The covered space is never too large, the exits never too wide, or the facilities of communication too great, in any building in which the public assemble, whether the object which impels it is taste, necessity, business, or pleasure.

Here we have a novel requirement, one which could never have arisen before the existence of railways and the wonderfully increased facilities of communication and intercourse. Listening sometimes to the grumblers who even condemn the prodigious works of street cutting accomplished in Paris and others of our great cities, we ask ourselves, What would have been the state of things if our towns had been left in the state in which they were twenty years ago? Should we have been able to live, to move about, to buy and sell? It is retorted that in reality the feverish activity of our great towns is occasioned by new facilities for movement and the works they necessitate. That is the question. I do not think that the opening of a street is a sufficient cause why crowds and vehicles should immediately fill it. Louis the Fourteenth could never make Versailles a lively place despite the magnificent arteries that traverse it. But when we see crowds of people filling the issues made for them, we may say that such issues were required. And are any of those great new streets that have been opened in Paris, Marseilles, or Lyons, empty?

Another fact is also worth remarking : when the first railways were made, how often was it asserted that the great trunk lines would lose a considerable part of their returns as soon as the secondary lines were constructed! But with rare exceptions the result has been quite the contrary ; the more lines have been constructed, the more travelling there has been and the greater the amount of goods traffic. It would seem as if the population multiplied in a direct ratio to the increase of roads of various kinds. We observe the same result in our cities themselves ; it has often been said that such or such a new thoroughfare would injure another, that such or such a boulevard would cause another to be abandoned. On the contrary, in proportion to the number opened, the more are they all frequented, old and new alike. The fact of the matter is this : people now do in a day what they formerly took a week to accomplish, and in an hour what they used to do in a day. The result, as estimated by Political Economy, is the increase of wealth. I will not discuss the question whether this is a good or an evil; I merely note the fact, and remark that it must and does influence architecture. I cannot but say that when, in presence of such a social transformation, which is constantly tending to be more and more complete, I see sacrifices offered to certain of those jealous divinities who held sway in the architecture of the last two centuries ; when I see invoked as supreme arbiters the Greek orders, Vignola and Palladio, and the formulas of art recognised in the Greek capitals whose extent was not greater than that of our small provincial centres, while a few trifling changes, uncritically adopted, are regarded as bold innovations, I cannot repress a smile. In fact, we hear it discussed as an important question whether Corinthian columns ought to be single or coupled; whether the complete entablature should be placed on the column, and whether the lintel should be preferred to the arch, or the arch to the lintel! whether *marmoréenne* decoration is destined to produce a revolution in art, or whether any such revolution will eschew marble and gilding in the open air! The *really* important consideration would be for us to take the trouble to exercise our reason. But our magnificent new thoroughfares, which shorten distances and introduce light and air into the crowded centres of our cities, unquestionably ameliorate the material condition of our townsmen. Do they produce *citizens?* Never have such advantageous positions been accorded to artists; never has money been more liberally voted for building purposes, or a freer scope been given for executing the most extensive enterprises in a short space of time. Will this create an art? It is just as impossible to create citizens by opening streets—whatever their width—as to create an architecture by giving its professors sites and money at discretion. If, then, architects would not wish to be classed, in the next century, among lost species and extinct historical individualities—such as astrologers, alchemists, and men in armour—it is high time they set themselves resolutely to work, for the venerable mysteries by which their dignity has been sustained are beginning to be exposed to the gaze of the vulgar; and if the public should take it into its head some fine day to insist upon a rational explanation of what is being built for it, there will be a vindictive reaction against these ruinous caprices—these orgies in stone. It is not by the mingling of styles, and combining, without reason or principle, the architectural forms of various ages, that we shall discover the art appropriate to our own, but by making the introduction of reason and plain good sense into every conception our first consideration; making use of materials in accordance with their respective properties; with a frank and cordial adoption of industrial appliances, and instead of waiting for these to take the initiative, ourselves eliciting their production.

Even now there are persons who imagine that novelty in architecture must consist in some such devices as building inverted pyramids or columns with capitals at their base; and many of our professional brethren, finding no difficulty in exposing the imbecility of such notions, are apt to conclude that "all is for the best" in this "best of possible worlds," and in drawing the conclusion that nothing could be more disastrous than to lend an ear to reformers of this class. Some find fault with the study of certain styles of art, and while themselves engaged in combining, in their designs, architectural forms borrowed from the ages of Augustus and Louis the Fourteenth, accuse the study of other styles as leading to *exclusiveness*, causing art to retrograde, and so forth. I will not enlarge on these hackneyed indictments here, though they continually present themselves in various forms, and with as little of logical consistency as of good faith. A real novelty in architecture in these days would be to follow in the track of reason—a track that has long been lost; and the study of those ancient arts which proceeded according to a rational method is the only means of imparting to us afresh the habit of making use, before and above everything else, of that portion of reason which nature has allotted us.

Sanguine natures, optimists in architecture—and there are such—have long been hoping that from the strange accumulation of so many diverse elements, the confusion of methods, and the absence of principles, there would gradually arise an art proper to the nineteenth century. "See," they say, "what took place in the sixteenth century! The study of classical art undertaken without critical discrimination or scientific methods was introduced amid expiring Gothic art. To contemporaries of a philosophic turn, nothing but confusion and anarchy was apparent, but to us, viewing it from a distance, that French architecture of the sixteenth century presents all the credentials of a complete art; it is distinct from that of Italy, it has a character of its own; each province even has its special features. Let development have its free course, and we shall find that in our days a similar process is going on, which we do not distinctly appreciate because we are in the very centre of the evolution; but what you call *confusion* will turn out for our grandchildren to be only *transition;* and this transition will produce a result in art proper to the times, which will have a character of its own, and will perhaps be the admiration of future ages." Such were the views entertained thirty years ago; but the transitional state still remains only transitional, the confusion only increases, and our cities are being filled with public buildings deviating more and more in style from a common principle, instead of grouping themselves harmoniously round it. I might even go further, and say that each of our architects seems to aim at self-contradiction; here he adopts Romanesque forms, there he follows the Renaissance, elsewhere he conforms implicitly to the age of Louis the Fourteenth; while in a fourth case he employs the Byzantine style. It was not thus that the architects of the sixteenth century proceeded, and we may rest assured that in no period of civilisation has the birth of a new epoch in art been thus inaugurated. The architects of the sixteenth century were thoroughly sincere and consistent in their procedure. They preserved the method of construction adopted in previous ages, a method which was good, practical, and rational, while, to conform to the taste of their age, they clothed their constructions in a novel dress.

Whether wrongly or rightly, they judged that the new dress could renovate the old body, which they left intact. The idea may have been a mistaken one, but it was an idea, and they kept it constantly in view.

We cannot, in our days, lay claim to an idea, good or bad ; for when a programme is laid before an architect he does not know whether or not it can be adapted to Romanesque, Gothic, Renaissance or Roman architecture. Unless the authorities prescribe one of these styles—which, it must be allowed, they rarely do,—the architect is free to choose, and his choice is directed by mere caprice, the success of another, the wish to produce something different from what has been done before, or an equally trivial consideration. From this sceptical position nothing new, vital, or productive can arise ; it can issue only in such results as we see daily produced,—buildings exhibiting more and more display in point of sculpture or material ; for where ideas are wanting, nothing remains but to make an ever increasing extravagance of such display,—buildings in which we never see a programme clearly traceable ; rarely does sound reason intervene, and still more rarely are materials judiciously employed. And the public are sated with these architectural luxuries even before the scaffolding is removed.

And when the building is completed, and the purposes for which it was constructed have to be realised, a series of operations must be commenced which will alter the architectural effects and arrangements. Here the flooring of an entresol will pass across a range of magnificent window recesses. There a metal awning will cut right through a colonnade ; elsewhere balconies which had no place in the original plan will be placed in front of windows—they had not been thought of before ! Useless windows will have to be stopped up, though a glazed frame will perhaps be left to disguise the alteration. Sheet-iron stovepipes will be carried through the roofing, or chimney-pots be added to the stone stacks. The gasfitter too will pierce the walls and cut the pilasters to make room for his piping ; while other systems of pipes will wind in various directions, spoil the effect of the architectural lines, and alter the contours of the cornices for the purpose of illuminations. In the interior the alterations will be much more considerable ; staircases and, later, flues for *calorifères* not contemplated in the design will pass in front of windows. Down-spouts will traverse the walls ; apartments too large for their purpose will have to be divided; closets and passages will have only borrowed lights or skylights in the roofing. Halls that ought to be spacious will be reduced to narrow dimensions; while close to them will be unmeaning, useless, dark and gloomy spaces, in which lights must be kept burning at noon-day. In one part there will be no ventilation, in others dangerously chilling draughts. Swing-doors must be placed within outer ones, and the noise of opening and shutting will be a constant annoyance to the inmates. And many more such examples of want of foresight might be mentioned. Ought we not in building rather to consider the complicated requirements of our civilisation than how to combine styles of architecture, or how to erect façades that shall attract the gaze of loungers—who, by the by, pay little attention to them because they do not understand their use or meaning, and are irritated by the consideration of the vast sums lavished on these architectural caprices?

And would not a little reflection suggest that one of the most effective means for discovering that architecture of the age which is so much desiderated would be a rigorous adherence to the requirements of the case? As these requirements are in many cases novel, would not their scrupulous observance lead us to novel conceptions? And to these primary considerations thus suggested we may add those of a no less important character which result from the nature of materials not employed formerly, and which oblige us to adopt new forms adapted to their peculiar properties. May we not draw from these conditions thus presented inferences which, being strictly logical, will satisfy our reason and harmonise with our customs, and will not exhibit that strange contrast which is now presented between the habits and the buildings of the nation? From the appearance and arrangements of most of our public edifices, might it not be concluded that the population of France is tyrannised over by conquerors who are attempting to impose on it a form of art which is at variance with its tastes, requirements, and habits? Is not this imposition of an art upon a people, —which somewhat resembles that of a sacred language under a theocratic régime—a most extraordinary phenomenon? does it not in some degree remind us of the custom of speaking Latin persisted in by the ecclesiastical courts and parliaments, when the attempt was made to express ideas in that language, and indicate objects which were utterly unknown in the empire of the Cæsars? Fancy a railway director speaking of scrip, preference shares, rolling stock, working of the line, stations, tunnels, ballast, cuttings, and embankments, sleepers, and rails, locomotives and carriages, points and level crossings, in Latin! What a ridiculous jargon would be the result! Why then should that which would appear ridiculous in the case just mentioned be habitually adopted in architecture? And why torture ancient forms of art to force them to express requirements and appliances which had no existence when those forms were invented.

I know by experience the difficulties that will have to be encountered by those who make it their chief consideration to consult reason and follow its decisions, instead of yielding to the dictates, imperious as vague and undefined, of the powerful coterie which for its own advantage keeps watch and ward over all the communications between the profession of architecture and the public services. I can understand the weaknesses which such a régime encourages, and I sincerely sympathise with them; but let there be no misapprehension as to the fact that this is a question of life and death to the architect. This colourless scepticism, this absence of well-defined views, this utter ignoring of principles, this pusillanimous cringing to irrational dogmas, the mental inertia that urges us to swim with the stream that we may get a living and not make ourselves enemies, to shelter ourselves behind prejudices rather than examine them, is imperceptibly degrading the architect to the rank of a mere designer, if he has some little ingenuity, or a mere clerk, if he has not. It has been long a subject of complaint among architects that the engineering profession is constantly tending to thrust them into the background. And in fact it must be so, if there are not found among them some brave spirits, some men of sufficient resolution to determine that, cost what it may, they will get out of the grooves of routine and part company with that grovelling and hybrid art which dreads the intervention of reason and examination as bats dread the sun. It is not the diplomas of the school that can save them from the decay to which they are already succumbing; their diplomas will but enable them to obtain positions which the course of things is inevitably rendering more and more subordinate and degrading. The only thing that can raise them is the candid, free, and vigorous application of thoroughly clear and well-defined principles, and a confidence in those principles, sustained by a resolute spirit; for, to make an architect, as to make a physician or a barrister, in the first place we must have a *man*. This would seem to have been forgotten.

There are signs indeed that the day of sincerity is beginning to dawn. In the sciences the experimental method has definitively superseded hypothesis. Philosophy is tending more and more to base itself on physiology—the rigorous observation of the order of nature. Pure Metaphysics are in their dotage, and even religious systems where intelligence is not overborne by credulity, are subjected, no less than philosophical systems, the successive phases of human thought and the chief phenomena of history, to the sifting of criticism and reason.

It is high time for those who devote themselves freely and without prepossession to intellectual work,—perhaps it is presumptuous to rank architects among such,—to make their election; to determine whether they will remain attached to doctrines which are insisted on as indisputable, or whether they will make use of reason and reason only to show them their road. To remain outside the impulse that has been communicated to literature, to science and philosophy, is to condemn ourselves to a speedy dissolution. Academical regulations and apologetics, and administrative decrees cannot retard by a single day the ruin of an art and a science,—for architecture is both, —that should presume to base itself on doctrines which may not be discussed. Let us be at least consistent. Why should liberty of thought and the authority of reason, whose claims are asserted in the domain of literature and science, be banished from that of art? Most of the writers who profess liberal tendencies base their convictions on a profound and critical study of history and the observation of social phenomena. It is with good reason that authors of established repute among us rely on such conscientious research in maintaining their opinions respecting the destinies of man. And in fact the study of history would be only a futile compilation, if it were limited to the mere exhibition of facts,—if it did not endeavour to collect for our modern civilisation a body of acquired experience which may enable it to draw just inferences that may guide its judgment and direct its actions. Further argument is in fact needless. The political leaders of our times have learned the art of governing, and have acquired their fame and predominance through the study of the past, and of a past not very remote from our days.

But if an architect has followed that same method; if he has gone to search in the past for elements fitted to establish and develop certain invariable principles; if from these elements he undertakes to deduce practical appliances suited to our own times with all the consequences naturally ensuing, people say of him: "He is an antiquary, who would make us live in Carlovingian houses or habitations of the thirteenth century."

In the opinion of most of these writers, who, having deeply studied the history of civilisation, think it strange (and not unreasonably) that advantage is not taken of the knowledge which has been acquired of the past to aid in solving the difficulties of the present—the architect who would be considered a "practical man,"—a representative of the age—has no need of considerable knowledge, but may be expected to produce from his own unfurnished brains new forms, an experience enabling him to apply new elements, and all the inferences and solutions which the practice of his art may require. As for those who, having studied, link by link, the long chain of transformations and phases of progress through which art has passed, presume to add a link, they are to be classed as mere archæologists, capable of nothing but patching up the remains of former ages. And (I may observe, in passing) this epithet "archæologist,"—which is a flattering title, I allow,—is given to a certain class of architects only with a view to repel them from new applications of their art. Architects whose studies of the past have been limited to the period between the age of Pericles and that of Constantine, are specially excepted from this class of archæologists; consequently it is reckoned safe to intrust them with the architectural undertakings of our times. An architect is accused of making art retrograde only when his study of the past has not stopped short at the fall of the Roman Empire.

I have sometimes put the question, and I put it once more: "How is it possible for an architect whose studies of the past have been limited to the arts of Greece and Rome, to be qualified for erecting buildings characteristic of our times, and preparing the way for the architecture of the *future?* and why, if an architect has studied not only these arts, but also those of the periods that are nearer to our own, should he be so jealously suspected of wishing to take us *back?*" This question has never been answered after any other fashion than that of the Marquis in the *Critique de l'École des femmes.*

Having the good fortune to be able at the present time to contemplate these pitiable inconsistencies as a cool spectator; in fact, as far as I myself am concerned, being really under an obligation to the powerful coterie respecting whose influence on my own position I may say,

"Deus nobis hæc otia fecit,"—

I have certainly no personal interest to serve in combating these prejudices, which have their ridiculous and even their barbarous side (as have all prejudices); since there is nothing that, in my view, is worth consideration in comparison with that independence which the study and search for the true secures: the only motive that impels me is an instinctive revolt against oppression of any kind. There are some natures which are disheartened by the weakness and defection of those who should have aided them; others, on the contrary, deem themselves happy in being able to devote their leisure to the task of infusing a little courage into the irresolute, combating errors which are cleverly maintained, and throwing some light on questions which are purposely rendered obscure to an indifferent public and to studious youth. These efforts, however feeble their apparent results, bring with them their own recompence.

Only a weak judgment and a superficial acquaintance with the history of ideas could hinder us from perceiving that the silence or vacancy with which an opinion is surrounded is a margin that really adds to its importance.

Besides, what remains to be tried in architecture after the extravagances we have witnessed? Such aberrations inevitably provoke a reaction. Is it not the duty of all men—of all who are sincerely and earnestly interested in the matter—to endeavour, however little they may be able to accomplish, to give this reaction some fixed principles—a base of operation determined by reason and the conscientious study of what has been attempted in former times, and of the resources and requirements of the present?

We can understand how persons who are ignorant of the art of construction should maintain that certain materials—iron for instance—cannot be used for great public monumental building; for iron has not hitherto been used in our public edifices in ways accordant with its properties. It may be pleaded that what has never been discovered is undiscoverable; but it is somewhat difficult to understand how professional men should be willing to admit this view; or how, if they do accept it, they should apply forms to iron which the arts of bygone ages gave to other materials, such as marble or stone. The more reasonable view would seem to be that, if iron is incapable of being adapted to architectural forms, it should not be used in our public buildings; while on the other hand, if it is thought necessary to employ it, such forms should be given to it as harmonise with its qualities and indicate its use. This is not merely a question of art, but of economy. To use cast-iron for supports on account of its rigidity, and then to cover it with brick and stucco, or marble, is to pay for two supports instead of one which would have been sufficient. To disguise iron vaulting by burying it in masonry is to belie the construction, and to employ double the quantity of materials required. Would it not be more natural to endeavour to give these materials the forms suitable to them, and to arrange the architectural features accordingly? That this has not yet been accomplished I admit, but is its attainment an impossibility? and should we not endeavour to accomplish it? Forms proper to the nature of the materials employed may not have been discovered in a single day, or by a single artist, even though a man of genius; but it is desirable to begin. For in architecture a true and rational form reveals itself only after a series of efforts and trials methodically conducted. It was only after some years of endeavour that the Greeks, ingenious though they were, invented the Doric Order; but while advancing it to perfection they did not amuse themselves on the road; they did not seek hither and thither for a variety of æsthetic expression. Having adopted a principle they never lost sight of it for a moment; never separating the true from the expedient, and never imagining that the beautiful can manifest itself apart from sound reason, sincerity, and utility.

Is it not an extraordinary assumption that the architect is limited to the employment of certain materials, if he would obtain beautiful forms? Beauty, in our opinion, lays claim to a wider empire; it is the true and fitly chosen expression, in the particular material at our command, of the physical or moral requirements we have to satisfy.

To suppose that beauty can be the result of falsehood is a heresy in art which the Greeks would have repudiated. But, as we have frequently remarked, and shall probably have occasion to repeat, our "monumental" architecture is a perpetual falsehood. As a rule, all visible forms in our buildings are useless, serving only the purpose of ornament,—all necessary means are carefully disguised beneath an appearance which often contravenes them. In fact, were it worth the trouble, each of our public buildings might be shown on analysis to consist of two distinct works; one,—the true one—the structure; the other,—that which is exhibited to the eye—the outward appearance; very unlike each other, and a comparison between which would greatly astonish the public.

Those pillars, which you are led to suppose are of solid masonry, are really cases of bricks covered with stucco, enclosing cast-iron columns. That vaulting, whose structure simulates a work in stone, is only a skeleton of iron coated over with plaster. Those majestic ranges of columns sustain nothing; it is behind them that the real supports are erected. Those openings which are quadrangular outside, present in the interior a row of arches. Behind these pediments which simulate a roof penetrating another roof, passes a gutter. Of those enormous iron girders which you have seen hoisted up into the building, you will vainly seek a trace when the work is finished; those necessary means of construction which form the bony framework of the building are carefully disguised beneath a parasitical ornamentation. And since no one will ever see those essential parts, no one will be able to judge whether they are not much stronger than is needful; no one will be able to know whether those concealed appliances are judiciously and economically contrived. As the appliances in question are not exhibited, the architect has no interest in employing them suitably; he will be liberal or sparing of them according as he is at liberty to be extravagant, or fears to be lavish.

It is certain, however, that many of these architectural false-hoods—for what else can we call them?—originate in motives of economy. Our architects, to whom the system of instruction now in vogue takes good care not to impart principles, are anxious in every case to make a show of dignity even when this is quite out of keeping with the commonplace materials at their disposal. They do not dare frankly to exhibit the material used, because they make it a *sine quâ non* to adopt forms with which that material does not harmonise; and through indifference, or rather perhaps through fear of coming into conflict with the powerful defenders of so-called classical doctrines, they avoid seeking for forms appropriate to the material.

How often have I not ascertained that architects have submitted implicitly to the established routine, in order to get a plan "passed" by one of those administrative boards which are intolerant of any innovation, and full of indulgence for self-abnegation? The question is, *To be, or not to be.* It must not be supposed, however, that it is by active opposition savouring of persecution, that any show of boldness or new ideas exhibited in the works submitted to their appreciation are stifled by these Areopaguses. . . . By no means! Academical usages furnish quite other means. The few plans that presume to deviate from the vulgar track are at their very appearance overwhelmed with eulogies; a *"but"* however follows, skilfully inserted among these laudations, which crushes attempts at innovation. And the *"but"* is sufficient, with the help of an administrative body unwilling to assume any responsibility, to destroy whatever was original in the contrivances suggested. By those who have undergone experiences of this kind—and to whom among architects have they not occurred?—it is found more advantageous to preserve a prudent inoffensive mediocrity, secured against those troublesome *"buts;"* for this will procure for them the privilege in their turn, when they have been sufficiently saturated with vulgarity, of cleverly putting "spokes in the wheel" of professional brethren who would endeavour to emancipate themselves.

This is the way to make our successors compensate us for the annoyances which our predecessors have inflicted on us. And thus is transmitted from generation to generation the "damper" which has been contrived and carefully kept in condition by the *Académie des Beaux Arts* in *la belle France;* but this explains why we have no architecture, and why our governmental budgets allot considerable sums for the erection of public buildings that are utterly at variance with our social

COURS D'ARCHITECTURE

Coupe sur A.B.

Élévation

HÔTEL DE VILLE

Emploi du fer

Échelle de

0 1 2 3 4 5 6 7 8 9 10   15   20   mètres

E. Viollet-le-Duc del.

A. MOREL. éditeur.

Cl. Sauvageot sc.

Imp. Lemercier et Cie Paris.

condition, and which will offer insoluble problems to future generations.

But even now—and we must not allow the presence of a great evil to make us forget more favourable aspects, however small their proportion,—we can discern the first symptoms of a reaction against the excesses of triumphant vulgarity. Some architects who preserve a certain independence of character, and who are determined to adhere to principles, educate themselves as constructors : that is, they endeavour to give to the materials employed the forms which their nature dictates. These architects have not, it is true, a control over the most important works of our great centres ; but a nucleus of young and inquiring minds has nevertheless formed itself around them, who may control the destinies of the future if they will resist the seductive influence of easy successes. I would then reason a little with the scattered but tolerably numerous members of this school of independent students. Let us consider how we might proceed in making use of the means which modern manufacturing skill furnishes us, strictly carrying out a programme of requirements, and seeking for the forms appropriate to the nature of the materials employed.[1]

Let us suppose that we have to erect an *Hôtel de Ville* for a town of third-rate importance. We first determine on a plan such as all would recognise as suitable and presenting a certain variety of arrangements. In an *Hôtel de Ville* there would be required open spaces, office-rooms, large assembly-rooms, easy approaches and secluded apartments, with good ventilation and lighting everywhere. On the ground-floor there will be an entrance hall, a wide vestibule communicating with the various offices and committee rooms, opening on a flight of steps comparatively wide and easily ascended, conducting to the first story,—the grand hall for fêtes and public meetings.

It is evident that the great covered spaces should be amply lighted with lofty ceilings, and easily accessible, while the secondary apartments, the various office-rooms, should be comparatively low. The following therefore are the arrangements which such a municipal edifice would suggest. Plates XXII. and XXII. *bis* give the plans of the several stories of the building. The entrance hall has a wide opening on the street. It gives access to the municipal offices and the great staircase that conducts to the grand hall of the first story. The wings containing the offices are entresoled and have their own special staircases. The apartments of the entresol are put in communication by a gallery which surrounds the entrance hall

---

[1] It will be understood that in the examples which follow it is not asserted that the only suitable forms are suggested. It is a *method* that is in question.

on three sides, and which is itself entered by the great stair-case. On the first story, in the roofing of the wings, are the employés' rooms; in the centre the grand hall for public meetings with its vestibule, over which is a tribune communicating with a gallery going round the hall. Over the great staircase is erected the belfry with its own small staircase. During public meetings or fêtes the service may be kept up through the two staircases of the wings. Along the front of the grand hall is a wide balcony. Plate XXIII. shows the elevation and the transverse section of the building. Common sense tells us that a large hall should not present an exterior such as would be suitable for committee rooms, offices or mere living rooms. Uniformity of architectural features would be absurd in such a case, a fact which the ancients—who are set up as models, but who are not imitated in the matter— always recognised; and which the mediæval builders, whose methods are systematically repudiated, also recognised and still more frankly. The external features differed with the structure. While for buildings destined for offices and dwelling-rooms, a mode of construction should be adopted similar to that which is suited for private houses, it is on the other hand proper that in the part destined for public meetings a mode of construction should be employed of more dignified character and otherwise suited to this particular object. Here the amplest accommoda-tion should be afforded; supports should not be thickly crowded together, air and light should be freely distributed, and there should be ready means of access. It should be remarked that an oblong is not the most favourable shape for meetings and fêtes. A hall that is much longer than it is wide—as are most of the great halls of our châteaux—is most suited for courts of justice and banquets, whereas the square form suits balls, concerts, and public meetings. Few great rooms are better adapted for these purposes than the *Salle des Maréchaux* in the Tuileries, and this hall is square. But the area must be large. Now the hall on the first story of our *Hôtel de Ville* is fifty feet square. It is entered through a vestibule, but the partition between the vestibule and the hall rises only thirteen feet above the floor, and is only wood-work, to give more ventilation in the hall; curtains may, on occasion, be drawn across to intercept com-munication above. On the ground-floor, the two open spaces next to the interior flight of steps, to the right and left, and therefore raised above the pavement of the antechamber, would serve as cloakrooms for visitors at fêtes or similar gatherings. Besides the tribune which forms a ceiling over the vestibule, and is well suited for an orchestra, balconies surround the hall; these enable the public to see what is going on in the middle of the meeting,

COURS D'ARCHITECTURE

F. Viollet-le-Duc del.

Cl. Sauvageot sculp.

HOTEL DE VILLE
Emploi du fer

A MOREL, éditeur.

Imp. Lemercier et Cie, Paris.

and permit a supervision of the chandeliers, the windlasses for raising which are placed above, between the ceiling and the outer roof. The tribune opening beneath the belfry tower would be easily ventilated, and the ventilation may be regulated. Every one knows that galleries placed in halls of this kind, in consequence of the heat produced by the lights, become veritable ovens. If windows are made in their walls, the currents of air become so violent, when they are opened at the wish of the audience, that it is impossible to remain there. The belfry tower produces the effect of a wide chimney, the draught of which can be regulated so as to change the air more or less quickly.

Addresses are not unfrequently delivered to crowds assembled outside in the square fronting the *Hôtel de Ville.* Our ancient city mansions were always provided with balconies suited to this purpose, and frequently even with covered balconies. Such a balcony should be included in the designs for buildings of this kind. I have therefore drawn it of considerable length and with a width of about six feet. Moreover the balcony should be covered ; for public functionaries should not be obliged to hold umbrellas over them while speaking or reading proclamations to the public. Dignity is sacrificed by such accompaniments, and it is notorious that the public, especially in France, are disposed to turn into ridicule ceremonials whose accessories are undignified. Perhaps some of our highly imaginative architects, who in designing their buildings take account of the sun—*i.e.* a classical sun 45° above the horizon, but who do not condescend to notice such insignificant matters as rain or wind or heat,—may censure our programme, as entering into details unworthy of our noble art. Nevertheless I think it worth while to add that this balcony should not only be covered, but should be closed at the two ends, to give a sheltered and quiet retreat to any who wish to stay some time there. Our covered balconies of mediæval times were thus constructed.

Plate XXIV. shows a perspective view of the principal part of the front, with the balcony closed at the ends and covered by a glazed awning.

Having shown the principal arrangements of the programme, let us consider the construction in which we have thought it desirable to assign an important and independent part to iron.

If, as remarked before, iron is destined in our modern buildings only to serve as a security for imperfect masonry, or to disguise its presence beneath parasitical casings, it would be as well for us to let it alone, and to build as they used to build in the time of Louis the Fourteenth, taking forms borrowed from a doubtful antiquity and overloading them with a hybrid ornamentation. But if iron is *prescribed*—not *proscribed*, be it understood,—we should try to find forms suitable to its properties and manufacture; we ought not to disguise it, but seek for those forms until we have found them. I do not assert that this is an easy task, but the solution of the problem ought to be attempted. It would be better for architects to devote themselves to this endeavour, though the first attempts may be artistically incomplete, than to pass their time in designing "gingerbread" fronts.

The gist of the problem is the supporting of a floor 50 feet wide and 60 feet long. To effect this, four cast-iron columns (see the ground-plan, Plate XXII.) divide the entrance hall into three bays,—two of 24 feet and one of 12 feet. T-iron joists can be used for bearings of 24 feet; but transverse *girders* resting on the columns are required to receive the iron joists. As the bearing of these girders is only 24 feet, they are easily formed either with riveted plate-and-angle iron, or with some system of iron trussing of sufficient strength to support the joists and any weight they may have to carry. It must be acknowledged that girders of plate-and-angle iron have not a pleasing appearance in the interior of a building. An iron-box girder made in the shape of a wooden beam is all very well, but is very heavy and is expensive, and does not present the appearance befitting the nature of iron. These box girders are not easily fastened on cast-iron columns; they require very widely-spreading capitals. It would therefore appear that some other system should be adopted here. Accordingly we give a detail, figure 1, of the system proposed.[1] Cast-iron columns of moderate length are more easily procured than very long ones. The two columns which rise all the way from the ground to the underside of the gallery of the first-floor are therefore made in two lengths—one of 26 ft. 6 in., the other of 23 ft. 6 in., fastened together at A with four bolts (see plan of capital *a*). The two other anterior columns also consist of a lower part, of 26 ft. 6 in., and a junction part of 4 ft. 6 in. in height, fastened together in the same way. At B we have the horizontal section of the part of the columns which receives the transverse trusses *c* supporting the floor joists and the longitudinal bracing-trusses *g*.

The transverse trusses supporting the joists consist of an upper bar D of single T-iron, whose section is represented at *d*, and an under bar E of single T-iron, whose section is shown at *e*. These bars are connected at their junction with the columns, by vertical bands H, forming brackets, forked for the upper fastening as shown in detail G, to allow a passage for the vertical flange of the T-iron D. Similarly at the junction of the two half trusses

---

[1] This detail presents the joining of the girders or trusses with the columns under the floor of the great upper hall (see section, Plate XXIII.).

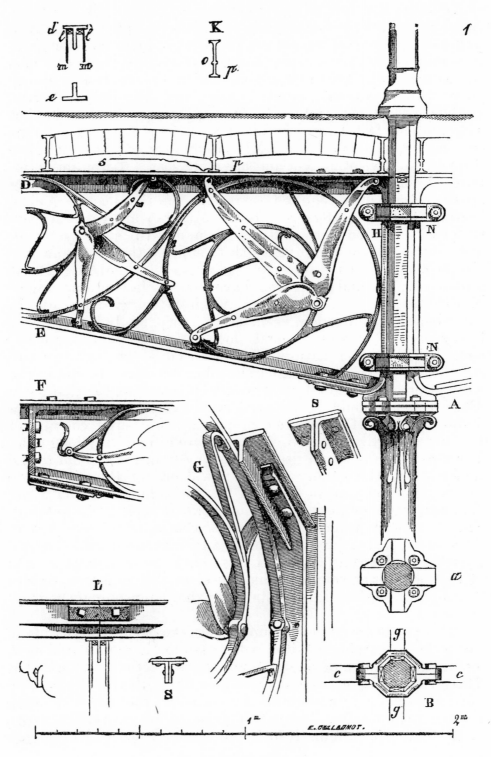

FIG. 1.—Details of the Great Floor.

(see detail F), bands, bent to an angle, receive the under T-irons, which abut against the face of these bands, and, forked, the upper T-iron, which alone is in one piece for the whole length of the bearing. The two bands, of which one is shown at I, are coupled by bolts. To render these trusses rigid, double scrolls (see section *d* at *l*) of $1\frac{1}{4}$ by $\frac{3}{4}$ inch iron are riveted on the flanges of the two upper and under T-irons; and the whole system is still further stiffened by leaf ornaments of sheet-iron *m* riveted on the outer faces of these scrolls.[1]

The longitudinal bracing trusses need not be so strong. Flat iron instead of T-iron will suffice, and single scrolls with ornaments of sheet-iron on the two faces. These trusses are secured to the columns, not by bolts, whose holes weaken the cast-iron of the supports, but by collars N (see also section B). On the flat of the upper T-iron D rest the joists end to end, connected by coupling plates (see L). These joists (see section K) are of double T-iron with additional flanges *o*, intended as a skewback for the hollow brick arching. There remains therefore an unfilled space *p* above the lower flanges, in which may be fitted either panels of moulded plaster or slabs of terra-cotta, or a filling-in of beaten sheet-iron *s*, or even panels of wood. The empty space between these panels and the arching will greatly contribute to check the resonance of these iron floorings; a resonance that would be disagreeable if they were filled in with hollow bricks or with cellular squares of plaster.

It is certain that trussed girders so contrived do not weigh so much as iron-box girders would do. They may weigh a little more than ordinary single plate girders with riveted angle-irons and flat-plates, but they have a more decorative appearance and are more easily fastened to the columns. If the architect contrives his ground-plan as we have done here so as to present equal spaces, and thus require only one or two patterns of scrolls and of sheet-iron ornaments, with the mechanical appliances now possessed by our large smiths' shops, these trusses may be cheaply made and will scarcely cost more than simple plate-girders with riveted angle-irons.

If we examine Plate XXIII. we shall see that the galleries are supported by means of the same system of open-work girders. But here, as the weights are less considerable, the trusses may be slighter and shallower and have scrolls on one side only of the T-irons,—the side facing the hall.

These brief explanations make it apparent that the iron-work is here independent of the masonry,—that it is nowhere con-

[1] We have seen trussed girders made on this principle tested by a relatively considerable weight without deflecting. When single T-iron does not afford sufficient strength or width of flange, angle-irons can be used, riveted together and covered by a plate as shown in section *S*.

cealed, and that it forms part, whatever its effect (for this is a matter of taste, and every one is at liberty to adopt the forms he considers suitable), of the interior decoration. Supposing the iron-work to be painted and gilt, we can readily imagine that the effect would be extremely rich. Objection might be made to the thinness of the forms proper to metal. This aspect of meagreness is in fact very unpleasing when the iron-work is placed in a position of competition,—when it is mixed up, as it were, with architectural stone-work. No such effect is produced when the iron is not put in competition with the architectural forms proper to stone-work. But here, in these interiors, we have only the four walls,—no ornamentation in stone-work. These walls should be decorated with painting and wainscoting; and both painting and joiner's work harmonise with the scale of ornamentation appropriate to the iron-work.

In the front, on the contrary, we have endeavoured to combine iron with stone, though leaving iron-work a distinct and independent part. The iron-work is not built in, but is simply rested or grooved in. The glazed awning of the balcony is terminated in front by a cast-iron gutter, which receives the T-irons that form the glazing bars. The gutter stands clear, with drips and overlaps. We shall presently examine the construction.

A glance at Plate XXIV., which gives in perspective a part of the front of the edifice, will show us that the iron balcony and the segmental curves between the piers beneath the windows, simply rest on projecting ledges left for that purpose in the stone-work. The curves consist of two plates of iron with angle-irons and braces; panels of beaten sheet-iron fill the spaces. As to the balconies, the flooring joists are fastened by means of angle-plates and bolts to the double T-iron forming a breast-summer on the outside. Supported by the stone brackets are pedestals, likewise of stone, into which are grooved the balus-trades, and on which stand the cast-iron columns that carry the glazed awning. To be efficient, however, the awning over a balcony should exceed the projection of the balcony itself. These cast-iron columns are therefore designed to receive cast-iron brackets, to which are fastened the trusses that support the bearing of the gutter. These trusses are not in the plane of the columns, but a certain distance outside them so as thoroughly to shelter the balcony. The ends of the gutter rest on the front of the stone projections enclosing the sides of the loggia.

Fig. 2 gives the heads of these two columns, and explains the fastenings of the cast- and wrought-iron pieces which receive the gutter and the glazing. At A is drawn the section through *a b* of the vertical support. The capital of the column has four

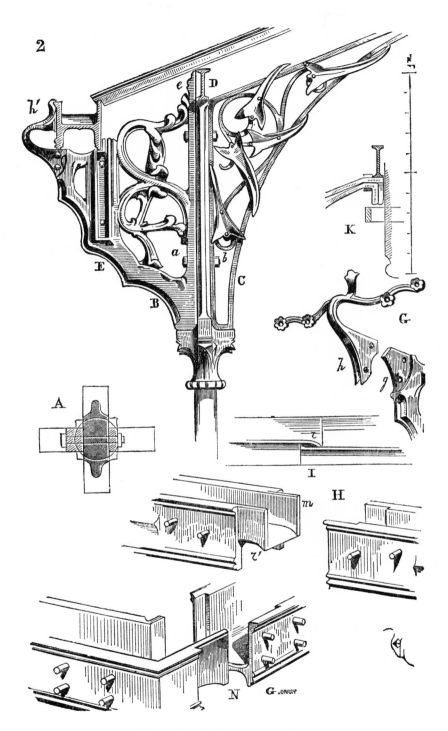

Fig. 2.—Details of the Glazed Awning.

projections forming corbels to receive the cast-iron brackets B, the half-truss C, and the two heels of the lateral ribs on which rests the double T-iron D receiving the glazing bars. The cast-iron brackets B have a shoulder at *e* which hinders the giving out of these double T-irons D; and at E, grooves with holes for bolts to secure the trusses that carry the gutter and stiffen the whole structure. These brackets are terminated at their outer extremity in the way shown at *g* in the detail G, so as to receive the wrought-iron supports *h* which secure the junctions of the gutter (see *h'*). The trusses C, at their upper extremity, hook into staples firmly fastened, or rather built, into the stone-work (see detail K). Thus the structure in iron is independent of the structure in stone; it may be put up or taken down without in the least affecting the latter.

The use of cast-iron gutters in buildings is very desirable; but the manner in which they are to be contrived and connected demands very careful consideration. The mere fixing of cast-iron gutters end to end, and jointing them with putty or lead, is only an expedient; it is not an efficient method. Cast-iron gutters should be isolated, and should not require either putty or lead to effect their purpose. In the example given here, the gutter of the glazed roof is made in five pieces, three in front, two at the ends; the longest of these divisions—the middle one—has a length of 25 feet, which presents no difficulties. The two cheeks of the gutter are of equal height all round, but the bottoms are inclined, and have at their points of junction a drip, shown at *r* in the detail I, and at *r'* in the detail H. Along the vertical cheeks, these lengths of gutter are connected —like down-spouts—with flanges. As the bottom of the under length I has a slightly raised edge, the water cannot run out between the joints. The angle junctions of the gutters are contrived as shown at N. As a means for connecting the gutters in front, we have indicated the wrought-iron fastening *h*; at the angles, flat plates are sufficient (see the perspective view, Plate XXIV.). But bolt-holes must not be made through the cheeks of these gutters; screw dowels, indicated in detail H, have therefore been cast in, and receive the nuts that will tighten the wrought-iron fastenings and angle-plates.[1]

It seems unnecessary to continue these examples, which are given, as I have said, merely to indicate a method, and not as architectural forms. Our architects are quite able to invent, if they will give themselves the trouble, better designs and more pleasing forms; but they must make up their minds utterly to

---

[1] This method of fixing pieces of wrought-iron in cast-iron, in running the metal, is much in vogue in England, but has hitherto been little employed in France. It is however an excellent plan.

abandon worn-out types, expensive and inconvenient common-places, and determine resolutely to consider the requirements of the case, and not less resolutely to make use of the materials and practical appliances which our age supplies. That in the time of Louis the Fourteenth the Physician-Architect Perrault should have been commissioned to design orders of architecture bearing the date of the *Grand Siècle*, and that it should then have been firmly believed that new principles were thereby founded and a new era commenced, is quite conceivable; but in these days it is not by giving a module more or less to a column that we hope to cause a revolution in the art of architecture. A revolution in architecture is to be brought about only by reverting to common-sense methods instead of adhering to classic formulas and the prejudices of coteries.

In art as in philosophy—and they are allied—even eclecticism has had its day; we no longer deem it advisable to welcome all views, but only those which are rational, dictated by the experimental method and by a course of logical deductions. We are absolutely obliged to proceed in this manner when we have to build warehouses, factories, and farm buildings; why change our method in the case of public buildings? By what right does the architect claim to inflict on the public architectural features which do not harmonise with its customs or its requirements, and for which it has to pay at a most extravagant rate? Will not the future reproach us bitterly for having thus wasted our resources by an expenditure out of all proportion to the results obtained? If architects suppose that the public will always remain indifferent to these questions, and that it will continue to remain in ignorance of, and to respect, those pretentious dogmas behind which "high art" ensconces itself, they are mistaken. The public will bring to bear on these questions, as on many others, the light of investigation; and its judgments will be severe in proportion to the pains that have been taken to deceive it. Has it not already remarked the cost of this purposeless architecture originating in the caprice of a few? Has it not seen, despite of boarded and canvassed partitions, that the design of entire portions of buildings has been altered during their construction, without any apparent reason for substituting one form in place of another? Now I would ask whether, if the original features had been the well-considered outcome of the conditions imperative in any rational construction, such an alteration could have been called for? Granting even that the appearance of the first was not satisfactory, had the architect no good reasons to give for adhering to them? But when mere fancy or caprice has originated a form in art, and it is alleged that such form is unpleasing, or too rich, or too poor, what grounds can you bring forward for retaining it ? Hence this irrational and capricious architecture of ours is at the mercy of the first comer, whether he be a mere ignoramus or a man of taste : any one may demand this or that alteration according to the fancy of the moment ! No longer based on essential principles, the rigorous consideration of the requirements of the case, and the material appliances available, it cannot assert the privileges claimed by art, but falls into the category of *objets de luxe*—the nicknacks that one buys or gets rid of according to the fashion of the day, and whose value is altogether conventional.

When the public first remark the appearance of iron employed as the principal means of construction in a public building, they are inclined to associate it with structures of the same material employed in a railway terminus, a market, or a factory. But is it by masking this material, as many of us have endeavoured to do, that the criticism thus arising can be obviated ? I think not ; rather, on the contrary, by rendering thoroughly apparent the veritable function of this material. It is evident that the attempts hitherto made in this direction are timid, showing a lack of courage to depart from certain time-honoured architectural forms which are not appropriate to the new appliances at our command.

Iron possesses very useful properties, and we should make it our object to utilise and manifest these properties, not to disguise them. A practical architect might not unnaturally conceive the idea of erecting a vast edifice whose frame should be entirely of iron, and clothing that frame—preserving it—by means of a casing of stone.[1] By means of iron the thrusts of vaulting can be almost entirely counteracted, and considerable strength can be given to slight supports. But it cannot too often be repeated : iron should be left independent ; it cannot be allied with masonry in large buildings. It possesses properties special to itself in point of resistance, elasticity, and expansion, and which are contrary to the very nature of masonry. Employed as a support, cast-iron is rigid and incompressible, while masonry, consisting of layers, always sinks a little through the drying of the mortar which fills in the joints. Hence a wall built behind a cast-iron column will sink somewhat, while the column will not yield.

---

[1] This idea is certainly dominant in the construction of the new Church of St. Augustine in Paris. It only wanted working out to be frankly accepted with all its consequences. If the architect of that edifice had taken advantage of the methods presented by some of the mediæval buildings which exemplify an analogous principle of structure, he would have realised effects far more satisfactory, because they would have been more in accordance with the means adopted. He would also have somewhat lessened the cost of the building,— a consideration never to be despised. In any case, however, it exhibits a step in advance —a hesitating step, it is true, but one which, in the present condition of our art, deserves to be noted as a symptom of returning independence.

What is supported by the column, therefore, must not at the same time rest on the wall, for there will result a difference of level between the two supports, and consequently a disturbance of whatever is supported. Hence we conclude that the rigid support ought to be placed on the outside, and the masonry inside; for then the sinking of this latter would only result in directing the pressure towards the centre of the building. But if we put cast-iron columns against the wall of a building inside, and rest iron trusses, *e.g.* on the columns and wall, we run great risk of causing partial and general dislocations in the building. If, therefore, we undertake to encase an iron structure with a shell of masonry, that shell must be regarded only as an envelope, having no function other than supporting itself, without lending any support to the iron, or receiving any from it. Whenever an attempt has been made to mingle the two systems, mischief has resulted in the shape of dislocations and unequal settlements. In this particular, a close examination of our great mediæval French buildings will supply us with a useful precedent, for in these edifices the frame (that is, the piers, arches, vaulting, buttresses, and flying-buttresses) is independent of the enclosure. But, through the blindest of prejudices, we prefer committing blunders to making use of well-tested principles; and in order not to *retrograde*, as our architects say, they deprive themselves of the knowledge gained by a whole series of experimental investigations—knowledge which would naturally lead them to give iron structure its veritable function. The determination not to benefit by these precedents, which are so favourable to the development of iron construction, is so very evident, that it would be amusing if anything less serious or costly than architecture were in question.

There is one of the systems of what is called Gothic vaulting, which seems to have been designed in anticipation of structure in iron, viz., that which was adopted in England towards the end of the fourteenth century, known as *fan-vaulting*, and which presents a series of arch-ribs of the same curve, radiating from a single support, or axis. This fan-vaulting, in the form of curvilinear concave cones, like the bell of a trumpet, consists of similar and equal ribs, between which are panels or soffits that are easy to fill in. I have elsewhere[1] given a minute description of this kind of vaulting which can be so easily adapted to structure in iron.

As machinery is now so extensively applied in the manufacture of large rolled iron, what should be avoided is the multiplication of patterns, which necessitates frequent changes in the operations of the workshop. A smith will make fifty pieces to

[1] See the article VOÛTE in the *Dictionnaire de l'Architecture.*

the same pattern more cheaply and rapidly than if each piece
required a special pattern; and when it comes to the fixing
there is less chance of the work not fitting, or of mistakes in it.

In some of the buildings lately erected, in which an attempt
has been made to employ iron as a means of vaulting, the iron
ribs are left apparent; they are centrings turned beneath the
masonry, and supporting it.   Hence the necessity for decorating
these ribs and making them of two concentric curves, the spaces
between which are filled with scroll-work, more or less rich,
strongly connecting the curves and contributing to the ornamentation.   But however well designed the scroll-work of these
ribs, it is scarcely seen from below, as it is in the plane of the
two curves, and masked from the spectator by one of them.[1]
When these ornamented ribs are viewed obliquely, they necessarily present an exceedingly meagre appearance beneath the

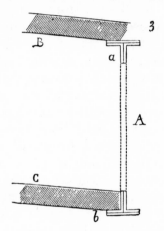

Fig. 3.—Iron Vaulting Ribs.

solid masonry soffits of the vaulting.   Moreover, this kind of
iron framing is expensive, because it demands complicated work.
It would seem more rational to regard the ribs as a framework
between which nothing more is required than the placing of
panels.   So treated the iron sinews would be above the vaulting,
and would leave nothing apparent but their inner curve, and it
would no longer be necessary to ornament them.

Let figure 3 be an iron truss.   Supposing we lay on this truss
vaults or panels B, it is evident that all the part *a, b* of the
truss will be visible inside the building and should be decorated;
but if we lay the vaults or panels at C, there will no longer be
any necessity for decorating the truss A, and it may be formed
in the most economical manner.   Moreover, there will not be
seen beneath the solid surfaces of the vault that skeleton-work

[1] Thus it is impossible to perceive the scrolls that fill in between the curve-ribs of the
dome of St. Augustine's Church in Paris.

of angle-iron, which at a certain height appears so meagre and weak. In this case trusses of thin plate-iron with T-iron strengthening are sufficient, and the part in sight may be easily and cheaply, though very appropriately, decorated.

According to the system of iron structure now adopted, when a vast space has to be roofed, parallel trusses connected by longitudinal braces or purlins are employed. These parallel trusses require to be of relatively considerable strength, in order to support themselves,—to say nothing of the weight they have to carry,—so as not to turn about or yield in any direction. It would seem however that the adoption of iron naturally leads to the network system for the covering of areas. Every one knows the strength of iron netting in a spheroidal form. If the weight of the iron of such netting were distributed in any other manner, the strength would be less. It is not easy to abandon old usages, so that having adopted iron in place of timber for roofing, we were for applying it in the same way as timber, *i.e.* in the form of bays and principals. Yet in the timber roofing or vaulting, the mediæval builders display a marked superiority over those of the seventeenth century; they distributed the weights over a wider extent of surface. When we began to employ iron for roofing, our architects never thought of examining whether certain elements were not to be found in the buildings of the Middle Ages, which might be of service to them; that would have been "retrograding," and to avoid "retrograding" they thought the best plan was to adhere to the methods in vogue among the Romans of the Empire, or, better still, the pseudo-Roman style of the seventeenth century,—an age when people built extremely ill. It was the seventeenth century that invented the heavy form of principal which bears the weight of the purlins, the rafters, and all the roofing. We did with iron therefore what we have been accustomed to do with wood; that is, for roofing or vaulting we set up a series of parallel principals or trusses, to which an inordinate weight had to be given to maintain them in their place; yet after all these trusses have sometimes given way, falling one over the other like a row of cards.

The network system has been attempted in cast-iron by the English; but as cast-iron has no elasticity, these endeavours have not been successful. With wrought- or plate-iron on the other hand, the system would answer admirably. In order to stiffen the plate-iron which we now employ for trusses or girders, and to maintain it in the vertical position, it has to be strengthened with heavy angle-iron riveted to it, and to be powerfully braced. The weight of iron structure might be very considerably lessened by adopting a network system instead of that of

COURS D'ARCHITECTURE

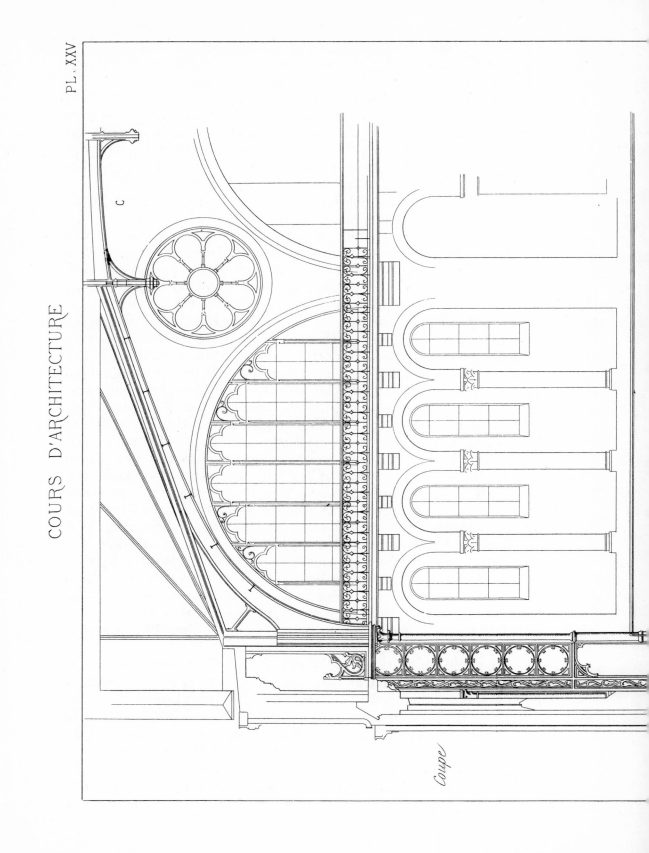

C

Coupe

VOÛTES EN FER.

¼ d'une
travée

E. Viollet-le-Duc del.

Cl. Sauvageot sc.

A. MOREL. — Editeur.

Imp. Lemercier et Cie Paris.

parallel trusses.   As I said before, the so-called fan-vaulting in
vogue in England during part of the fourteenth and fifteenth
centuries gives us the elements of this system.   I will endeavour
to show this.

We are required to vault over a large hall 70 feet wide in
the clear ; and this hall must be closed in with walls of masonry.
It is understood that we shall employ iron for the entire frame
of the edifice, and masonry only as a casing.

In the preceding Lecture I explained how vaulting of
masonry could be carried on iron supports or trusses.   Here the
case is different ; we have to construct the vaulting itself of iron,
or by means of a framework of iron resting on supports, likewise
of iron, and the interior iron structure must be completely independent of the casing.   This is a principle which cannot be
departed from without incurring grave risks, as proved by some
recent attempts where it has been disregarded.

Plate XXV. gives the plan of a quarter of one of the bays of
the vaulting.   The entire system rests on the detached columns
A (see the general plan of the ceiling of the hall at B), and the
walls merely serve as an outer shell sufficiently strong to support
itself, without aid from the cast-iron supports A, but also
without affording any aid to these supports.   The width of
the hall between the columns is 70 feet.   The truss $a\,b$ is the
pattern of all the other radiating trusses $a\,c$, $a\,d$, $a\,e$, $a\,f$.   The
section gives the vertical elevation of the trusses.   They each
abut against upright pieces b, c, d, e, f, whose shape and function
we shall presently describe.   The lines fg, bg, are the ridge
lines which rise slightly from f to g, and from b to g.   The
section shows at C the diagonal pieces $d\,g$, which also abut
against a central upright g.   These trusses $a\,b$, $a\,c$, $a\,d$, $a\,e$, $a\,f$,
are equal and similar to each other.   There remain the portions
of trusses $k\,i$, $k\,l$, etc., which are merely portions of principal
radiating trusses.   These half trusses are held at the feet, at h,
and at k, by bracing struts, $h\,m$, $h\,n$, $k\,n$, $k\,o$, etc., which direct
their pressure on to the principal radiating trusses.   These segments are divided by concentric braces into panels whose surface
does not exceed three yards.   The surface $a\,b$, $f\,a$, therefore,
is a quarter of a curvilinear concave cone, and the surface b, g, f
is a ceiling slightly elevated at g.   The truss $a\,f$ takes the place
of a wall-rib, but it is 5 feet clear of the wall, and only connected
with it by braces fixed so as to afford them liberty of movement.
To maintain the cast-iron columns upright and resist the thrust
exerted by the trusses, we need not depend on the wall ; an
open work cast-iron buttress serves that purpose (see the
section).   Thus, then, the entire framework can be erected
before or after the building of the enclosing walls.   We come

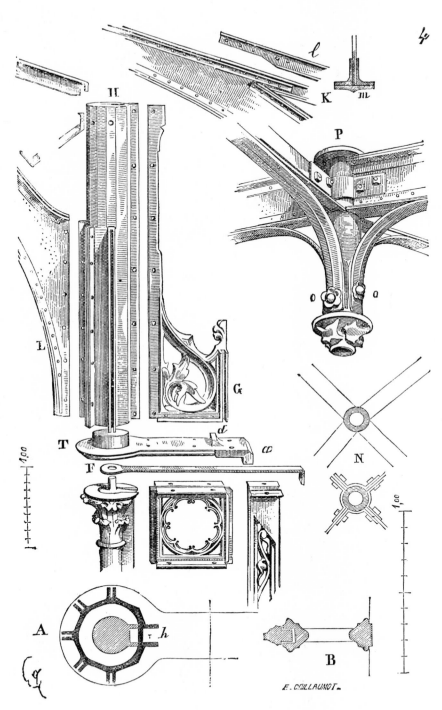

Fig. 4.—Details of Iron Network Vaulting.

E. Viollet le Duc del.

A. MOREL._ éditeur

Cl. Sauvageot sc.

Imp. Lemercier et Cie Paris

now to the closing in of the vaulting, the filling in of the network.   Instead of resting the soffits *on* the trusses, we suppose
them to be placed on the flanges of the lower angle-irons of these
plate-trusses ; so that from within the building all that will be
seen will be the under line of the trusses, the thickness of their
angle-iron flanges and the soffits, which can be made in the
workshop, either of plaster of Paris, sheet-iron beaten out, or of
terra-cotta with grille-work, and present a decorative appearance
as rich as may be desired.   These soffits are merely panels
which will be readily fixed and will have been prepared beforehand.   Plate XXVI. shows the interior perspective of this hall.

It is necessary to give some further details and explanations
of the methods employed, in order to show that the system is
practicable with the aid of very simple means.

A, figure 4, gives to a scale of $\frac{1}{25}$ the section of the column
and that of the vertical springer to which the trusses are fastened.
Running up the side of the column are two flanges forming a
groove, to receive the cast-iron panels that constitute the
buttresses.   An upright piece of cast-iron set against the wall,
and whose section is drawn at B, also grooved, receives the other
edge of these perforated panels.   This upright portion B may
be in one piece or in two, joined at the level of the lintel over
the openings of the lower passage-way (see section Plate XXV.).
It is held at its upper extremity by the heel of the abacus of the
capital, as shown at a by the perspective dissection of these
pieces (fig. 4).   The column may be in one piece or in two, likewise joined at the level of the lintel above mentioned.   The
capital is cast on the shaft, as are also the flanges of the latter.
The abacus of cast-iron is a separate piece, and is provided with
the heel a, which grasps the vertical grooved piece, and a little
shoulder d, to stop the foot of the cast-iron abutting piece G.
A wrought-iron brace F ties the column to the wall ; but without
its being possible that a settlement of the latter should in any
way affect the column or other cast-iron work, as the brace can
yield.   The abutting piece G enters into the groove h of the
vertical cast-iron fastening springer H.   This springer, whose
horizontal section is drawn at A, also carries the five grooves
which receive the five radiating trusses whose lower part is
drawn at L.   These trusses of plate-iron, strengthened, as I have
said, with angle-irons, are furnished at the point where the
curve becomes abrupt with a T-iron K, shown separately at l, to
carry the roofing.   The trusses, the braces that connect their
extremities, and the diagonal pieces which constitute the main
frame of the ceiling, all unite against the cylindrical cast-iron
king-posts P, which are hollow for the passage of the cords or
pipes for pendant lights, and are held in place by angle-plates ;

moreover the under covering-plates *m*, which, quitting the trusses
and braces at a certain distance from the king-post, bend down
in the form of curved struts and are bolted at *o*, against these
king-posts above the lower termination. At N is given to a
scale of $\frac{1}{25}$ the section of the king-posts across these fastenings.
The pieces G are furnished with lateral grooves to receive the
iron balustrades of the upper gallery (see the section).

The roof covering may be placed immediately on the vaulting,
as the soffits rest on the lower flange of the vaulting-ribs, and
thus the air can freely circulate between the soffits and the

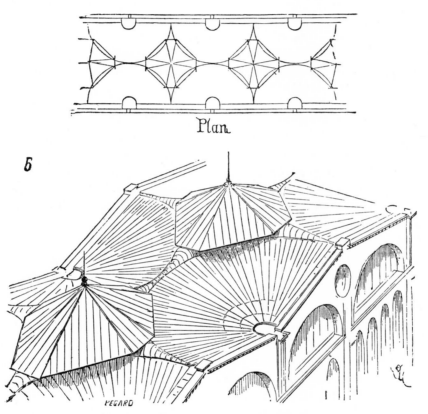

Plan.

FIG. 5.—Roof over Iron Network Vaulting.

sheets of metal which compose the covering. The conical shape
of the roofing is in fact well adapted for a metallic covering;
at each bay there is a gable or pediment of masonry. Only
the middle parts forming the flat ceilings require a special roof.
Fig. 5 represents the appearance this roofing would present.

These few details suffice to exemplify this system of iron
structure in combination with the structure in masonry, but independent of it, a system which would seem to merit the earnest
consideration of our architects. But I remark once more that
these illustrations are not intended as models to be followed, but

merely as examples of principles, and of the method in which they might be applied. It appears more sensible to revert to those precedents which best adapt themselves to structure in iron—as we have done in this case *à propos* of English fifteenth-century vaulting—and to make use of the appliances there suggested, than systematically to object to certain architectural forms because they belong to a particular period or style, and to adopt others which manifestly contravene the employment of novel materials, simply because they are reputed classic. We may be well assured that classic, or so-called classic doctrines, are utterly alien to the architecture which the public is justified in requiring from us.

The network of iron which constitutes the fan vaulting illustrated in the preceding engravings presents, like the English vaulting from which its principle is derived, a special advantage, namely, that the iron-work becomes slighter in proportion as the vaulting recedes from its supports. Consequently this framework has its greatest strength of resistance where it has to bear the greatest weight. Not long ago, for instance, there might have been seen in course of construction some flat vaulting circular in plan, consisting of radiating irons of equal section, *all* converging to a central hoop; so that this central part, which is furthest removed from the supports, becomes relatively the most weighted. When such vaulting is intended to carry, besides its own weight, a considerable addition, such as that of a number of persons, a superficial yard of the weakest part, viz., that furthest removed from the supports, will have to bear ten times more strain than the same extent of surface in the neighbourhood of those supports. Why not in such a case adopt the network system so well adapted for structure in iron?

A diagram will explain this. Here is a circular hall which has to be covered by a very flat vault to economise height,—a vault intended to support a considerable weight—a compact audience. If, fig. 6, from the circumference to the centre of the hall, whose diameter is 80 feet, we have a series of girders of similar section all converging to a small central circle (see A), it is evident that although we may reduce the weight of these girders near their extremity, there will nevertheless be a weight of metal around the central circle out of proportion to that which is distributed near the circumference. To sustain this weight in addition to that which the vaulting has to bear, it will be necessary to add enormously to the strength of the girders near the circumference—greatly to increase their weight, and consequently their cost; the strength of the walls too must be proportionately increased; but if we proceed as shown in drawing B, only bringing eight of the principal girders to meet the central circle, and putting between these eight principal girders portions of slighter girders with strut-braces, we shall secure quite as much strength as in drawing A, and much less weight of metal—especially at the centre—and consequently greater bearing power.

We shall thus have applied to structure in iron the network system of which the mediæval architects made such judicious use in their stone vaulting. I do not know whether we shall be "classic," but I am certain that we shall be sensible, and that we shall not have employed the money of the public or of our

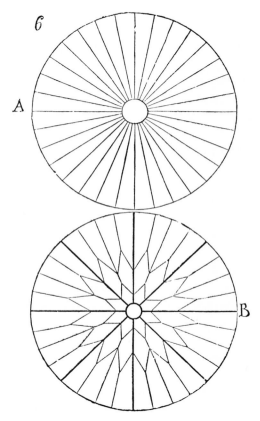

FIG. 6.—Iron Network Vaulting.

clients uselessly. I am even disposed to think that the reticulated frame B would be quite as suitable for decoration as the frame A; that is, if we determine to show the structure, and not encase the iron-work in a mass of plaster of Paris, which would conceal the construction, according to the fashion of the day. It seems useless to enlarge further on the method it would seem reasonable to adopt when iron is employed in large buildings, the construction being left visible. To give more examples would oblige us to exceed the limits of this work, whose purpose is not the teaching of construction. Having explained the principles, we leave it to those to whom they may commend themselves to study their application. Of course, if we would adopt these rational methods in employing iron in large structures, we must rid ourselves of certain prepossessions, and be guided only by reason; at the same time carefully analysing the methods suggested by former precedents which may afford us valuable hints, and being ready to lay aside architectural forms that are reproduced without consideration, and which are by no means suited to the novel materials which our manufactures place at our disposal. The future of architecture depends, we are convinced, on the prompt adoption of these rational methods.

We have been told more than once, when the subject has been mentioned, that we are aiming at nothing less than destroying imagination and inspiration in the architect; that in assigning to reason so important a function in architectural conceptions, we are putting an extinguisher on the sacred fire; and that the acquisitions in point of knowledge, habits of analysis, calculation, and method which we urge upon students would be gained at the expense of taste and the instinctive appreciation of the beautiful. This style of argument—if I may be excused for saying so—reminds one rather too vividly of that of the rustics who take care not to clean their children's heads because, as they say, the parasites which swarm in their shaggy polls are good for their health. It is not the first time that people have been found ready to inveigh against all those who incline to have recourse to reason, science, and the appliances it furnishes. When gunpowder was first used in war, was it not said that there was an end of bravery? When printing was invented, was it not affirmed that by rendering knowledge popular, true science would be annihilated? What unfavourable presages were not uttered when railway locomotives were first started! The human mind is naturally inert, and will sometimes give itself more trouble to combat a truth whose recognition would cost it something of an effort, than would be required to make that effort. I cannot help smiling, *e.g.* when I see the infinite pains taken by most of our craft to avoid the appearance of borrowing anything in their constructions from the well-digested methods adopted in certain cases by mediæval builders. They approach these methods, and they would gladly take advantage of them, and thus avoid useless complications and expense; but prejudice —something perhaps of fear, lest they should incur the censure of the *Académie des Beaux Arts*—restrains them, and then we see how they distort a simple idea—a really rational process— and evade the truth with the hesitations and reticence of conscious guilt.   It may be well asked whether these infantile pre-possessions which remind one of a pedagogic tutelage, and which at any rate show no great independence of character, are not more prejudicial to the development of imagination and to inspiration, than appeals to reason, calculation, and method could possibly be.   On the contrary, those who have manifested the most complete independence have been always those in whom reason, knowledge, and judgment had reached a fair degree of development.   And since imagination—or inspiration, if we choose to call it so,—is essentially independent in its nature, independence of character is absolutely necessary to its manifestation.

LECTURE XIV.

ON THE TEACHING OF ARCHITECTURE.

WE are evidently close upon one of those critical eras in the history of civilisation, when each in his several sphere feels that an effort has to be made, *i.e.*—if I may be allowed the expression—a " belling of the cat" to be undertaken ; but in which each is waiting for his neighbour to take the initiative. We can well understand that architects who have their way to make,—who are forced, in order to live (for this is the real state of the case, and young men who devote themselves to architecture are not generally millionnaires), to seek powerful patronage, and to submit to exigencies often of a painful kind, supposing they have settled convictions, should be disinclined to make a parade of these convictions if they happen not to be in accordance with prevalent ideas. We can also understand that after a certain time the most steadfast minds become habituated to the oppression to which they at first submitted with reservations ; that their submission, though only apparent, may procure them certain advantages, and that at last, when they are their own masters, they find it more convenient and profitable to range themselves in their turn on the side of the oppressors.

A writer who addresses the public—who produces a book which the public reads—a painter who produces a picture, or a sculptor who models a statue, has really no need of any one's patronage to bring him into notice. Their talent, if they have any, will sooner or later give them popularity. It is not so in the case of the architect ; for his productions something more is required than a little ink and paper, a piece of canvas and colours, or a few clods of earth. This needs no demonstration, and that combination of favouring circumstances which can alone enable an architect to demonstrate his ability, if he has any, is rarely presented. And if this combination of circumstances depends on the will of a corporate body, such as that of the *Académie des Beaux Arts*, of which we shall have to speak, it will evidently never be presented to any one who has not the advantage of sharing the opinions and ideas of that body. This is also clear. But, it may be objected, how can a body composed of artists possess in this year of grace 1868 the power we impute to it? There must be some exaggeration in our estimate. Is it an administrative body? No. Does it control a teaching of the art? No. Has it the revenues of the State or of our great cities at its disposal? No. On what then do you ground your estimate of its potency?

Simply on the fact that it is a body enjoying the protection of the State. The State, inasmuch as it is the acknowledged protector of an intellectual corporation, becomes, in assuming that position, the arm, the executive, of that corporation. Some intelligent persons, whose clear-sightedness no one can deny, are demanding the severance of the Church from the State, and they can bring powerful arguments in favour of that demand; and reasons quite as powerful, at least, can be alleged in favour of a separation of the Academies from the State. Of these reasons I will discuss one only, viz. that every body that recognises a fixed system of doctrines, which is otherwise irresponsible, and is connected with the State, will infallibly make use of that impersonal force called the State to secure the triumph of that system.

It was with perfect logical consistency that Louis the Fourteenth founded the Academy of the Fine Arts, because the State under Louis the Fourteenth professed, or made a show of professing, dogmas in all branches of investigation. There existed then a State Religion; it was natural that there should be a State Art, a State Philosophy, and a State system of instruction. The bonds uniting the throne and the altar being closely knit, it was logically consistent that no discord or contest should be possible between what belongs to the domain of intellect or conscience and the Executive. And just as in that age the mandate went forth to all, " Be Catholics, or leave the kingdom," with even greater reason the command might be issued, " Think as we wish you to think, or a *lettre de cachet* will prove to you that independence is no longer in fashion." The Government of Louis the Fourteenth therefore was quite justified, from its point of view, in establishing the *Académie des Beaux Arts*, for it recognised an official architecture,—the proof of which is that the plans of all the public edifices erected throughout the kingdom were subjected to the examination of the *surintendant* Lebrun. I may even add, that the *Académie des Beaux Arts* was the necessary complement of this organisation; a body must be created which could define the principles sanctioned by the State, preserve them, and unite around them those who were capable of following and developing them. The Academy of the Fine Arts must consequently have its seminary, which was the *École de Rome.* I repeat it : there is nothing to find fault with in this perfectly logical concatenation, the first datum being granted,—that is, the interference of the State in the domain of intellect.

The organisation thus created by Louis the Fourteenth's Government undeniably presented an aspect of grandeur, and we can easily understand how it must have dazzled, not only contemporaries, but many intelligent men of later times. The attainment of this unity of thought and action, the having cemented together so firmly the moral and material elements of an entire people without the assumption on the part of the monarch of being the *Pontifex maximus* of his empire, as well as its temporal sovereign ; the having developed under the shelter of corporations which were *independent,* since they selected their own members—arts, letters, and science, while subjecting these bodies to the *protection* of the State,—is a result which cannot but excite our admiration. The Church too was Gallican, that is to say, national, and the Academies preserved a unity in their proceedings which perfectly harmonised with the general tenor, the tendencies and usages of the Government.

But in this world of ours, logical inconsistencies cannot be hazarded with impunity. That magnificent *ensemble* could only retain its unity on the condition that even its slightest feature should not be modified. A single cog displaced, and the whole of this magnificent machinery would give way. It is not my business here to write the history of the close of the last century. The Revolution did more than remove one of those cogs ; it broke up the whole machine. And though an attempt has been made since to gather up and reunite the pieces, these fragments only embarrass us. Instead of forming the harmonious whole which they presented—apparently at least—in the eighteenth century, such gearing of the old machine as has been preserved grates harshly and turns the wrong way ; presenting to all, but especially to those who have wished to make it serve its purpose again, an incessant cause of difficulties and even of dangers.

As the State is neither priest nor artist, it is soon obliged, if it undertakes to protect orthodoxy or art, to commit the power at its command to one or other of them.

The State however ultimately discovers that its protection is abused ; then it undertakes to interfere in questions of dogma or art, with a view to define its action and guard its responsibility ; but it does too much or too little ; it is ignorant in such matters, and however careful it may be not to seem to lay a hand on the sacred ark, it is denounced as tyrannical. Thus it is always between the horns of a dilemma : it must either be regarded as an oppressor, or it must accept the part of an executor of decrees of whose rectitude it has no authority to judge. As regards the subject in question, have we not seen this to be exactly the case in reference to the reforms attempted by the State in the teaching of the Fine Arts ?

The State thought it perceived that the *Académie des Beaux Arts*,—which had no legal power to control the teaching of art, but to which in point of fact that teaching was subject,—was endangering the studies in question ; it undertook, as the responsible *protector* of that study, to reform this system of teaching, —to modify it (though, be it observed, very slightly) in some of its details. We can remember the chorus of vehement expostulations on the part of members of the " Institut." The Republic of the Arts was declared in danger, and manifestos, protests, and memorials fell thick as hail on the Administration, which sustained the first fire, but was not very long in acknowledging itself beaten in this unequal contest, and aimed at nothing more than an honourable retreat under the appearance of conciliation and respect for interests which it confessed it had perhaps not duly appreciated. This however, we may observe, does not prevent the *Académie des Beaux Arts* from maintaining a sulky and mistrustful attitude towards that civil authority which had thus encroached on the domain over which it claimed jurisdiction. At present the two powers, one of which is the protector, and the other the legally protected, are officially reconciled ; but this reconciliation has been secured only at the cost of a more and more manifest compliance of the protector with the wishes of the protégé, which latter is becoming so decidedly the master that it abuses its position—as corporations of this order always do— so egregiously as to provoke a reaction. If that reaction takes the shape of measures of reform in their administration things will always return to their original condition. There is only one method of reforming the bodies placed under the protection of the civil authority, namely withdrawing this protection from them,—that is, not attempting to convert them to the ideas of the age by regulations, but leaving them alone. If the *Académie des Beaux Arts* ceased to be, as under Louis the Fourteenth, placed beneath the protection of the State, if it were left to shift for itself, perhaps it would render some services ; but at any rate we may be certain that it would not present embarrassments either to governments or to the governed, and that the arts would be the better for the change, especially architecture.

These truths appear to many people so simple, that they are inclined to ask why they are not carried out in practice.

Why? Because in the whole affair that which is least cared for is art itself; personal considerations are in the ascendant, and in art, as in everything else, when personal considerations take precedence of principles, no worthy or durable result can be realised.

Besides, the *Académie des Beaux Arts* finds itself now in a novel position; it no longer recognises a definite doctrine in art; what it seeks to establish is not a principle—an orthodox belief —but merely the predominance of an interest. All its efforts tend, not to the propagation of doctrines, whether true or false, but to the maintenance of its position and the exclusion from it of those who are not Academicians, or do not aspire to be so, or who are unwilling to acknowledge its supremacy. In this respect the *Académie des Beaux Arts* is departing from the traditions of those corporations which purpose to perpetuate their existence, and has been attacked by the worm that settles on bodies whose decay is imminent.

When the guilds and fraternities—whose origin, be it observed, was quite democratic—were more taken up with maintaining their antiquated privileges than raising their several industries to the level of the knowledge of the times, when they became exclusive, and desired to drive away competitors instead of excelling them, they were marked for death. When it became clear that the *Inquisitio pro fide* made a point of accusing rich people of heresy to confiscate their wealth, the days of its power were numbered.

The history of the architectural section of the *Académie des Beaux Arts,* since the manifesto issued by it in 1846, will be instructive on more accounts than one, when the time comes for its being written, and when we shall be able to reckon what it costs, and to show how, by degrees, it has attained to its irresponsible supremacy, while leaving to Government boards the task of hiding or defending the blunders or costly fancies of most of its alumni. Meanwhile, it is, we think, desirable to raise a corner of the veil interposed between the public and an organisation which may be paralleled with the most firmly established corporations of a similar kind in the Middle Ages.

The architectural section of the *Académie des Beaux Arts* consists of eight members—not too large a number; that of Painting comprises fourteen; that of Sculpture eight: in all, thirty members. And as architects frequently have the opportunity of bestowing commissions for works of sculpture and painting, a community of interests very naturally arises among these thirty members. The *esprit de corps* which prevails among the alumni of the *École de Rome* is roused on the occasion of a nomination to the vacant chairs of the Institute, and so we cannot be surprised that of these thirty members, eight architects, nine painters, and seven sculptors, formerly belonged to that school —a respectable majority certainly.

There would certainly be nothing to find fault with in this if the *Académie des Beaux Arts* was an independent association, not enjoying State protection. It is quite natural that the members of that academy should prefer to recruit their body from among their familiar circle instead of giving themselves the trouble to seek out talent from various quarters ; especially as they are justified in regarding their comrades as very capable men, since they obtained the Roman Exhibition by a competitive examination. But it must never be forgotten that the State is their *protector*, and thus makes itself the passive instrument of a body which recruits itself from an element that is unchanged and unchangeable. In fact you enter the " Institut " *because* you were at Rome, and you obtain admission there, and (which is most important), you cannot leave it with any chance of obtaining commissions, except on the condition that you have followed the course marked out by the Institute.

Attempts have frequently been made to break through this . . . profitable circle, but the protected and privileged, and consequently irresponsible body has easily frustrated the attempts at emancipation. The few younger men who may have wished to emancipate themselves, relying on the liberal tendencies of an administrative body, have learned to their cost what such emancipation must involve. If they will not walk along the beaten path prescribed by the coterie, they find every door closed against them ; if they do not encounter open hostility, they have to cope with a conspiracy of silence. Do they betake themselves to that administrative body, whose extrinsic liberality of view they thought they had discovered, and which has had the tribute of their best wishes and humble efforts ? They are received with promises and attentions of every kind ; they are even commended for their independent attitude towards the corporation in question ; but the commissions they solicit, often with a good title to receive them, will be given to those who, more discreetly, shall have *valiantly* compromised themselves by defending against those liberal efforts of the administration the privileges of the corporation. Such are the acts which that administration, in its controversy with the " Institut," reckons to the score of measures stamped with the mark of impartiality. Such being the state of things, and more emphatically now than ever, we can sufficiently understand the extensive influence which an irresponsible corporate body may acquire over an executive.

And, in fact, what can an administration which is not competent to judge of such matters bring to bear against the opinion of a body considered by the State itself—inasmuch as the latter sustains it—supremely competent ?   How can we expect that an administration not laying claim to discernment in art should take the responsibility of intrusting the construction of a public building, *e.g.*, to one who is excluded from a body supposed to recruit its members from the very *élite* of artists ?   An easier and less compromising course for it will be to shelter itself behind the opinion of that body which is nevertheless not a responsible one, and is by no means bound to render to the public an account of the motives that guide its action, and which it takes good care not to furnish.   We can understand that, in view of these scruples and that timidity which is very excusable in an administrative body having no acquaintance with the specialities of art, the coterie in question will carry all before it.   Thus the government boards soon find themselves completely at the mercy of the chiefs of that corporation, and surrounded by its adherents, who are candidates for every post. These latter become so much the more numerous and so much the more submissive to the influence of the body in question, as they perceive its influence increasing and its authority strengthened in all government undertakings.   And as the authorities constantly hear the same opinion expressed with regard to all that is done—since they have allowed those who do not share that opinion to be removed from their councils— they sincerely believe that the views they hear expressed are correct, until some accidental circumstance rudely awakens them to the truth.   Then the responsibility which the administration thought it might devolve on an irresponsible body falls back upon it with all its weight, and the State-protected corporation retires beneath the copula of the "Institut."   I would have it clearly understood that I am preferring an indictment not against persons, but against an institution which, connected with the State, is to it a cause of embarrassment, and to art a source of weakness ; while it places artists in a position as undignified as it is inconsistent with the tendencies of the age and the require- ments of our social condition.   I have no intention to discuss matters that concern painters and sculptors ; it is for them to decide whether the "Institut" promotes art in their department, or is advantageous to their personal interests.   I have here only to do with the position of architects who, as I have just shown, find themselves in a peculiar situation as regards the public and the public service.   And without exaggeration it may be main- tained that it is an undignified alternative for men who are intrusted with interests often of great importance, to have either to repudiate their opinions and ideas,—if these opinions or ideas are not favoured by the corporation protected by the State,—

or to be condemned to a kind of ostracism, if they hold to such ideas and opinions. Temptation should not be made too strong; firmness and constancy are rare virtues; moreover, with most men the consideration how they shall procure a living is a very influential one. And corporate bodies which have no longer the power to incarcerate or burn those who do not share their opinions are still able to impose on them the protracted torture of isolation, silence, and embarrassment, obstacles of all kinds, polite manifestations of ill-will, disappointments, and so forth. In our opinion there is still too much of such displays of power. If this could possibly be a benefit to art; if art gained thereby in dignity and strength what artists lose in independence and security, it would not be right to complain. We should heartily exclaim: "Let artists perish rather than art!" But the fact is that there can be no art without artists; in fact, none without artists of independence and character. By degrading its professors we necessarily degrade art itself.

For this deplorable state of things there is but one remedy, viz., to regard the *Académie des Beaux Arts* (its architectural section at least) as an independent society, and to sever the bonds that unite it with the State. And sooner or later it will come to this. The period will arrive,—and the time for such a change of aspect comes at certain crises in the history of nations,— when questions of principle will take precedence of personal considerations; when we become aware that nothing of the old machinery of the seventeenth century can be retained.

Not till then will the teaching of architecture be free, and begin to develop itself. But how? This is a question we shall examine presently.

It is quite natural that the architectural section of the *Académie des Beaux Arts* should assume that good architecture in France dates from 1671,—the era of its foundation; but this opinion is not shared by the public in general, and many persons of intelligence believe that before that epoch buildings of some merit were erected in France. But supposing this opinion to be erroneous, it is a sincere one, and on that account alone it has a title to respect in a country which for the last seventy-five years has placed freedom of conscience and opinion at the head of the numerous constitutions it has adopted.

But at its commencement, be it observed, this Academy of Architecture had not the character it assumed in later days, especially after the Restoration. I will cite here the words of a writer whom assuredly no one will accuse of systematic hostility towards the Academies.[1] "Before the Revolution, which put

---

[1] See the "Réponse à la lettre de M. Ingres," by M. Ch. Giraud, of the Institute. Paris, 1864, p. 2.

an end to the ancient monarchy, the chief depositaries of the traditions of art in France were an Academy of painting and sculpture founded, not by Lebrun, as has been said, but by Mazarin, in 1648, and an *Academy of Architecture* founded by Colbert in 1671. At their foundation, these two institutions had by no means the æsthetic character with which we should be inclined to credit them if we considered their names only, and interpreted those names according to the ideas now prevalent. The guild and corporation régime formerly gave law to the profession of all the arts in France. None could practise the art of painting or sculpture unless he belonged to the corporation of *maîtres peintres* and *sculptiers*, and, to be enrolled among its members, six years must be passed with a master, three as a *rapin*, and three as an apprentice; at the end of which term the candidate had to produce a *chef-d'œuvre*, on the completion of which he was received. No one outside the circle of privileged persons was allowed to use the palette or the chisel freely or publicly, on pain of forfeiture of his work wherever the syndicate of the masters might find it. Only the artists directly commissioned by the king, the princes or very powerful nobles, could escape the jealous surveillance of the corporation. It was to liberate artists from the tyranny of the guilds that Mazarin and Colbert founded the Academies in question. In fact it was the privilege of their members to be exempted from the necessity of becoming free of the guilds, and to be able to practise their art without restriction.

But in conferring this novel privilege, Mazarin and Colbert did not make the two *Academies of the Arts two public institutions;* this last idea also is foreign to the intention of the founders. They established two *new private corporations*, elevated above the others, I admit, and liberal in status, while the others were connected with trade, but presenting the same character fundamentally; for none who did not belong to the Academies or to the guilds could exercise the art of painting, sculpture, or building. The Academies of the Arts, therefore, were organised on the *model of the trade corporations;* this was at that time the customary and obligatory type of every association of this kind. Thus the government of the Academies was left to a kind of syndicate; the first twelve who were inscribed on the list of Academicians formed the supreme council of the *Anciens*. The other members, whose number was not limited, had no share in the direction; but they participated in the honour or privilege of the free exercise of their art; the charges *for rent, models, and even prizes, were defrayed by the contributions of the Academicians generally, who furnished each his quota towards these expenses. The State never gave any aid except in the way of trifling and occasional subsidies.* At a later date the king gave them a local habitation. Besides the free exercise of their several professions, teaching constituted another privilege of the Academies; but the Council of the *Anciens* had the exclusive right of naming professors, of regulating the discipline, and determining the conditions of the régime of the school. This constitution lasted till 1793, when the last vestiges of the ancient trade corporations were obliterated. . . . When the Revolutionary storm had passed over, Vien succeeded in procuring the re-establishment of the ancient Academies, under the new and more apposite title of *École des Beaux Arts.* His influence availed even to restore their former prerogatives to the *Anciens;* but it was only for a short time, for a decree of the 11th of January 1806 assigned the nomination of the professors to the Emperor, and allotted them a salary out of the coffers of the State. . . ."

This review of the history of the *Académie des Beaux Arts,* from its foundation down to 1806, suggests some general remarks deserving of consideration.

The corporate bodies of the Middle Ages, which were democratic though far from liberal, could not, however, continue to exist under the government established by the ministers of Louis the Fourteenth. What course then did those ministers pursue? They raised side by side with, or above them, a privileged corporation, though leaving to that corporation the quasi-republican prerogatives of the ancient guilds.

The government of Louis the Fourteenth grafted a privilege on old established privileges. And whether the corporate body were called Academy or guild, the effect was in the first instance essentially the same or nearly so; but we can understand how much more easy it was for the State speedily to render an *Academy* founded by itself a docile instrument—an instrument all its own—than to exert an influence over the ancient guilds. In this the government of Louis the Fourteenth was consistent; it proceeded in matters of art in the same way as it was proceeding in regard to feudalism. It raised a new order of privileges which were more valid, and at the same time more submissive to itself, above the ancient order of privileges which were capable of raising obstructions in the way of absolute power.

Nevertheless, this superior corporation, under royal protection, preserved the republican forms of the ancient guilds. But, objectionable as were the abuses attaching to those ancient guilds, they were amenable to no external authority, they existed in the city, lived its life, and were obliged to take account of prevailing opinion, and were influenced by its changes. It could not be so with a corporate body under the control of royalty; sheltered behind the special privileges it enjoyed, it necessarily soon became isolated, and formed a kind of aristocracy more powerful than the oligarchy of the guilds had ever been able to become. In fact, "these Academies were at the same time teaching, professional and Academic bodies, in the modern sense of this term; as in fact were the Academies of the same kind that existed in Italy—whence Mazarin had taken the idea and plan of them—and whose influence was so disastrous to Italian art from the close of the seventeenth century downwards. It is to them in great measure that the decline of that art is owing. . . . The Academic professional body had everywhere originated a kind of style which has become notorious, and which is not always that of grace and good taste.

The supreme Academic honour at that time was the Professorship; and so, as the *Anciens* sincerely believed they could not do better, they always nominated one of themselves. Academician and Professor were, in their view, convertible terms, for one was inseparable from the other. . . ."[1]

The decree of the 11th of January 1806, in re-constituting the *Académie des Beaux Arts,* purported to restrict its authority within moderate limits; its professors were selected by the emperor, and its expenses were charged to the State. This arrangement was a kind of concordat, followed, at various periods, especially in 1863, by regulative enactments. But we know what regulative enactments are to corporate bodies which accept a concordat only in the hope of evading at least the spirit of it, so that at the present moment that body, which is a relic of institutions foreign to the ideas of our times, has, in spite of all limitations, the control of teaching in the Fine Arts, and of most of the Boards which regulate the State expenditure and that of our large cities, for Fine Art purposes; consequently it determines the destiny of artists, and more particularly of architects who have scarcely any scope for exhibiting their talents apart from the works controlled by those Boards.

We might well ask why the *Académie des Beaux Arts,* which is only a concentrated representative of the guilds of the Middle Ages, professes such an utter contempt and even aversion for all that belongs to that period, if we did not consider that corporate bodies are wont to repudiate their origin, and to assume that they owe their dignity to none but themselves. But this is no excuse for the ingratitude thus displayed. In undertaking to make the *École des Beaux Arts* a public institution, the State almost quarrelled with the Academy; it did not realise the object proposed, and cannot attain it as long as there exists a connection between it and the Academy. In the judgment of the Academic body, the intervention of the State in the teaching of the Fine

---

[1] "Réponse à la lettre de M. Ingrès," by Ch. Giraud of the Institute, Paris, 1864.

Arts is as great a breach of privilege as its interference with the instruction given at the *Seminaire* could be from an episcopal standpoint.

But, it may be objected, with some show of reason, since it is the State that is responsible for the employment of the public funds, it is but fair, at least as regards architecture, that it should require a guarantee of the quality and character of the instruction given to the architects who will be commissioned to expend those funds in the construction of public buildings. And this is not merely a question of economy but of security; to say nothing of the honour which redounds to it—the State—if such edifices are handsome, and the disgrace attaching to it when they are badly designed and unsightly.

"No," replies the corporate body in question, and with not less reason, "I have been instituted by you, the State, to maintain art at the highest level it can attain in our times; in virtue of the position thus assigned me, and enjoying your protection, I recruit myself from among the most capable of all the artists of the day; I am assured of the competence of this selection, since I, a *corps d'elité*, am the chooser of those who fill up such vacancies as occur; it would therefore be to belie my constitution, which you acknowledge to be excellent, since you are its creator and protector, if you were to deprive me of the means of forming those competent artists from among whom I am to recruit myself,—if I could not fashion them in my own likeness; or if, having so fashioned them, you should not implicitly receive them as excellent.

"You, the State, are no judge in such matters; you cannot know how an architect should be trained; and the best thing you can do is to intrust the affair entirely to me who have been instituted by, and are maintained by you—let it be remembered —for the very purpose of maintaining art at an exalted level, and not allowing it to lose its way amid certain studies which I declare dangerous, because I have little familiarity with them, or amid novelties which I do not think proper to sanction."

The public would certainly have good reasons for making the above representations; but the Academy would be justified in returning such a reply as we have attributed to it.

For these contradictory positions, the truth of each of which may be asserted according to the point of view from which we regard them; for these conflicting arguments which will go on for ever without in any degree modifying the opinions of either party, the State may some day find a simple, harmonising solution, to which nothing could be objected. It would only have to express itself thus: "Your constitution dates as far back as 1671, I freely admit, and the Academy may be proud of this;

but since 1671 some events of the gravest importance have
happened in France. Since that day many other institutions
have been created or changed; many traditions have been forgotten or annihilated; privileges sanctioned by former governments have been abolished: these are facts which existing
authorities are forced to recognise. I do not object to your
having the amplest liberty, for I do not wish to restrict that of
any individual or even of any society, fraternity, or corporation.
But you must be aware that the Revolution of the last century
abolished privileges and monopolies, and that in France the
principles of equality have come to pervade our moral and social
existence; I cannot therefore protect or support you, because
my special and exclusive protection is a warranty that binds and
compromises me; and, which is more important still, it is an
infringement of the principle of free competition. If I give you
exclusive protection and support, either that protection must
oblige you to a compliance with my wishes,—and you object to
these as arbitrary,—or I must give you absolute liberty, a
liberty which, entrenched behind my protection, may overbear
that of others. I clearly perceive this dilemma, and am unwilling any longer to be caught in it. Take your part fairly with
others, preserve your institution even, if you think proper, but
henceforth I shall not be its protector or responsible chief.
Determine to have a school or not to have one; make the theory
or the practice of art your study, give medals and exhibitions, if
generous donors provide you with the means of so doing;
give lectures or publish books for the benefit of any who
are willing to listen to or read them; I will not interfere to prevent you. Provided you make no disturbance in the streets, nor
obstruct the thoroughfares, and do not exhibit or publish anything morally reprehensible, you may do what you like. But if
to-morrow, one, two, three, or twenty Academies of the Fine Arts
should endeavour to establish themselves in this country, you
must not object to my allowing them the same liberty, to which
in fact they are legally entitled, since from this date, 1868, the
State can no longer sanction privileges or privileged bodies. If
you train capable men, I shall be grateful to you, and shall
employ them as occasion offers; but you must allow me to
select them from other quarters also, if other institutions can
furnish me men of greater ability. You wear dresses embroidered
with green silk; I have not the slightest objection to your doing
so; but I shall not be able to prevent other Academies from
wearing embroideries of red or yellow. That is a trifle, I know,
but I mention it that you may thoroughly understand the spirit
by which our relations will henceforth be guided—equality and
equal protection to all, but no subsidies, endowments, or salaries;

I cannot allow the minority of the Fine Arts to endure for ever; they have attained their majority, and ought to know how to manage their affairs; I cannot suppose that they will always require the aid of a family council. However, I am not a State inclined to limit myself to a passive attitude incompatible with my functions. I provide a school of the Fine Arts free of charge, to which are annexed a Museum of models and a good library. This school will be a public one like the *Collége de France*, and I reserve to myself the right of naming the professors who shall occupy its chairs, either according to the results of public competitions, or from among a certain number of candidates elected by artists.

"Of course I shall not have the mere elementary branches taught from these chairs. That is the province of the special schools, and I do not undertake to be a schoolmaster; I concern myself only with the higher part of the teaching. Moreover, the course of study will not be the occasion of examinations or distributions of prizes. Medals and degrees are likewise the business of the special schools. Do not suppose that I am wishing to be meanly stingy in my expenditure on the Fine Arts,—an expenditure which is trifling enough in all conscience for a great country; no, such is not my idea; but inasmuch as the resources I have to dispose of are barely sufficient, I am pledged to employ the public money to the best advantage. I shall abolish the *École de Rome*, which is an institution, to say the least, of no utility in the present day. That school may have served a good purpose when it took three months to journey from Paris to Rome, when travelling in any part of Europe was a difficult matter, and when the governments whose successor I am, regarded this institution as a convenient pretext for maintaining the influence of France in the Eternal City. In our times these political motives are out of date; travelling is an easy matter almost all over the globe, but especially in Europe; artists, and architects in particular, can find something to learn everywhere; and to provide them an establishment at Rome, where they lose that energy and initiative faculty which are so desirable in the present day, and to habituate them to the easy life of the Villa Medici,—to stimulate that spirit of coterie among young people which leads them thus to transmit to each other the antiquated traditions of former generations,—is neither wise nor conformable to the spirit of the age. I must observe that in suppressing the *École de Rome*, I do not propose to restore to the treasury the money it costs. This is how I propose to employ it. If I no longer maintain your monopoly, several Schools of Art will be immediately formed in France, nay, even private studios, in which, stimulated by free competition, an endeavour will be made to give the students the best instruction in the shortest possible time. It would be evidently contrary to my interest not to make inquiries respecting these private undertakings and their results. I shall therefore invite those private schools or studios to send every year one of their pupils to take part in a general competition (observe I speak now of architects only). The syllabus of subjects for the competition, including two or three grades, shall be chosen by lot from among a certain number of such syllabuses prepared by the architects connected with government works. The results of the examination shall be submitted to a jury chosen by the competitors, excluding, of course, the teachers who shall have sent students to the examination. The awards shall be accompanied by the reasons for them ; they shall be printed and exhibited in public with the designs. We shall see whether one or more prizes can be given annually. The laureate (supposing there is only one) shall have the opportunity of travelling, if he thinks proper, and where he thinks proper, in the course of the first and third year. At the end of the first year it will be obligatory on him to send in a study of some existing monument, ancient or modern, accompanied by a critical and analytic memoir. This study will be submitted to the jury elected, to decide on the competition of the following year : if the work is approved, the laureate will enjoy the emoluments of a second year, which will have to be employed in some commission assigned him by government. The results of this will be judged of as before. If he is deemed competent, the privileges attaching to the third year will be granted him ; at the end of which he will present a study, not of a public building, but having reference to an *ensemble* of structures belonging to a certain country or period, at his discretion ;—this study to be analytic as well as graphic, and to be fully developed. After these trials,—which however engage me to nothing, and do not constitute any claim on their part, but which merely establish the fact of their ability,—I give these laureates a certificate of merit. It will evidently be my interest to employ those who are thus certificated in public work ; but, I repeat it, I shall consider myself at full liberty to do so or not."

If the State should come to make this announcement, and sooner or later it will, there will be the advantage, 1*st*, of consistency and of bringing our practical administration as regards the Fine Arts into harmony with the principles on which our social constitution is based ; 2*d*, embarrassments would be avoided —difficulties of minor importance I allow, but which are not altogether insignificant ; 3*d*, the State would cease to be the responsible guarantor of an irresponsible body ; 4*th*, it would stimulate the development of serious and practical study, and would not have on its hands, as is the case now, a number of mediocrities assuming to have acquired a right to the patronage of the State, because it educates, directs, and pensions them, and marks out for them the several stages they have to pass through; *5th*, it would restore to artists, and to architects in particular, that initiative which is indispensable in every liberal career, which alone can issue in practical results, but which is carefully suppressed at the present time, beneath academical influence; *6th*, it would give precedence to those general questions in which society is really interested, before merely personal questions, which are interesting only to a privileged body, . . and in this it would be conferring a great boon.

I must not pass over in silence the arguments that are brought against such radical changes. These arguments are substantially as follows, and I acknowledge that they have some weight : " If the State abandons the teaching of architecture to private enterprise, that teaching will sensibly degenerate. From these schools and studios will come the strangest doctrines : the good sense and right reason which you regard as entitled to the supreme direction of that teaching will be met with only exceptionally. Europe envies us our Academy and Fine Arts School, and the countries which claim to be the leaders of civilisation have for the last sixty years made it their constant endeavour to imitate these institutions of ours which you would destroy. If your advice were taken, France would find itself immediately relegated to the lowest rank in art production. If the influence of the Academy—whose effects you exaggerate—cease to exist, we should lose all that remains to us of taste, feeling, unity, and grandeur in our architectural works. Architects would no longer be artists, but mere builders, skilful and ingenious, it may be, but destitute of that nice appreciation of the beautiful which is sustained by the influence of the Academy amid all the fluctuations of fashion.

" By destroying an institution which, like all other things of earth, is not exempt from abuses, though these are fundamentally inconsiderable, you would abandon the study of the arts to the influences of fashion, you would sacrifice invaluable traditions, while, for the schools you allow to be established, you would not have that directive principle which is necessary for teaching of every kind, and which, though it may sometimes appear to hinder its progressive tendencies, prevents it from losing its way amid vagaries which you yourself would be the first to deplore. There is no danger in allowing to a body which by its very constitution is not and cannot be composed of any but distinguished men an influence purely moral ; and the influence of the *Académie des Beaux Arts* has not and cannot have any other character. The weight it has acquired in the teaching of art and in public works is owing solely to the value of its doctrines ; or, if the word doctrine seems to you out of harmony with the spirit of the age, to the real merit of the works produced by each of the members composing that body. You cannot prevent talent and merit from encircling themselves with a halo of distinction ; and you will not surely deny that such a radiation is among the most legitimate and salutary of influences. Besides, the *Académie des Beaux Arts* has no power to forbid the establishment of Schools of Art ; and if it had the power, there is every reason for believing that it would not exercise it. Its interest would lead it rather to favour the opening of Schools of Architecture, as it would be well assured that sooner or later these schools would become branches of the *École des Beaux Arts*. We think, therefore, that the inconveniences—to use no harsher term—that would result from the suppression or the diminution of the status of the *Académie des Beaux Arts* would be far from being compensated by the very doubtful advantages that would arise from the withdrawal of State protection. As regards the *École de Rome*, since the decree passed in 1863, the period during which the laureates enjoy their scholarship is reduced from five to three years, and of these three years students may spend a considerable portion abroad ; there is therefore no very great difference between what you propose as an improved arrangement and the one now adopted, while the residence of the students in the Villa Medici brings them into companionship, and affords them an artistic environment which may produce the best results on the development of their talents and their future course. Isolation is not good for any one ; in fact it is positively bad for youth, and the criticisms and encouragement of fellow-students are among the most influential means for forming the tastes and the intellect, especially if traditions of vigorous study influence this life in common. In short, we should leave to time gradually to improve what is defective or contrary to the spirit of the age in the *Académie* and the *École des Beaux Arts* in their architectural branches ; but it would be imprudent to make abrupt changes."

To such representations, which every one has heard or read, for they have been uttered or written again and again, in various forms reproducing the same arguments, it may be replied : If an institution having no political character requires for its maintenance the special protection of the State, it must be because it has not a vitality of its own to sustain it, and is consequently regarded by the public as unnecessary. We do not ask for the suppression of the *Académie* and the *École des Beaux Arts*, in its architectural section ; we only ask that the State shall cease to protect the one and direct the other on its own responsibility.

We know indeed that, in the view of that Academy and School, to withdraw from them the support of the State is to deprive them of the influence exercised by that body; but it is from that very influence, which we consider deleterious, that in the interest of art itself we wish it to be delivered. Time may improve or modify free associations; it brings no new element into corporate bodies that shelter their own irresponsibility behind the responsibility of the State. Liberty is essential to continuous progress. But a protected body cannot be more free than the protector of that body. In this case the State and corporate body are attached to the two ends of one chain; and as the State is little able to occupy itself with the details that particularly interest the corporation, the latter, whose sole business these are, draws the chain towards its side. There is therefore no other means of assuring the independence of the two parties than cutting the chain. The *Académie des Beaux Arts*, which in our opinion exerts so injurious an influence on the teaching and practice of architecture, would probably become a useful association as soon as it was completely independent, and had to struggle on a footing of equality with other societies. It would always have its time-honoured associations in its favour; but it could no longer make these smooth the path for mere mediocrities. Having no personal interest in the question, since we have always preferred our own independence to the advantages attaching to the title of member of the *Académie des Beaux Arts*, we have attentively regarded the course of those events which might have had the effect of modifying the spirit of that institution. Within the last thirty years the *personnel* of the architectural section has been, it must be observed, completely renewed. Not only is the majority of the members of that section selected from among the *élite* of our architects, but it consists of men who previously to membership, and ever since, have manifested individually the most generous and liberal tendencies. Among these distinguished individuals there are even some who may have passed for *revolutionary, i.e.* disposed to very radical modifications in the system of instruction approved of by the academy and the course adopted in reference to public works. But such is the inherent force of circumstances, that these liberal and enlightened spirits, once admitted into the fraternity, have not been able to modify its character, but have been compelled to reduce their opinions or personal tendencies to that dead level of uniformity which is the law of the body. In fact, this liberal and enlightened majority is subjected to the yoke imposed by the minority, because the minority, which does not consist of men of distinguished genius, has no other object than to keep up the *esprit du corps*, has a wide-spread connection in the higher administrative bodies as well as among the members of the school, and is thus able to preserve the power which the protection of the State has enabled it to acquire.

Thus the *Académie des Beaux Arts* (the architectural section) is really outside the institute, and therefore we call it a fraternity (*congregation*). It follows in the wake of a coterie consisting of actively influential mediocrities, all whose power consists in the protection accorded by the State. Withdraw that protection, and the very remarkable result will follow that this class of the institute restored to independence will enter on a liberal course, and will become as helpful as it is now obstructive to progress.

We must therefore expect nothing from the effect of time, if the State remains the protector of the *Académie des Beaux Arts* and the director of architectural training. Rather we must expect a more and more marked degradation in the character of the body itself, and of the studies it presides over. Do we suppose that in the present state of society the level of literary philosophical and scientific studies would be raised if ecclesiastical corporations had the monopoly of teaching in France? or if, in rivalry with such institutions, we had not the University and private schools, and the *Collége de France?* Yet all that concerns instruction in architecture, and the destiny of individual architects, is in the hands of a corporation subject to influences which are concealed from the light of day, and whose action is sheltered by the " Institut."

A time is sure to come when corporate bodies can no longer be directed by men of genius,—when they become subject to the rule of a mediocrity which looks no further than satisfying interests, and has no ambition to secure the triumph of principles. When things are come to this pass, talent and even genius, which are unhappily betrayed into such an environment, cannot impart to it any vivifying element, but are the first to be subjected to the tyranny of conceited mediocrities.

In reference to the course prescribed by the *École de Rome,* the following is what every cool and impartial observer must have remarked. While life and study in community may suit very young people, they are most injurious to the development of superior talent when that second youth begins which sees the growing fruit ripening. Let those who have followed with any success a career in arts or letters question their own memories, and recall the period that intervened between their earliest studies and that in which the results of those studies began to be realised. What uncertainties and anxieties! . . . The mind at that time full of ill-defined cravings, knows not where or how to satisfy them. It has need of calm reflection that it may classify the elements it has not yet been able to assimilate. It requires to perform a process of 'clearing,' as we may call it. It feels the need of a method, though it know not as yet what method is. It is in this crisis of fermentation that real talents develop themselves, but on that very account they must be left to themselves, and not have placed before them a ready-made path, for they would probably follow it. It is only fools who at twenty-five believe they are geniuses. At this age true merit (without supposing it to amount to genius) is, on the contrary, anxious, disquieted, and self-distrustful, because it has a vague glimpse of toilsome work before it, and feels its strength without knowing to what to apply it. Such natures, the only ones we need to consider in the commonwealth of arts and letters, do not develop themselves in a seminary of art or of literature ; on the contrary, they pine in such an atmosphere. From the very circumstance of their feeling that doubt, anxiety, and shrinking modesty which foresees the length and difficulties of the task, they soon allow themselves to be seduced by the plausible offers of easy and quiet study ; they are inclined to believe in the advantages of associated work, and perhaps more than others they feel grateful for the protection offered to these doubts and hesitations ; and unless they are endowed with rare energy of character, they are apt to abdicate individual responsibility. How many students of the *École de Rome,* who promised brilliantly at starting, produce works of a more and more spiritless character ! On the other hand, this *régime* is admirably well suited to mere mediocrities ; it gives them that security, confidence, presumption, which are often an element of success . . for themselves, . . . but of grievous disappointment to that part of the public which is interested in art. The French Seminary of Architecture in Rome is therefore in our judgment the origin of those preposterous and costly vulgarities which fill our cities. And the few distinguished artists who issue from that school—there are certainly some whom we might name—form a class without influence,—respected perhaps, and certainly most estimable in character, but obliged to deplore in silence that predominance of certificated mediocrities who are compromising the future of our art. The real sentiment of this class of artists is, we are assured, identical with our own in this matter ; but as they are members of the fraternity themselves, they consider it incumbent on them to submit to its tyranny without complaint.

Let the State, therefore, which cannot inquire into these trifles, but which suffers from the mischief thus occasioned, apply the only remedy possible ; let it put complete liberty, unlimited competition, in place of the *régime* of protection. It will be the first to benefit by the change, for in giving liberty to all, it will regain its own liberty, and will no longer be obliged, in contravention of its own interests, to humour a monopoly which, moreover, the present state of society cannot long tolerate.

No real competition is possible with the existing organisation of the *École des Beaux Arts*. The gratuitous character of the education given, the series of prizes culminating in the *Prix de Rome* and a kind of claim to employment on returning from the Villa Medici, and the support of the coterie whose head is at the *Académie des Beaux Arts*, which is mistress of the situation, are enticements too seductive for young men not to yield to them. But it is evident that at the present day intellectual work of every kind which has not the stimulus of free competition must soon degenerate, and that every monopoly conduces to inferiority in production. It is therefore a mockery to tell us that the teaching of architecture is free; inasmuch as the protection of the State attracts students to a single privileged school, and which by the influence of circumstances is itself subjected to a privileged body. Let the resources of the State be applied, not to maintaining a corporation and a particular organisation, but to making use of proved ability wherever it may come from; this is all that can reasonably be asked of it, and it is the only means of elevating the teaching of Art.

The meshes of the net spread by the corporate body in question around all the positions to which architects aspire, are not so close as to prevent the introduction among them of architectural *free-thinkers*. The latter do not indeed reach the elevations which are carefully reserved for submissive adepts, but they sometimes find an opportunity of showing their capacity. And it is interesting to observe that, while the greater part of the more important architectural works executed in our day exhibit the strangest and most expensive assemblage of incoherent elements, works of a more modest character often bear that stamp of knowledge, reasoning power, and exact acquaintance with the value and nature of materials which we should be glad to recognise in our more pretentious edifices. The authors of the designs in question are not, it is true, laureates of the Institute; they have not passed the ordeal of the *École des Beaux Arts;* their name is scarcely known, and they will never be members of the *Conseil des batiments civils,* now that the Council has become a mere branch of the *Académie des Beaux Arts,* in contravention of the spirit of its organisation; they will never occupy a chair beneath the dome of the Quai Conti; but they are leaving works which are some consolation to sensible men in view of those orgies in stone to which their more privileged fellow architects commit themselves. Their modest talent occupies itself with practical appliances, seeking to perfect and make the best and most economical use of them. It is they who bring into use certain industrial appliances connected with building, because they condescend to give reason and the interests of their clients the precedence before the satisfaction of their own fancies. Whence, then, did these architects get these methods, —this often precocious experience ? Was it at the *École des Beaux Arts ?* Certainly not ; it was from their own intelligence and private studies, pursued with scrupulous care and without prepossessions. It is therefore not correct to say that outside that school no teaching would be possible, or that it would degenerate if that privileged school ceased to exist. Make the teaching of architecture really free by ceasing to maintain a privileged establishment, and you will immediately see those intelligent and conscientious men, with their modest knowledge and practical experience, take the lead in imparting instruction fruitful in results, free from the prejudices of coteries, and not slavishly following routine. You will see this instruction developing itself not in forming a disciplined and exclusive body, aspiring only to the rewards that will provide comfortable positions for its members, but in training for the public service men who will have only their personal merit to recommend them, who will be independent and careful, because if they commit blunders, they will not be able to fall back upon the influence of a powerful and irresponsible body to cloak them.

Twenty years ago, exterior to and side by side with the *École des Beaux Arts*, there existed what were then called *ateliers, i.e.* societies of young men working under the direction of a master. In these *ateliers* architecture was really learned ; the elementary branches which should precede the study of this art being taught everywhere. These *ateliers*, in competition with each other, and even directed by teachers whose principles were often opposed to each other, occasioned a ferment of intellectual activity which has produced distinguished talents and independent characters. The whole of the school that was subject to the " Institut " was at that time endeavouring to counteract these liberal tendencies, to reduce these minds to a dead level beneath Academic influence ; but it did not always succeed in doing so. If these *ateliers* still exist in name, they no longer exist as far as the spirit that directed them is concerned. The Academic levelling apparatus, in spite of the decree of 1863, has passed over them, and has reduced the heights and filled up the hollows. Those institutions showed us not merely isolated students, but whole bodies of them, revolting against routine, giving proof of juvenile freshness, determining to be no longer satisfied with unexplained conventions, but to follow those laws which examination and reasoning had revealed to their minds. Thus, from an intellectual point of view, we have been retrograding instead of advancing, for there is always retrogression in teaching, as in everything else, when a single corporate body is allowed to open and close the doors at its will.   To those principles and ideas which nourished the intellect of our students and nerved them to enter resolutely into the arena, ready to struggle even to the detriment of their interests, has succeeded a ravenous greed for positions.   Thus, in the various boards intrusted with the management of architectural works, we have seen the number of those places multiplied to satisfy the requisitions made for them on behalf of those who had the support of the privileged frater-nity.   In most of the *offices* connected with public buildings and those of the city of Paris, the staff is twice as large as it need be.   Here again persons take precedence of principles ; and there is far more anxiety to find places for the protégés of the fraternity at all stages of their career than to procure those who would best execute the work.   These numerous agents receive but small salaries, it is true, but their labour is not considerable, and their number tends to divide that moral responsibility which ought to rest on each several agent.   The sum total of their salaries, given to a body proportionate to the work, would pro-duce more satisfactory results and a better guarantee of their adequacy.   But this is not the object contemplated ; the demands of the fraternity must be satisfied, and the more fully they are satisfied, and the more numerous the fraternity becomes, the more its influence extends.   Only the profound ignorance in which the public have been assiduously kept respecting all ques-tions that relate to the practical applications of architecture could have brought things to such a pass as we behold them in at present.   It is therefore the public that I appeal to here ; for its opinion alone will be able to counteract the abuses I have pointed out, and which it will make head against as soon as it clearly recognises the fact that it is interested in the highest degree in the right and wise direction of the architectural works undertaken for it.

Supposing the Academy of Architecture separated from the State or the administrative boards, *i.e.* supposing there were complete liberty, it would no longer be necessary thus to pro-vide places, half of which at least are useless, for this army, recruited by the Academy to confirm its power.   Why, we may ask, should government boards burden themselves with the nomination and direction of this numerous staff ?   Why should they encumber themselves with a hierarchy of architects, from the architect in chief down to the actual clerk of the works ?   Before the law these agents have no responsibility ; the architect alone answers for the execution of the work.   Then why not leave him the privilege attached to responsibility, that is liberty? The administration gives an architect a commission; at the same time it assigns him a staff of agents. I grant that it consults him respecting the choice and even the number of them, though this is not always done, and there is no obligation to do so. Why does it not allow him the option of making a selection (since he is legally responsible) of the staff he requires, both as to capacity and number? Or, if he thinks proper, should he not be allowed to dispense with such a staff altogether, and to do all the architectural work himself? And I may observe that this is the case sometimes; I could mention certain cases of the kind in which the architect alone works, taking upon himself the design, the details of the execution, and the accounts, going to the works in the morning and not leaving them before the workmen; while his staff are attending to their personal affairs or doing nothing at all. And we can easily understand why this should be so in the present state of affairs. In the first place, it is disagreeable to have to play the usher, to mark the absences or shortcomings of employés who are not directly dependent on you, and whose remuneration is often insufficient,—who in fact could not keep themselves and their families on what they receive. After a few hints and remonstrances the architect decides to say nothing, but to do all himself, as he is the responsible party. I have seen architects whom I could name going to take memoranda at their works while the appointed clerks were leisurely enjoying themselves. And even supposing one had the good fortune to possess a staff of conscientious clerks, it would be a matter of further anxiety to know whence they came, what was the extent of their acquisitions, and what were their aptitudes and tastes. Too often such employés have not the most elementary notion of practical building; having come from the School of Architecture thoroughly imbued with the illusions which that institution fosters in the minds of pupils, they regard the practical side of our art with disgust. They fancy themselves tied to an occupation which is unworthy of their merits: have they not gained prizes? have they not (on paper at least) erected splendid edifices which have called forth the admiration of their companions and gained them the Prix de Rome? Do they not feel themselves called on to dazzle the public by superior conceptions? Are these young men to superintend excavations, to direct the composition of concrete, to choose materials and satisfy themselves that the stone-dressers are doing the work according to the designs? As well ask a captain in the army to perform the extra duties and sweep the barracks! Supposing again that this staff of clerks were inclined to aid you, that they were willing to make themselves of use at the works, it is still a question whether they have followed your methods, are imbued with the principles that guide you, and would act as your pupils and assistants. In most cases they are almost strangers to you; or they may come to your office imbued with ideas and methods the very opposite to your own. If you give them anything to do, you soon perceive by the way in which they set about it that you will either have to yield to their ideas, or that you will have to begin a new course of instruction with them; and then it will happen, nine times out of ten, that you can do without their help, or that you have in your works a person disposed to criticise everything, and who is delighted if something goes wrong. Let the administrative boards cease to give themselves so much trouble; let them leave to architects the task of selecting their agents where and how they think fit; then we shall have excellent instruction without wanting a privileged school. In fact every building-yard will become a school, the best possible; for there is no architect of merit who would not be inclined, when he undertakes a building, to establish his *atelier* of pupils at the works, and to make them execute, according to their capacities and grade of acquirements, work useful to himself and profitable to them. This is the case in private building enterprises, and so it happens that from the building-yards in connection with them there issue men who are really capable and useful; and thus, in contrast with our public edifices, our private habitations are generally well planned, economically built, and skilfully constructed.

We can understand an organisation such as that of the "Bridges and Highways" (*Ponts et Chaussées*), which consists of a select body, and of superintendents who (with rare exceptions due to extraordinary capacity) remain superintendents for life. It matters little to an engineer whether the superintendent of his works is Peter or Paul; he is a superintendent of recognised capability; if he is not so, a change is made, but the superintendent of *Ponts et Chaussées* is not an aspirant to the rank of engineer; he does not regard the period he passes at the works as a necessary stage to his admission to higher functions. He performs his work honestly and frankly without any *arrière-pensée*; he has not been intoxicated by successes at the *École*, and does not consider that the time he has passed at the works is so much lost to the pursuit of that art to which his aspirations are urging him. I am far from suggesting that such an organisation—one, moreover, which is not in harmony with the habitudes of the day—should be applied to practical architecture; but the middle course adopted by the administration, in reference to the direction of architectural works, presents the inconvenience attending all plans not deduced from a logical principle; it has neither the advantages of the system adopted in the *Ponts et Chaussées* nor the advantages of liberty. But, as I said before, the point least considered in all these matters is art and the public interest. The chief object is to secure to the *Académie des Beaux Arts* the perpetuation of its influence, and, with a view to this, positions for those who put themselves under its protection. It is only by degrees, and unconsciously I may say, that our administrative boards have been reduced to this absolute deference to those encroachments on the part of the architectural section of the "Institut." The time has been, and at no distant date, when men high in office were sensible of those encroachments, and showed some tendency to free themselves from this increasing dependence on the Academy. That time has passed away; in our days those high functionaries have other cares, perhaps of a graver kind, and they leave to subalterns that of providing for these interests. It is unnecessary to add that these subalterns have become the allies of the all-powerful fraternity, since they can derive nothing but advantage from their compliance with its increased craving for influence, and neither honour nor profit can accrue to them from a struggle against it.

Persons of matured and vigorous character never allow themselves to be seduced into such compliance with a corporate body, and it must be allowed that men do not reach the higher officers of State, or at any rate do not maintain such positions unless they possess a certain amount of dignified impartiality which revolts against being mixed up with the interests of a coterie; but in these times men in high places are too much occupied with graver matters to be able to exercise their impartiality in all the trifling details of their administration. They leave these details to subordinates, and it is evident that these have neither the will nor the power to resist the persistent influence of a body which has its connections everywhere, and is placed under the protection of the State. Even a minister (in the present state of things) would scarcely have sufficient authority to enable him to break through the Academic network that envelops his administration. Should he attempt it, he would soon bring upon himself a world of opponents, and his own ministerial staff would be an obstacle in his way. Of this fact the Academic fraternity are well aware, and all its efforts, especially during the last few years, have had this consideration pretty steadily and continuously in view. There is thus only one method, as simple as it is effective, of breaking the charm, and that is a complete separation of the State from the Academic fraternity,—the liberty of teaching in architecture, and the resolution on the part of the Government to give up playing the schoolmaster: in fact, the substitution of free competition for the *protective* system; the responsibility of the architect for State direction everywhere and over everything,—a responsibility which, moreover, is imposed on him by the law. Then, and then only, will a really thorough system of instruction arise, without any obligation on the part of the State to trouble itself in the matter; just as the system of instruction at the Central School of Arts and Manufactures was formed.[1] It would be unreasonable to bring university teaching as an argument in favour of State superintendence in the teaching of architecture. I will not discuss the question whether our university system is favourable or unfavourable to the intellectual development of the youth of France; I maintain only that there is no analogy between the two kinds of teaching. It may be reasonably maintained that it is the duty of the State to maintain a uniform system in the teaching of our Public Schools (Lycées). In these we have to take children from their families and make citizens of them; to prepare them for entering on the various careers open to them, while subjecting them to that régime of equality which is the fundamental principle of our social state; but when they have quitted this intellectual gymnasium which has made, or ought to have made of all these children, citizens in the germ, the State has fulfilled its task. We can also see the reason for the State maintaining special schools besides the lyceums, such as those of Saint Cyr, of the *Ponts et Chaussées*, those of Law and of Medicine; because that of Saint Cyr is the nursery of the army, that of the *Ponts et Chaussées* a training institution for our engineers, who form a regular organised body; because the State deems it its duty to protect the health of the citizens; because Law is immutable, and the Magistracy is a function of the State; but we cannot continue this reasoning in regard to architecture. This art is subject, or ought to be subject, to all the changes that supervene in the habits of society. Nothing is more rational than that a Professor of Law should teach law under the protection of the State, since it is the State which makes the law and presides over its execution; but that a Professor of Architecture should teach a particular architectural form under the protection of the State, is almost ridiculous. I, a private individual, cannot make a law; but I may invent an architectural form; and if it is a desirable one, why should the State intervene to prevent me from teaching or applying it? The State in our lyceums teaches literature, history, and the

---

[1] The *École Centrale des Arts et Manufactures* is now placed under State control, which, in the opinion of many, is to be deplored; but it was originally established and obtained the influence we witness by private effort.

sciences according to an approved method ; that is all very well ; but the State does not teach the writing of novels, comedies, or histories. From Havre to Marseilles we should hear a shout of ridicule if the State was to set about opening a School of Literature ; if it made young people write novels or comedies at certain hours ; if it put them in cells to give themselves up to their inspirations ; if it gave them prizes and sent them to Rome to make them better acquainted with Tacitus and Cicero, or to Spain to study the old Spanish theatre.

Architecture is an art based upon several sciences. And these sciences—geometry, mathematics, chemistry, mechanics—are taught everywhere. But at the point where art comes in, the State has no more to do with directing the teaching than with inquiring how novels and comedies are produced. At this stage, each artist, each author, must find out his own path. There is no such thing as official architecture or official literature ; and between the public and the artist or writer no power can intervene to any good purpose. Such an intervention may have been tried under Louis XIV., but it must be relegated to the same category as the *machine de Marly.* Unfortunately we have still many *machines de Marly,* and we can understand how those whose business it is to grease them, and who get their living by this employment, should assume that the world will come to an end if those machines are touched, or if steam-engines take their place.

Many sensible people complain that our age has not an architecture of its own. We have heard such complaints from very distinguished persons.

But how can our age have an architecture in France when the State keeps up and protects a body whose instrument it has gradually become, which maintains, in defiance of and against all comers, those particular forms of art which suit its purpose—a body which, in spite of all endeavours to the contrary, is the supreme director of instruction, and insists on limiting it within the narrow field which it cultivates and from which it derives a considerable profit ? In the precarious position occupied by architects, how is it possible that new ideas should be developed ? They can barely secure recognition on paper ; how should they succeed in getting translated into stone ?

It is for the development of the artist's independence, and securing him that independence, that we should strive, if we would have an art special to our age. It is not sufficient that discussion should be free ; it is necessary that all the methods suggested by such discussion, as far as they are compatible with public safety, should be capable of being followed without embarrassment to those who pursue them, or, worse still, their entire failure to secure a position.

There was a time when every one was obliged to dress according to certain regulations or edicts, and when it was not permitted to a burgess to wear a cloak such as covered the shoulders of a baron. There was a time when the burgess was not allowed to build a house resembling that of the noble. Now-a-days every one dresses and houses himself according to his good pleasure—every one selects his tailor or his architect where he likes. Why then should the State continue to encourage and sustain a monopoly which has the effect of circumscribing a *useful art,* such as architecture, within the limits prescribed by a corporate body? What advantage can it derive from this state of things? It is the first to complain of those enormous expenses which the most devoted associates of that corporate body impose upon it.

Now-a-days the State cannot and ought not to be otherwise than indifferent as to dogmas; it has everything to lose and nothing to gain in supporting one at the expense of the other. In this, as in many other things, the State is only the epitome of the various opinions that are held, and its duty is simply that of protecting all in such a way that the new may, if necessary, take the place of the old. And while the State complains of the great expenses entailed upon it by the architects whom it prefers to call in, and justly, because they have been pupils of the school it maintains, the public are not always satisfied with the style which these architects seem to favour; and the censure which, wrongly or rightly, is applied to the buildings erected for them, falls back on the administration itself. So that no one is satisfied unless it be the Academy of Architecture; and the State can neither get rid of its responsibility, nor reply to the public that the blame ought to be laid on the artists who are its own creatures. If a play is hissed at the theatre, no one finds fault with the government, but if the State maintained a school of dramatic authors, and if from that school there issued laureates pensioned by it, the case would be different; in hissing the piece disapproved of, the State would be censured.

Let the State cease to trouble itself about the teaching of Architecture, and there will arise a sound system of teaching adapted to our age and its requirements.

Let the State sever itself from the *Académie des Beaux Arts* and we shall have an Architecture of this Nineteenth Century in France, as there was in Athens, in Rome, in Byzantium, in Florence, in Venice, and among ourselves from the twelfth to the sixteenth century before the *Académie des Beaux Arts,* or its architectural section, was invented. But, I repeat once more, the chief object aimed at is not consulting history and profiting by its teachings; it is not art, or the few who would wish to practise and teach it freely, that are considered; it is the conservation of a fraternity that has succeeded in attaching itself to the State, like the moss to the rock, to such a degree as to conceal its real nature and quality.

LECTURE XV.

DOES an architectural conception comprehend its ornamentation, or is the ornamentation an after design of the architect? In other words, is the ornamentation an integral part of the edifice, or is it only a clothing more or less rich with which the edifice is covered when its shape has been determined? Among the various civilisations which have had a characteristic architecture, these questions have probably never been consciously proposed; but they proceeded as if these questions had been mooted, which, as far as our purpose is concerned, comes to the same thing.

The oldest known architecture whose history affords us any reliable data is the Egyptian; and this architecture derived its ornamentation, in the first instance, from primitive methods of construction which are not those we find employed in the oldest monuments extant. Thus we cannot doubt that the earliest Egyptian edifices were built with materials supplied by the vegetable kingdom (wood and reeds): yet there no longer exist any but stone buildings on the banks of the Nile, and the ornamentation of these stone buildings is in great part proper to timber structures. At what distant period did the transformation of that structure take place? We do not know; at least we have not yet discovered it. But dates are here of secondary importance; as in the geological transformations of the crust of the earth, the succession of the strata is demonstrated, though we cannot ascertain how many centuries it took to effect the changes in question.

We can have no doubt that at the time when the most ancient Egyptian buildings whose remains still exist were erected, the tradition of those primitive wooden buildings was not obliterated, since we find them portrayed in sculptures and paintings. But those structures of vegetable material were not timber buildings such as are erected by the Northern races.

Timber of considerable length and hardness must always have been wanting in Egypt itself, and the hills that border the Nile were never wooded. We readily perceive that the system of construction adopted by the primitive architects was that of reed-work, frame and pannel-work—such as belongs rather to joinery than timber-work—and pise, that is, mud dried in the sun.

Whether Egypt was occupied by aborigines who hollowed out their dwellings in the calcareous rocks in the neighbourhood of the river, or whether the hypogæa of Nubia appeared to the conquering races good models to follow in a burning climate, the primitive buildings of reeds and slight timber would certainly seem to have had an interior core of earth in their walls and ceilings; that is, they were so constructed as to form artificial crypts; supports and casing of wood, with filling in and top covering of puddled clay. In Assyria, again, the traditions of this kind of construction are found in buildings of recent period as compared with the most ancient Egyptian remains. But we shall revert to this subject.

As Egypt possessed only reeds and light wood suitable for joinery, such as sycamore, fig, and a few resinous trees, but which are unfit for timber framing, when (for instance) a straight, stiff, and rather long support—what we call a prop—was wanted, the only means of obtaining it was by forming bundles of these reeds with fillets, and setting them upright on a socle; since strong timber was not to be had, these bundles of reeds were necessarily placed rather near together to receive lintels of short length, or even other reeds put across—a kind of watling that was filled in with puddled clay. Ceilings were formed in the same manner. As to the walls—the upright enclosures—nothing prevented their being built of unburnt bricks. Hence, when later on, stone buildings take the place of these structures of reeds and mud, the ornamentation of the columns and lintels borrows its forms from the vegetable kingdom, while the walls remain even or are covered with paintings and sunk carvings. These sunk carvings, which belong especially to Egypt, are an evidence of the means of construction primitively employed. In fact when we build a wall of earth—of pise—a strong coffer of wood is necessary for ramming in the earth; and thereby two even surfaces are obtained which can easily be rendered perfectly smooth when the work is dry. But if we wish to decorate these surfaces with delicate carving or hieroglyphics, it is not possible to plant such carvings on the smoothed wall, or to leave them standing out by depressing the surface around them; it is natural, on the contrary, to trace these figures on the smooth surface, and to produce the design by sinking their outline. It is none the less strange that an architectural ornamentation should be continued when the method of building which suggested it has been replaced by others. This can only be explained by the influence of tradition. We observe the same phenomenon in the Hindoo buildings, and in those of Asia Minor, attributed to the Ionians. Forms have been hallowed, as it were, by a primitive method of structure : when the method was changed, it was not considered necessary or advisable to change the form. In some of those Ionian monuments hewn in the rock are seen imitations of round logs, which had originally served for supports, shelters, and enclosures. Remarkable as were the arts of Asia,—and we class those of Egypt with them,—the spirit of criticism and logical method is wanting. It was the Oriental Greeks who, in architecture, as in all the expressions of art, were the first to proceed on a basis of reasoning and critical investigation. It was they who first made tradition subordinate to the intellectual power which seeks to give every human creation its appropriate expression in harmony with the purpose and the material means employed. Why is it that the thorough good sense of Greek art is not now perceived even by those who affect to draw their inspiration from it ? We have here one of those inconsistencies which would appear laughable if the consequences were less serious ; an inconsistency which I shall not endeavour to explain, and which certainly will never be explained by those among us who have arrogated to themselves the sole right of understanding that art, since they never deign to enlighten the public as to the reasons that guide them. It is nevertheless true that a very distinct line of demarcation may be drawn between ancient Asiatic art and Greek art. The former proceeds only in an uninterrupted course of tradition, each generation reproducing the forms adopted by preceding ages. When necessity dictates a change in the method of construction, or in the materials, the immutable form is not thereby affected, but is perpetuated in spite of the novel conditions ; so that the architecture of a country which does not possess building timber, continues to reproduce with stone or bricks the forms which previous generations dwelling in forests had adopted. Greek art, on the contrary, like Greek philosophy, proceeds by the method of investigation and criticism. Thus Greek genius is the pioneer in progress ; and though it may have halting-places, it does not fix limits. Facile, intelligent, attached to the form, but still more to the spirit, it rejects hieratic conventionalism in art as it opposes theocracy and fixed dogma in religion and philosophy. Who can tell what the development of Christianity would have been if it had not come in contact with Greek genius, which gave it life and expansive force ; not at once confining it within the limits of an immutable hieratic dogmatism, but by discussing it and causing it to undergo transformations as rapid as they are profound. It needed all the uniting and centralising spirit of the Empire, and the barbarian invasion of Islam, to arrest the diverging and probably fruitful development of which the new religion gave promise. If there had been no interference on the part of the Imperial power, and Mohammedanism had extended its conquests in the direction of India, instead of over-spreading Egypt and Asia Minor, the School of Alexandria would have been a focus of illumination for the West, and would have advanced civilisation by ten centuries. Perhaps in that case we might not have suffered the protracted intellectual oppression which weighed so long and so heavily upon Europe during the Middle Ages, and the deplorable results of which are still affecting us. It is owing to the long-continued persistence of intellectual tyranny under which the West has been suffering since the fifth century, that the essential spirit of the Greek genius is lost sight of. We appreciate its brilliancy; but in most cases we are incapable of using its clear light to guide us, and, like persons who having lived long in a dark cell are unable to bear the sun's rays, when we take any work in hand we are obliged to seek the shade.

We architects, clinging to certain spurious traditions which have never had the force of dogmatic belief; subject to caprices the least explicable; reproducing forms that are meaningless, and which, even when they first appeared, were produced without reasoning or serious consideration; stammering out a corrupted dialect, we talk of the Greeks! we go to study architecture in Greece! but for what purpose, unless it be to imbue ourselves with their daring spirit, their accuracy in reasoning and judicious use of knowledge?

Greek genius is not found, in architecture more than in any-thing else, in one corner of Europe only. It is not confined to the shape of a capital or the profile of a cornice. Greek genius is human genius *par excellence;* consequently it lives still and will live for ever. Any one of us may find a spark of it, if he chooses, in himself; and the builders who raised some of our Western Mediæval edifices were more thoroughly imbued with the principles constituting the essence of Greek genius than the frigid copyists of Greek forms can be.

Various principles have been adopted in the ornamentation of buildings. The first, or oldest—that which most naturally occurs to the mind of the decorator—consists in deriving the ornamentation from the objects and materials employed in building.

The dweller in the forests erects his buildings with the trees he has felled ; and the combination of the timbers, and the leaves with which he covers them, afford the earliest and most natural ornamentation.   Accustomed to the forms thus suggested, when later on he migrates to countries that are not wooded, we may be sure that he will give the new materials he employs forms which are derived from timber-work.   We need no further proof of this than that which has been furnished by the examination of the ancient remains of a great portion of Asia.[1]   The second principle of ornamentation is the result of a more perfect state of civilisation : it consists in giving to the several members of the building forms not dictated by an unreflecting adherence to tradition, but, on the contrary, by thoughtful consideration ;— features deduced from the nature of the materials employed, the requirements to be satisfied, and the exigencies of the climate. The first method of decoration only was followed in ancient times by most of the Asiatic nations, with which we class Egypt.   The Greeks were probably the first to adopt the second method.   The first is not in conformity with logical deduction ; the second is thoroughly rational.

For example, it is evidently quite illogical to give a column, a monostyle of stone, the form of a bundle of reeds.   This is nevertheless what the Egyptians did from an early period. Imitating in stone, fig. 1, bundles of reeds, which are moreover represented in painting or graving in their actual shape on the buildings themselves,[2] they perpetuated this kind of ornamentation in their architecture for many centuries.   Thus they hewed sarcophagi of granite or basalt, giving their sides the appearance of a piece of carpentry.   This mode of ornamentation is explicable among a people who seek to preserve certain traditional forms hallowed by religious associations and maintained by a powerful theocracy ; but it has been inadmissible in our Western civilisation ever since the supervention of Greek genius.   And in fact, while the Ionians of Asia believed they ought to continue this transmission of forms, the Dorians did not proceed in the same manner.   Even their earliest buildings display forms that are appropriate to the nature of the material employed.   I am well aware that there is a strong inclination to regard the Doric temple (for instance) as an imitation in stone of a wooden structure ; but this we may regard as one of those

---

[1] See Lecture II.

[2] Our figure 1 represents at A graven pictures dating from the fourth dynasty.   The bundle of reeds is there figured in its nearly actual form.   It is the delineation of the primitive arrangement of the column.   At B is the stone column (eighteenth dynasty), but which exactly reproduces all the characteristics of the bundle of reeds.   The ornamentation of this column and its capital is merely a rendering of the primitive work composed of vegetable growths.   The plan C shows at a, the sections of the column at its base ; at b, at the height of the binding ; at e, at the height of the swelling of the capital ; at d, at the height of the summit of the capital (see *l'Histoire de l'Art Egyptien*, by M. Prisse d'Avenne).

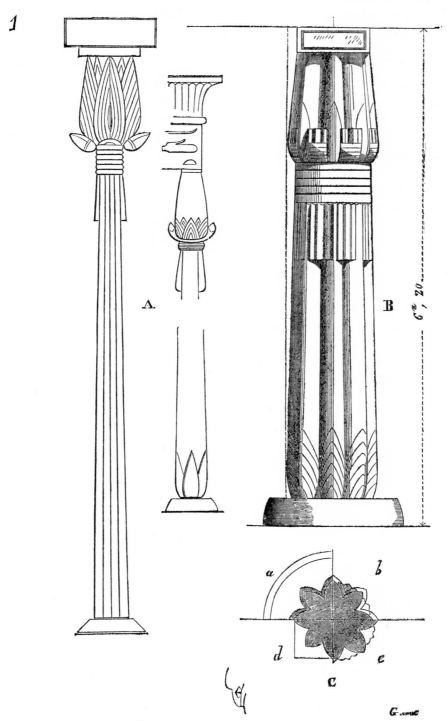

FIG. 1.—Origin of the form of the Egyptian Column.

hypotheses that are more ingenious than correct; we believe we have demonstrated this in the second lecture,[1] and shall not revert to the subject; especially as all that can be urged will not prevent the repetition of the assertion for a long time to come, that the Doric Greek temple derives its origin from the primitive wood hut. What, however, cannot be disputed is, that the shape of the capital and the mouldings of the cornice have no analogy whatever with shapes derived from the fashioning of wood. The primitive Egyptian capital is evidently an imitation of the lotus-flower, or of a cluster of lotus buds; but the Greek Doric capital is not an imitation of any vegetable form; and it would be very difficult to find such a shape in a piece of wood-work. Its graceful outline displays the form that rightly belongs to a stone support. This is evident to the least experienced. In the triglyphs again, we are asked to see the ends of beams: but besides the fact that the ends of beams could not show on the four sides of a building, how can we account for the wood being fluted at the ends? It is easy to flute wood in the direction of its grain, but across the grain this would not be an easy or rational process. We see in the triglyphs uprights of stone between which are placed the metopes, these being merely a filling in. This seems much more in accordance with common sense: and since the Greeks fluted their columns to express distinctly their function as vertical supports, it was natural to flute the uprights of the architrave, whose function is similar. Here wood has nothing to do with the origin of the forms given to the triglyphs. But we will not further discuss these somewhat commonplace trivialities.

In the buildings erected by the Dorian Greeks, painting was always employed as a means of ornamentation, internal and external. In the best period of Classic Art, the Greeks did not use coloured marbles in their large buildings. They built them of stone or white marble, coating the monochrome stone with a fine stucco and colouring it; when they used marble they selected white, and coloured its entire surface. Colour, therefore, was one of the most effective means of ornamentation; it served to distinguish the architectural members, and to give the several planes of the structure their due relief. But,—and in this particular the delicacy of Greek genius is manifest,—as it is necessary, especially in such a climate as theirs, to consider the effect of the sun's light, the Greek artists felt that in a building whose dimensions were never very considerable, greater relative importance should be given either to the vertical or to the horizontal lines: all their mouldings therefore are made in the horizontal members; here they are strongly marked; they

[1] See Vol. i. p. 35, and following.

are even deeply sunk, in order to obtain sharp shades like strong ink-lines in a drawing; while the vertical members are left bare, or only very slightly moulded. The shafts of the columns are but faintly streaked with shallow flutings, whose only effect is to render their cylindro-conical surface more distinctly apparent. If we examine a Doric Greek temple of the best period, we shall not find a single vertical moulding; all the mouldings are horizontal and very sharply cut. The result of this system was that the surfaces were distinguished by different shades, and that in the general effect the building was banded with strongly marked horizontal shadows, quieting to the eye, and clearly separating the various tones of colour. In these temples there is very little sculpture; it only appears in the metopes and the tympanums of the pediments; moreover, it is not ornamental sculpture, but represents independent subjects. For the most part the ornamentation, properly so called, consists of painting. Sometimes the horizontal mouldings are finely beaded in the most careful and effective manner.

It was only about the time of Pericles, in Attica, that sculptured ornamentation became a feature in buildings; and then it is flat, thin, and delicate, and appears as if it were intended to throw the painting into relief. It may therefore be asserted that, as a general rule, the ornamentation of the best Greek architecture consisted entirely of horizontal mouldings, very skilfully designed, with due regard to the effects of light and shade, and tones of colour, whose harmonious arrangement we shall have occasion to consider later on.

If the Greeks did not always preserve that admirable sobriety which nevertheless produces such a striking effect, they were at any rate never betrayed into those eccentricities into which their would-be imitators allowed themselves to be led. And even when the Roman Empire came to be established among them, they still had the ability to devise for the imperial architecture a style of ornamentation appropriate to the systems of construction then employed; for if there is an architecture in which the decorative method is out of harmony with the structure, it is certainly that of the Empire; and despite its intrinsic worth, which is sometimes incontestable, this decorative method has the defect of falsifying a structure which is nevertheless sufficiently beautiful and rational to render it an excellent theme. The ornamentation adopted in the buildings of the Cæsarean period—when those buildings are really Roman, and are not an imitation of the architecture of the Greeks,—has the great fault of dwarfing the building, whose real grandeur only becomes apparent when its dress has been removed.

Among the Greeks all ornamentation, so far from falsifying,

emphasizes the structure ; moreover, it is always proportioned to the size of the building ; it never breaks up the parts which should preserve an appearance of solidity ; and it is effective in proportion to its sobriety and moderation. In the Roman buildings ornamentation is lavished without sufficient judgment, and aims rather at richness of effect than fitness and clearness. While the Greeks of the Classic period made only a very moderate use of sculptured ornamentation, and confined their statuary to specially determined places, they covered the surfaces of their buildings with a colouring which, when required, gave relief to the supports, while it subordinated the parts that did not support but served only as enclosures. The Romans of the Empire, on the contrary, made it their chief object to employ if possible, all together, every decorative appliance,—granite, jasper, porphyry, marble, painted stucco, bronze, and mosaic ; they used all these with more profusion than discernment. With them, to charm meant to dazzle, to astonish ; and they appreciated but slightly the refinements of Greek genius. Besides, it was a matter of no concern to them whether the ornamentation suited the material made use of or not ; or whether that ornamentation belonged to the first or second of those two modes between which we have established a marked distinction, or borrowed at the same time from both. Every kind of decoration pleased them, provided it was rich.

But before tracing the consequences of Greek *rationalism* and Roman *eclecticism* in decoration, we must briefly consider the singular phase of art displayed by the civilisation of the Medes or Assyrians, and which incontestably exerted an influence over the art of Greece, and a much more powerful one than that attributed to Egypt.

Mesopotamia furnishes through its whole extent a plastic earth admirably adapted for making bricks ; it possesses very productive bituminous springs ; and on some of its ridges limestone, gypsum and even soft marbles. In that sunny clime it was possible to make with the mud of the Euphrates large quantities of bricks, which could be dried in the open air. With these materials therefore, thus easily obtained, the main body of their buildings was erected on a basement of stone. The walls were faced with fire-baked bricks, often enamelled or plastered ; on these walls were constructed either vaults, likewise of dried earth and covered by terraces, or ceilings consisting of beams of resinous wood, with soffits of brick, terraced and plastered. Sometimes bitumen served to unite these unburnt bricks, and would naturally aid in the formation of terrace-roofs. Excepting for basements, stone was only employed for doorways or for interior linings, and was then covered with carvings and inscriptions. The purport of these inscriptions is invariably a minute narration of the martial achievements of the person who had caused the erection of the building.

For several centuries the Assyrian kings did little else than plunder their neighbours. From the conquered countries were carried away not only the flocks, herds, and treasures, but, as we learn from the inscription of Sardanapalus III.,[1] iron, bronze, timber, wrought or unwrought,—everything, in fact; and in addition, whole populations, which were to augment in Mesopotamia the number of slave workmen who were employed in making and bringing together those enormous masses of bricks, in quarrying gigantic blocks of stone, and transporting them by main force to the royal buildings. This barbarous policy was moreover coincident with a refined state of civilisation. The Assyrians thus absorbed all the vitality and vigour of the neighbouring countries, and the prodigious splendour of their empire stood forth amid an environment of ruins and desert. When the Ninevite power, in its turn, crumbled beneath a Median invasion and the efforts of remnants of long-oppressed nations, there no longer remained anything of its glory but the piles of bricks that are still to be seen on the banks of the Euphrates and Tigris. Nowhere on the surface of the globe could there be instanced such an abuse of monarchical power, and nowhere so complete a fall; such, in fact, that no new civilisation has since then been able to found itself on that soil, exhausted by the most terrible despotism ever known.

It is certain that the mountains which form the boundary of Mesopotamia were once covered with fine forests; for in the inscriptions collected mention is often made of kings who sent to have cedars cut in considerable quantity for the building of their palaces. These mountains are now bare of timber; and everything leads to the belief that they have been so ever since the Assyrian devastations. The Assyrian monarchs concerned themselves but little with the reproduction of the vegetable wealth they were consuming; they took everything,—men, things, animals, and forests; thinking that lands would never be wanting to their successors for a continuance of their reckless spoliations. It might be supposed that in point of art a civilisation thus constituted would erect buildings correspondingly exceptional in kind, extent, and character. Nothing, however, in the remains of these buildings leads one to suppose a condition bordering on barbarism; on the contrary, they manifest all the refinements of an extremely advanced material civilisation. In the general arrangements everything is co-ordinated, designed,

[1] See *Expédit. scient. en Mésopotamie executée par ordre du gouvernement* 1851-1854, by MM. Fresnel, Felix Thomas, and Jules Oppert, 1853.

COURS D'ARCHITECTURE

E. Viollet-le-Duc. del.

A. Leve. lith.

Vve A. Morel & Cie Editeurs.

Imp. Lemercier &Cie, Paris

PALAIS DE KHORSABAD

Porte Sud-Est.

preconsidered, and executed with that sequence and regularity of working which is the mark of an administrative organisation as complete as it is powerful.   The water-courses were regulated with scrupulous care; in every direction are found traces of dikes raised to check the periodical inundations of rivers, and dams designed for the irrigation of the plains; for while those fierce Assyrian monarchs created a desert around their empire, it was their pleasure to live amid pleasant gardens and verdant fields.   The people whom they carried away from the neighbouring countries into bondage were employed in tasks for which our modern appliances would scarcely suffice.   Of the argillaceous earth taken from the numerous canals and streams, these labourers fabricated vast accumulations of sun-dried or fire-burnt bricks, and with these materials were raised veritable hills or plateaux, on which were built vast and lofty palaces, surrounded by rampart walls flanked with embattled towers.   These plateaux the were perforated by conduits, and passages for leading off water.

In accordance with an Oriental custom which still prevails, these palaces were more like towns than residences arranged in a symmetrical manner; they were groups of buildings designed for the uses they had to serve, with numerous rooms surrounding courts or cloisters.   Water flowed through the meadows and gardens.   Terraces of puddled clay, plastered with cement or bitumen, covered the buildings and afforded places for the enjoyment of the cool evening air after the hot days of those regions. The massive walls, built of sun-dried bricks, made with extreme care and united together by a thin bed of wet clay or of bitumen, were faced externally with plaster and brightly-coloured glazed bricks.   In the gates colossal sculptured figures of winged lions, or bulls with human heads, like those in the British Museum and that of the Louvre, or of men killing lions, formed the jambs, and supported semicircular vaults built of unburnt bricks with archivolts of glazed bricks.   At the palace of Khorsabad, M. Place has found existing one of those gates with its vault, a discovery which has caused no little astonishment to archæologists, who insisted that vaulting was a relatively recent invention, scarcely dating further back than the sixth century before our era.

Plate XXVII. represents a perspective view of the south-east gate of the palace of Khorsabad, restored according to data supplied by the discoveries of M. Place, and the meritorious graphical labours of E. Thomas.   The basement of the portal, consisting of winged bulls of colossal size, is of marble, and each figure is a monolith.   Above rise the masses of sun-dried brickwork forming the archway and the two towers.   The whole building was covered with plastering, most probably coloured, if we may judge by some analogous portions preserved, and the descriptions of Herodotus. There were besides friezes and an archivolt of bricks enamelled with colours, representing ornaments, human figures, hunting scenes, and combats.

It is worth while to observe the ornamentation on the outside of the tower walls,—an ornamentation employed in all parts of the palace of Khorsabad, and consisting of a series of portions of cylinders in juxtaposition, like the pipes of an organ, or, more accurately, like trunks of trees placed vertically close together. This style of decoration is a last reminiscence, as it were, of the timber stockading, which had originally served to keep up and preserve the tempered earth or pise before the regular use of sun-dried bricks. It must be remarked that with this exception of the tradition of a system of structure which had ceased to be employed, all the ornamentation is perfectly rational, and in accordance with the mode of building. It consists, in fact, in all the part erected of brick, merely of an inlaying or veneering of enamelled bricks set flush with the plastering. Sculpture is confined to the parts composed of calcareous materials, forming the basements whose aspect is so striking and grand.[1] And when we examine the character of this sculpture, we cannot help perceiving how much the early Dorian monuments resemble it.[2] In the Assyrian architecture, therefore, conformably with the testimony of Herodotus, Xenophon, Quintus Curtius, and Diodorus Siculus, painting played the principal part in the system of ornamentation, since, independently of the overlaying of enamelled bricks, the plastering was coloured in various tones, among which blue, yellow, and red were conspicuous. We can imagine the effect produced by those large coloured vertical surfaces, relieved by the most brilliant enamels, the whole resting on a basement of finely hewn or richly sculptured stone. Masts, overlaid with gilt bronze and terminated with large round shields or with palms, likewise gilt, were fastened to the sides of these portals, as shown in Plate XXVII.[3]

The East is that part of the globe in which the habits of the people are least affected by change; accordingly the buildings erected in Persia during the fourteenth and fifteenth centuries of our era still preserve the same decorative features. Externally large and even vertical surfaces, some friezes of enamelled tiles or impressed stucco; flat roofing, from which rise cupolas; upper loggias, for fresh air and coolness; and basements relatively rich and wrought in hard materials.

[1] See the work of MM. Place and Thomas, *Ninive et l'Assyrie.*

[2] See the Selinuntian metopes in the Palermo Museum.

[3] In the Assyrian Museum at the Louvre, there are fragments of gilt bronze from these platings, besides representations of them on the numerous bas-reliefs in which buildings are portrayed.

Assuredly the Dorians did not copy these architectural features, which neither suited their habits nor the materials they had at disposal; but they coloured the surfaces of their buildings, and began by imitating the character of those sculptures which were already buried beneath ruins when Xenophon traversed Mesopotamia; at that time, however, Greek art had emancipated itself, and had ceased to draw its inspiration from any other source than its own genius.

It would be superfluous to give examples of the ornamentation of Doric buildings here, since it is so well known and has been so frequently reproduced and commented upon. Even in these Lectures the ornamentation of Greek architecture has been frequently discussed,—an ornamentation which is invariably sober in character, and which depends more on painting than sculpture. Roman ornamentation under the Empire is also familiarly known. Luxurious and too often commonplace, its chief merit consisted in the profusion of costly materials, and the accumulation of decorative appliances with more prodigality than taste. It must be acknowledged, however, that both in their exterior and interior decoration of buildings the artists (generally Greeks) exhibited skill in giving to the richness of the materials employed, and to the style of the sculpture, an air of dignity that should not be disregarded at a time like the present, when an attempt is made to produce analogous effects.

The chief defect in the architectural decoration of the Empire is the want of repose. I will explain my meaning: when, as in the architecture of the classic period in Greece, ornamentation occupies only well-defined positions; when the architectural members are so carefully considered, proportioned, and shaped that they themselves constitute the principal decoration; when, to put it more clearly, the structure of the architectural features constitutes the ornamentation; that structure necessitates parts presenting greater resistance, parts of greater strength, which limit the sculptured ornamentation to the less strong or less resisting parts. Thus, in the Doric temple, it is perfectly evident that the only parts fitted to receive carving or sculpture are the metopes, the friezes, and the tympanums of the gables. Everywhere else it is the actual members of the structure which assume a decorative shape, resulting from their faithfully expressing their function. But if we replace the Doric capital, which perfectly indicates its function of support, by the Corinthian capital—an architectural member which, to the eye, is wanting in expression as a support—which seems as if it must be crushed beneath the weight it is intended to carry, we are obliged to give a lighter appearance to the members supported; we must richly decorate the frieze, and even the architrave and the cornice. The result will be a want of congruity between this florid upper part and the smooth column shafts ; we must deeply flute the latter ; and the shafts themselves must rest on a base corresponding with the richness of the capital. But we cannot stop here ; the same process must be extended to every part of the building. When the artist decorates an architectural member, which in virtue of its function should preserve an appearance of special strength, he is soon led to make the ornamentation general ; particularly in the case of the smooth surfaces, whose function as supports is not very manifest. Hence the Greeks were slow to adopt the Corinthian capital, and at first used it only in buildings of very small size, such, *e.g.*, as the Choragic monument of Lysicrates. The Ionian capital, though richly ornamented, does not lose its expression as a support,—a remark applying especially to its earlier forms. Its wide volutes curve round beyond the diameter of the column shaft, which is carried up to the abacus ; they do not conceal the support, but only gracefully terminate it.

A Roman hall, without supposing variations in the structure, might be ornamented, externally and internally, in very different ways ; and in fact, given one of those edifices completely stripped of its decoration, ten architects might imagine ten several modes of ornamenting it. This would not be the case with a Greek building, since its ornamentation is determined by the structure itself. In this the variations would concern only details of minor importance, or the style of painting ; and even for these subordinate parts, there are laws deduced from the structure familiar even to architects of the most limited attainments.

Let us suppose the rotunda of the Pantheon at Rome entirely stripped of its interior orders, its marbles, and its band mouldings ; that no trace of this superadded ornamentation remains ; that even the knowledge of what it was has passed away, and that several architects are commissioned to re-decorate the bare interior. It is evident that each would produce a different design. Will it occur to any of them to shut off those great recesses with a screen of columns ? Shall there be two or three orders superposed in the height of the circular wall ? Or shall there be only one order, or none at all ? There is in fact nothing in the structure to indicate what that decoration should be, which, though only an overlaying, is nevertheless of extreme importance.

Every architect possesses illustrations of Roman edifices, —edifices built according to the veritable Roman, not the Greek method ; for the two must not be confounded. I will ask him, then, to suppress in imagination that which constitutes the ornamentation of these buildings, and consider only their struc-

E. Viollet-le-Duc, del.

Vᵈᵉ A. Morel & Cⁱᵉ, Éditeurs.

MAISON GRECQU

SYRIE CENTRALE

Imp. Lemercier & Cᵢᵉ, Paris.

ture ; and, forgetting, if possible, all knowledge of what the ornamentation was, to endeavour to re-decorate them in a rational manner. We may confidently predict that he will design something very unlike the existing ornamentation. I shall not, however, enlarge on this question, which has been already discussed in these Lectures. We may admire the architectural decoration of the Empire ; but it can only have originated in the desire to accumulate costly materials and make a display of luxury, however striking or grand the effect. Exception should certainly be made in favour of some buildings of a mixed character, such, *e.g.*, as the basilicas, in which the ornamentation was appropriate to the object, and was an integral part of the structure : but the Basilica is not a veritable Roman edifice ; it is a composite of Greek and Oriental origin.

In proportion as the Roman Empire tended to shift its centre towards the East, Greek genius regained the influence it had exerted on architectural art before the culmination of the imperial power. It also, we may observe, had conformed to the times,—to the needs of the social condition created by the Romans. It did not restrict itself to reproducing or reviving the forms in vogue when Pericles lived. It had perceived the advantages to be derived from the Roman system of construction, and after having long submitted to being merely the decorator of that structure, proceeded to improve it by bringing it into harmony with the mode of ornamentation. I grant that the decoration of the Pantheon of Agrippa is much superior in point of execution to that of the Church of St. Sophia at Constantinople ; but a brief examination will suffice to show that, between the ornamentation and the structure of the latter building, there is much closer connection than in the Pantheon : though in the Church of St. Sophia we find ornamentation that is superposed, it merely forms a kind of tapestry, and the orders serve a useful and even necessary purpose.

Before we begin to consider Byzantine ornamentation, it will be well to inquire how decorative art was conceived by the Greek populations of Syria not far distant from Constantinople. We will take one of the most simple examples of Syrian architecture,—in fact one of the most ordinary type, so as more clearly to manifest the essential character of that Greek genius which could so readily adapt itself to new conditions without departing from true principles. Every one has seen the Greek-Italian houses of Pompeii, or is at any rate acquainted with them through the medium of fairly exact representations ; there is no need therefore to direct special attention here to the practical side of these examples of domestic architecture, or to its grace and elegance, so perfectly in harmony with the requirements and habits of the people.   Ornate or simple, the houses of Pompeii have an equal value in point of art, and their ornamentation is the expression of those habits.   Those straggling towns on the shores of the Gulf of Naples, built in a charming environment, rich in materials and resources of every kind, offered to their inhabitants an easy and elegant existence which displays itself in their buildings.   Different in character were the small towns scattered about the neighbourhood of Antioch in the route followed by the caravans which maintained the commercial relations of Persia and the Arabian Gulf with Constantinople. Built in an arid region, whose climate is burning in summer and capricious in winter, the sole reason for their existence was the continual passing of the caravans.   In the country in question there are no rivers, scarcely even torrents ; no timber, but stone everywhere.   The ruins of many of those small cities still exist, and exhibit dwellings almost intact ; since, as a great portion of the district they occupied was completely devoid of timber, every part of the building was made of stone, even the doors themselves.   The floors consisted of large slabs laid across lintels or arches.   The terraced roofs were made in the same way.   It might be supposed that with appliances thus limited, these habitations must resemble mere burrows.   Not at all ; the Greek still knows how to introduce art into his primitive buildings, and how to make the ornamentation expressive of the requirements, and in perfect accord with the mode of structure.

Plate XXVII. represents the interior of one of those small dwellings in Central Syria.[1]   Could construction be more frankly expressed, or could ornamentation be more simple and truthful ? The principal apartments occupy a ground-floor and a first story, and open into the two low and comparatively deep porticos, so well adapted as a shelter from the sun's heat and the storms of winter, which are terrible in those regions.   The portico of the ground-floor, which is without any mouldings, and which was perhaps decorated with a few paintings, consists of single stones on end, supporting lintels which receive in a rebate the slabs that form the first-story floor.   All the ornamentation is reserved for this story ; it is the *loggia* of the dwelling,—the part in which the family associate.   The wide moulding that environs the portico and terminates in volutes, is surmounted by the projecting cornice formed by the ends of the slabs that cover in the building.   A gutter sunk in the cornice receives the water of the terrace, which is thrown off by gargoyles into the court.   Three columns, with capitals of various forms, give to this upper portico an aspect of graceful strength, which is increased by the

---

[1] This house, situated in the district of Refadi, bears the date August 13, 510 (see *la Syrie Centrale par M. le Comte Melchior de Vogüé, dessins de M. Duthoit*).

solid balustrade whose panel moulding deviates to enable the column bases to abut against a plane surface. Where a lintel is placed at right angles to another, the monolith is hewn with a projecting corbel to receive the bearing of that lintel. These are small matters I allow : but in architecture these small matters are very nearly everything ; and the satisfaction we experience in observing them is greater than the pleasure we feel in looking at a façade covered with ornamentation, whose use or meaning we do not comprehend. In this unpretentious dwelling, more-over, is not the sense of proportions profoundly manifest ? Are not these in just relation to the human size ? Does not the house distinctly indicate the habits of its occupants ?

In other parts of the same country, more favoured by climate, there was timber. And here we find another system of con-struction, and consequently another mode of ornamentation. Yet these tribes who built so differently were neighbours living only a few miles apart ; and they were building their villages at the same time. How was it then that they did not proceed as we are now doing ? we, who in our villages try to imitate the buildings of our towns, and who, so far from endeavouring to vary the mode of ornamentation, according to the nature of the materials, the climate, and the customs of our several localities, reproduce *ad nauseam*, from one end of an extensive country to the other, designs whose only justification is the unreasoning fashion of the day ? Why was it ? Because the tribes in question preserved the essence of Greek genius, which is based on common sense. And, incredible as it may appear, it is actually in the name of this genius of the Greeks that we have lost what constituted its essential quality. A few worthy persons once formed for themselves what they called a Greek style, a Greek taste, a Greek art, in accordance with their own special fancies and interests ; and the indifference of the public favouring them, they constituted themselves the sole interpreters of Greek art, and succeeded in persuading us that outside the pale of their own little church there is only con-fusion and barbarism ! It is quite certain, however, that if Greek genius could be impersonated and return among us, it would be not a little surprised at seeing the garb in which the pretended Classical school has wrapped it, and the senseless things done in its name.

At Byzantium the force of Roman traditions was too strong to allow Greek feeling to exert so radical an influence on art ; nevertheless that influence is largely manifest. The first thing that strikes us is that it establishes a decided correlation between the ornamentation and the structure ; in the Church of St. Sophia at Constantinople we should search in vain for an architectural member, even a decorative one, that does not serve a necessary purpose. It would not be possible to remove from this edifice whole orders—columns and entablatures,—as has been done in Rome, without causing the ruin of the building. In the Church of St. Sophia the columns and their capitals are not merely ornamental; they really support the structure. The latter even assume a novel form, appropriate to the purpose, which is to receive the springers of arches and vaulting. As to the interior plane surfaces, they are covered with slabs of marble on the vertical parts, and with mosaics in the vaulting.

We said that the Greeks of Classic times did not employ coloured marbles, but coloured the white marble or stone. They thus controlled the colour-harmony of the exterior, as well as of the interior of their edifices. And the first requisite for securing colour-harmony is to employ only the same substances, or substances that will readily blend. Applied colour has the advantage of presenting surfaces similar in appearance, if not in point of tint, at least in point of material, uniformity of grain, smoothness, apparent hardness, brilliancy, and so forth. But when we employ in a building materials such as coloured marble or jasper, or red or green porphyry, painting can never ally itself with these substances which are coloured by nature, and present reflective effects and remarkable intensity of tone.

No painted decoration will harmonise with these natural colourings. Coloured marble demands marble or coloured substances analogous to it in appearance, or metals such as gold or bronze. The Romans of the Empire did not hesitate to combine the two modes of colour-decoration, that resulting from naturally coloured materials, and that produced by painting. But we must not take the Romans for models of refined taste in art. When Roman architecture was introduced at Byzantium, among Greek communities, it was not long before the latter made their instinctive taste prevail. Ornamentation and structure were intimately united; and since the Empire required the employment of coloured marble, the whole system of colouring was made to consist of the use of marble or substances of similar appearance, such, *e.g.* as glass mosaics. The walls were therefore covered with large marble slabs of harmonious shades; the columns were made of marble intensely strong and warm in colour, porphyry and jasper; the capitals and bases were worked in white marble, and were covered with delicate carving, which did not destroy their expression as supports, and the vaults and curved surfaces, which it was not possible to line with marble slabs, were overlaid with mosaics made with small cubes of coloured glass, forming a translucent enamel on a gilt ground. Thus the general aspect of the decoration was that presented by brilliant, hard-looking substances having analogous colour effects; when painting was employed, it was only secondary, on detached parts of the building, and did not enter into the general effect. Moreover, there was no sculpture except delicate diaperings, or very slender tracery which could not affect the repose of the general lines. This is a principle of essential importance when we wish to give an aspect of grandeur to a building; hence the interior of the Church of St. Sophia appears still more vast than it really is, while the interior of St. Peter's at Rome appears comparatively small on account of the colossal sculptures and mouldings which constitute its decorations.

Though the style of the architecture of St. Sophia is open to much criticism, though the construction of that edifice, despite the grandeur of the conception, is not perfect, and even shows in many parts carelessness and a decline in art, when compared with that of the buildings of the best period of the Empire; nevertheless, as regards the right conception of interior ornamentation, this vast church would seem to have resolved the problem. The theme is so perfectly rendered that nothing could be added, nothing could be taken away; and this because the plan adopted is so frank and clear, and is so rigorously pursued from the basement to the vaulting; because the manner in which the exterior light is distributed adds still more to the effect by completing it,—by throwing over the whole of these surfaces analogous in material, and having similar colouring qualities, a shimmering light, whose intensity is equal through the very similarity of material on which the light strikes. Both the great central dome and the apsidal vaults of St. Sophia's are, as is well known, perforated at their base by a series of windows pretty close together, thus making these vaults appear like sails fastened at certain points and bellied out by the wind. Independently of the effect produced by this mode of structure, these openings at the base of the vaulting have the further advantage of illuminating a stratum of air beneath the intrados of the cupolas. This sheet of atmosphere, thus lighted, interposes a luminous haze between the eye of the spectator and the upper mosaics, which, without this interposing medium, would appear hard and too bright; whereas they thus assume a transparent tone which raises and softens them. Here again is manifested the genius of the Greek, who, in architectural decoration, never fails to take advantage of light in producing the effects.

In the present day these subtleties would probably be considered fanciful; and if an architect were now to speak of the disposition of the lights as capable of producing an effect of grandeur, repose, or cheerfulness in the interior of a building, he would most likely be deemed insane. He would scarcely be thought better of were he to present designs in which he had considered the effects which perspective would produce in execution. This would be to apply reason to decorative design; and in the opinion of a certain school such an application of reason is " unsound."

Nevertheless, when the outer and inner ornamentation of buildings is in question, it would seem—and very many architects of former times have been of this opinion—that light, perspective, and therefore orientation, and the greater or less distance of the spectator, should be taken into account by the architect. By an intelligent consideration of those two conditions—whose effects we cannot ignore,—light and perspective,—and with a little common sense, we may obviate vast expense and produce desired effects with certainty. Generally, however, the architect is content to produce satisfactory effects on paper; and then discovers, to his great surprise, that when carried out his attractive designs produce but a poor result. Much expense might, I maintain, be avoided, by taking the trouble to realise beforehand the exact effect of perspective and light on buildings; and I say further that the more we are able to avoid such useless expenditure, the more we add to the value of a work of art. The main consideration is to put things in their proper place: ornamentation lavished in a façade till it becomes wearisome to the spectator would be pleasing were it confined to a few points in which it would find its appropriate position. In this respect the Orientals excelled us. In their buildings, however ornate the decoration, it never injures the effect of the masses; it invariably leaves points of repose,—points moreover that are dictated by the structure; so far from wearying the eye, this decoration engages it, because it is put where it tells to advantage. We have departed so widely from the decorative methods of the East, that it is necessary to point out wherein these methods differ from those which prevail among ourselves.[1]

Ever since the seventeenth century, both in Italy and France, elements for decorative features have been sought in classical architecture of a kind the least appropriate to the exigencies of modern architecture. Thus, *e.g.* the *Orders* adopted during the empire of the Cæsars, and which, with certain exceptions, constitute the edifice, we, in most cases, only employ as a superposition, whose least defect is that it divides the front or surface by vertical and horizontal lines which are offensively monotonous. The otherwise inappropriate use of these orders

[1] In speaking of Eastern buildings we refer here only to those of the schools of Persia, Asia Minor, and Egypt, excluding Hindoo architecture, whose æsthetical character requires a special consideration that would take us beyond our limits.

has a perhaps still more serious disadvantage in front of ornamentation.   The architectural orders have a scale, a modulus,
of their own, which the architect cannot disregard, so that when,
for instance, he adopts superposed orders for a large edifice, he is
obliged to subordinate the ornamentation of the whole, which is
on a great scale, to orders which are comparatively small.   This
ornamentation therefore appears mean and diminutive in proportion to the edifice.   When, on the other hand, the architect
adopts on a façade a colossal order, through whose divisions he
will be obliged to cut openings, to make windows in the several
stories, and to carry string-courses, the scale of the ornamentation
of that order will not accord with the scale of ornamentation in
the intercalated features, and there will be a want of harmony.
We have recently seen an instance of the disadvantages resulting
from this system in the *Pavillon de Flore* forming the corner of
the Palace of the Tuileries on the quay.   Despite the unques-
tionable ability displayed by the architect in this large building,
he has not succeeded, and no one could have succeeded, in
making the ornamentation imposed by the small orders, correspond with the general scale.   And the architect himself was so
well aware of the insurmountable character of the difficulty,
that he endeavoured to correct this want of accord between the
scale of the small orders and the size of the edifice by crowning
the angles and the middle of the fronts of the pavilion with
colossal sculptures, which are themselves in scale with the entire
building, but not with the stories of the building.   The following
circumstance will show exactly where the difficulty lay.   On the
side of the quay the able architect had introduced niches between the central piers,—niches in which statues were placed.
These niches, with their statues, were perfectly in scale with the
ordonnance of the stories ; but when the upper tympanum and
angle-crownings which are in scale with the building as a whole
were uncovered, the statues and their niches appeared so mean
and out of scale with the mass that they had to be removed ; the
effect was intolerable.   We have cited this example, not for the
sake of criticising an otherwise creditable work, but to exhibit
the vice inherent in the system adopted in architectural ornamentation since the seventeenth century,—a vice whose evil
results no ability can obviate.   And when the architect is less
gifted or less scrupulous, less inclined to correct his work, then
the case is much worse ! Starting with false conceptions, there
is no extravagance or caprice of which he is not guilty.   He
covers the fronts with carvings, some flat and quiet like
arabesques, others prominent and striking in effect.   The more
he puts, the more he needs to put, and every bare place seems
to trouble his spirit.   Having exhausted the means which stone

affords him, and having adopted every scale at the same time, or rather having disregarded every scale both in relation to the whole and the parts,—having failed to produce a satisfactory result, and feeling instinctively that all his striving and all his accumulation of detail only presents a disconnected whole,— he has recourse to decorative appliances of another order, to marbles, or metallic lustre, with no other ultimate result but that of manifesting the utter absence of idea. According to the truthful Greek saying, Unable to render his work beautiful, he has made it rich. This feebleness on the part of the artist, when he ceases to be guided by right ideas in architectural ornamentation, is not of modern date. The Romans of the Empire fell into similar aberrations, and into such all do and will fall who regard architectural ornamentation merely as a question of caprice,—a pure work of imagination independent of the limits traced by sound judgment or common sense, and a delicate observation of scale and perspective effects.

But it would be undesirable to select examples for criticism solely among those works which in the general opinion are justly considered the feeblest. In every system of architecture it is the *chefs-d'œuvre* which should be compared ; not an excellent building on the one hand, and on the other one of mediocre stamp : for even granting the inferiority of one system relatively to the other, ability may be shown in the manner of applying principles vicious in themselves, or rather in treatment, while the laws prescribed by reason are neglected, and the dictates of fancy alone are followed. It would be unjust not to acknow- ledge, for instance, that there is much excellent work in point of ornamentation in the edifices erected since the seventeenth century, under the influence of a false application of Classic art. Thus the fronts of the buildings of the Garde Meuble on the Place de la Concorde in Paris exhibit a successful application of the orders in a building of our own age. Besides the fact that the junction of these fronts with the sides is cleverly managed, and that they do not present that mere super- position of features which is so common in the present day, the large-columned portico, resting on a ground story whose rela- tive proportions are excellent, expresses its purpose as forming immense loggias sheltering two stories. We have here an idea that is truly architectural, and which lends itself to ornamental effect by giving an opportunity for the most pleasing contrasts of light and shade, and by affording a magnificent covered terrace for the apartments situated on the level of the portico, and an isolation of these from the public road that is per- fectly justifiable and dignified. This style of decoration has no need of marbles or gilding to produce its full effect ; and despite its sumptuous character it has an air of repose and dignity befitting the place it occupies. The great loggia opens, as reason would dictate, in the middle of the building, and terminates at either extremity by the two pavilions which, forming square returns, connect the principal front with the two lateral fronts in a natural and harmonious way. The scale of the colonnade is large enough to admit of its details being proportioned to the general scale of the palace, and in conformity with the method of the architects of the best periods, and with the best examples, the architect was wisely sparing of sculpture on this front. He reserved the delicacies of enrichment for the central loggia, carefully avoiding the least approach to sculpture on the open-arched basement. This work therefore is—in our opinion at least—really beautiful and excellent, because it bears the impress of sound reasoning, of thorough consideration, and of that sobriety from which the architect should never depart, even in the most sumptuous buildings. Had he expended thousands more in covering the lateral pavilions and the under portico with decorative sculpture or statuary in groups or single figures, he would have lessened the general effect of grandeur which is now so powerfully expressed.

One of the conditions of beauty in an architectural work is that it should impress all who see it as having been produced naturally without effort,—without occasioning trouble or anxious consideration to its designer, that in fact it could not have been otherwise. In particular, it should be free from those expedients that betray paucity of ideas,—those *bits* which bear the mark of studied effort, and the aim on the part of the designer to astound and engage the attention of the passers-by without being able to satisfy his mind. To be clear, to be comprehensible without requiring an effort : this is, and always will be, the aim which the architect should have in view. The highest praise to which the public speaker can aspire is the remark on the part of the hearers: "That is just what I thought; he exactly expressed my feeling." Similarly, in viewing the work of the architect, every one should experience the impression that the materials in combination do but reflect the anticipation of the beholder,—that the conception as realised is the only one that was appropriate to the circumstances of the case.

However richly ornate a building may be, the ornamentation must be subordinated to the conception, in order not to weaken, disturb, or obscure its expression. I grant that in such a case the more lavish the ornamentation the more vigorously should the idea be expressed, and that it can be more easily manifested in a building which is simple than in one that is loaded with ornament. But it is plain that where an idea is wanting the temptation is strong to conceal feebleness of conception beneath a parasitical embellishment.

I remarked that the Orientals are our superiors in architectural ornamentation, because among them that ornamentation never obscures the dominant conception ; on the contrary, it always powerfully aids its expression, and is its natural manifestation. It must indeed be observed at the outset that among them such dominant conception is never wanting. Talking without having anything to say is one of the innovations for which the Academies are responsible, and whose injurious results

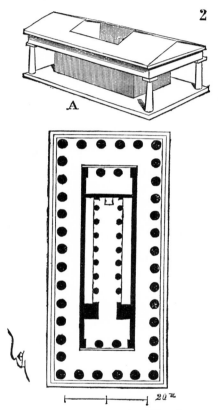

FIG. 2.—Idea of the Greek Temple.

are too often conspicuous in the architecture of these latter days. I am aware that by a certain school idea in art is regarded as of secondary importance; but the fact is that idea in art has an imperious aspect, or at any rate a far from subordinate one ; its manifestations not unfrequently savour of freedom and an unwillingness to make concessions ;—characteristics that are displeasing to those corporate bodies in whose esteem self-obliteration is the highest excellence.

Architectural ornamentation is, however, attractive only as far as it expresses an idea with great clearness. We have seen how, in certain classical buildings, the idea is indicated by the work ; let us pursue this investigation. We will take a Greek temple of early age : the great temple of Pæstum, for instance, fig. 2. What is the thought or idea of the architect ? It is clearly indicated by the plan. Here the temple is a chest, a *capsa* containing the image of the special or local divinity, and the offerings by which that image is surrounded. Around this chest or enclosure, if we like to call it so, is a portico,—an ambulacrum, a kind of screen covered, but open, in order that the cella, or enclosed part, may be visible. In what then consists the ornamental part of the edifice ? It is the open screen itself alone that constitutes it. The Greek architect made this outer screen the groundwork of his architectural design, and in working out that design he sought for the most harmonious system of proportions and forms he could possibly find. Figure A, in which for greater clearness we have shown only the corner columns, explains this so simple conception—that of a *box* surrounded by a covered screen. Whether the tympanums are embellished with sculpture, whether the angles of the pediments are crowned by statues or *acroteria*, or the metopes decorated with bas-reliefs,— such embellishment in nowise affects the idea nor the accordance of the ornamentation with the idea. And when once the architect has succeeded so admirably in establishing this harmony at the very outset, he has full liberty to perfect the details of his original conception, and in such a way that while perfecting them, he is only expressing that first idea in a better and more attractive manner. But it is not often that the opportunity is given of expressing an idea so simple ; or rather most of our modern buildings necessitate a combination of various ideas.

It is none the less evident that, however complicated the programme may be, there is a dominant idea. Is it a Palace that has to be built ? There will be the principal hall,—the centre of gathering. Is it a Church ? There will be the chancel. Is it a public library ? From the central reading-room there should be every facility for ready reference. Is it a market ? There can never be too many openings for passing in and out. These chief requirements necessitate architectural features in accordance with them, and consequently an ornamentation aiding the expression of these features.

Let us now take a building of quite another kind. In the Greek temple, a divinity—or a jealously exclusive feature of a divinity, according to the Pantheistic idea—is in question : some fraction or attribute to which a special worship is rendered ; the cella is closed ; no one enters it but the priest, the initiated —the intermediary between the God and the people. Widely different is the mosque. Here it is not an attribute of the

supreme deity that is worshipped, a jealous God, who only communicates with man in the closed sanctuary which he prefers:
the God of the Mahometan is everywhere; he could not be
represented by an image: he may be adored on the desert or
on the ocean as well as within a sacred enclosure. But before
approaching him the supplant must purify himself, collect his
thoughts, meditate and render himself worthy to commune with
him. His God prescribes charity and serenity of soul. . . .
What then is a mosque? There are no images, there is no
ritual, no outward pomp. A mosque is nothing more than an

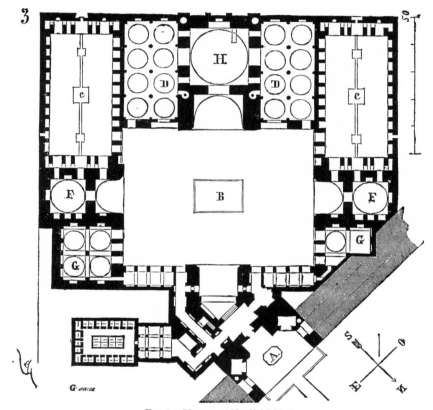

FIG. 3.—Mosque of Mesdjid-i-Shah.

enclosed space, with recesses, enabling each to collect his thoughts
in silent meditation; and in this enclosure is one particular spot
which indicates, not the presence of God, but the single thought
in view of which every Mahometan should direct his prayer.
Let us then examine one of these buildings. Here, fig. 3, is the
plan of the mosque of Mesdjid-i-Shah at Ispahan. Its principal
entrance opens on one of the galleries of an immense bazaar
whose orientation is north and south; but, as the mosque itself
must be placed in such a way that every true believer may direct
his prayer towards Mecca—"Turn thy face towards the temple

Haram; wherever thou art, direct thy gaze to that august sanctuary "[1]—the axis of the mosque alters its direction, so as to present its sacred front to that point of the horizon. At A is the first basin; at B the second basin for the ablutions, in the midst of a vast court; at C other basins in two lateral courts surrounded by recesses serving for shelter. Though every believer without distinction of rank may meditate or pray wherever he pleases, in the lateral courts, or in the halls D, F, and G, there is nevertheless at H a central dominant spot which calls attention to the unity of the Deity. By its configuration alone, the plan indicates the decorative system that plainly expresses the ruling idea. Easy access on every side, retired places for those who wish to pray and meditate in solitude; but the unity of the Deity is denoted by the great building that occupies the middle of the sacred part. And in fact, the elevation of this front has all the frankness of the plan. A lofty porch, a high and wide archway giving entrance to the hall H, covered by a pointed dome, all the other parts of the building, are subordinate in height to this principal structure. Fig. 4 presents a view of the middle part. The building constitutes in itself a magnificent groundwork of ornamentation,[2] because it exactly fulfils the requirements of the case, and clearly explains the ruling idea. Nevertheless these surfaces must be embellished. Shall it be by columns and entablatures so admirably appropriate to the requirements of the Greek temple, but which would serve no purpose here? Shall it be with projecting sculpture, large in scale, tending to distract the minds of the faithful? Or lastly, shall it be with a pile of small features accumulated without meaning, overloaded with mouldings, useless members, niches and pediments? No. A facing of glazed faïence will overspread, as with tapestry, all the plane surfaces of the building, both within and without. Harmonious tones of colour, and admirably distributed designs relatively small, will alone compose the decoration of this edifice,—a decoration splendid in effect, but with perfect unity of aspect, leaving the chief lines their full importance, and the building generally all its simple grandeur and repose. The porch, or rather the enormous opening which admits light and air into the central part of the mosque, symbolises to the Mussulman his idea of the One Divinity whose sanctuary is the universe, whose dwelling-place is everywhere, yet nowhere, and to whom each believer may pray without an intermediary: " What is better pleasing to the Lord than to lift up our faces to Him, to do right, to follow

---

[1] Coran, chap. ii.
[2] For the details of the mosque see the work of M. Coste: *Monuments modernes de la Perse.* The Mosque of Mesdjid-i-Shah was built about the year 1580 of our era.

4

FIG. 4.—Mosque of Mesdjid-i-Shah.

COURS D'ARCHITECTURE

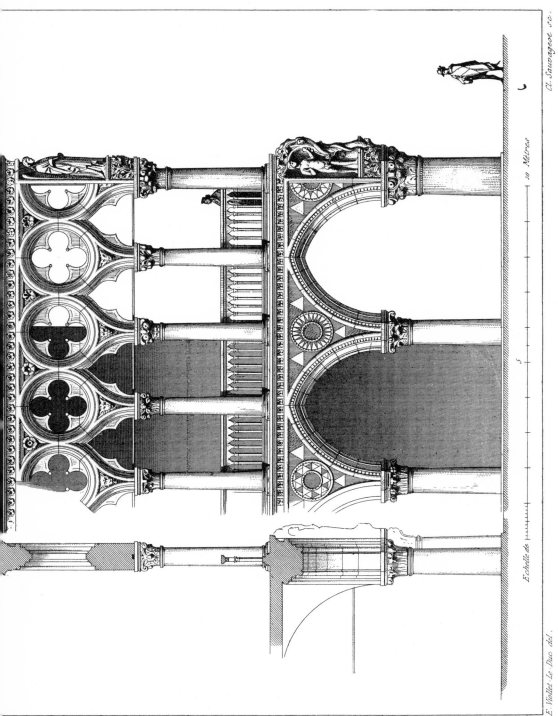

E. Viollet-le-Duc del.

Cl. Sauvageot sc.

A. MOREL — Editeur

Imp. Lemercier et Cⁱᵉ Paris

Echelle de |⊢⊢⊢⊢⊢⊢⊢| 5   10 Mètres

DU PALAIS DES DOGES (VENISE)

the faith of Abraham who worshipped only one God, and was
worthy to be called his friend! God is king of the heavens and
of the earth. He embraces the universe in His immensity."[1]
Two towers—two minarets, flank the great opening. From their
summits the hour of prayer is announced. The dome that covers
the central hall, at whose furthest side is a recess indicating the
direction of Mecca, is itself covered with glazed bricks of light
tones blending with the brilliance of the sky.

Here then we have two kinds of edifices greatly differing in
purpose and requirements, but in whose execution the idea that
produced them is clearly expressed. Whether we prefer Greek
architecture to Persian, or Greek pantheism to Mahometan
monotheism, is little to our purpose; but it cannot be denied
that these distinctly various decorative forms are each perfectly
appropriate to their object, that in both cases the form expresses
the idea, and that we cannot take any form that comes to hand
from the architectural repertory to express a special idea. Moreover we cannot fail to perceive that the ornamentation is not a
commonplace enrichment suitable for the embellishment of any
building whatsoever; that the ornamentation is contemplated
in the very plan, takes shape in the first conception of the
programme; that it is already indicated in the structure, if that
structure is a sensible one; that it fits the edifice, not as the
dress, but as the muscles and skin fit the man; that the method
which consists in ornamenting a building as we ornament the
walls of a room or hall with medallions, arms, or pictures, is a
method of somewhat recent date, since it was never employed,
either by the ancients during their best periods of art, or during
the Middle Ages; so that in fact those who employ this method
must either condemn the best works of the ancients, or condemn
themselves if they appreciate the excellence of those works. The
kind of ornamentation employed in the mosque of Mesdjid-i-
Shah, a facing of enamel that clothes the walls as with a
tapestry, is all the more appropriate there because the edifice is
built of baked brick, and the decoration is laid on the same
material as that employed in the building, and because with
brick it is not possible to obtain greatly projecting members.
The basements only are faced with a reddish marble.

Let us now consider an edifice of a totally different order.
Let us go to Venice and examine the old palace built of stone.
We need not concern ourselves with the decorative detail, which
is not irreproachable in point of taste; but let us look at the
general features. The old ducal palace of the Piazzetta of St.
Mark consists externally of two porticos, one over the other,
supporting the actual mansion, which is composed of lofty and

[1] Coran, chap. iv.

spacious rooms. Here again the requirements of the case are as frankly met as in the Greek temple and the mosque of Ispahan. The box, the enclosed part, is supported on the uprights of the porticos, at the back of which are the secondary offices. The rigorous interpretation of the programme, supposing the edifice erected of wood—that is, by the readiest and most economical means—would give figure 5. But the intention is to build a durable edifice, to employ solid materials, and to produce, without contravening their properties, the appearance of an enclosed habitation, containing vast apartments, and placed upon a covered ambulacrum of two stories.

The Venetian architect has scrupulously fulfilled the conditions of this programme, and his work owes all its decorative effect to the genuine and forcible expression of the structure. There are few to whom this edifice is not familiar, either from engravings or photographs, or actual inspection. Now, whether

5

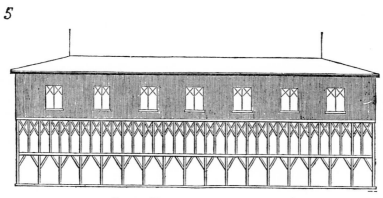

Fig. 5.—Idea of the Venetian Palace.

we admire the style of the architecture or are indifferent to it, the general design of the building never fails to produce a very strong and lasting impression,—the sure mark of special excellence and a truthful expression. The details of the ornamentation, whatever be their merits or demerits, have nothing to do with the impression produced, and any architect might, while modifying the style in accordance with the prevailing taste, produce as marked an effect, provided he as scrupulously rendered the general idea. In point of decorative detail also, this edifice, such as it is, presents some remarkable characteristics. By his skilful treatment of the angles—a delicate point—the architect has succeeded in giving an aspect of sturdy strength to the system of props that support a box of massive appearance. Plate XXIX., representing the angle, shows the excellence of the design. In order to lighten the heavy appearance of the unrelieved wall over the galleries, the architect built it of materials in two colours—red and white—forming a regular pattern like a kind of broad mosaic. Here again the Venetian architect found his precedent in the methods of the Orientals, those great masters in decorative art. Leaving wide plane surfaces in contrast with deeply-recessed parts full of dark shades and bright points, and covering these even surfaces with a colouring that engages the eye without destroying their unity, is one of the means of ornamentation most frequently and felicitously employed by Oriental artists. Small but apparent imbrications of the simplest character, bricks mingled with white materials, suffice to produce the always pleasing effect of plane surfaces affording a colour value contrasted with features covered with detail, and presenting projections and recesses. Opposite this palace there stands another building of nearly similar destination (the Procurazzi), where Renaissance taste displays itself in all its splendour, and the ornamental details are charming. But the stamp of frankness and dignity is wanting, and our gaze always reverts to the old ducal palace, whose exterior indicates so well the destination of its interior, and whose decorative system is so perfectly in harmony with the structure. On looking at the façade do we not see that the lower portico is vaulted, and that the upper one supports a timber floor—the floor of the apartments above—and that the ceilings of these apartments are of wood ? No projecting buttresses or pilasters for the upper story, which is nothing other than a box perforated with great windows.

Perhaps, however, our Western architecture of the North before the period of the Renaissance, is still more frank in its decorative features. The relations of the ornamentation to the structure are more harmonious, and the ornamentation itself is more artistic : it is true that in these buildings are not to be found those parasitical decorations which abound in our modern architecture ; and this must be regarded as a deficiency if we are to accept the judgment of the intolerant school now dominant. Not that this school takes the trouble to pronounce such an opinion candidly ; that is not its mode of procedure ; it does not discuss principles ; it is content to hinder their formation by every means in its power, for principles are troublesome—they entail obligations.

In our opinion the best architecture is that whose ornamentation cannot be divorced from the structure. Whatever be the merit of a piece of carving—or of a decorative composition—if such piece of carving, or even such composition, can be removed without making it apparent that the edifice lacks something essential, that accessory is of small value, and perhaps even prejudicial. It needs no great practical knowledge to recognise the decorative features which an architect has added to a building, and which are not necessitated by the structure. For instance, ornamented panels are perfectly justifiable in wood-work, but they are utterly out of place in a stone pier. Medallions stuck against a plane wall, like pictures in a room, are evidently not an ornamentation suggested by a requirement of construction. Surmounting a door or a window with symbols more or less ingeniously designed, making the cornice of the opening remind us of a collector's chimney-piece covered with curiosities, cannot be considered veritable architectural ornamentation. Groups of figures placed *on* a pediment, and which appear to have escaped from it in order to be more at ease on the roof, make sensible persons long to push these escaping figures back into their frame. Little circular openings, filled with busts on their stands, may perhaps suit a gallery of portraits, but have a most unmeaning appearance on an external façade. Curved or triangular pediments surmounting window jambs, keystones of arches whose exaggerated projection supports nothing, may be called, without too much severity, decorative make-weights. Apart from the expense they occasion, without any advantage to art, these commonplaces so greatly in vogue have a still graver fault—they weary and nauseate the spectator, and gradually lead to a distaste for all architectural forms ; in fact, to such a degree is this the case that he comes to abominate these unmeaning ornaments, and even ceases to find any pleasure in those with which veritable masters of design in past or present times have embellished their works. Bad classical tragedies have hindered many from going to representations of the masterpieces of Corneille and Racine. And yet, as my friend Sandeau used to say : " It is so easy not-to-write a tragedy in five acts and in verse !" It would be so easy to spare us these repetitions *ad nauseam* of architectural ornaments, dictated neither by structural form nor respected tradition. What meaning have those classic symbols, those worn-out insignia on a building ? What meaning have Greek masks and lyres on the walls of a theatre where neither lyres nor masks are used ? What meaning have Roman trophies with Lebrun's improvements on palaces whose doorways are guarded by soldiers armed with Chassepot rifles ? But it is needless to enlarge : these worn-out commonplaces have scarcely any interest except for carvers, and impart no real value to an architectural work; and yet how few architects there are who have the courage to abstain from these vulgar superpositions, which, apart from their senseless character, are no credit to the imaginative powers of the designer, and have no attraction for the public. Accordingly when an architect manifests sufficient ability and good sense to emancipate himself from this thraldom, we cannot too heartily congratulate and praise him, or too strongly commend him to the waning attention of a not unnaturally sceptical public.[1] However noble the materials employed, the decorative method now in vogue always reminds one of the moulded plaster or composition ornaments lavished on cheap showy buildings. What advantage is there in cutting an ornament in solid stone if it looks exactly like one that is moulded and stuck on? And what merit is there in employing costly materials for an ornamentation that may next day be reproduced in plaster on the front of a neighbouring gin-shop? True richness is that which beneath an appearance of simplicity exhibits elegancies that are not to be imitated by cheap means. It corresponds to that which in society the French call *distinction*—a manner marked by good sense, discretion, and unaffected simplicity, and which is natural to some, independently of wealth or rank.

One of the charms of good architecture consists in a close relationship between the external and internal ornamentation. The external ornamentation should prepare the spectator for and prefigure to him that which he will find within. It is not the part of architecture to surprise. Besides, the architect should not give promise on the outside of more than he can perform. When he has lavished every species of ornamentation in the front, what will he have remaining to show inside? In this respect again we may learn something from the nations of the East. Exteriorly their buildings affect great relative simplicity, and the architecture becomes richer and more elegant the farther we penetrate into the interior—a kind of legitimate coquetry, as we might term it, and one that never fails to be seductive. They are skilful in making transitions,—in gradually leading the spectator's gaze to the culminating splendour, so that one never feels a desire to go back. In ornamentation, nothing is more fatal to effect than a too pompous prelude—an over-presumptuous promise. It is of the same order, and leads to a similar unfortunate result, as the bombastic prologue of the poet. To give more than one seemed to promise is the true way to engage and retain the attention of the listener and the gazer. At the same time the prelude should be in direct accordance with the body of the discourse,—it should prepare for and lead up to the chief point of interest. The best means for attaining this end is

[1] Some few of our Paris buildings are indeed free from this vulgarity. Among others may be cited one of the most remarkable : the new part of the Palais de Justice, whose ornamentation is integral with the structure, accentuates it even, and hence is not wanting in dignity or originality. The Salle des Pas Perdus, both within and without, is one of the buildings that will do honour to our age. Here everything is in keeping ; one clear idea runs through and connects the whole. As always happens in such cases, the execution is worthy of the design ; it is good and careful. Everything testifies to an artist who respects his art and the public, and such are not commonly met with in our day.

to be truthful,—to adapt the ornamentation to the requirements of the case. As before observed, there is in every edifice one part of special interest; and this would not be on the outside, for I cannot suppose that buildings are erected only to be seen from the street. We shall therefore so dispose our means as to concentrate the interest—the decorative effect—on that special part. In a palace it would be the audience chambers; in a theatre, the hall and the boxes; in a church, the chancel; in a town-hall, the assembly-room; in a court of justice, the law courts; in a mansion, the reception-room. From the outside to the interior, therefore, the introduction should be gradual, and there should be nothing to make people inclined to stay in a lobby or on a flight of stairs. It is not much to the architectural credit of a building that the reception-rooms should be accounted dull or bare-looking, but the staircases magnificent; probably those interior rooms appear uninteresting in great measure because those staircases promised too much.

It must be acknowledged that in most of our modern buildings the ornamentation is redundant when it should be scanty, and scanty when it should abound. The fronts are overlaid with decorations; surprising ornamental effects are sought for in the designs for the lobbies and staircases; and all this display by way of introduction to rooms that are comparatively mean of aspect. The visitor sees fronts embellished by lofty columns, passes beneath stately peristyles, ascends flights of stairs of magical effect covered by domes enriched with carvings; and after this imposing introduction, which gives promise of halls rivalling those of the hôtels Lambert, de Maine, or Mazarin, or of the Farnese palace, what do you in reality find? Rooms that are very commonplace in the general design, but overloaded with gilded stucco-work, sham wood-carving, mean paper-hangings and vulgar upholstery. Less pompous display on the outside, and more dignity and real richness within would appear more rational,—more in conformity with the principles of true ornamentation.

But what shall we say of those pretentious classic orders, overspreading the upper stories of our city houses,—pilasters, which rest on wooden shop-fronts? How ridiculous this inappropriate decoration will appear, when, sooner or later, the public taste shall revert to simpler and more sensible forms, after so much profuse extravagance; when the time shall arrive for restoring harmony between the character of our architecture and the manners of the times. What sense is there in ornamenting the exteriors of mere lodging-houses more richly than the mansions of the great nobles in the seventeenth century? Is it not the most egregious vanity—covering walls and window-frames with ornament while the closely-packed families within are suffering every kind of discomfort in rooms whose scanty dimensions scarcely afford room for a crib and a chair?

In the style of architecture adopted in the public edifices and mansions of the seventeenth and eighteenth centuries, there was a certain harmony with the manners of the times. At that time, all—the great in particular—sacrificed the comforts of life to outward grandeur. Without were spacious courts and grandly ornamented façades; within, magnificent vestibules, noble staircases, and vast saloons; but this imposing display was obtained at the expense of comfort. The bedrooms were generally small and close, constructed in entresols; and the passages and back staircases narrow and steep. The servants were huddled together in wretched garrets beneath the roofs. Except in the state-rooms there was nothing like convenience or comfort. This was in conformity with the habits of the times, and no one complained. But in a *democratised* age imitations of a departed and little regretted aristocratic state and splendour are so much the more ridiculous as being merely superficial and confined to external appearances. The manners·of the times run counter to this superannuated art, and in adapting our habits of comfort to this external grandeur, truth has to be contravened in the strangest ways. In private dwellings we may still to a certain extent reconcile the arrangements dictated by necessity with the decorative display of the street front. Their stories are divided, and their windows disposed in accordance with the dictates of commercial speculation, in despite of classic orders and symmetrical grandeur; but in the case of public edifices it is otherwise. Here commercial speculation does not intervene; there is no question of a profitable return, and consequently we have imposing fronts concealing interior arrangements utterly at variance with those they appear to enclose. We have one design for the passer-by, another for the occupant; and if an architect should ever have occasion to draw the plans and elevations of one of these princely dwellings, he will have a difficult task to make them agree. This window which he has sketched in the elevation will have nothing in the interior to correspond with it; what to the passer-by appears a square window will be an arched one to the occupant; in fact, he will find a double case in the building,—one for outward show, the other to suit the interior arrangements. What becomes of architectural ornamentation in this costly farrago? Like the structure, it is double, that of the exterior having no kind of relation to that of the interior. To these observations, the justice of which all may perceive, many reply: "What does that matter to us? provided the building is beautiful outside and beautiful inside, it does not seem necessary that the two beauties should accord. What we want is an edifice which shall appear splendid, imposing, symmetrical and perfect to passers-by, while at the same time we are comfortably housed, and find within a profusion of luxurious adornment. We ourselves are not occupied with looking at the façades that are erected to attract the gaze of the vulgar ; we live behind these façades and have our taste and luxury apart." That people who have no concern with art should speak thus is not surprising, but that architects should lend themselves to such singular conditions, and, while doing so, still consider themselves architects, is more difficult to conceive ; for if there is one thing worthy of the architect's best considerations, it is the perfect agreement between all the parts of his building, that correspondence between the case and what it contains,—the frank expression outside of the arrangements within, not only in point of structure, but of ornamentation, which ought to be in close alliance with it. We observe a doctor of medicine setting himself up for an architect in Louis XIV.'s time, and erecting the colonnade of the Louvre as a mere ornament, without thinking what he was going to put behind that imposing screen. In fact he put nothing, and his successors were sadly embarrassed to know what to put that would be of any use. We are not to suppose that the most enthusiastic lovers of the architecture of the *grand siècle* have felt more than a Platonic admiration for this front, or have attempted to explain the meaning of this plaything in stone. But are caprices of the kind congenial to our times ? Are they acceptable to a public which sooner or later asks the purpose for which this or that building was erected ? That buildings should be splendid is all very well ; but at least let them be sensible and not designed chiefly for mere external show ; for that public which is good-natured sometimes, and which for a long time has accepted—I recall the term—*tolerated* a certain style of architecture which is loftily proclaimed the glory of French art, one day may assert that it is not rich enough to pay for this glory. Our young architects will do well to anticipate this change of feeling, and may rely upon it that it is not taste based on reason that provokes reaction, but ostentatious luxury, obtrusive wealth, that makes a useless parade of itself. The architecture suited to our times is not an art that is a mere luxury, for the delectation of a few amateurs—a select portion of society ; it must be an art which belongs to all, since in the case of public buildings it is paid for by all. It should therefore conform to the manners and habits not of a coterie,—not of *a* public, but of *the* public. Let us then, while duly admiring—as we may do—the ostentatious splendours of Roman architecture or of that of the time of Louis XIV., cease to reproduce them ; and endeavour, not to impoverish, despoil, and humiliate ourselves, —which is unbecoming a great country,—but to gain respect by a display of taste, thought and good sense, rather than by an unjustifiable abuse of wealth. To bring the ornamentation of our buildings into accord with the sterling qualities of our national character, which is opposed to exaggeration and want of proportion, is a noble problem, to the working out of which the rising generation of architects should devote their best powers. It is the careful thinking-out of the problem which can alone give birth to the architecture of the future ; not the servile imitation and undigested mingling of features borrowed from previous times and previous styles of architecture.

There is an influence altogether modern which must necessarily be taken into account : it is criticism, not the criticism of the partisan, envious and destructive—of this we should take no heed—but the criticism which appertains to the spirit of the age, favouring careful investigation and based on reason. This spirit of investigation which in science discards hypotheses and systems founded on *a priori* reasoning, and requires proofs based on experience and observation, is tending to penetrate into the domain of art, especially when art is connected with science. Our days, and ours alone, have witnessed the application of the novel critical method to the study of the past in the material, as well as in the immaterial sphere. This method is not satisfied with conjectures, however ingenious, or opinions based on an impression or a sentiment ; it requires proofs logically deduced. To ignore this tendency of the age is not to argue against the method ; it is simply to give proof of ignorance. But though in former ages it may have been permitted to consider the architectural remains of extinct civilisations, merely in reference to the forms and appearance, without regarding the causes that had produced those forms, this is not admissible in the present day. It is the same with History : a writer who should attempt to review the various forms of government, adopted by past civilisations without investigating the causes which among some produced theocracies or monarchies, among others oligarchic or democratic republics, would be considered at best a mere chronicler not a historian. From the tendency of the spirit of the age, it results that in practical modern politics the analytical knowledge of the past, the philosophy of history, becomes necessary, since it is continually appealed to in discussion. The last century had already introduced the critical method with the study of history : Montesquieu[1] and even Voltaire[2] were not content with

[1] *Grandeur et Décadence des Romains. Esprit des Lois.*
[2] *Dictionnaire philosophique. Essai sur les Lois.*

narrating; they sought to compare, to appreciate, to draw deductions, which, when based on careful observation, acquire the form of axioms—of fixed laws—in regard to civilisation. The same phenomenon next presented itself in the study of the sciences. But in this respect the arts lagged behind, and with the exception of a few unexplained dogmatic systems, the critics in their appreciation of architectural works were scarcely influenced by anything more than individual liking or the instinctive tastes of the society amid which they lived. Winckelmann in Germany was the first who attempted to apply critical methods to Classic art. And though the scope of his investigations was very limited, the result of his endeavours was to strike a blow at empirical procedure. There arose a desire to discover in the monuments of antiquity something more than the outer forms. But our French architects were not easily induced to adopt critical methods. Confiding in their ability, there were many who clung to the belief that ignorance of everything not professional was an essential characteristic of talent. When young, I had fellow-students in architecture who piqued themselves on not being readers. And in fact they knew nothing besides how to ink-in a plan or colour-up an elevation, and the little that was then taught in the School. Since then, however, things have somewhat changed.

The study of the arts of past times, and especially of architecture, caused no little consternation in the numerous band of architects whose library consisted of Perrault's translation of Vitruvius, a Vignole, a Palladio, Rondelet's *Construction*, and Périer and Fontaine's *Palais de Rome*. The most active-minded hastened to fill up their bookshelves with everything that was published, good or indifferent. The result was that all these examples of architectural forms, compiled at hazard without method, added, as it were, a prodigious number of words to the vocabulary of persons who were unacquainted with their meaning, and who knew nothing of syntax and grammar. The jargon that ensued may be imagined. The venerable conservators of the *bases* of good architecture beheld with dismay this invasion of documents gathered from every quarter, and uttered anathemas against what they termed "archæology" encroaching on Art. They were not entirely wrong. But the thing to be deplored is the persistence of the belief that the study of the past is injurious now that we can apply analytical methods to architecture as we do to the sciences.

This study—of course supposing it does not stop short at the forms, but investigates the causes and principles,—supposing it not to be exclusive or prejudiced *a priori*—soon enables us to distinguish among examples of architecture those which are original from such as are only more or less successful plagiarisms; to classify the examples that have resulted from an unbroken course of logical deduction; to detect the principles common to certain civilisations, and thus found rules not on the application of such or such a form of art; but on immutable reason. I grant that this is a labour of greater complication than the system in vogue thirty years ago, and which consisted in applying certain forms of art without considering the reasons which originated them; but it is a procedure that will have to be employed, because it will be dictated by serious criticism (and it will not be long before serious criticism will make its appearance), when the critic, better enlightened respecting the essential conditions of architecture, will ask the architect: "Why are Classic columns that are made to rest on a socle, raised on the first floor of a building? Why are these columns, which moreover serve no purpose since they only support themselves, divided by two stories? Why are these window-openings made so high, since you have to divide them by a floor? Why this imitation of a small Italian palace-front stuck against an enormous building containing nothing but vast halls? Why are superposed columns forming buttresses set against a thick wall that only supports ceilings having no outward thrust? Why this reproduction, on a new building erected all at one time, of a front which is the production of different periods and various requirements? Why two campaniles and two clock-faces on the same front of a building and only two yards apart? Symmetry, do you say? But where is this symmetry to stop? and in what way does it constitute art? Why build porticos where no one passes or can pass, since they lead nowhere, and which darken a useful ground-floor and entresol? Why erect buildings of such a width transversely that you cannot light the central part? To these and many similar questions, which a serious critic might put to an architect in many cases, will it be sufficient to reply that the critic is an archæologist, exclusive or enthusiastic? For wherein lies the archæology, the exclusiveness, or the enthusiasm? Youthful architects will do wisely to anticipate the day which is not far distant, when their works will be brought before the tribunal of a criticism, which is not archæological, exclusive, or enthusiastic, but which simply demands the reason of things. They will do wisely to prepare themselves for that judgment by studies that are in accordance with the modern methodical spirit, and by works in which the outward form never contravenes the dictates of reason, and the correct and judicious appreciation of the requirements of the times in which we live.

LECTURE XVI.

ON MONUMENTAL SCULPTURE.

NEVER, I imagine, was architecture an art easy of execution. The very fact that architecture is a combination of various arts causes an accumulation of difficulties when we have to compose, and proceed to the execution of this complex whole, so as to satisfy all requirements. These difficulties are insurmountable if the combination cannot be guided by one presiding intelligence,—if each artist who is called to contribute his share conceives and executes independently. We should not therefore be astonished, nor should we blame the architects alone, if most of our buildings present only agglomerations of art products, not works of art. When we consider how matters are managed—in our day still more than formerly—when a building has to be erected, the wonder is that there is not even more confusion than actually prevails in the heaps of objects of all kinds which are complimented with the title of public edifices. Sculpture, which once bore a sisterly relation to architecture, tends to become more and more estranged from it, and sometimes even hostile to it; it insists upon choosing its own place as it would in an Exhibition or a Museum. What it desires is to be seen, and that there may be nothing in its neighbourhood to distract the spectator. And not only does this sculptor wish to be conspicuous himself, but he wishes to throw into the shade another who is engaged in a theme side by side with his own. A very desirable competition this, if they were producing works destined to be displayed in a public exhibition, but disastrous when occurring in works intended to compose a united whole. Should the architect then,—it will be objected,—presume to direct the sculptor,—to fetter his genius by certain formularies he may please to dictate, to make the statuary a mere workman, a mere cutter-out of images, whose composition he is to determine? It is no slight privilege,—and sculptors are not sparing in their complaints on this score,—that the architect should have the right of assigning such or such a place, defining such or such limits, dictating such or such degrees of projection, and

such or such a scale.   Is not the sculptor's art at least equal
in dignity with that of the architect ?   Why should the former
be subjected to the latter ?   Such an anomaly might be expected
in those barbarous ages from which we are far removed, when
the name of artist was unknown, and when the loftiest positions
in the arts were occupied by mere artisans. . . . I know—everybody knows—what may be urged on this score ; the name is a
matter of indifference ; the workman who sculptured statues I
could name at Rheims or Chartres, possessed in my opinion talents
equal to those of many of our modern artists.   But was he as
independent and free in the expression of his talent ?   We may
suppose so ; only he did not endeavour to produce a discord in
the concert in which he was called to take part, and did not
suppose that his merit could be enhanced by eclipsing his
environment.

It must not be supposed that I wish in any degree to
detract from the real merit of our statuaries, for the amount of
talent represented by their works is very considerable.   Few
periods of art in modern times have produced so large a number
of very good works, and it needs no great discernment to perceive that the sculptor's art has reached a higher level since
the beginning of the century ; but it must be acknowledged
that, in rising, it has become more and more at variance with
the sister art of architecture, so that we may regard the time as
not distant when they must part company.   What then is the
cause of this want of harmony ?   This is what we are concerned
to investigate.

In regions where the plastic arts were subjected to hieratic
formulas, as in Egypt for example, these arts moved only within
certain narrow limits which it was forbidden them to transgress.
The harmony established between their relations could not be
disturbed by the innovations of a man of genius.   The functions
of architecture, sculpture, and painting, defined, I may say, from
the very commencement, were exercised under a kind of rigorous
archaic control, and the pre-established harmony was such that
it is difficult to say, on seeing an Egyptian building of the best
period, where the expressions of these three arts, which are so
intimately associated, severally begin and end.   How and by
what efforts of genius had this intimate union been first
established ?   This I shall not endeavour to explain.   I will
take the fact simply as it stands.   Its consequences are such,
even in the view of the least intelligent observer, that the
monuments of Egypt are not only distinguished from all others,
but exhibit a stamp of unity so complete that architecture of
any other order, even the most perfect in its kind, seems to want
cohesion when compared with that of Egypt.   Roman buildings

themselves,[1] however concrete, solidly built, and well balanced, seem to be wanting in vigour and unity by the side of the least important of the Egyptian monuments of the best period. The reason is that in the Egyptian building, while the construction gives the idea of stability and strength, because it is suggested by a principle which is the simplest and the most easy to conceive, the intimate union of the arts of sculpture and painting with the form adopted by the architect, concentrates the attention of the spectator on the absolute unity of the whole, instead of turning it away. The colossal statues that flank the opening in a pylon exhibit in their composition the appearance of buttresses. The caryatides, standing against the piers of the portico, make a part of these pillars in virtue of their form and the monumental manner in which they are treated. If historic sculpture occurs on the walls, it assimilates with the structure ; it presents a kind of tapestry which covers it without altering its surface. Although minutely careful in the execution of his work, and though he observes nature with a rare subtlety of penetration, the Egyptian sculptor makes considerable sacrifices to the monumental principle. He is marvellously well acquainted with the form he is rendering, but he takes good care not to express all its details, and contents himself with a liberal and simple though always true interpretation, notwithstanding the archaic appearance which he gives to that form. This absolute harmony between the sculpture and the architecture causes all other buildings when compared with Egyptian art to present an appearance of pieces of furniture, and involuntarily recalls our attention to this powerful and unique expression of the intimate union of the three arts. Do we then recommend an imitation of the monuments of Egypt along our own streets ! Certainly not : but however remote Egyptian art may be from our own times and customs, we may find instruction in it, if we are willing to preserve in the various expressions of art in general something more than the apparent form,—if we seek in them the generating principle, the reason of that diversity of expression. The leading characteristic of the sculpture applied to Egyptian architecture, we cannot too frequently repeat, is its intimate union with the forms of that architecture,—its participation in those forms. Whether the statuary is colossal or on a very small scale, it never, in the former case, disturbs the dominant lines of the building, nor in the latter case appears mean or detrimental to the grandeur of the whole. This appears simple enough when we see those monuments of the

[1] Here, as in all other references, it must be understood that in speaking of Roman buildings, those of genuine Roman structure are intended, and not the false imitations of Greek art introduced under the Empire.

shores of the Nile; it might be supposed that this so perfect result cost no effort; it is, in fact, the peculiarity of complete works of art, not to suggest to the spectator any idea of effort or study: but to him who knows how much knowledge and intellectual labour are required for every product of art which can attract and retain our attention without troubling the intellect, the architecture of Egypt in its best period will certainly seem the most perfectly correct on the face of the globe. It must be allowed indeed that such a result could be much more easily obtained with simple necessities such as those which Egyptian civilisation presented than with the complicated ones furnished by such a civilisation as ours. The principle however is applicable everywhere. The artist is always free to make use of nature without servilely copying it, and to subject the composition and the execution of the sculpture to the monumental idea. I am far from blaming the institution of Museums, which so greatly further the preservation of works of art and the instruction of artists: but it cannot be denied that Museums tend to obliterate from the artist's mind, unless he is richly endowed with genius, and has a well-developed critical faculty, that idea of the intimate union of the arts, which is one of the prominent characteristics of the best periods of art. The contemplation of isolated masterpieces may certainly contribute to the production of fresh masterpieces, also isolated, but they do not suggest those broad and comprehensive ideas which are so necessary to architecture, and to those who are called on to lend their aid in giving it expression. In a still greater degree these Museums tend to distract the attention and taste of the public, which soon acquires the notion that to become a connoisseur in art it suffices to have examined with some degree of care a few fragments taken from ancient monuments, without the power of restoring them to their proper place, even in thought. To become really instructive, to be something more than a mere show-room of archæological curiosities, more or less duly classified, or of fragmentary *chefs-d'œuvre*, Museums should exhibit along with these remains the complete works from which they are taken, were it only in drawings, and with *catalogues raisonnés*. But in these matters everything remains to be done, and many prejudices have to be got rid of. Our neighbours in England have already attempted something of the kind, but our singular vanity rather than any want of resources stands in the way. Confiding in our readiness of apprehension and natural taste, we think we have supplied all that art requires if we have exhibited a beautiful picture or a fine piece of sculpture; but we scarcely care to inquire what place shall be found for the painting or the statue. It was not thus however that the Greeks proceeded during the best period of their art, when they had not begun to carve and paint for wealthy Roman amateurs, but were building and decorating those monuments which are among their glories. Nor was it thus that the artists of the Middle Ages and those of the Renaissance proceeded. To speak of statuary only,—the habit which our most distinguished artists have acquired of working independently in the isolation of their studies, that sort of disdain which they manifest for the arts which they do not profess, and their absolute ignorance of the conditions of monumental art, occasion the most singular deceptions on their own part, and on that of the public the severest criticisms when they are called on to contribute to the decoration of a building. Are we to understand then that the sculptors consider themselves to blame for the disappoint-ments and criticisms thus occasioned ? By no means ! It is always the fault of the architect or of a competing sculpture in the immediate neighbourhood. The position is bad ; the archi-tecture spoils the effect of the statuary by its mass, arrangement, or details; or the rival sculptor has endeavoured to "kill" the work that competes with his own. It must indeed be acknowledged that these mishaps, which so frequently occur in the present day, are in some measure caused by the architect. In adopting those arrangements which furnish the artist with a kind of frame or pedestal for the reception of the piece of sculpture regarded as a sort of addition, the latter has thought simply of *exhibiting* his work, and does not trouble himself about a general effect which he does not understand, and which is not explained to him because, for the most part, it is not provided for, and he is not consulted about it. It is true I never saw the Greeks at work, but I am persuaded that they did not proceed in this way ; indeed, every-thing leads me to believe that Ictinus and Phidias worked in combination. And yet, notwithstanding the beauty of that Greek architecture at its culmination, it must be allowed that in the buildings which have remained to us the statuary is far from presenting that monumental combination with the archi-tecture of which Egypt presents so complete a type. That unity very probably existed in the primitive Doric architecture, *e.g.* in that basilica of Agrigentum, known as the Temple of the Giants, and in other buildings of an archaic character; but it seems to me already near its extinction in the Parthenon, if not as re-gards the execution of the sculpture, at least in point of principle.

In fact, in monumental statuary two conditions must be observed,—appropriate design in reference to the whole, to the general scale ; and also execution, which should bear a relation to the style adopted, the position and destination. Now, with all due respect for Phidias, it does not seem as if the subjects represented in the metopes were exactly adapted to the scale of the building ; and those figures in alto-relievo must, at the height at which they are placed, have appeared paltry, especially on the anterior and posterior fronts, that is, beneath the colossal figures which filled the tympanums.　But if we look at the execution, it is impossible to find statuary better harmonising with the destination and the place.　The exquisite delicacy of certain details does not injure the effect of the mass, which is always frankly rendered and expressed.　One may pardon an artist such as Phidias, who probably exhibited some of the figures of the tympanums in his studio, for carrying minuteness in the execution of certain details to excess, details which could only be seen by the swallows, if this minuteness does not injuriously affect the simple dignity of the masses.　It is not the less true that in this elaboration, designed to please a few amateurs, we can already trace the beginnings of an abuse which will soon manifest itself,—the separation of the two arts, architecture and statuary. When the artist works with the view of satisfying a few *dilettanti* he is approaching decline, he is losing the right path ; he thinks he is attaining perfection because he is pleasing a select body of connoisseurs, while in reality he is deteriorating. Perfection in art implies the power to impress all,—the ignorant as well as the fastidious.　When the sculptor's art is limited to the gratification of the taste of certain privileged persons, of certain distinguished amateurs, it has lost that monumental signification which alone can stir the masses.

　　Is it not evident also that statuary must have a meaning for all if it would produce a tolerably profound impression ?　Among the Greeks, mythologic, heroic, or historic sculpture represented something which had a very vivid interest for every one. Similarly, in our mediæval monuments, statuary had a meaning perfectly understood by all ; it was a means of instruction.　The iconography of our great northern cathedrals is a veritable encyclopædia instructing the multitude through the eyes.　I admit that in our days such means are unavailing.　Allegory is a poor resource,—a frigid enigma which very few take the trouble to guess, because it interests no one and answers to no sentiment of the human heart.　Personifications of qualities or abstractions —such as Peace, War, Abundance, Commerce, Art, etc.—all this is too abstract, or savours too much of puerile metaphysics to interest any one.　They are mere pretexts for making statues, bas-reliefs, or groups, in which no one sees anything but a more or less well-arranged collection of figures,—academical works savouring of the studio, which do not correspond with any living fact, intellectual movement, or emotion of the soul.　We may admire the form if it is beautiful, but an art which possesses such power as does statuary is not destined merely to gratify the eyes and conduct the mind to a purely material criticism. Form is, after all, only a means of calling up an idea or a sensation; if it stands alone, or rather if it has not sprung into existence under the inspiration of a thought which it is destined to diffuse, form leaves in the mind only a very fugitive trace, and quickly wearies us. Our most eminent sculptors know this well; and so not being able to diffuse a general thought over a whole edifice they content themselves with embodying the idea, if they have one, in a statue or a bust; and they sometimes succeed. But this *idea*, concentrated within more and more narrow limits, in proportion as art is more and more confined to the studio, is absolutely null in monumental statuary. Must we say then that the injurious conditions now prevailing are fatal and irremediable? that with the very abundant and distinguished talent which our age can boast, monumental statuary is condemned to give us only detached fragments, injuring each other by their proximity, having no relation to the architecture, and presenting sometimes masterpieces in point of execution consigned to oblivion through the vagueness or commonplace character of the thought? Assuredly not; an art that possesses so many elements of vitality, which produces not unfrequently works of considerable merit, is not destined to perish for the public, and place its isolated productions on scattered pedestals, or in mansions, palaces, or museums. It is easy to lay our finger on the evil, and it is well that the public should be accurately acquainted with its cause. Now the public do not know how the Republic of the Arts is administered, and the critics who are willing to undertake to instruct them know little more than they do, or have too much personal interest in such questions to say all the truth.

If a building is being erected in which statuary will have to occupy a place of some importance, the architect devises the plan, submits it to the proper authorities, and proceeds to the execution; immediately he is assailed by applications from sculptors who wish to have a share in the work. As a matter of course he refers them to the board of management, who will undertake to have the work done when required. Meantime the building advances, and the architect assigns the places which the statuary is to occupy. Here there are to be statues. But what? He does not know, and it is of little importance to him. They are to be six feet high; this is his main consideration. For that place there is to be a bas-relief. . . . What is it to represent? . . . We shall see by and by. On this pediment, or in front of these piers, there are to be groups. . . . What are they to designate? . . . Industry, Agriculture, Music, or Poetry? . . . This will be settled when the time comes. The day arrives when the sculptors are to set to work. Then comes the mêlée. . . . Mr. So-and-so gets a commission for a statue ; . . . he is furious because his more favoured *confrère* is to supply two. The latter in his turn anathematises the board which accords a group to Mr. M., and Mr. M. is beside himself on finding that his group will have an inferior position to that assigned to Mr. N. If the architect enjoys the favour of the board, his friends will have good commissions ; if the board does not make a point of obliging him, his advice will not even be asked for, but he will be informed by an official letter that such or such sculptors having been commissioned by the board to execute such or such statues, bas-reliefs, and groups, he is requested to arrange with them concerning the execution. If, in such an assignment, the sculptors who have been rejected are not satisfied, most of those who have obtained commissions are scarcely more so. This one, who has the honour of being a member of the Institute, thinks it unseemly that he has been placed on an equal footing with a sculptor who is not ; he considers himself wronged, and asks for compensation. Another, who has manifested a rather independent spirit towards the board or the Academy—it comes to the same thing,—has only plaster medallions for the interior assigned him, or one of those busts which are the small coin reserved for candidates or artists who are out of favour, but who must not be allowed absolutely to die of hunger. The perpetual secretary of the *Academie des Beaux Arts*, who is fond of introducing Phidias, ought to beg him to tell us what he thinks of the method of procedure when the decoration of our buildings is in question. However this may be, every one sets to work, on the condition that all the designs will have to be submitted to the architect, or, most frequently, to a commission, so that they may be approved before being executed. Of course each sculptor makes his model in his studio ; he has his programme and the dimensions assigned him. As to the style of the monument, the place to be occupied, and the effect of the whole, he rarely takes them into consideration. If his work is to occupy a good position, he hopes he shall eclipse his *confrère* and produce something . . . striking. If he has been favoured with a mere second-rate commission, he patches up a design simply that he may get the order to proceed. He produces a Muse or a Season, or something or other that reminds one of some antique statue or other. The number of female forms in this official statuary is considerable ; there are very few male ones ! Glory, War, Faith, Charity, Peace, Natural Philosophy, Astronomy,—all are feminine ; but even if Commerce, Spring, Summer, or Autumn[1] are to be represented, it is still woman that is intrusted with these parts. If, some two

---

[1] The reader will remember that the French equivalents of these words are masculine.—*Tr.*

or three thousand years hence, when the grass grows on the sites of our public buildings, learned antiquaries should make explorations, they will certainly suppose, finding so many French statues, that a law or a religious dogma interdicted us from representing man in sculpture; and they will read long dissertations on the subject before the Academies of those days, and which will probably be "crowned." At length the designs are approved. But observe that a model to the scale of one-twentieth, or even to that of one-tenth, gives no idea of the effect when a place in a building has to be filled. These little rough models of clay or plaster can give even the most practised artist only an idea of the design of the work itself; they cannot enable him to form an opinion as to the effect which this model enlarged will produce (even supposing its principal features to be rigorously carried out) when placed upon or in front of the building: approval follows, and the board has nothing more to do. Then the sculptors who have received these commissions shut themselves up once more in their studios with their model and work separately.

Some of them—I have known such, but they are the exceptions—visit their colleagues; but generally they abstain from such visits, that they may not subject themselves to an influence which might derogate from the originality of their work. In the case of those who have groups or bas-reliefs to carve, screens of boards, such as any one may have seen, are raised in front of the portion they have to decorate, and they set their employés to work on a model which is generally half-size. It may be supposed that they do not visit one another's works, for the reasons above mentioned. One fine morning the screens fall, wagons bring the statues, which are then placed in their niches or on the pedestals; and all these works, in which, separately considered, there is a great deal of real merit, produce when combined the strangest assemblage. The statues executed in the studio far from the building look thin and poor; the groups overpower all that surrounds them, both sculpture and architecture. One bas-relief is full of shadows, another, its counterpart, is only a luminous blotch. Each artist brings his friends to look at his work, and these friends look at his work alone, just as if they were in the studio; the round of compliments is exhausted; the public are not much enlightened, and the critics who chance to have no prepossessions endeavour to discover an intention in the whole, which is no easy matter.

As I said in a previous Lecture, what chiefly concerns so many people who are intrusted with the building of our public edifices,—from the members of boards to the artist who executes the designs, but especially the former,—is not the question of art, but that of persons. The fraternity and fellows severally have to be conciliated, such or such a patron must be humoured, such or such a situation of great interest must be respected; and all this must be managed with discreet patronage, the greatest number possible must be satisfied, so that one's importance may be increased, and a body of canvassers and clients may be secured, men of talent not be disgusted, while mediocrities, who are the majority, are not offended. It would seem reasonable that an architect intrusted with the erection of a building in which sculpture occupies an important place should be also commissioned to choose and direct the sculptors; but if that is to be the case, architects must be empowered to dictate arrangements, and sculptors must be willing to accept them; but we are still far from being able to fulfil these two conditions. Few architects, it must be confessed, are competent to give a criticism on a piece of sculpture based on clearly understood grounds; and very few could put such ideas, even if they had them, on paper. Or if, on the other hand, it were permitted them to choose a single artist, and intrust to him the arrangements for the statuary designed to decorate a façade or a hall, entirely on his own responsibility, perhaps the result would not harmonise with the architecture, but there would be a chance of its being in harmony with itself. This would not suit great administrative bodies, and the happy object of the architect's choice would have enough to do to defend himself against the recriminations and hatreds which he would thus bring upon him. The state of the case being thus, prudent architects avoid, as far as possible, any prevision regarding the statuary to be placed on the buildings they erect; those who are bold enough or sufficiently inexperienced to dare to ask of statuary an important decorative element are sure to repent of it.[1]

Next to the Egyptians, and in a quite different order of ideas, no epoch of art in our view has better known how to apply statuary to architecture than the best period of the Middle Ages. We have so little Greek statuary forming part of a monumental work that I could not venture to say whether in composition, in comprehensive harmony, the Greeks were superior or inferior in their sculptured ornamentation to the mediæval masters. We can only speak of what is extant, of what we see, and are therefore able to analyse. And while the sculpture in the Greek buildings extant is superior in point of execution to all that has ever been produced, we are compelled to admire exceedingly the uniform compositions and the formal compartments occupied by the statuary in Greek temples. Evidently (I speak only of the temples) the sculpture is sacri-

---

[1] See the seventh Lecture.

ficed to the architectural composition ; it plays only a restricted part, and one which cannot have any considerable influence, advantageous or to the contrary, on the general effect. We may suppose—and we have a specimen of the kind in the Pandrosium at Athens—that the Greeks erected buildings in which sculpture had a preponderating influence on the architectural composition ; but as these monuments no longer exist, we can only form more or less ingenious conjectures respecting them. I am inclined to accord an absolute superiority to the Greeks in point of art generally, but as regards architecture we can discuss only what exists, and not what we may suppose to have existed—at least this is not the place for so doing. We have not much to say of the sculpture connected with the architecture of the Empire. Sculpture was alien to the genius of the Romans : to them it was an exotic art, an affair of luxury ; the beauty of a truly Roman edifice consists exclusively in its admirable construction. I freely admit that on the basilica of the Forum of Trajan the sculpture occupied an important place, and was very well arranged, if we may trust the data supplied by medals and some remains ; but it would be difficult to restore that edifice, as far as this point is concerned, with any degree of certainty. The triumphal arches—for I should not take into consideration the Roman temples, which are merely a modification of the Greek—are nearly the only Roman monuments extant in which statuary is closely connected with architecture. Although in these structures the combination does not present a perfect harmony, the general effect is unquestionably majestic, the relative proportions are often happily determined, and the unity of composition between the statues, the bas-reliefs, and the dominant architectural lines is specially commendable. Evidently the architects and the sculptors understood each other perfectly, and we may surmise that Rome had not a board of public works which was expected to give commissions to a dozen sculptors to decorate an edifice. And as regards the expression of the idea, the Romans are not behind the Greeks. The designs have a relation to each other ; they mean something, and form a clear and consistent whole. In this respect the column of Trajan, which we mentioned above,[1] is a masterpiece, and the triumphal arches, the only monuments extant that exhibit complete examples of the intimate union of sculpture with architecture among the Romans, do not less clearly express the causes in which they originated. It may be replied that with the ancients this was easy enough : that the Greeks had no difficulty in designing statuary for a sacred monument whose meaning would be comprehensible to all,

---

[1] Fourth Lecture.

by selecting subjects from mythology and heroic story, nor the Romans in finding subjects suitable for a triumphal arch, battles, trophies, treaties, captives, victors—this was perfectly easy, and the subjects spoke for themselves; the artists of the Middle Ages, who lived amid a society in great part based upon and animated by a religious belief, could decorate the exterior of a church with the subjects taken from any part of the sacred hierarchy, from Old or New Testament history. But to what repertory shall the sculptor have recourse in decorating an Exchange, a Court of Justice, or a Theatre? Are we not in these cases forced to adopt those stupid and monotonous abstractions which have no meaning for the multitude? The public may form an idea of Jupiter, of the Fates, or the Virgin; in fact it may possibly personify a virtue or a quality, such as Courage, Patience, Faith, Force—even a city or province, but under what form can we represent Industry, Commerce, the Constitution, Physics, Astronomy, Poetry, lyrical or fanciful? That Muses should be the patrons of Tragedy, Comedy, or Astronomy is intelligible, as we may suppose a Deity presiding over the rain or the harvests; the multitude recognises the myth, and no further explanation is needed; but how personify an abstraction? Are we then condemned to the unvarying reproduction of myths that have no meaning for us, or to give a form to ideas which are incompatible with a form? Or, on the other hand, must we keep to cold and inevitably ridiculous Allegories,—show Despotism crushed by Emancipated Thought, or Anarchy vanquished by Order, or Religion sheltering the suffering beneath its immortal mantle, or Liberty breaking a pile of fetters? Can we not do something else, and something better? Cannot we find in the past elementary ideas which it would be possible to develop? In art, poetry, and sentiment no absolutely new invention is possible, because the human heart has been ever beating in the same way. And what we call new can only be a fuller or wider development of an idea which is usually quite an old one. Two sentiments—love and hatred—supply, and will long supply, poets, novelists, and dramatists with materials for moving the passions of readers and hearers, if they only present these passions under a new phase.

I grant that if we have to produce a programme for the composition of a general work in sculpture for a public building, some ingenuity and some tact is needed, and boards of works are not responsible for these conditions, but architects at least might take account of them, for their reputation is often at stake in the matter. The sculptural commonplaces with which they cover the buildings confided to their skill are imputed to the barrenness of their imaginations, their want of knowledge, or to prejudices derived from the school, which, whatever may be alleged to the contrary, are confined to a very narrow coterie. Nine-tenths of our sculptors and painters confine themselves to their own narrow circle, and manifest a profound contempt for all who do not handle the chisel or the brush ; architects, who are perhaps less exclusive, are nevertheless afflicted with this malady of caste which has been introduced among us by the institution of the Academies. This world of artists reads little, and takes no trouble to make itself acquainted with the progress of thought. On the other hand, the public are absolutely ignorant of the grounds on which artists proceed. As contact between them rarely if ever occurs, the indifference of the public towards the questions which interest artists increases in direct proportion to the contempt exhibited by the latter for all criticism outside their caste. But it is artists themselves who lose most in this state of things, and it would be well if they were to be convinced of it for the sake of their own interest. Those of them who covet success, perceiving that the public does not understand their language, flatter the equivocal taste of the multitude, not giving them credit for anything but unwholesome fancies. Whatever talent they may therefore display in their works, these artists debase the level of art and tend to make it a contemptible calling. I would not be mistaken here : I am not one of those who admit that there can be high or low art ; there is only *one* art, and if the public shows a preference for representations of an equivocal kind, it is because it finds at least ideas in such productions, while it can discover none in those of an elevated order. What is now called, for example, religious sculpture and painting, whatever be the merit of the execution, is utterly commonplace and uninteresting, and is absolutely wanting in thought and idea. It is not because their works represent what are called religious subjects that the public has no interest in them, but because their works are stale copies, having no religious or other ideas in them. All subjects are good, provided they present a clear thought to the public ; but in order to paint or carve subjects of an elevated order, the artist who conceives them must have an elevated mind, and must not take his inspirations from a depôt of traditional commonplaces. Every painter who undertakes to paint a religious subject is immediately haunted by the productions of Raphael or one of the masters of the Renaissance. Every sculptor who is working at a bas-relief, an allegorical group or figure, or one belonging to a doubtful mythology, is similarly possessed by Classical works, or, what is worse, by those which are mere imitations of them. The public is weary of this, and not unreasonably ; at any rate such productions cannot attract its attention. At the first glance the multitude recognises the work as belonging to the merely conventional order; to use a common phrase, they do not believe any such thing ever happened, and they pass on. Apart from the merit of the work, it was not thus among the Greeks; and the sculptures that decorated the Parthenon or the Temple of Theseus had a very distinct and even, so to speak, living meaning for them. Nor again was it thus with those who in former ages stopped to gaze at the portal of a Cathedral; for not only did they find there a whole world of thought which was familiar to them, but saw in what was represented the eternal struggle of good against evil, the ruin of the wicked, the apotheosis of the just, and the glorification of virtue, however humble. It was thus with the help of an idea, or a succession of ideas, understood by all; if the form was beautiful the eyes became accustomed to be interested in things of art, to love them, and to become familiar with the beautiful. There is no other means of habituating the public to the beautiful, and making it loved by them, but presenting beautiful forms as the expression of an idea which arrests their thoughts, engages and interests them. But an idea must not be wanting; it must be comprehensible and must strike a right chord. Looking away from those vapid allegories or abstractions in sculpture, if we take, for instance, a bas-relief of our own days representing the Last Judgment—supposing this to embody a generally received belief,—it must not be left out of consideration that we are now far advanced in the nineteenth century, and that the idea which religious people form of the Last Judgment cannot be the same as that which occupied people's minds in the thirteenth. But if we compare the bas-reliefs that represent this scene on our old Cathedrals with that which adorns the tympanum of the Madeleine, it is in the older sculptures that we shall find a philosophical, delicate, and true thought developed, whereas in the latter a material and coarse idea will be exhibited, or rather no thought at all. Let us examine first the bas-relief of the thirteenth century. Christ is represented half-clothed, showing his wounds,—pointing out the redemptive sacrifice, the Divine endeavour to redeem the sins of the world. This suffices to indicate that those who are condemned are not excusable. He is accompanied by angels bearing the instruments of the Passion as a testimony against them. Then we observe the beloved disciple St. John and his mother on her knees at his side interceding for man. The elect, all in the same dress, and crowned, are of neither sex,—which, in point of art, obviates a great difficulty; the condemned, on the contrary, preserve their characteristic features. We have a crowd in which are people of every condition—labourers, traders, soldiers, women, popes, kings, priests: there is no distinction among the reprobate. Certainly, granted the belief, it could not be rendered by a more just expression, or one at the same time more conformable to the requirements of the plastic art. But what does the bas-relief on the tympanum of the Madeleine exhibit to us ? A fully draped Christ, who seems placed there merely to separate the crowd ; and on one side personages—chiefly women—with a sanctimonious expression, who seem to be addressing the Saviour to thank him for separating them from a posse of demoniacs going off on the other side, making horrible grimaces, and pommelling each other. I appeal to any unprejudiced judgment as to which of these two designs contain the religious thought fit to impress the multitude ? Better certainly not to produce statuary—to repudiate it altogether like the Mussulmans—than to place on the front of our churches designs so destitute of all thought,—I will not say religious, but even right or sensible. I shall be told that the bas-relief of the tympanum of the Madeleine was not designed for the purpose of converting people, but to show to future generations how well our sculptors can model and drape figures. . . . But what interest has the public in the matter, if these figures, however well modelled and draped, teach it nothing—say nothing to it,—produce no moral impression upon it ? It will prefer to betake itself to the Museum of Antiquities, and justly. In spite of restricted belief,—and though I have never seen any one stop to look at the tympanum of the Madeleine,—in crossing the square in front of Notre Dame (as I have sometimes had occasion to do), I have not unfrequently perceived groups of persons stopping before the central door and interpreting in their way the bas-reliefs on the tympanum over it. Even in our day this piece of sculpture elicits ideas, makes people think of something, while that on the Madeleine may perhaps interest a few sculptors, but utterly fails to engage the eyes of the public, for which, however, we must suppose it to have been produced. Yet even here that shade of an idea exists, though poorly expressed ; but what shall we say of the statues perched up one neither knows why nor wherefore, on most of our modern churches, and which are apparently carved with no other purpose than to give self-styled sculptors something to do ?

But leaving these abortions, let us see whether there is not a means of escaping from the worn-out mythologies, insipid allegories, and the sickly or vapidly sanctimonious religious styles that have intruded themselves for some time past. There is one subject which is eternally true, and which as long as there are human beings on this earth will always have the power to interest them,—the antagonism between good and evil, the struggle of the good against the bad, of truth with error.

Though error and evil often triumph, the defeats sustained by truth and goodness have not been able to diminish the respect which every one cherishes for them in his own conscience. This antagonism offers to artists an inexhaustible fund of subjects, especially to sculptors, who have but a limited number of forms for expressing an idea. The theme in question always arrests attention, because it reminds every one of his own history, encourages the victims of wrong to persevere in the right, and condemns error or wickedness in the public view.

The sculptors and painters of the Middle Ages were well aware of this, and have left us many illustrations in plastic arts of this antagonism, as well in religious as in civil monumental structures. To personify a virtue or some other abstract quality, and to oppose to it the contrary of that virtue or quality, is an idea which has at least the merit of ingenuity from an æsthetic point of view. We have here an occasion for displaying contrasts which cannot fail to attract the eye and occupy the mind. We have moreover an element of plastic compositions. This suggestion is not equivalent to having recourse to allegory,— exhibiting, for example, as I was just saying, the personification of Order crushing the personification of Anarchy, or that of Liberty trampling on Despotism. But I foresee the objections that will be brought. . . . How, it will be said, will you represent those correlations on our public buildings ? . . I fully admit that with our present conceptions of architecture this would be impossible ; and this is exactly the point to which I wished to come. When statuary is to be placed on a façade, certain tympanums, niches, or pedestals which are evidently supererogatory are contrived, and the band of the elect are summoned. " Here," they are told, " are the places allotted you ; there might be more or less, or none at all ; for this sculpture is no essential part of the building, it is nothing more or less than a superfluous decoration, a surplusage of luxury. Between the group placed there on a pedestal near the ground, the statues perched up in these niches and the bas-relief which fills a tympanum, we do not contemplate establishing any relation in thought, subject, or even execution. If these works have any signification, it belongs to them individually ; no general iconography exists, no dominant scheme is recognised. We have pieces of sculpture and nothing more ; do not look for anything else.

Let us, however, examine the subject in detail. Three distinct systems are recognisable in the styles of architecture known to us which have called in sculpture as a decorative accessory, and it seems hardly possible to imagine a fourth. The first, and most ancient, is that adopted by the Egyptians, but it is probable that they were not its inventors.

This system consists, as is well known, in covering the bare spaces with a kind of continuous tapestry representing religious, heroic, or historic subjects,—a tapestry which in nowise alters the principal lines of the architecture ; and in placing colossal figures before pillars or pylons, or as ornaments ; figures which are an essential part of the architecture, both in composition and method of treatment.   Here sculpture and architecture seem, as it were, to have grown up together.   The Greek monuments may be comprised among the off-shoots of this system.   Though much less lavish of monumental sculpture than the Egyptians, the Greeks also considered this kind of decoration as forming an essential part of the architecture.   The metopes, the tympanums, and friezes of the Parthenon are panels or tapestries in sculpture having no influence on the structural lines ; and though we may not be acquainted with any Greek temple the walls of whose *cella* were covered with bas-reliefs from top to bottom, such may have existed, and the fact would not contravene the Greek idea of the application of statuary to architecture.   The Basilica of the Giants at Agrigentum shows also that colossal statues of a purely architectural character, and according exactly with the architectural lines, as among the Egyptians, were adopted by the Dorian race.   Next to this primitive system, of which we find specimens in Asia, we may class the Roman system.   And by this we mean that which strictly belonged to the Romans, not their imitations of Greek art.   The Roman system regards sculpture only as a decorative accessory, without any connection with architecture.   Except in certain monuments whose characteristics in this respect we have particularised, viz., the column of Trajan and the triumphal arches, the Romans adopt sculpture as a kind of spoil with which they ornament their buildings : and in fact such was their actual procedure.   They were perhaps the first who had the taste of amateurs for objects of a certain marked value, and who took a pride in collecting them.   Even during the Republic we find Cicero forming a museum, and asking his friend Atticus to send him from Athens copies or casts in default of original Greek statues.   It would seem that except in the above-mentioned monuments of a particular kind, the Romans did not concern themselves with iconography.   Their architects, like our own, used to prepare niches and raise pedestals here and there, and would then go to Greece for statues fitted to occupy them.

Lastly, we have the system adopted by the mediæval artists —a system which restores to iconography the importance it had acquired in Egypt and in Greece, but which proceeds differently as regards the composition.   This system does not allow of colossal sculpture,[1] and groups the figures so as to present a striking scenic effect at a particular point.   Bas-relief does not comport with it, as it does with Egyptian and Greek sculpture; the subjects have the effect of a tapestry covered with slightly projecting figures, but are all represented in full relief, except at some points near the eye of the spectator, and which are intended to appear as a kind of hanging.   It does not seek, as do the Egyptian and Greek systems, to develop the sculpture on wide spaces or long friezes, but on the contrary to concentrate it on some points whose excessive richness and brilliant effects contrast with the less striking parts.   It makes the sculpture form part of the structure more decidedly than the Egyptian and Greek systems; brings the former into close association with the latter, and even makes it accentuate the construction; in proof of which may be cited those portals which are so richly decorated, and whose lintels, tympanums, jambs, or relieving voussoirs are clearly indicated by the sculptured arrangements, so that each object or figure is a piece of stone with a definite and useful function.   The mediæval artist in France, as much for reasons founded on the nature of the climate as from considerations of art, shelters his statuary, and seldom allows its outlines to cut the sky.   Moreover the statuary of the Middle Ages, like that of Egypt, India, and Greece, is always painted.   This is equivalent to saying that those civilisations which really had schools of sculpture considered that this art could not dispense with painting.

It is pretty clear, I think, from what has just been stated, that statuary applied to architecture has accommodated itself to two distinct systems of composition: the one adopted by the people of Asia, Egypt, and Greece also, the other proper to our mediæval art.

The Romans did not adopt either decidedly; their method, in fact, may be said to consist in having none.   It would seem that we in the present day prefer this neutral position,—the absence of iconography, and of any decided system of decoration,—though accompanied by pretensions which the Romans certainly did not make.   Why then should we extol the Greeks if we are so little concerned to resemble them in their desirable qualities?   And what have our architects to do with Athens?   Do we wish to resemble those rogues who are constantly appealing to honour and probity?   For my own part, I prefer the candour with which some members of the *Académie des Beaux Arts,*

[1] We cannot give the name of colossal sculpture to any other than that which appears such by its relative proportions.   The statues of the kings in the galleries of Notre Dame at Amiens, which are thirteen feet in height, have no pretensions to appear colossal, and are of this size only on account of the height at which they are placed.   In fact, they appear of natural size.

twenty years ago, when travels in Greece were beginning to be undertaken by our artists, declared that a residence in Greece was useless if not injurious to architects. They were of opinion that a residence in the country of Pericles,—though in this experience proves that they were mistaken,—might give them ideas contrary to the principles on which the Academy was founded, and seduce them from the loyalty to that mongrel Roman style which is the only one approved by that institution, and of which Lebrun's age has supplied the only recognised types. In fact, we are reduced to that meaningless Roman style, with some indications even of further enfeeblement,—which is natural enough; and if our architects bring back anything from Attica, it is merely descriptive matter; for of principles they bring nothing at all; or at least they take good care not to apply them in their works.

I am by no means desirous that one of the Theban buildings, or even the Parthenon, should be reproduced in Paris; what use could we make of them? If we are to imitate an ancient building absolutely, I would rather see one of the veritably Roman structures erected,—the Basilica of Constantine, for example; we could at least make some use of that. But then let us be unpretending; let us regard the façades of our public buildings as mere exhibitions of works of art,—museums or bazaars in the open air, where each sculptor presents his production to the gaze of amateurs; but let us not presume to make believe that we know how to apply statuary art to architecture. *A propos* of this matter, allow me to relate an anecdote, which, however, shall not be a long one. At seventeen, X. was a pupil in the studio of an architect, a member of the Institute, a most excellent man, whom he venerated on account of the uprightness of his character. This master made his pupil copy and shade in Indian ink many fragments of Roman buildings; and the youth would amuse himself by completing on the margin of his drawings— according to his notion of them—the buildings of which only a part had been shown him. It will readily be imagined that these restorations had no resemblance to the reality. He made them up out of reminiscences from every quarter, and heaven only knows what singular farragos they were! The Eclectics would have been charmed with them! A gate of the Temple of Cora would be attached to a house-front of which a glimpse had been gained at Rouen or at Dreux; a row of columns from the Theatre of Marcellus would be surmounted by an attic covered with bas-reliefs, and rested on a basement borrowed from some Florentine palace. At first the master seemed to pay no attention to these fantastic restorations, but seeing the thing continued, he said, "What's all this?" The pupil stammered out an explanation of his intention. No further notice was taken, till, seeing the malady was chronic, the master one morning called the pupil into his study and addressed him as follows : " My dear fellow, you are losing your time ; if you have the means, I recommend you, as it is summer-time, to take a run along the banks of the Loire or in Normandy, copy the buildings you see, and show me your drawings when you come back." The youth did not require to have the advice repeated. On returning,—in fact he hastened as quickly as he could to show his master his portfolio. Having looked at the contents in silence,—" Well," said he, " what conclusions have you drawn from all this ?" The tyro architect had drawn no conclusions, as may be imagined, and said nothing. The master added : "As you used to presume to construct the whole of a building from a fragment or a range of columns which you copied in the studio, how is it that you deduce no inferences from the numerous buildings and parts of buildings which you have been drawing ? A house, a mansion, a church, each has a guiding principle of construction, and everything that contributes to the ornamentation of these buildings must also have its why and wherefore. Have you asked yourself whether the various edifices you have drawn have attracted you, whether they have given you a desire to copy them because they very obviously harmonised with their objects, and whether their decoration was what it ought to be ? I see that you have made a good selection as the result of natural good taste ; but that is not enough. You should know why and how a work of art gives pleasure. Travel again, if you can manage it, and let your head work more than your hand, both in your journeys and in the studio." This advice harmonised too well with the pupil's taste not to be followed ; he continued his travels in France and other parts of Europe, constantly remembering the last words of his excellent instructor. And the final conclusion to be drawn is this. If it would please, whatever be the dress in which architecture exhibits itself, the expression must result from a thought perfectly clear and definite ; it should never wander into dreamy vagueness under the pretext of giving utterance to a sudden inspiration or metaphysical penchant, or a mere sentiment. Such emotions as music and poetry are able to call forth in the soul of the hearer can only be produced by the contemplation of an architectural work, when it affects the mind through the medium of reason. As far as this point is concerned we must be " exclusive," as our modern enthusiasts would call it, *i.e.* we must exclude from art all that does not fulfil this condition.

The disposition to transpose the arts is somewhat indicative of decadence. The writer pretends to paint ; he exchanges his pen for a brush, and he makes the words of the language his palette.

He gives every bramble in his landscape leaf by leaf, spares not a single technical term, and marks every point of light and shade ; he gives you a catalogue of the pebbles on the road,—he knows that this one is composed of the purest granite, and that one of a fragment of quartz ; and he supposes that in giving you this inventory he has transported you to the locality he has described ; he deepens the backgrounds and heightens the foliage. The roughest pencil sketches would make us better acquainted with the landscape.   On the other hand, there is a certain school of painters who try to make a philosophic or social manifesto of a picture.   Not a bit of drapery or the slightest accessory but conceals a profound signification.   A picture thus becomes a riddle ; and if we do not take in the most subtle intimations of the artist at a glance, if we do not penetrate with him into the labyrinth of the morbid fancies he has thought proper to bring upon his canvas, he thinks us idiots.

In architecture also we have artists similarly misguided.   They are but few, I allow, and considering the want of ideas manifested by most of our modern architectural conceptions, I am inclined to be very indulgent to these aberrant seekers ;—they are at least seekers.   Nevertheless, our younger students should beware of them ; they are dangerous.   A whole page of a romance or novel occupied with the description of the corner of a dirty court or the bottom of a staircase abandoned to the rats, is nothing worse than a useless page ; it may be borne with.   A dashing style, happy turns of expression, a jingle of words, a selection of piquant antitheses, may still keep the reader awake ; but in architecture no such resources are available, and transpositions are tiresome.   Even on paper this art is obliged to express the thought by common-sense methods regularly deduced from inexorable laws ; and when a vague cloudy idea lying outside the domain of plastic art has to be expressed in stone, wood, or iron, the result verges closely on the ridiculous.

Is it not strange, that while writers of a certain school are making a point of minutely describing a spot, a room, a hovel,—to add interest and reality to a narrative,—architects, disdainful of the imperatively material side of their art, unmindful alike of the most ordinary requirements, the nature of materials and manner of using them, and of relative proportion between the cost and the importance of the object, should pretend to express with stone and iron a complex thought, which is difficult to render even by the most subtle analysis ?

Architecture cannot pretend to anything of the kind ; it speaks only the language of plastic art.   It is evident that if the architect erects a wall without an opening, he conveys the idea of a place that is strictly shut up and defended, and consequently suggests distrust; that if, on the contrary, he pierces a façade with numerous openings, and ornaments it with sculpture, he gives his building an appearance of hospitality, and attaches an idea of ease and luxury to it. Mistrust and its opposite—luxurious hospitality—are, moreover, very simple notions, comporting with expression by plastic art, because they have to do with material, visible, and sensible facts. But how can we give architectural expression to the *love of country*, the *sense of duty, tolerance,* or the idea of *fraternity and union?*

These latter are complex emotions of the heart and of rational reflection, lying entirely outside the domain of plastic art; so that if an artist happens to try to render these metaphysical ideas by means of stone and iron, he is led to compose veritable enigmas, or to sacrifice absolute essentials and imperative necessities to the expression of a philosophical idea which, when all is done that can be done, nobody discovers, and which would require several pages of explanation or the aid of a cicerone to make it intelligible.

But to return to sculpture: it seems to me that the name of monumental statuary can be applied only to that of which all the parts are connected with the architecture both in the idea generally and in the details of the execution. Egyptian sculpture, that of Greece and that of the Middle Ages, succeeded, by different means, in fulfilling these imperative conditions, and the last in date, the Mediæval, without abandoning the principle, furnished probably the greatest variety of expressions that can be obtained. From the middle of the twelfth century to the end of the thirteenth, this French art produced in unparalleled abundance a multitude of architectural works in which the statuary, even when of mediocre execution, produces effects whose grandeur is incontestable. Need I mention the doorways of the abbeys of Moissac and Vezelay, the lateral porches of Notre Dame at Chartres, of the Cathedral of Bourges, of the church of St. Seurin at Bordeaux, those of the portal of the Cathedral of Amiens, and the façade of Notre Dame in Paris? Who is not familiar with or does not possess engravings or photographs of these conceptions, so marvellous both in architecture and sculpture,—conceptions in which the iconography is so well designed and the scale-relations so intelligently observed? But let us consider specimens of less pretension. The merit of a style of art is exhibited, not in certain magnificent conceptions in which resources of all kinds have abounded, but in works of a secondary rank. An age which side by side with edifices of unparalleled splendour, excessive luxury, and an exaggerated display of wealth, erects contemptible constructions worthy of barbarians—so ill designed are they, so ill executed and shapeless—cannot pass for an age of art. Art requires a breadth of atmosphere to enable it to exist. If it is reared in a hot-house it is only a curiosity, an amusement, or an object of study for the privileged few. Imagine a landlord building a magnificent conservatory, and devoting all his means and employing all the labour at his disposal in raising the rarest plants in that conservatory, but letting thistles and briers cover his fields; should we not rather see the conservatory destroyed and the land producing fine woods, harvests, and vintages? Our position as regards architecture is in this country something like that of such a landlord; we have a magnificent conservatory, but too many thistles in its neighbourhood. The life of this art, which was formerly diffused throughout our land, is concentrated in a conservatory heated and cultivated at great expense; yet after all we should certainly prefer to take our walks in groves flourishing in the open air than beneath foliage protected by glass.

As regards sculpture,—supposing that we are even too severe in our judgment in the case of two or three of our great cities,—when it makes its appearance, as it sometimes does, in our provincial municipalities, is it not grotesque? Or if, thanks to the liberality of some corporate body, it figures on a façade, has it any kind of connection with the building? Buying a statue at an Exhibition, packing it up, sending it a couple of hundred miles to be placed in a niche made in a wall ready for anything to fill it,—this is what is called encouraging the arts! Certainly it is encouraging the artist to produce a second statue, in the hope that it will have the same good luck as the first. . . . But art,—what has that to do in the matter? Yet that is what most of our sculptors are working for; I am speaking only of those who have real talent. To make a statue, or a group, at leisure in their studios, and to see the article purchased by a corporate body to be set somewhere—neither the artist who sells it, nor the corporate body that buys it, knows where. Some place or other will be found for it! And *"à statue donnée. . . ."* Are such methods of procedure likely to form a school of monumental sculpture?

Are these methods in vogue, or are they not? Is there any exaggeration in the above? Lately some reforms in the domain of the arts have been talked about. Do the public know what questions have been raised among artists in consequence? They have talked about an Exhibition,—that is, the organisation of a vast bazaar. Some are of opinion that all should be free to exhibit, others wish for a selecting jury; several—and they are not the most illogical in their proposal—supposing that the way in which the republic of arts is governed at present is reasonable—

COURS D'ARCHITECTURE.

E. Viollet-le-Duc del .

Cl . Sauvageot sc .

Imp. Lemercier et Cie Paris .

DE L'ÉGLISE DE Sᵀ PIERRE SOUS VÉZELAY

Vᵉ A. MOREL et Cⁱᵉ Éditeurs .

claim special Exhibitions for the Institute and . . . its associates ! Such a suggestion has actually been made ; it is no invention of mine. But no one has thought of inquiring whether there is not something of more urgent importance to be tried : whether the State ought to continue to act the schoolmaster towards artists, under the tutelage of a coterie, or whether it would not be more reasonable to leave this function to private enterprise. A Minister is found who undertakes during an impulse of liberalism to give liberty to artists. Each coterie in art begins to think how it can *organise* that liberty to its own advantage ; the Institute first, of course. *Organise Liberty!* A strange combination of terms. To organise liberty is equivalent to saying to any one : " You will be at liberty to get up at seven o'clock, to go at eight to the Boulevard des Italiens, to break- fast at ten at the Maison d'Or, and to go to Mr. X.'s at twelve, who will give you lessons during the rest of the day."

Thanks to the régime under which artists have long accus- tomed themselves to live, this is what they are asking under various forms. But there is one very natural way of giving artists this liberty, if there is really a wish to give it, *i.e.* for the Government to say to them : " You are free . . . and so am I. Work, enjoy all the success you can, give yourselves heartily to your calling ; I shall be the first to encourage such talents as manifest themselves, and to consider those who pro- duce works having a value recognised by all, as citizens useful to the State. But in the name of Art, I beg you to provide yourselves with instruction and tutorage in your own fashion, if you wish to be tutored !"

It follows therefore that during those periods of slavery, when the arts were not organised by the State, and when the State had neither an Academy to protect or to humour, nor a School to maintain, nor Exhibitions for Rome or Athens to be arranged for, nor directors or inspectors to appoint, nor criticism to be experienced on the part of the artists themselves or of the public respecting matters of art, there were nevertheless monuments erected in which statuary was not spared. On some of these erections sculptured figures may be reckoned, not by hundreds, but by thousands. The number is not the important considera- tion ; it only shows that the sculptors had plenty to do. But what is more to the point is that this vast quantity is so distri- buted as to give effect to the whole, and that the whole being satisfactory, clear, and easy of comprehension, its general character is reflected back in each detail, and that these works which might be considered mediocre when isolated, are not prejudicial to the general effect, but take their position in it without offending the eye. There is no need, I say once more, to give representations of these gigantic works, thoroughly familiar as they are to every one, in order to make these excellencies of combination manifest. It will serve our purpose better to select a modest edifice in a remote quarter between Burgundy and the Nivernais. In its restricted limits we shall be better able to appreciate the relations of the architectural composition, in which sculpture plays an important part. I refer to the front of the little church of St. Pierre sous Vezelay.[1] Plate XXX. gives the whole of the upper part of the front, the lower part of which has been masked by a very projecting porch of a more recent period. This front belongs to the middle of the thirteenth century, and is built of a hard stone with a fine golden tone. Originally it was painted all over. The general subject scarcely needs to be explained. At the top, Christ, seated, is being crowned by two angels; beneath his feet is St. Stephen, the patron of the diocese; at his side the Virgin and Saint Anna; next St. Peter and St. Paul; St. John, St. Andrew, and two other apostles. Nothing is wanting in this composition; neither the complete connection with the lines of the architecture, which, far from disturbing, it emphasises; nor the due relation of the statues to the whole composition; nor clearness, nor execution. The gable, arranged with a view to mask the roof, surmounts a rose window which lights the nave; which rose window, with its strong archivolt bearing this gable, is pierced above a beautiful doorway formerly ornamented by three statues. Two spires—one only is complete—terminated this dignified composition, and entered into combination with its principal lines. As will be observed, all the figures are sheltered, and are thus prevented from being stained by the rain, as too often happens in our modern buildings. Clearness, which is the chief requisite in every work of art, is indisputable here.

That the style of the building is not, as we allow, to the taste of some architects—the reason being that it possesses excellencies in which they are absolutely wanting—does not affect the point in question. I am calling attention to the general arrangement, scale-relations, the harmony between the lines of the architecture and the character of the sculpture; I am intending to show how those mediæval artists, even of the humblest order, were able to come to an understanding with each other, so as to obtain a general effect for which two arts must concur. This and none other is the principle to be observed. The sculpture is not here a superaddition,—something not contemplated from the first,— a collection of pieces taken from various studios: it belongs to the architecture as the members of the buildings itself belong to it. This is all we wish to demonstrate.

It is not in their buildings alone that this intimate union of

[1] Department of Yonne, ten miles from Avallon.

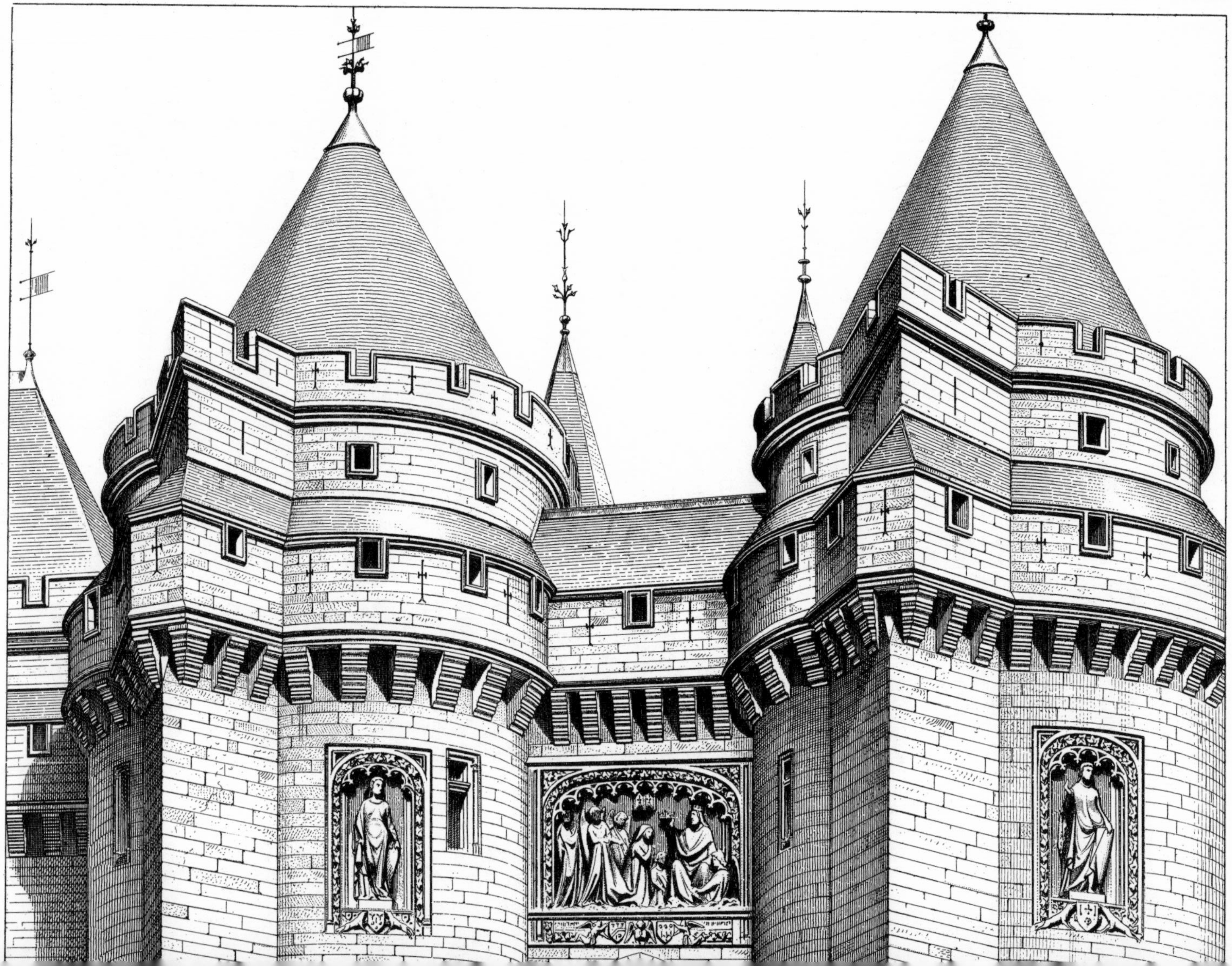

E. Viollet-Le-Duc del.

Cl. Sauvageot sc.

PORTE DU CHATEAU DE LA FERTE MILON

Vve A. MOREL et Cie Editeurs.

Imp. Lemercier et Cie Paris

FIG. 1.—Sculpture Ornamentation in the Middle Ages.

the two arts among mediæval workers can be traced—a union
tending to enhance the effect of both,—but also in many compositions to which they certainly attached no importance : we
find it in the vignettes of manuscripts, for example.   And it is
when the arts reproduce their expression in works of every kind,
not in some exceptional objects only, that we can appreciate their
real value, and say that they have become a kind of habit, that
they emanate from a principle recognised and understood by all.

In the Bibliothèque Impériale there is a manuscript of the
close of the fifteenth century, filled with miniatures of no great
account in point of execution, but in which the artist has
thought fit to introduce a great number of buildings.   It is a
Livy in French.   The painter, doubtless under the impression
that the buildings of ancient Rome were covered with sculptures, thought himself obliged to put a great number of bas-
reliefs or statues on his architecture.   Moreover, the buildings
he portrays belong entirely to his own age, and are Northern
French in style.   Well, this miniature painter has in every
case succeeded in placing the statuary on his houses, palaces,
temples, towers, etc., in the happiest and most picturesque
manner possible, to such an extent was the habit of doing
so still preserved among our artists.   A belfry tower, for
example, was to be drawn ; the miniature painter, who could
afford to be lavish of sculpture, conceived the idea of adorning
this tower (fig. 1) with two zones of statuary in full relief.
Have we not here a true idea clearly and frankly expressed ?
Certainly this artist, who was no great genius, did not ransack
his brains to invent this design : it was only the unconscious
expression, so to speak, of the art-ideas current at the time, and
these ideas were just.   Besides, he did nothing more than reproduce compositions similar to those which met his eyes.   The
gateway of the Château de la Ferté-Milon furnishes proof
of this.   This portal is one of the finest conceptions of feudal
architecture in the Middle Ages, which is so varied in character,
and in which the decorative parts harmonise so well with the
imperative necessities of defence, and the severe aspect which
is appropriate to buildings of this kind.   Plate XXXI. gives
the perspective view of this gateway, whose plan and section are
given, to make the whole more intelligible, in figure 2.   This
drawing shows that the large archway which unites the two great
towers is an immense machicolation adorned outside with a bas-
relief representing the crowning of the Virgin.   In the castles
built by Louis of Orleans, about the year 1400, there is always a
design taken from the history of the Virgin on the façade.   At
Pierrefonds it is the Annunciation.   This is, however, of little
importance ; it is the composition viewed as sculpture with

FIG. 2.—Gateway of the Château de la Ferté-Milon.

which we are here concerned. Each of the towers was moreover adorned with a colossal statue of one of the nine *Preuses*,[1] in the same way as in the Château de Pierrefonds the towers were ornamented by the statues of the *Preux:* this was a method of designating them,—giving them a name. It will be observed that the niches which surround these statues are placed laterally, and on the same side relatively to the salient projections or buttresses which fortify these towers against sapping, and strengthen the flankings. An arrangement suggested by defensive precautions has caused these buttresses to be placed obliquely (see the plan), and the architect has placed the statues on the side which fronts that part of the neighbourhood whence the castle was most seen. We have artists here who concern themselves little with symmetry, but who have a marvellous appreciation of picturesque effect, which the Greeks did not disdain. This placard style of decoration on the walls of a tower may seem strange to some, and will appear not to have required any great effort of imagination. But it is precisely this audacity (if I may be allowed the term), this defiant simplicity of design, which infallibly produces its effect. This is one of those *naïvetés* which characterise people who know very well what they are about, and what they mean to accomplish ; and it is by no means so easy to be *naïf*—in the modern acceptation of the word—as many persons suppose, without falling into a false simplicity, which of all affectations is the most intolerable. And while the composition of sculpture applied to public buildings during the best mediæval period in France is noteworthy in respect of the frankness with which the design is carried out, and its perfect accordance with the structure, the execution is not less worthy of attention, for the execution always harmonises with the place and the object. The artists worked on the edifice itself, or close by it, without ever losing sight of the position their work was to occupy ; and, careful to make their works accord with the architecture, they seemed to conceive and to execute their designs under the influence of one single idea. I should not dare to assert that the architect had authority and knowledge sufficient to superintend the sculptural design and the execution himself ; but the result shows that the understanding between him and the sculptors was sufficiently perfect to suggest the idea of a single directing power. We cannot doubt that such an understanding existed among the

---

[1] The *Preuses,*—nine feminine types of knighthood in the Middle Ages ; their names (partly recognisable in Classic story) were : *Tammaris,* queen of Egypt, *Deifemme, Lamprédo, Hippolyte,* queen of the Amazons, *Semiramis, Penthesilea, Tancqua, Deisille,* and *Menalippe.* The *Preux,*—nine masculine types of knighthood ; their names were : *Joshua, David, Judas Maccabæus, Alexander the Great, Hector of Troy, Julius Cæsar, Charlemagne, Arthur,* and *Godefroy de Bouillon.*—*Tr.*

Greeks—a circumstance which in no way detracted from the value of the sculpture. Sculptors are therefore mistaken in supposing that they should confine their attention to the piece of statuary intrusted to them, and that the merit of their work is independent of the place assigned it. But we will quit the subject of general adaptation, on which enough has been said, and discuss the execution.

The larger the scale of a work in statuary, and the farther from the eye it is destined to be placed, the more simply ought it to be treated. I know that the production of the grand and simple is no easy matter, but I believe that I am justified in saying that the accomplishment of such a result requires very simple means in the execution. Let us revert to Antiquity. The Egyptians treated statuary with a simplicity proportioned to the size of the scale. And we observe the same principle in the few really Greek works we possess. Those admirable artists pushed to its utmost limits the art of sacrificing in the execution all that is not indispensable to the expression of the form. None of their monuments give a clearer idea of the way in which the Ancients were able to treat colossal sculpture than the statues cut in the mountains forming the entrance to the great Speos at Abou Sembil, on the banks of the Nile, in Nubia.[1] The grand characteristic lines of the figures are alone preserved; the type only is retained intact; all that is mere detail is suppressed. And yet if we examine these colossi attentively, we shall perceive that the execution is extremely delicate; the shaping is at once broad and fine, treated *con amore*, but without the artist allowing himself, though master of his chisel, to be led into doing more than was absolutely necessary. Some fragments of colossal Egyptian statues, cut in granite and deposited in the British Museum, exhibit the same excellencies in a still higher degree. We have always a simple profile, easy to be perceived and engraven in the memory, and a shaping which seems to clothe the details with an envelope, allowing them to be surmised, but clearly exhibiting only the principal features.

We find also these essentially monumental characteristics in the nude figures on the tympanum of the Parthenon, with a beauty in the selection of the forms which human genius cannot surpass.

Moreover, in the best monumental sculptures of Antiquity, we never see a violent or false gesture, or an expression savouring of grimace. We have here a sifting, as it were, of the works of nature, in which insignificant details and vulgar points are put aside so that the principal idea,—that which

---

[1] See the *Atlas des Photographies de l'Egypte*, published by M. Felix Teynard.

deserves to arrest the mind, and which manifests the conception by the simplest process,—may alone be expressed. To fulfil these conditions, the artist must not only possess manual skill but have comprehended the philosophical aspect of his art, if we may so term it ; he must have analysed the effects produced on beings animated by instincts, passions, and feelings, and must have known how to distinguish from among such effects those which have really an immediate connection with the individual organism, from those which result from social habitudes. The lower animals never make a false gesture ; we cannot say as much for man, whom his education, social environment, dress, and the fashion of the day, often reduce to the condition of a cleverly-jointed puppet. But he who can look within this puppet—and we may take for granted that there were some such at Athens—will discover the man, the reality ; as, beneath caprices, follies, and vices we may find the human conscience. Skill, in the case of the sculptor, as in that of the mental philosopher, consists in searching for and discovering, the former the true gesture, the real material expression of a feeling, the other that innermost recess in the soul which does not change, and to which we accord the name Conscience. Some critics are severe in their condemnation of *Realism*, and perhaps their severity is justifiable ; but they should say in what respect it is blameworthy, a thing they rarely do. To blame *Realism* because it assumes to take Nature just as it is, and to reproduce it literally, is to reply by repeating the question itself, and to offer no solution. The fact is that *Realism* is no nearer to Nature than is a mere academical model. The one perceives and reproduces nothing more than an appearance, which is not the truth ; the other puts in place of it a conventional form understood only by those to whom that form has become familiar, and for whom it can be substituted for Nature. I will endeavour to make myself understood by an example.

You see a person who is in appearance vulgar, and whose features are irregular : but beneath these features and appearance there is an expression, a result of habit, which dominates the whole ; we have what is called the physiognomy. Now the painter or the sculptor who possesses talent can produce a real portrait of this person,—a portrait more true than nature itself, —if he seizes that physiognomy, that dominant expression ; if he brings it into prominence while disregarding the vulgar or repulsive details through which it has difficulty in making its way ; and he will produce a work of art. The Realist, or at least he to whom this epithet is applied, will allow himself to be so dominated by the coarse envelope ; he will render it with so absolute a material truth,—a scepticism so absolute,—that his production will exhibit no trace of that passing flame which sometimes illuminates the original. He will not, it is true, have substituted a conventional type for the original, but he will have painted the lantern without introducing the light it holds. One of the most profoundly cherished pleasures of the artist is to regard with attention a person who passes for plain, awkward, or uncultivated, and to discover in this model, presented to him by chance, springs of beauty and grace which escape the notice of most people, and to say to himself that with these imperfect elements a remarkably beautiful work might be produced; and to consider by what succession of efforts, and with what labour of elimination and selection, he could arrive at this result. This is the method of observation according to which the Greeks proceeded. For they were as far removed—*i.e.* during their best periods —from commonplace conventionality as from coarse realism. While they knew how to seek for and discover the beautiful even amid the repulsive—and to find the beautiful, one only needs to be a passionate lover of it,—they had an aversion for mere copying. The beautiful lives in the Greek; it is not merely embalmed, but it lives in virtue of a careful selection, by setting aside what might tarnish it with affectation or vulgarity, contemptible details and puerile refinements; and it is as much in point of execution as composition that Greek sculpture entered on this path, being, however, the first to abandon archaic traditions and to emancipate art from them. It was indeed not long able to maintain itself in this lofty position, but the value of a period of art is not limited to its duration. It remains for us to treat of the conditions under which monumental statuary produces certain preconceived effects.

We need scarcely remind our readers that it is light which gives its effect to statuary. The sculptor should therefore take account of the result it will produce in his work. It is evident, for instance, that a statue illuminated directly by the sun's rays will have quite a different appearance from what it would have if lighted by reflection; the execution of the statue should therefore be different in the one case from what it would be in the other. But if, as often happens, the statue is carved without the artist's knowing the place that will be allotted it, how can he take account of this difference in executing it? and if he does not take account of it, will chance be sufficient to rely on? I do not believe the Greeks carved statues without having their destination precisely determined, before the time of the Roman dominion,—*i.e.* before the invasion of the Roman amateurs, who had more vanity than taste for art. I am certain, from the examples now existing, that the sculptors in the Middle Ages never carved a statue or a bas-relief without knowing where their works would be placed. In this respect it is they who might justly regard us as barbarians. Beneath the sky of Attica the atmosphere is so perfectly transparent, and the light so brilliant, that the artists of that country could reckon on constant effects of light and shade which are unattainable in our less favoured climate. But it must also be observed that to give their statuary its full effect, even when cut in white marble, they required the aid of painting. Thus the grounds of the metopes and tympanums were always painted, and the figures themselves were at least set off and adorned with painted, gilded, or metallic accessories. There was therefore no reason to fear lest at a distance these sculptures should be lost in the shadows thrown by the projection of the cornices. Besides, we can easily see that the sculptors took account of the position and of the difference between direct and reflected light, from the manner in which the figure is treated. This is clearly evident, for example, in the interior friezes of the portico of the Parthenon, which could never be lighted except by reflected rays, or seen except from immediately below. The surfaces intended to catch the light so as to bring the form into due relief are often inclined in a contrary direction to the natural shape. The caryatides of the Pandrosium placed in full light are treated in such a manner that the parts which strongly exhibit the posture present wide smooth surfaces, while those which are to be kept in the background are covered with details which always give shadow wherever the light may come from.[1] The same principle may be observed in the beautiful fragments taken from the little temple of the Wingless Victory, which was likewise exposed to full light.

But the north of France is not under such favourable atmospheric conditions. Sunlight is often absent; and thick fogs make the solar rays feeble and pallid. If bas-reliefs were placed on one of our buildings in the same position as the friezes of the portico of the Parthenon, we should see them perhaps for a fortnight altogether in the year; during the rest of the time these sculptures would be plunged in obscurity. In our country therefore, sculptors would be obliged to adopt a very different plan. While on account of the intensity of the light the Greeks thought it necessary to colour the backgrounds of their bas-reliefs in order that the parts of the latter which were in light might not be confounded with those backgrounds, this expedient in our country would not be sufficient from the contrary cause, viz., the diffusion of the light. The figures themselves must have a relief sufficiently strong to enable them to detach

[1] See the seventh Lecture, fig. 15.

themselves from the backgrounds independently of the colouring of the latter; or the backgrounds themselves must have an intensity distinguishing them well from the figures by diaperings or powderings. The free surfaces of these backgrounds must also have been reduced as much as possible, in order to cover them with shadows by the strong projection given to the figures. And this the sculptor of the twelfth and thirteenth centuries never failed to do.

These artists had observed that a statue isolated in front of a line of wall in our climate soon gets a darker colouring than that of the background, and that instead of standing out brightly on it, it forms a dark spot,—a very disagreeable effect; so they very rarely placed statues in such a position, and when they thought necessary to do so they always accompanied these figures by supports or very salient uprights and canopies, which, while they sheltered them, gave them a sufficiently toned surrounding to allow them to stand out clearly. We may also imagine statues advantageously placed along a smooth line of wall though destitute of a surrounding that would give them a dark background, because the shadows thrown by these figures themselves on the line of wall will detach them and give them sufficient relief. But what effect do we suppose can be obtained if we place statues in front of a wall pierced with windows, for example? These statues stained with damp and casting no shadow on the distant wall, standing out sometimes against a pier, sometimes against a window, will produce in perspective only the appearance of confused and disagreeable spots, offending the eye. This unfortunate effect is only too evident on the interior façades of the new Louvre above the portico, and we may rest assured that the architecture would gain by the removal of an ornamentation as inappropriate as it is costly. The execution of figures thus placed must at any rate be treated with extreme simplicity; it must present to the daylight broad surfaces adapted to arrest the sun's rays, conditions to which the sculptors who have cut these figures in their studios have not thought proper to subject themselves, and which the architect, occupied with other cares, has not thought fit to impose on them.

We could wish that architects and sculptors who consider the study of the antique as the first, most essential, and most fertile in results—in which they are right—should at least put in practice those principles which ancient works most clearly exhibit. But they are far from doing so. This love of the antique is purely Platonic; or rather it establishes a kind of privilege or monopoly, under cover of which those who turn the monopoly to their own account with the sanction of the Government allow themselves the most singular eccentricities. They make their appeal to antiquity and pronounce pompous eulogiums on its arts in academical discourses,—but without examining their merits, which it would be dangerous for them to do, as it might lead to unfortunate comparisons; they usurp, as it were, an exclusive right of speaking of ancient art, and affect to despise all that lies outside the pale of that art embodied as a dogma which must be believed without examination. They profess to consider the schools of Rome and Athens as corner-stones of education in the arts; but when it comes to practice, the instruction thus derived seems to have been of scarcely any use to those who extol it so highly. This reminds us of that kind of hypocrisy which is pretty much in vogue nowadays, which consists in observing religious duties as far as appearance goes, *i.e.* before children, the poor people in the village, and servants, but throwing off the mask in the society of our equals. If you admire ancient art, why not adopt its most essential principles in your own works? On the other hand, if you do not adopt them, why set yourselves up for high priests of its arts and the sole participants in its mysteries? Observe, I do not insist on its being necessary to imitate antiquity servilely, but only to build on its principles, which are, moreover, the principles of art in all its best periods. We must, however, have a clear understanding in the matter, and not be constantly equivocating. I would not say that you are intentionally speculating on the credulity, ignorance or indifference of the public, and behind the respectable announcement that appears on your house-front, allowing yourselves all sorts of extravaganzas,—laughing at the simple public which was to pay for them; but we might easily believe it to be so. For you certainly will not find in any ancient building, or even in the Renaissance period, and most assuredly not in the Middle Ages, decorative expedients in any way analogous to those you generally adopt in your architecture. I see in the latter—and I am not the only one who does so—only a feeble reminiscence of the work of the seventeenth century, without its grandeur and unity; and in addition an aggravation of the defects inherent in the arts of that period, with an absolute confusion in the design, and a not less absolute want of comprehension of decorative effects. What, for instance, is the meaning of those heaps of twisted conglomerations of figures on those copings, distorted to such a degree, that with the help of damp and moss it soon becomes difficult to make anything of those convolutions of bodies and limbs? Do we see anything like this in ancient work? Certainly not; anything intended to stand out in profile on the sky is treated in the simplest and most easily comprehensible manner, both as a whole and in its details. Have we here anything new? Does this belong to that Art of the Future which has been promised us? No; for we have discovered similar abuses in the worst designs of Italian art at the decline of the renaissance. Is this what you have gone to Rome to study? It may be so; but then do not say anything about ancient art, least of all that of Greece! What then are your principles? Where have you obtained them? From no quarter. Are they derived from your own imagination? That is equivalent to saying you have no principles at all! Then do not talk to us of great traditions and the necessity of preserving them. Do not set yourselves up for licensed defenders of those traditions if you are the foremost to disregard them; but frankly come out with the confession that you are making a monopoly of this uncritical study of Antiquity for your own advantage, under the protection of the Government which is simple enough to believe you, on your own unproved assertion, to be the indispensable defenders of doctrines which you do not practise, and which are only a mask.

Rarely has any period so much used and abused sculpture in public buildings as our own. Has the result to the public been a more delicate taste or a more determinate judgment in matters of art? The contrary effect has, I fear, been produced. The public take no interest in the separate designs which interest the studios, unless attention is loudly called to some particular works; it only sees and judges of entire compositions. If these want clearness or harmony it passes by with indifference, and in its function as the public it does so with reason. Artists find fault with it, despise it as ignorant, and groan over the decline of taste; but they are in the wrong. What the public requires— and will always justly require—is that it shall comprehend without effort what is produced for it,—that is, that the parts of a building shall not be isolated from the whole. It wishes to find its gratification in the whole, and has not the leisure to find out whether in a work which to its eyes and thoughts is confused, there are some creditable parts, any more than it will listen patiently to five acts of a drama which is on the whole ill-conceived and obscure, but in which two or three good scenes occur.

Finding fault with the public is an easy method of criticism; but when a country like France possesses Academies of Art, and keeps up a school of art at great expense, if that public, instead of finding an interest in the productions furnished by those schools and academies, seeks satisfaction for its tastes elsewhere, —if it attaches a continually increasing value to nicknacks to which time has given in its eyes a kind of consecration; if fashion turns to works of second-rate merit, it is because you— academies and schools—do not fulfil the mission to which you were called; in fact that you yourselves are useless. If therefore the State continues to support you, it is from motives foreign to art ; it is in deference to certain traditions respecting whose worth it is mistaken, or more manifestly—much more manifestly, I might say—from personal considerations. We must not hoodwink ourselves in the matter ; whenever the State occupies itself with questions pertaining to the domain of intellect outside the political sphere, it regards persons alone. Its interest is not to quarrel with certain corporations which might give it trouble, but to humour them so as to make use of them in case of need. As to principles beyond the sphere of politics and public morals, it has but a trifling interest in them, or rather it does not at all understand them—it finds them troublesome. The State is consequently made a tool of by the corporate bodies which it professes to protect and hold in tutelage, and on that account it should not give them any special countenance other than that which is due from it to all citizens.

LECTURE XVII.

DOMESTIC ARCHITECTURE.

THE disastrous events which have just taken place, long fore-seen by those who did not allow themselves to be dazzled by a prosperity more brilliant than solid, must exert a radical influence on our moral and social existence, and our system of instruction, if we would not see our unfortunate country abandoned to rapid decay. We cannot but be convinced now that luxury does not constitute true greatness, and that privileges accorded to an official system of instruction, relieved from responsibility, are far from satisfying all the requirements of our times, and only insure us, when a crisis comes, the exposure of our inferiority before our rivals, by giving us a confidence in our resources which actual experiment fails to justify. How often during these unhappy days, marked each of them by deplorable miscalculations, have we not had to witness the incompetency of those privileged bodies which, as their partisans asserted, were to have secured us in every department a superiority over our neighbours. Government, war, arts, and sciences, everything in fact, was placed under the control of irresponsible bodies infatuated with confidence in their doctrines and regulations—rejecting the aid of private enterprise, assuming itself capable of sufficiency for everything and preserving us from all dangers. In the face of disasters which successively have overwhelmed us, what have our institutions—the envy of Europe, as it was as-serted—done for us? They have not only left the country absolutely destitute, but have obstructed the action of private enterprise; in the very presence of the enemy they have still found time to bring personal squabbles into the foreground and to defend privilege and routine inch by inch. Not having been able to prevent or even to foresee these disasters, but having with proud disdain opposed all reform and resisted all appeals on the part of liberal minds, they have dragged down with them-selves to ruin even those who were combating their despotic doctrines. All they think of is their own safety, and we must consider ourselves fortunate if they do not make us solely responsible for the disasters of which they are among the principal causes.

Even now, when a humiliating peace has been imposed upon us, and a vagabond horde has all but destroyed the capital of France, and has played a drama before the eyes of Europe, in which folly and brutishness have succeeded by violence in producing a reign of terror, there are still those who venture to thrust their foolish personality into the foreground. Only a few months have passed away since the disastrous interval when our country—crushed beneath the heel of Germany—and dishonoured by bands of drunkards, was at the point of desperation, yet already the same pretensions are beginning to show themselves. Those who had disappeared during the storm, reappear, like flies after a summer shower, to trouble us with their importunate assumption to govern the domain of thought, which, as they affirmed, they were officially commissioned to protect, but which they have exposed to the utmost peril. Let us not deceive ourselves: our country needs a regeneration, and it is by sound instruction alone that this can be accomplished. Crushed beneath the weight of our errors, our indifference and moral weakness, overborne by an enemy whose power equals his animosity, it is from ourselves alone that we must look for retaliating power by means of education, instruction, and labour. To hide from the country at such a time the gravity of the evil which has long been eating out its life, is to determine to perpetuate that evil,—in fact it is to fall into the lowest grade among civilised people. We have reached that period of decline which has manifested itself in former civilisations. If what is called the Latin race does not make one last effort, its fate is sealed. Let us have the courage to examine the wound in clear daylight, to sound its depth, and, if necessary, to apply the red-hot iron; otherwise the mortification will advance. Incapacity and mere routine in the higher strata of society, effeminacy and nonchalance in the middle class, and envy and ignorance at the lower extremity of the scale,—this is a fair general view of the state of our affairs. And it is at the lower extremity that the regeneration must begin; the general level of a nation is raised only by the instruction and education of the lower strata. In rising they force the rest to rise. To work therefore! and without delay! It is for men of energy and intelligence—if any such are left among us—to abandon all those prejudices which up to this very moment may have seemed to be valuable traditions, to leave sterile discussions to the unemployed, to regard serious, practical, rational study as the true element of all intellectual work, and to diffuse the love of study of this kind around them, and no longer to deal with colleges or corporate bodies, but with capacity—wherever it may spring from.

And what can we as architects do ? Are we going to continue our old courses in the midst of a ruined country, still shuddering at the insults that have been inflicted, despairing and seeking some way of safety—(the courses, I was going to say, of the past century,—so great seeming to be the distance between to-day and the opening months of the year 1870) ? Are we—regardless of what our actual necessities and the administration of the public finances counsel—to continue to translate into stone the most ridiculous caprices, to mock with ill-timed display the mourning aspect of the country, and flatter the follies of that part of the public which sees in our recent misfortunes only a temporary check on its love for appearances, vain pomp and a leisurely and easy-going existence ?

I am aware that there will be found among us some of those who have always taken refuge behind these three words :—I am paid !! (panders too are paid), and who are always flatterers of the most perverted intellects, the most foolish vanities, and the most unwarrantable presumption ; and who, clever as well as compliant, will contrive to carry out the most ridiculous schemes. But I believe that there will also be architects,—and they alone are worthy of the name,—who will persistently oppose the evil tendencies of the past, and respect the dignity of their profession. The position of an architect towards his client is not that of a mere executor of the ideas, fancies, and whims of the latter. He is also an adviser ; and the talent he possesses should never be prostituted to the carrying out of an idea that is false, ridiculous, or injurious to the real interests of his clients. This talent should never condescend to satisfy foolish conditions. Talent is invested with a certain dignity ; and, as a writer, if he is an honourable man, will not lend his pen to the expression of thoughts whose tendency is unwholesome, or which seem to him erroneous, I do not see how an architect can, without dishonour, use the money of his client to the detriment of the interests confided to him, even at the express order of the man who pays him.

I hear it said on all sides, since the sad experience through which we have been passing, that every one ought to endeavour to stimulate the intellectual vigour of the country, which has long been depressed. But assuredly it is in great measure to the enfeeblement of the moral sense,—to shameful compliances with what conscience really disapproves, that we owe our misfortunes. However subordinate may be the part which the Architect has to sustain in this indispensable reformation, he ought to make a point of sustaining it well ; and if all those among us who have preserved a love for their country, who do not make the gain which a commission offers them their chief consideration,—who retain some dignity of character,—comprehend the duties incumbent on our profession, perhaps they will lose some of those capricious clients, but they will consolidate the position we ought to take, and will avoid being subjected to that contempt which sooner or later will overwhelm buffoons and parasites.

There has been a good deal of building in France both on the part of the State, municipal bodies and private persons, during the past twenty years. Do the results answer exactly to our social condition? No reflecting person will fail to answer in the negative at once. But if we examine that social condition or rather its external appearance carefully, we shall soon observe that the love of the false, the vulgar luxury, the shameless display of vanity, that appear in our public and private buildings, correspond with one of the most strongly marked tendencies of recent times. Indeed, a vigorous temperament and a singularly firm character is required for resisting the tendency to snatch at easy successes gained by any means whatever. "Making an appearance" has been the order of the day; for appearance has been readily taken for reality, and the tailor has made the man more perhaps than at any other time. The question has been who should make the most show. If some were contented to remain inconspicuous in the midst of this factitious splendour, many who understood the world better, or who were less scrupulous, were content with this brilliant surface. A downfall more sudden than ever occurred in the midst of a highly polished society has laid bare the vices of this social condition; and Paris presents the singular spectacle, unique in history, of a city partly laid in ruins in the very midst of its splendour, and exhibiting among the débris new public buildings, mansions and ordinary houses (untouched by the barbarians whose mission it has been to recall us to the reality of existence), but whose *raison d'être* no longer exists.

History has seen rich and prosperous cities gradually falling into oblivion,—cities whose life seems to have slowly abandoned them; which—Venice for example—present to the traveller's gaze their empty and ruined palaces, slowly corroded by time, without care on the part of man, distracted by thoughts of other things, to suspend its action. Their present aspect is melancholy; but these palaces, which now appear empty sepulchres, were once peopled by young and vigorous beings: they recall a brilliant past—a firmly established splendour; and though in presence of such desolation we are naturally induced to meditate on the fleetingness of human things, there yet remains in our minds the certainty that all we see has had a rational basis of existence,—has really lived. We have before us an old and dusty book, with many a discoloration from decay, but which we may still read with profit. But our poor Paris presents to the eyes of the philosopher a much more depressing spectacle. Amid its ruins, blackened by incendiary fires, arise public and private edifices whose apparent splendour seems an anachronism. We begin to ask ourselves for whom and why this luxury has been displayed. Is it for those barbarians *within the walls* who regret that they have not been able to destroy the whole city? Or is it for an extinct race—a proscribed aristocracy? What can be the meaning of this splendour, side by side with these ruins? Why has it been paraded? These mansions are empty, these public buildings serve no clearly defined purpose; these luxurious houses shelter only a few scattered tenants who seem ashamed to inhabit them. The magnificent portals remain closed. Silence reigns in these newly built mansions, which have no time-honoured associations, but remind us of enchanted palaces, silent and deserted, whose state is kept up by invisible genii. It must be acknowledged that this luxury is of a debased character: it did not correspond with the realities of our social condition, it formed a veil for the most corrupted part of its surface.

This we may regard as indisputable, and let it serve as a warning to us to produce no more anachronisms in stone.

If we inquire into the history of the past, we shall find that however debased any period may have been, there was not a private house that did not answer to the requirements of the civilisation under whose auspices it was built. In the Ancient World, both in Asia and in the West during the Mediæval period, the dwellings were the veritable garb, so to speak, of the manners, customs and modes of living of those who occupied them. It is not till we come down to our own times, whose aspect presents so much of confusion in all departments of culture, that we find a schism often manifest, and always inexplicable, between the daily occupations and needs of the people and the character of their habitations. I will not pursue the question as to the false ideas that have conducted us to this point; it is sufficient to prove the fact that nine times in ten the habitations erected among ourselves do not accord with our requirements, customs or incomes. This it will be easy to demonstrate.

We must first classify the dwellings of the period according to the various kinds.

In the cities we have, *first*, mansions, *i.e.* houses occupied by a single family, belonging to the wealthy; *secondly*, houses of less pretension, but which are also intended for single families of moderate income; *thirdly*, houses occupied by more than one tenant, which form the majority of private dwellings in Paris. Suburban habitations comprise, *first*, villas, *secondly*, country houses. Châteaux we need not remark upon, as they have been already considered in this work.

It need not be observed that the arrangements of these various kinds of dwellings differ essentially from each other, and that consequently their appearance ought to present various aspects.

But let us consider domestic architecture at an earlier epoch, without absolutely going back to antiquity, to which we have paid sufficient attention in the course of these Lectures, and whose features less concern us, inasmuch as—though we have positive data respecting the houses in a provincial town such as Pompeii, and though we know that there were at Rome houses several stories high, whose suites of rooms were let to several tenants—we have only very vague information respecting the latter.

Large houses with several flats do not date from a high antiquity; until the sixteenth century, each house in France was occupied by a single family. Those who had no house of their own used to lodge in hostelries or groups of houses belonging to feudal lords, chapters, or convents which let such premises, often furnished. In fact there were no special arrangements for providing hired dwellings. The custom of building premises for such a purpose does not date further back than the seventeenth century. Have the requirements of such buildings ever been satisfactorily met? Certainly not; though in this respect our modern houses are better arranged, as far as such requirements are concerned, than were those of the time of Louis XIII. Can it be said that they fully supply the desideratum? Not yet. Can the problem be solved? Assuredly: but we must abandon routine and æsthetic traditions, which have no place here, if we would solve it. But let us pursue the order just indicated, and begin with what we designate mansions.

Mansions are generally isolated, that is to say, are not connected as buildings with a neighbouring edifice; or at least the points of connection are of trifling importance. They have their roadways, and often their gardens. The sixteenth, seventeenth, and eighteenth centuries erected mansions in great numbers, which completely satisfied the requirements of their inhabitants; we have some still, but we may assert that the most ancient are the best arranged—those built at a time when the mania for symmetry had not yet seized the court and the city.

The mansion was erected between the courtyard and the garden, had all its openings for light on the inner side, and had only its entrance gate and some outbuildings on the public way, which at that time was often narrow.   It was a rare thing for its buildings to be more than one room deep, so that the chief apartments opened on the court and the garden.   Private life was less retired than it is now among persons of high rank, and it was not necessary to provide those complicated arrangements for privacy, which, entering as they now do into our requirements, are out of harmony with the monumental grandeur which is some-times affected.   The arrangements in those mansions were very simple : a vestibule, from which rose the principal flight of stairs, the hall in which the friends of the house assembled, and the ante-chamber which then actually led to the bed-chambers, with their dressing-rooms and wardrobes.   The ancient arrangement of seigneurial habitations, which were always divided into two distinct parts, was still kept up : there was a part more open to the public, and a part reserved for family habitation.   This custom might even be traced to classical antiquity.   In the wing were the pantries, kitchens, servants' hall, butler's room, etc.   The kitchens were as far as possible from the rooms for the family, and were well ventilated.   The servants' staircases were numerous, and always placed so as to allow attendants to reach rooms in the upper stories easily.   The *Hôtel de Lionne*, built by Le Vaux, in the *Rue des Petits Champs*, presents a typical habitation of this order in the seventeenth century.   The plan of this mansion is given in the *grand Marot*.[1]

We gain a living glimpse as it were of the manners and customs of the persons who inhabited such dwellings, on seeing this plan.   We observe that a great number of domestics were needed, for the ground is very extensive.   We see great care shown to isolate the private apartments from the noise of the streets without, and that caused by the servants within, and there are easy communications from these apartments by private staircases.   The stable and coach-house yard is entirely separated, with issues conducting to the street, and a roadway to the grand court.

The front is well arranged, so as to command the garden, with flankings which give various views, and make the most of the sunlight.   Square returns, well managed, so as to furnish the lights required for each department, and an ingenious arrange-ment of the partition walls so as to avoid too great bearings.   As regards the façades, their ornamentation is sober and the lines pleasing to the eye.

At the present day we are building mansions whose extent and importance are equal to those of the *hôtel* we have selected from amongst a hundred similar ones.   Now, will these

[1] *Architecture française.*   Paris, 1727.

new constructions give future generations a perfectly exact notion of the habits of our higher classes ? I fear not. In them we observe many reminiscences of the past : a remarkable affectation of sumptuousness, often accompanied by mediocre execution ; an outside of monumental appearance concealing *bourgeois* habits, which are far from censurable, but which should, for that very reason, not be disguised ; comfort, of no very dignified type, ensconcing itself as it may beneath exteriors of simple grandeur having no correspondence with that luxuriously snug privacy which society in our days most covets. We observe no form presenting the true expression of our actual manners and customs, and but little of invention. A single example will show the truth of this criticism.

Until nearly the middle of the last century, the higher classes rarely paid visits except in sedan-chairs. Coaches were employed only for journeys into the country, or for traversing the city. If visits of compliment were to be paid or invitations had been accepted, the sedan-chair was the usual vehicle for both sexes. These chairs were brought into the vestibules, where the visitors or guests were set down without having to fear the crumpling of their toilets or inconvenience from rain ; at that time there was no need of awnings to preserve visitors or guests from the inclemency of the weather, and the façades displayed their majestic proportions to the courts.

When sedan-chairs were abandoned in favour of coaches, as the latter were not able to enter the vestibules, the arrangements of the grand entrances had to be changed ; awnings projecting from these vestibules had to be put up to preserve visitors from rain and wind ; and this was done. These awnings were called *marquises*. The grand fronts were somewhat the worse for the change, but the interests of wigs and costly toilets had to be consulted, and architectural requirements must yield to necessity. The Revolution of 1792 followed, and then more mansions were demolished and pillaged than were constructed. But when the regular course of things was resumed—*i.e.* when for equality in misery inequality in wealth was substituted by the nature of things—when some were a little less miserably poor, and others had become very rich, mansions began to be built again for the latter. This was towards the close of the Directory. There was then an impulse given to art, which though not a very powerful one, at least bore in the direction of attempting something new, and particularly insisted on not imitating the style immediately preceding the Revolution. But architects were for introducing too many of the columnar *orders* of Pæstum, and convenience suffered from it. With the help of a hearty good-will, however, some tolerably successful attempts were made.   And, as a substitute for *mar-quises*,—to obviate the necessity of putting them up, and thus spoiling the rows of columns,—they opened entrances to the vestibules under the passages of the court gates, which insured sufficient protection against the rain, but not against the currents of air.   Inflammation of the lungs was therefore much in vogue.   Gradually, at the Restoration, but more especially immediately afterwards, the opinion prevailed that every build-ing which did not resemble the ancient hôtels of the Faubourg St. Germain was unworthy of the name.   Architects again set themselves to copy those ancient dwellings.   But what of the *marquises*? . . . They continued, and they continue still to put them up in a way suggesting that, in building the mansions, they had not been contemplated.   They were tacked on, just as the case allowed, to the architecture.   Very few architects endeavoured to introduce these accessories into their original designs as an absolute desideratum dictated by a constant and imperious necessity.

I fancy if the great architects of the age of Louis Quatorze, who built such handsome mansions, had been required to consider the *marquise* in their plans they would have in-vented something better than those glass and iron cages which combine so awkwardly with architecture in stone.   This is a mere detail, I freely admit ; but this detail itself indicates how little inventive faculty we possess, and how easy it is to acquire the name of architect ; since, to gain the title, it is considered sufficient to imitate forms belonging to a period whose habits differ from our own, and to seek for arrangements and distri-butions behind these forms which any one might draw with a stick on the ground, simply following his own particular ideas of things.

What architect is there who has not had a visit from a client exhibiting a plan, and addressing him in some such words as the following :—"Here, sir, is the plan of a mansion which Madame —— and myself have thought out : it corresponds exactly with our wishes.   Each part of the building occupies the place which our habits of life require ; be so kind therefore as to build us this : we wish moreover that the parts should be built in the style of Louis XVI. and the interiors to be Renais-sance."   Take care not to tell such a client that his arrange-ments are utterly absurd, that the fireplaces cannot find flues and the staircases are impassable, and that the Renaissance and Louis XVI. have nothing to do with each other.   Or if you do thus expostulate, you may be sure your client will find another architect more complaisant and more sparing of his criticisms.

All clients indeed are not of this stamp, and many (having

furnished a programme of their requirements) leave the architect to do the best he can with it. In such a case it is his duty to endeavour to make architecture comply with the programme and not to insist on emulating mansions built in the time of Louis XIV., Louis XV., or even Louis XVI.

We might compile a long catalogue of the blunders caused by this mania for imitation,—this obligation to subject arrangements, absolutely new in character, to external appearances which have no longer a sufficient reason for their reproduction. The English, who are a little less vain than ourselves, and more practical, although possessing only a mediocre natural taste, understand better than we do how to make the best of conditions suggested by their daily habits. At least they rarely affect in their exteriors that monumental grandeur which is so out of keeping with the domestic habits of our times.

One may pass ten times in front of mansions in London which are sumptuously furnished and wonderfully well arranged to suit the requirements of their occupants, without suspecting that their so simple fronts, of no architectural pretension, belong to premises which are admirably distributed and ornamented, and in which life can be very conveniently passed.

Each nation has its particular tastes, and we do not assert that it is binding on us to affect in the exteriors of our mansions a puritanical simplicity which contravenes our natural dispositions ; but let us at least avoid absolutely excluding common sense (which is never detrimental) from our dwellings, even though they be of princely splendour, and let us try to make their external appearance—since we make a point of external appearance,—correspond with the arrangements within. Nations quite as much inclined as ourselves to love external splendour and to show their taste, perhaps also their vanity, have succeeded in producing that agreement. We ourselves have not always thus repudiated reason and common sense ; we have been able to display invention and a judicious application of architectural art to our needs and habits. If we go to the Grand Canal in Venice, we shall observe that the palaces built at the same epoch present a striking analogy.

There is no need to enter these dwellings to divine at once the internal arrangements or to know how the inhabitants lived in them, or what were their daily customs. Never were the requirements of the case more faithfully complied with. It is well known that the mansions or palaces of Venice generally overlook on one side a canal and on the other a *calle* or road for foot-passengers. A long vestibule traverses the building from one side to the other, with one or two water-entrances and one on the land side. On the right and left are the dependencies : the porter's

E. Viollet-Le-Duc del.

COUPE PERSPECTIV

Vᵉ A.MOREL et Cⁱᵉ Editeurs

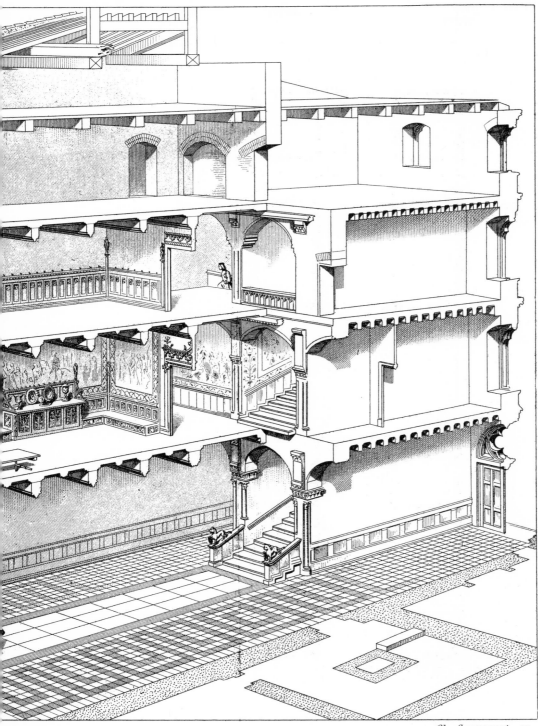

CL. Sauvageot sc.

N PALAIS DE VENISE

Imp. Lemercier et Cie _ Paris

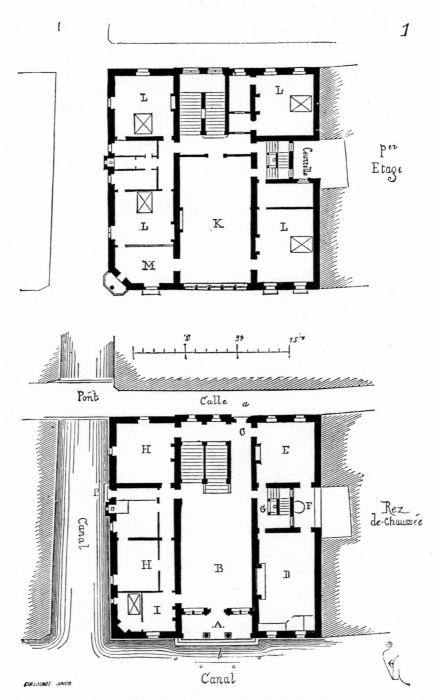

FIG. 1.—Ground and First-floor plans of a Venetian Palace.

lodge, the servants' apartments, kitchen, pantry, storerooms, etc. On one side, or sometimes even at the further end of the vestibule, is the grand staircase, which terminates on the first story in a large hall corresponding with the vestibule. At the right and left of the hall open the private suites of apartments. This arrangement is reproduced in the other stories.

The plans, figure 1, show concisely with what frank simplicity the conditions are fulfilled.[1] The main front of this palace commands a wide canal, its posterior façade overlooks a *calle*, and one of its sides a narrower canal. This is an arrangement frequently adopted. At A is a portico serving as a place of embarkation. The great vestibule B is immediately behind it, giving access directly to the grand staircase. At C the back entrance opens on the *calle*; at P, a postern on the narrower canal for bringing in provisions by boat. At F is a little court with a cistern receiving the rain-water from the roofs. At E the pantry, and at D the kitchen. The porter's lodge is at I. At H are the offices, provision stores, cellars, etc. A back stair is placed at G.

The first-floor plan shows at K the great hall, at M a study or small receiving room, and at L bed-chambers with wardrobes.

This plan, which is so simple—so readily understood—was perfectly accommodated to the requirements of a noble family in Venice ; and the domestic habits of the higher classes of that beautiful city have certainly changed but little since the period in question. We observe the hall,—the place of meeting for the family where strangers are admitted ; and next the apartments destined for greater privacy, completely distinct from that principal hall. It is in this latter that meals are taken, in accordance with an ancient mediæval custom. Quickly cleared after the repast, the same table once more assembled the family around it during the winter evenings. In the summer the family enjoy the coolness of the night in their gondolas. Around the great hall are ranged the buffets containing the plate ; and on its walls are hung the family portraits and memorials of honour and distinctions connected with the house. The elevations express these internal arrangements with singular clearness ; a wide arcaded opening for light crosses at the end of the great hall. As regards the secondary apartments, they are lighted by windows proportioned to their dimensions.

To exhibit more clearly the general aspect of the architectural method adopted, we give a perspective section through the broken line *a b*, Plate XXXII., showing how frankly the exterior corresponds with the internal arrangements.

[1] This plan gives a résumé, if one may so term it, of a certain number of those dwellings belonging to the commencement of the fifteenth century, which are designed on the same type though of various dimensions.

At Venice it was a matter of importance to economise every inch of soil. Courts or gardens could scarcely be thought of in a city where every site had to be conquered from the lagune.

The edifice must always show in plan an agglomerated mass of constructions—what we call a *pavillon.* This spacious reservoir of air in the interior, with a wide opening for light at one of its extremities, being cool in summer when the heat is overwhelming, and warm in winter when the cold is pretty severe, presented advantages which a court could not have offered; and it was really utilised, a point of supreme importance where ground was so difficult to obtain. Towards the close of the sixteenth century, the Venetians, without deviating from the arrangements of this plan in the main, determined, according to the prevailing fashion, to erect symmetrical façades presenting ranges of columns with no break from one extremity to the other.

Thus from this *penchant* for the "orders" they perverted the plan. Windows of equal dimensions and similar form lighted the central hall and the lateral apartments, which was absurd; but it is not for us to find fault with this inconsistency, since we are constantly doing the same thing.

In Italy the family bond was formerly and is still very powerful. The impress of this characteristic feature is strongly marked in the programme so skilfully carried out. We observe one locality for all to assemble in, as in our own mediæval châteaux, and still more remotely in the Roman houses; though with this difference—that among the wealthy Romans the wife and young children occupied a separate part of the dwelling, whereas here all the members of the family are grouped around the common hearth. We observe, however, in these Venetian palaces entire liberty left to each. The means of retirement are numerous and convenient, and the ways of issue by land and by water allowed the inhabitants to go out and return without attracting attention.

The Roman palace of the fifteenth century is on an entirely different plan. In Rome there was no lack of space, and the ancient tradition was in greater vigour. The Roman palace usually consists of an interior court, surrounded by porticos with apartments one room in depth all round, whose doors open on these porticos, which are found at every story. We have, in fact, an arrangement in accordance with the impluvium of the houses of classical antiquity. Here, too, we find a great hall, but under the form of the *gallery,* whose function is not that of the Venetian great hall. The gallery is an affair of ostentation. Ceremonial receptions and fêtes take place there. It is not a place of assembling for the family; the gallery is not in a central position, but, on the contrary, is connected as little as possible with the private apartments. We observe magnificent flights of stairs, occupying a space which is considerable in proportion to the whole building, and symmetrical façades without projections, and which offend by their dreary monotony.

We find the same arrangement at Florence, and in most of the cities of Southern Italy. There is no appearance of comfort, but an evident intention to appear magnificent; in fact, all the dwellings in question ape grandeur. What is censurable in them is, that they do not show the imprint of the habits of those who occupied them. Whereas one seems actually to live with the citizens of Pompeii, and would in a few hours be quite familiar with their daily habits and customs, these palaces of modern Rome appear not to have been built with a view to being lived in. They are vast and sometimes magnificent edifices; but they seem to be waiting for a generation of human beings that will never present themselves, to give their walls that stamp of living humanity without which every building leaves the spectator cold and indifferent. It is this stamp that gives our ancient French houses so real a charm. Here in the old manors of the Marais, we find ourselves transported back to the midst of a society that has really lived, and has left in every corner the trace of its habits, passions and endeavours.

It cannot be denied that one of the most powerful of the attractions possessed by the Arts of olden times is that they enable the spectator to live amid the civilisation that has produced them. A great many works of art attract and touch us profoundly, simply because they recall the circumstances that gave them birth, and because, in examining them, we see pass before us, as it were, those generations which have examined them with curious eyes, in times long past. Suppose this charm obliterated—were this possible—and the work, however beautiful, will lose much of its attraction. On this account mere imitations, marvellous though they may seem, never produce much impression on the mind, and can no more deeply affect it than apocryphal memoirs. On this account, also, no epoch that has not the determination and energy to model its architecture according to its habits will leave more than a fugitive trace in the history of the arts. Even should it rack its intellect to reproduce a collection of the finest of anterior creations, its architecture will count for less in the judgment of the future, than an unpretentious house of wood belonging to our old cities; and the verdict would be just. We tender no thanks to an author who wants imagination, though he may borrow splendid passages from a brother author to adorn his pages: but we shall thank him if he is true, and relates simply what he has seen and known.

The principal charm, to my thinking, in the domestic buildings of our French architects down to the seventeenth century is due to the fact that they never went out of their way. They frankly satisfied the requirements of their times, and by the simplest means. But to be ingenuous and simple in the arts it is necessary to be strong ; and in fact all the borrowed splendours with which our own age glorifies itself—its eclectic refinements —conceal an incurable feebleness, to say the least, and often a profound ignorance.

One of the most interesting works on the subject that can be studied is Pierre le Muet's book.[1] This architect begins by exhibiting the house of the poorer citizens with a single window in front ; and advancing to houses of more and more pretension he comes to notice the smaller mansions, then the larger ones, such as the Hôtel Davaux, built by him in the Rue Sainte-Avoye. In these habitations, whether accommodated to the most restricted or to princely incomes, we find the faithful imprint of the manners of the times. The whole of society from the lowest to the highest grades is depicted in this ingenious collection of buildings. There is a connection between all of them ; each holds the place it ought really to occupy, and assumes the importance suitable to it. The buildings are generally only one room deep ; their simple stately arrangements would not suit our habits, but were quite suited to the requirements of the period.

Every one knows that at that time the widest streets in Paris were only thirty feet wide. It is thence inferred that the houses were narrow, wanted ventilation, and were consequently unhealthy. In this as in many other things our judgment is rather hasty.

The space that was wanting in the thoroughfare was made use of to the advantage of the houses themselves. Many of these mansions, and even of the smaller dwellings which lined streets scarcely wide enough for two carriages abreast, possessed courts and gardens.

When our modern municipal authorities cut those great arteries (whose utility and desirableness we are far from contesting) through quarters of the city which appeared to consist of squalid abodes, whose only light seemed derived from narrow streets, people were much surprised to see behind these blocks of building, consigned to destruction, gardens or ample spaces

[1] *Manière de bâtir pour toutes sortes de personnes ;* par Pierre le Muet, architecte-ordinaire du roi, et conducteur des dessins des fortifications de Sa Majesté ; Paris, 1681. In-folio en deux parties.

known only to the inhabitants of those dwellings. In the most crowded quarters even, the top of a neighbouring building—the Tower of St. Jacques, for instance—would enable one to see trees whose existence was quite unknown to those who passed through the fetid and narrow streets. Old Paris, seen from a balloon, would have presented innumerable spots of verdure in every direction,—vestiges of the ancient arrangement of the houses of the city.

Paris must certainly have been rendered more healthy by the broad currents of air which now circulate through its most populous quarters, and especially by the improved arrangements for house and street drainage; but can we suppose that our massive and lofty constructions, which often have no courts, or which have only wells of air between their party walls, will continue to be wholesomely conditioned when time shall have produced its disintegrating effect on the materials of which they are built? I have heard doubts on this head—and which I myself share—expressed by men who have made sanitary matters their special study. All circumstances considered, the blocks of houses in our great modern cities, particularly in Paris, present agglomerations much too compact and uniformly built to allow of such masses of buildings having a sufficient, free circulation of air. Miasmata fatal to the health of the inhabitants must be developed amid these masses in consequence of the fermentation produced by time in masses of material of various kinds.

Similar considerations show us that buildings one room in depth, of which our mansions consisted down to the end of the seventeenth century, had the advantage of being easily aërated. The plan adopted presented difficulties in regard to internal arrangements; but it cannot be denied that our ancient architects showed skill in overcoming them, and did not lose the space we are now obliged to sacrifice to sombre passages and communications which cannot be well ventilated and are in every respect objectionable.

In studying those ancient plans we observe how exactly they rendered the programmes dictated by the habits of the higher class. When the desire for symmetrical openings and axial arrangements took possession of our architects, towards the beginning of the seventeenth century, they could comply with the new requirements, thanks to the simplicity of their plans. Buildings one room deep could of course be accommodated to those symmetrical arrangements; and although architects often employed artifices to humour the exigencies of art, they did not go to the extent of perverting the plans and deranging the internal arrangements.

These arrangements were but little modified during the sixteenth and seventeenth centuries; we observe them in the Hôtel de Cluny and the Hôtel de la Trémouille which date from the end of the fifteenth century, and in the mansions erected during the reign of Louis xv.

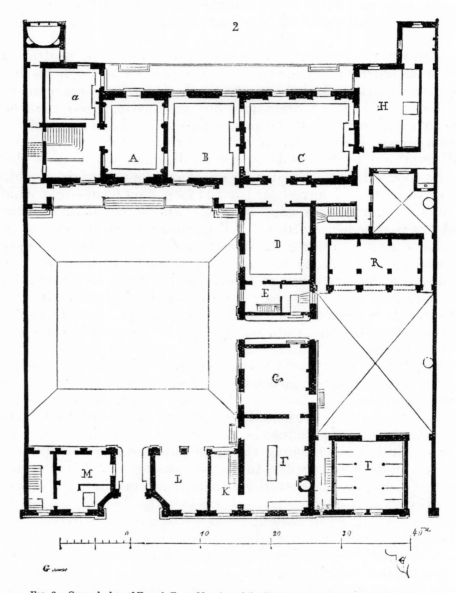

FIG. 2.—Ground-plan of French Town Mansion of the Sixteenth and Seventeenth Centuries.

The plan, figure 2, gives the type of the arrangements observed in mansions of the north of France. The principal building stands, where possible, between the court and the garden. The inferior courts are placed laterally in direct communication with the great court (*cour d'honneur*). A wide vestibule, A, opens in front of the axis of the court. The sedan-chairs were carried as far as the interior of this vestibule. On one side is placed the principal staircase and the room *a*, in which persons who came on business were received. On the other side, at B is what was called the antechamber, *i.e.* the waiting-room preceding the apartments. Next to this at C is the chamber which served as a private drawing-room. At D the dining-room with the buttery at E. The kitchens are placed at F, and at G the *salle de commun*, which corresponds with the modern servants' hall. At H is a bedroom with its great alcove, dressing-room and wardrobes.

The coach-house R, and stables I, fronted the back court. Near the kitchens, at K, is the store-room for provisions, at L a coach-house for carriages or chairs awaiting the departure of guests: at M the porter's apartments.

The ground-floor was therefore occupied by the rooms for the household. There was no grand reception hall; the dining-room was small, for during that period—except on certain very special occasions—only intimate friends were invited to repasts.

The reception-rooms are arranged on the first story. They consist, fig. **3**, of what was called the hall A, an antechamber B, which in fact, serving the purpose of an ordinary drawing-room, usually, was arranged for grand receptions on gala days; the gallery G, and the chapel C. Two apartments, D, for the use of the family, were connected with these reception-rooms, and had their separate services. Other suites of apartments were placed at E over the entrance buildings, and were for the use of friends. The domestics were lodged in the attics, and the grooms over the stables.

We find these arrangements adopted with trifling variations in most of the mansions of the seventeenth century. There is a marked distinction between the apartments connected with the outside world and those reserved for domestic privacy. There are special stairs for all the apartments, and on the first story the large reception-rooms serving for means of communication between these private apartments. Along the public road are the outbuildings or secondary apartments. The rooms for the family and the halls reserved for receptions look on the garden and the *cour d'honneur* only. All this is frankly and clearly expressed, and the grandiose arrangements of symmetrical architecture adopted in the seventeenth century accord with this simplicity of arrangement.

The requirements of the present day are evidently more complex; they imply more specialised arrangements and more numerous private communications and minor adjuncts: they would consequently demand an architectural style less grandiose in aspect but less simple in its dispositions, and cannot be easily accommodated to symmetrical composition.

3

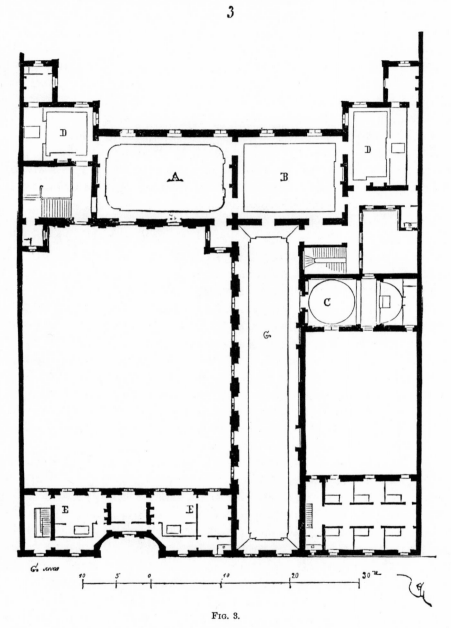

FIG. 3.

The works of Le Muet and De Marot are in the libraries of all architects; it is easy therefore, without enlarging on the architectural arrangements of the great mansions of the seventeenth century, to understand the pompous style adopted in the construction of these dwellings.

In order to be adapted to our present requirements, the plans we have just given must evidently undergo important modifications. We could not now make a carriage-way the communication between the kitchen and the dining-room. We should want at least two drawing-rooms on the ground floor, dressing-rooms and wardrobes attached to each of the bed-rooms, and a number of minute arrangements which are here omitted. The broad continuity characterising the life of persons belonging to the higher classes of former times has been, so to speak, broken up into a number of minute occupations and consequent desiderata, the complete satisfaction of which does not comport with those grandiose arrangements whose uniformity renders them comprehensible at a glance.

A social condition of aristocratic character introduces intimate, and, so to speak, familiar relations between superiors and inferiors, which disappear in democratic societies. Domestic architecture bears the impress of this change in manners. When the classes of society are separated by distances that cannot be crossed, those of the higher grades, assured that neither personal merit, nor intrigue, nor violence, will be able to rob them of their distinction, do not raise useless barriers between themselves and the subordinate classes; on the contrary, the very need of companionship soon gives rise to intimate relations connecting all ranks from the lowest to the highest.

Both in the châteaux and in the mansions the life of the noblesse was quite unsecluded; it was not deemed singular or reprehensible for the inmates of the dwelling, even those of an inferior class, to go in and out in every part of the building. Life was lived in common without inconvenience, because there was no reason to fear that subordinates would ever forget the social distance that separated them from their superiors.

It is not so in a democratic state of society; there the higher class require material barriers to protect them from the presumption and encroachments of inferiors. Such serious alterations in the habits of society are reflected in domestic architecture, in a number of precautionary details devised with a view to secure the independence of the master of the house, and to secure his domestic privacy from the curiosity of subordinates whom no moral tie attaches to the family, who are little devoted to its interests, if they are not unfriendly or envious.

We conclude from the above that domestic architecture in an aristocratic state of society may affect a breadth and simplicity in its arrangements which would be intolerable in a democratic condition, where each department in the dwelling must be distinct and definite, in proportion to the equality before the law that exists between masters and servants. In ancient times the slave was considered as belonging to the family, and the master could the more freely admit him to intimacy with himself, as the law gave him but little protection. And though slavery had no legal existence in that elder period of French social life, the servants were in fact so absolutely dependent on their master,—they were so absolutely his chattels,—that he soon came to consider the domestics attached to his house as forming part of the family,—that is to say, as interested in the preservation of what down to the sixteenth century was called the *maisonnée* (household).

Neither the city nor the country mansion had any need to take precautions, except against the world outside. Within, everything was, as it were, in common.

This state of things is impossible in a social condition in which the servant is a stranger hired by the week, and whom no other lien but wages attaches to the family with whom he lives. Then not only must the house be closely walled in, but the life of each of the family must have its privacy secured against the curiosity of these mercenary strangers. In the "hôtels" of former centuries there appeared nothing unseemly in listening through the doors to the talk of the valets in the ante-chambers or courts, any more than there would now in listening to the prattle of children playing in a neighbouring apartment. But in our days this is not, and could not be, tolerated. Thus, whatever can be done to hinder it, what we gain in social conditions on the one side we lose on the other. Judging of things superficially, our ancient "hôtels" seem to be adapted to democratic customs, and those of the present day to aristocratic usages pushed to excess, since we require that each apartment should on occasion be a kind of isolated and independent sanctuary, secluded from observation. Thus democratic institutions, whose intention is to establish equality between citizens, and obliterate distinctions of castes and classes, produce an effect diametrically opposite in many points, and particularly in the dwellings of those whom fortune favours. If we have no longer any reason to fear a servile war, we may have to count upon enmity on the part of those who are paid for their services against those who pay them. And it is certain that whereas in ancient times, many masters might reckon on the devotedness of slaves born in their houses, and who from infancy had been in servitude in the family, there is scarcely a master or employer of labour now who has not an enemy, or at least a person indifferent to his interests, in the servant or work-man whom he pays.

The inference is—for I am not wishing to enter upon the discussion of a vexed social question—that we must adopt a style of domestic architecture in accordance with this state of manners,—these complicated, often somewhat paltry, considerations and requirements, showing an excess of distrustfulness; and that it would be irrational to endeavour to combine the grandeur of our ancient mansions with the fastidious refinements of modern domestic comfort. Symmetry admitted of being allied with the stately arrangements presented by the plans of mansions in the sixteenth and seventeenth centuries; but it becomes a source of extreme embarrassment in our modern constructions, since it obliges us to distort the plans and adopt inconvenient and sham arrangements and to lose valuable space. When, *e.g.* apartments of nearly equal dimensions occurred along a façade, it was natural to light these apartments by windows of equal dimensions; but when the requirements of the inhabitants of a mansion are such, that very large and very small apartments must be in close proximity to each other, it is not only in very bad taste but very inconvenient to give all these rooms windows equal in size and the same height of ceiling. The true principle, whose importance and value cannot be disputed, had been frankly applied down to the sixteenth century, when in the arrangement of the several parts of the building very large halls were erected and rooms of very small dimensions close to them. With a freedom which cannot be too much commended, they made liberal use of corbellings and projections to secure varied prospects and favourable positions, of open or closed loggias, of entresols quite conspicuous from the outside, and of openings in the rooms, not for the sake of symmetry but to establish ready communication and free views. Such a liberty would greatly simplify the task of architects commissioned to build mansions if they would avail themselves of it, and if their clients did not insist, before all things, on displaying outside an architecture pompously symmetrical. I may add that buildings would then be secured of a better and less expensive construction than those which are now erected on irrational principles.

I am aware that many well-meaning persons look upon the disregard of what are called the *laws of symmetry* as a kind of impiety, a contempt for ancient and sound traditions : as if the most ancient traditions, and consequently those which should be most respected by believers in traditions, were not in flagrant contradiction with these supposed laws, which are in fact very recent. There are some of these observances and ideas which each in his secret judgment or on the slightest reflection recognises as absurd and false, but which no one ventures to contravene. Each is waiting for his neighbour to display the requisite moral courage. All would gladly follow the movement, but are very careful not to provoke it. Symmetry is one of these unhappy ideas to which we sacrifice our well-being as far as our dwellings are concerned, and sometimes our common sense, and a considerable amount of money always.

It is desirable that architects of repute should take advantage of the occasions which present themselves for beginning the reformation, when they meet with a client whose ideas are just and reasonable. The example would soon be followed, for the advantage resulting from the abandonment of their pretentious follies would soon be manifest. Many have ventured to disregard the laws of symmetry in building houses in the country, but it seems there are more difficulties in the case of mansions in the city. In fact it is matter of fashion. People think it necessary that their houses in the city should be irreproachable in point of symmetry, in the same way as they make it a matter of conscience not to appear in the streets with anything but the usual hat on their heads, and the customary dress on their persons. Will the rude shock we have recently experienced lead us back to more correct ideas and induce us to abandon puerile prejudices? I wish rather than hope for it. It is not the less incumbent on us to endeavour to show the advantages that would result from abandoning these prejudices, which, while they run away with our money, are entirely alien to art. The very essence of art, as far as architecture is concerned, consists in knowing how to clothe every object with a form appropriate to that object, not in making a magnificent case, and afterwards considering how the requisite arrangements can be accommodated *in* that case.

Every one who wants a mansion built for him submits a programme of his requirements. If he is incapable of doing so, it is for the architect to make up for his incompetence, or the indefiniteness of his ideas, by explaining his presumed wants to him and himself preparing the programme. And to every architect worthy of the name, a programme that is well drawn up and clear, and which is not liable to any false interpretation, is half the battle; on one condition, however; that he complies with it in every particular, that he completely satisfies it, that he will not content himself with mere approximations, nor seek to conceal his failure to perform certain conditions of it under the seductive appearance of architectural prescription.

Many clients are deceived by this stratagem, and have to repent, when the building is finished, that they have allowed themselves to be seduced by an outward show which flattered their vanity as proprietors.

Few in number are those clients who know exactly what they want; while on the contrary great is the number of those who have what they call *an idea*,—sometimes a mere dreamy conception, impossible to realise; or perhaps (as mansions are in question) this idea consists in getting a house whose exterior shall present the appearance of that occupied by Monsieur L. or N. Whether such a case will be capable of suitably containing what they need is an inquiry that has not even crossed their minds. They want the columns, the cornices, the windows of the *hôtel de . . .* and likewise the flight of steps in front, and the attics, and the chimneys, and the oval drawing-room, and the grand staircase. "It is a copy of the *hôtel de . . .* then that you wish," the architect responds. "Oh no; that is much too large for me; besides, I want only two stories, and that has three; and it has a garden, whereas I cannot have one in the ground at my disposal; moreover, the kitchens are on the wing, and I want my offices below ground; its reception-rooms are on the first story, and I wish mine on the ground-floor; besides, I am anxious to have an entresol for the servants, the children, etc." "Then be so kind as to give me your programme of requirements."—Now it is certain that this programme will no more accommodate itself to the *hôtel de . . .* than to the great Temple of Baalbec. If the architect have a little good sense and conscience, and the client is in any degree obstinate—which sometimes happens—they separate without anything having been accomplished. But what may surprise us is that such a client will find, as I said just now, an . . . "architect" who will do all that he likes, who will produce a plan similar to the *hôtel de . . .* with its oval drawing-room and columns; he will cleverly manage to introduce the entresol and the underground kitchens required, and all that is wanted. The thing that is built will be uninhabitable; there will be fundamental errors of construction: and the proprietor will go to law with his complaisant architect, and will apply to the one who was less so—as an expert—to give evidence against him. But let us not be too sweeping in our censure; there are some clients who have intelligence and common sense, who apply to competent architects and place entire confidence in them, and who when they have determined on their programme commit the affair entirely to them. And it is with such clients that it would be worth while to see if something reasonable could not be attempted.

A modern mansion, though it presents complicated details,—a series of arrangement much more broken up than was the case with the ancient ones,—exhibits certain fundamental similarities. There is one part reserved for the reception of visitors and relations with the world outside, and another part for domestic privacy. Though on certain occasions these are connected, in the ordinary course of life they are perfectly distinct. Convenience and economy both suggest that they should not be intermingled with each other. It will be observed that in the mansions of former days this principle was the predominant one,— a principle which is perhaps more imperative now than it was of old. Whether a mansion be divided into two distinct sections, one composing the reception-rooms, and the other those for the family, or whether one story is allotted to the former service, and the others to the latter, the condition in question is a dominant one. But there are always inconveniences and difficulties, as regards the construction, in placing apartments relatively small, and complicated arrangements, over large rooms. This is probably one of the reasons which in the old mansions led to the placing of the reception-rooms on the first story, and the dwelling-rooms on the ground-floor. It was desirable for the sake of the building to put what was comparatively light over what was heavier, on account of the number of partitions. However, the flues required on the ground floor in a great number of rooms could not readily pass through much larger rooms above. Besides, our modern habits are better suited to dwelling-rooms on the first story than on the ground-floor; for very few mansions can boast those extensive courts and gardens which render living on the ground-floor agreeable. There are therefore nine chances to one that the programme given to the architect will require reception-rooms on the ground-floor, and living-rooms on the other stories. We require—so large is our circle of friends—for the generally very thronged receptions of our times, spacious apartments, easy of access, so that those galleries which were so much in vogue in the sixteenth and seventeenth centuries no longer suit us. We require means of free circulation on account of the multitude of guests; and that every part may be readily accessible without the necessity of crossing the apartments. These requirements imply at the outset buildings two rooms wide; on the other hand, for private habitation these very broad buildings are very inconvenient; they leave apartments or at least passages dark and unventilated, and they necessitate aspects injurious to health, leaving those gloomy recesses which in plans are disguised as *dégagements*.

Whenever you see the word *dégagements* in a plan, be on your guard! This word generally indicates a space that cannot be usefully employed. On the surfaces occupied by these *dégagements* in the mansions of Paris and other cities hundreds of families might find a lodging; at any rate if they were wisely used the mansions in question would give much more comfortable accommodation to their inmates.

This brief review therefore shows us that in fact the programme of a mansion which had reception rooms on the ground floor, and private rooms in the upper stories, presents no trifling difficulties, since the part supported has no similarity to that which supports it, not only as regards the arrangement, but also the construction.

It is not by studying the houses of Pompeii which have only a ground floor that we can solve this problem. Nor can this be accomplished by copying the architecture of recent centuries, since it is evident that the plans given, 2 and 3, cannot satisfy our present requirements. It is therefore to the resources supplied by our own common sense and reason that we must apply for the solution of the problem, proceeding as our predecessors had the wisdom to proceed : that is, by adopting new arrangements without troubling ourselves about the forms applied to old ones whose conditions were different from those we have to deal with.

Although we might mention many mansions in Paris and in the provinces which exhibit much talent and careful attention on the part of the architects who have designed them, the mansion exactly suited to modern requirements still remains to be discovered ; and among the best I do not know one whose construction shows a real enfranchisement from the bondage of traditions which are in the present day very embarrassing, which nothing compels us to respect, and adherence to which robs these private dwellings of that character which each period ought to impress on buildings of the kind still more than on public edifices.

There have been times when public architecture, having lost all character of its own, followed in the wake of enfeebled art ; but during those very periods domestic architecture, not subjected to the narrow ideas of a Government or of an Academy, was still able to imprint its own seal upon its designs.

It has been reserved for our own age to allow this last vestige of originality to be lost. Let architects of ability, therefore, who have not the ambition to secure a *fauteuil* at the Institute, or who have not set their minds on forcing open for themselves the doors of administrative boards which are entirely under the control of a privileged body, set themselves to work and seek for a solution of the problems suggested in the domestic architecture of the day. What we say respecting mansions applies, as we shall presently see, to ordinary houses in the city and the country, whose programmes are far from being satisfactorily treated. A vast field of study and labour is presented here, and we may even assert that the clear and practical solution of these problems would be the best means of preventing the shameless perversion of principles exhibited in the construction of our public buildings. We should thus form the taste of the higher classes, which has been all but utterly corrupted by the sight of the architectural vagaries exhibited by the public edifices with which our cities have been filled.

We shall content ourselves with seeking for the right way, and indicating the means of discovering it according to the plan hitherto adopted in these Lectures.

The English, who are a practical people, and who have not the classical prejudices familiar to ourselves, but for which we pay dearly, have in many cases adopted in their country-houses, and even in some city-mansions, an arrangement which may have its advantages. This consists in the adoption of a great central hall lighted from above, and around which the family apartments and those of the servants are grouped. We have in fact the *patio* of the Moorish house under cover.

But the English have preserved to a certain point those arrangements for life in common in the household to which I recently referred. Domestic life in England, as in every aristocratic state of society, is kept in that condition approximating to that of the family, strictly so called, which is the best guarantee for internal well-being and tranquillity. The great central hall, provided with galleries or balconies above, which establish communication with the private apartments, is thus left visible to all the servants of the country or city mansion. This is the "hall" or court, accessible to all and open to all. This would not suit our French habits ; besides, such large halls lighted from above are gloomy,—remind us somewhat of a prison,—whereas we, as curious people, like to see what is going on ; and when we are placed between four walls without openings to the outside world at the height of our vision, our first impulse is to escape as soon as possible. The arrangements of English mansions, therefore, though they deserve to be studied, and may furnish some details which it would be well to imitate, do not suit our customs.

We French do not like this contact with the servants of the household. Each of us wishes for isolation ; and there is no country where *individualism* (if I may thus use the word) is in more vigorous force. And it is not for architects to undertake to reform our habits and manners in points in which they are objectionable or carry good principles too far, but to make their buildings conform to them, or refuse their concurrence if, as may happen in circumstances that need not be particularised, conditions are presented to them whose fulfilment would be repugnant to their reason and conscience.

Our modern requirements are multiplied, complicated, and in some respects even undignified ; yet we pretend to something like state when we invite our friends and acquaintances to our mansions, though generally they are mere strangers, or such as we only know through having seen them once or twice in society.

But, I repeat it, it is not for the architect to remonstrate with his clients on this point, or to protest against these odd customs, but to manage as well as he reasonably can to render the buildings with which he is commissioned conformable to them. The task is not an easy one, I allow. But have energetic efforts been made to perform it?

We may remark in passing that the display required, as well as the complicated exigencies of daily life, generally have to be provided for at the lowest cost. People wish to make a show, and to have their comforts; but they wish it to be understood that no very great expense is to be incurred,—another difficulty. When the ground is paid for at the rate of £20 per square yard, at the lowest figure, and the building costs, on an average, for a mansion, £40 per yard, there must be economy both in the construction and in the space it occupies. The great point, therefore, is to manage so that there may be no surfaces lost, and to avoid external magnificence which adds nothing to the merit of the work, but which on the other hand draws largely on the client's purse without contributing anything to his comfort. This might be done in the construction of those ancient mansions which were very simple in point of plan, and whose unsophisticated arrangements cost little to provide for; and besides it must be observed that the exteriors of those old mansions, with rare exceptions, do not present a very rich or ornamented appearance. But in the present day there is really no reason for the magnificent displays of frontage, and they interest no one. But I must recall this last statement: they do tend to keep up that brooding hatred which the less wealthy classes cherish against opulence and against those who make a foolish display of it to their own prejudice. I do not assert that we ought, as the Orientals do, to disguise the internal splendours of a palace behind bare white-washed walls; but between that hypocritical semblance of poverty and the luxurious display which leaves no impression except in the mind of the envious, a rational *via media* may, I think, be found.

And the same may be said with regard to that symmetry whose abuse should be reprobated. It would be still more ridiculous to proscribe it absolutely and to design irregular plans for the mere love of irregularity. When the tenor of a programme lends itself to symmetrical arrangements, it would be puerile not to take advantage of it; for we cannot be blind to the fact that circumstances often present themselves in which a symmetrical disposition is a satisfaction to the mind and to the eye. But the mind and eye must be able to take in this symmetry whether in a public or private building: a result which is often produced in the interiors of houses, but seldom on the outside, especially in dwellings which, like large hotels, can only be seen in parts, and not altogether. However this may be, it would seem reasonable never to sacrifice absolute requirements, or rather arrangements which ought to comply with those requirements, to symmetry. A bad arrangement is a nuisance felt constantly, while the pleasure which a symmetrical arrangement produces is soon forgotten.

In regard to symmetry, then, we should observe a reasonable medium ; and it is for men of talent, who know their business, to discover that medium. What should not be tolerated in any case is symmetrical rows of windows on a façade which internal arrangements oblige us to cut by floors, partitions, and staircases. And architects can bear witness how excessively these hypocrisies and insults to common sense and to the most elementary laws of our art are indulged in.

In the building of our mansions there is also another important condition, which it is not always possible to comply with : the orientation, *i.e.* position as regards aspect. In our temperate climate a position north or south offers serious inconveniences. There will be excessive heat during some months on the south side, and cold and absolute deprivation of sun during the other months, on the north. But the architect who has to build on a certain ground is not free to choose the position most suitable to his erections in a city where space is often limited and where the entrances are on the public thoroughfares.

These are the cases, however, in which we must proceed with skilful caution, and endeavour to discover such an arrangement as will allow us to avail ourselves of the advantages, and avoid the inconveniences, of such or such a position. If a site stretches from north to south, it is evident that a building erected across it, between the court and the garden for example, will have one of its aspects deprived of the sun for nine months in the year, and the other exposed to its rays from the 1st of January to the 31st of December. The apartments opening on the former will be very difficult to warm, and unhealthy in winter, while those which open on the latter will be uninhabitable during the summer.

One last remark suggests itself in reference to the building of mansions answering to our requirements. While we wish to prevent the intrusion of our domestics into our daily life, and desire that the former should as little as possible come in contact with the latter, on the other hand we have not so many servants as were kept in the mansions of former times. In fact, we may say that as compared with those days their number is now reduced to a minimum. We must therefore avoid the necessity of their having to traverse long distances. When we do not need their services, their presence is undesirable; but when we require a servant, we wish that there should be no delay in giving our orders. These habits require an easy and rapid concentration of the service, and communications specially reserved for it.

Let us attempt, if not the complete fulfilment of this programme,—to which it would be ridiculous to pretend,—to indicate at least the method to be followed in satisfying it. To do this we must present definite plans; this is the form of expression that excludes vagueness and ambiguity. Criticism is easy, but the realisation of ideas which seem at first of the simplest and clearest order is a task of no small difficulty.

At the present day, still more imperatively than was the case in former times, we desire that the reception-rooms of a mansion should be distinct from those reserved for privacy, simply because we receive a good many people with whom we have but the slightest acquaintance. The ground-floor of a mansion should therefore be reserved for those receptions, and the first story for family privacy. But as crowds of visitors are sometimes entertained, the rooms destined to receive them must be so arranged that it may be easy to move about in them, and that the means of entrance and exit may be easy; and that isolation may be possible if, amid the crowd of persons we have to invite, there are, as generally happens, a select few who are more intimately connected. People should be able to find some better place of rendezvous than the embrasures of doors, if they wish to talk about their own interests or affairs. If we give a dinner, the hall in which we give it should be quite separated from the apartments reserved for evening receptions: for nothing is more disagreeable for those who come at nine or ten o'clock, than to be witnesses of the clearing away of a large table, even with a side glance; yet the dining-room must be very near the drawing-rooms, so that one may pass directly from one into the others. Many other things are requisite: we want an awning to shelter the carriages; but those who come and go on foot,—for in a democratic state of society there will be such, as well as people who keep their carriages,—must also be able to come into the entrance-hall without passing under the horses' noses; and there must be a closed vestibule where overcoats may be deposited. Between this vestibule and the reception-rooms there must be a room where ladies may assure themselves of the state of their toilet, and where guests may prepare to be introduced. These antechambers must communicate readily with the servants' rooms of various functions. There must be a waiting-room for attendants who receive overcoats and mantles, and who have to call the coachmen when the guests leave. A dressing-room will be required for ladies whose attire may have been somewhat disarranged. But this antechamber must not be directly in view of the reception-rooms, nor *vice versâ*. The guests must not be imprisoned in one part of the public saloons, but be able to make their escape at will. It should also be remarked that festive sounds and lights should not attract attention in the street.

As regards the private apartments, which we suppose to be in the first story, there must be a sufficient number of servants' staircases, besides the grand staircase, to insure the rapid and easy communication of the kitchens and servants' rooms with those apartments. And besides bedrooms with their wardrobes and dressing-rooms there must be a waiting-room, an ante-chamber, a dining-room and a drawing-room for the family and intimate friends. Sun and air and light should be arranged for in every part, with aspects as favourable as possible, and ready exits and entrances, so that every inmate may come in without attracting attention.

As regards the servants' offices, underground kitchens should be avoided, as being unhealthy for those who live in them, and undesirable as spreading the odour of cooking through the house. The kitchen however should not be too far from the rooms allotted to repasts. The pantry arrangements should be on a large scale, communicating directly with the kitchens and dining-room. Of course there must be a back yard for the stables, coach-houses, and kitchen ; and so placed that the washing of carriages, or the grooming of horses, or the occupations of the scullery, may never be visible from the grand court.

Such at least have been the requirements of a well-planned mansion up to the present moment. And I do not suppose that a republican form of government (supposing it established in France) would in any degree lessen the extent of this programme ; on the contrary, a republican government can maintain its position only on the condition of allowing individual distinction to develop and assert itself, and consequently great fortunes to be accumulated, with the results they bring with them in the shape of luxury, high life, fêtes and grand receptions. A republic may establish and maintain equality among citizens before the law, but it does not favour the levelling of mental capacities or of the wealth and personal influence thence derived ; and on this ground we must consider ourselves little fitted for a republic—at any rate, as yet. In the view of many of our countrymen who profess themselves republicans, a republic means equality, not before the law,—for among us every one endeavours to escape from its dominion,—but an equality implying mediocrity ; the triumph of envy, which inevitably leads to despotism ; the despot looks with no favourable eye on great capacities, and the ample independent fortunes that result from them in a State which is really civilised ; men of ability are swept down as were the poppy-heads by Tarquin, to the great satisfaction of *soi-disant* republicans who sooner or later take the side of absolutism from jealousy towards superior natures.

Architects and contractors need therefore be under no apprehensions from the establishment of a government truly republican,—that is, a government which does not fetter the development of intellectual worth. Under such a government —and may Heaven favour its establishment in our poor distracted country !—mansions will be built in greater number than ever, if not for dukes and marquises who have no other title to distinction than ancestral name and fortunes, yet for citizens of humble or noble birth, who by their intelligence, industry, and devotion to public affairs, will have acquired, together with their wealth, a preponderating influence in the State, and an elevated position in society. But if this state of things is to be realised, the republic must have other supporters than drunkards and idlers, and must not be managed by people who see in its establishment only the means of getting the places quitted by the Monarchy or the Empire, and retaining them in connection with all the abuses which those places brought with them, and against which they had recently inveighed with the greatest bitterness.

But let us consider our *hôtel*, the programme of which we have just given in a summary form.

There is in every building, I may say, one principal organ,— one dominant part,—and certain secondary organs or members, and the necessary appliances for supplying all these parts, by a system of circulation. Each of these organs has its own function ; but it ought to be connected with the whole body in proportion to its requirements.

The plan, figure 4, is sketched according to these principles, exhibiting the ground-floor of a mansion of medium pretensions, taking the mansions in Paris as a standard.

We suppose the ground it occupies to present the conditions most frequently met with in the midst of a great city,—that is, with a frontage comparatively narrow and becoming broader towards the back. We need not insist on the advantages which buildings of this kind offer, built between a court and a garden, far from the noise of the street. But unless we have a very large space of ground at our disposal, mansions built between a court and a garden form a barrier separating them ; the result of which is that on the side of the court the aspect is generally cold and gloomy, while on that of the garden there is complete isolation with a monotony of view and position. Besides,

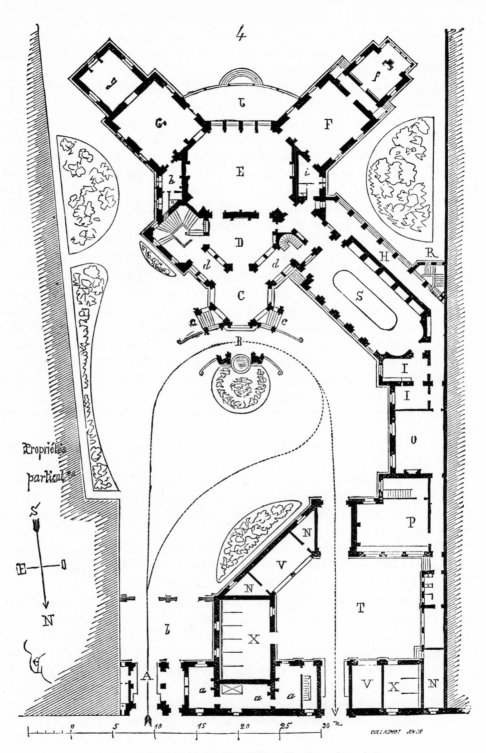

FIG. 4.—Design for a Modern French Town Mansion.—Ground-plan.

long rows of apartments or square returns make the arrangements of the house difficult, lengthen communications with the offices at certain points, and cause much space to be lost, if we would have a free circulation for the family and servants.

If, in order to avoid the inconveniences resulting from having a large building crossing the site,—the building being two rooms deep,—we adopt the *block* arrangement, we must provide air and light in the centre; which cannot be obtained except by means of that objectionable English "hall" which our French customs will, I trust, not tolerate.

The above-mentioned considerations have suggested the plan, figure 4, which consists of an octagon 65 feet in diameter, with two oblique wings on the garden side, and a third wing, likewise oblique, overlooking the court.

Whatever the aspects of the site, the sun would thus dry and warm three-fourths of the walls at least; and supposing the position of the mansion be as marked in the plan, there would not be a single aspect deprived of sun; each would have the benefit of its rays in turn.

At A is the grand entrance, with the porter's lodge at *a*; at *b* a fore-court closed by a railing; an arrangement frequently required if, for instance, the family are absent or are not accessible to visitors before a certain hour. At B is erected an awning for carriages, with a central entrance in the vestibule C. Two other side-entrances with steps are provided at *c*. This vestibule C opens into a first saloon D and two galleries *d*; one of which —that to the left—communicates with the grand staircase, and the other with a servants' staircase, the lobby of the dining-room and the passages leading to the pantries. Under the grand staircase, in the basement, is the room for attendants on guests. Glazed doors give entrance from the first saloon D, into the galleries, which are themselves glazed, so that when a levée is over the guests may easily disperse in the vestibule C, whence they can depart through one of three doors, two of which are for those on foot, who thus avoid encountering the carriages. While the first saloon opens on the vestibule through a principal central door, it gives entrance to the great central drawing-room E by two doors, both to avoid the direct view referred to above, and to enable the guests to go out and in without passing through the same entrance.

It is customary for the master or the mistress of the house to present themselves at the entrance of their drawing-rooms to receive invited guests or callers; it often happens, moreover, that only a few moments can be devoted to visits of this kind, and it is a very awkward thing to pass before the master or mistress of the house in departing when we have paid our respects to them on entering only a few minutes before. The two passages out enable us to avoid the inconvenience, either of failing somewhat in politeness or remaining prisoners.

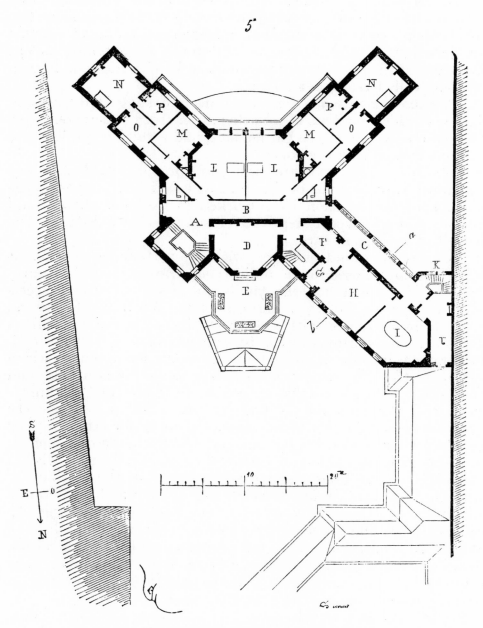

FIG. 5.—Design for a Modern French Town Mansion.—First-floor plan.

The great central drawing-room E opens on a conservatory or winter garden J, and obliquely on two saloons F and G on the wing, which open likewise on the conservatory.   The saloon G, more particularly appropriated to ladies, is terminated by a small parlour *g*. The saloon F opens on a gallery with two doors into the garden, and a smoking-room *f*, the odours of which therefore cannot penetrate into the other apartments. At *h* is a dressing-room with a closet for ladies; at *i* a similar arrangement for the other sex. These rooms may also serve as retreats in case of indisposition, or to conduct to the upper stories, either by the grand staircase or that of the servants. From the large drawing-room E or the first

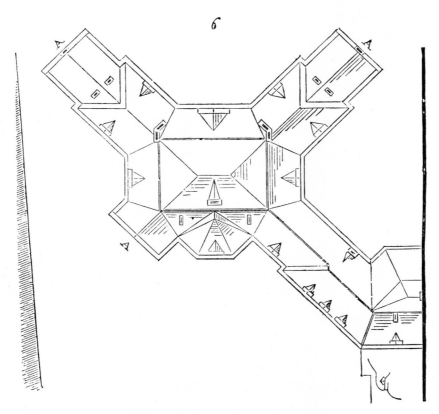

Fig. 6.—Design for a Modern French Town Mansion.—Roof plan.

saloon D we pass into the great dining-hall s, which has a passage communicating with the kitchen H and pantries in its vicinity I. The servants' hall where they take their meals is at o, and the cooking kitchen and its appurtenances at P. The servants' passage H is entresoled; and the entresol and the gallery of the first story is reached by the servants' staircase R. But we shall return to this arrangement directly. Around the servants' court T are coach-houses V, stables X, and harness-rooms N.

Let us ascend to the first story, allotted to family privacy,

E. Viollet-Le-Duc del.

Ve. A. MOREL et Cie. Editeurs

Cl. Sauvageot sc.

'UN HOTEL

Imp. Lemercier et Cie Paris

figure 5. The grand staircase leads at A to a wide landing on the same level with a gallery B traversing the central part of the building, and leading to another gallery C, communicating with the offices. At D is a large study or parlour between the grand staircase and the servants' stairs, appropriated to the master of the house. This room opens on a terrace E covering the vestibule and the lateral galleries. At F is an antechamber with a small waiting-room G, and a private drawing-room H and dining-room I, with a pantry J in direct communication with the servants' staircase K descending to the kitchens. The gallery B therefore separates the apartments to which strangers can be admitted from the two rooms L with their dressing-rooms M, and from the two apartments N, each furnished with an antechamber-saloon O and dressing-room P. Above, in the attics, are rooms for the children and for servants whose duties attach them more closely to the family. The roofing, figure 6, is arranged in these buildings in the simplest manner and with no complicated combinations. The wings A terminate in gables, an arrangement which allows of chimneys on gable walls and windows to light the attics, without adopting lateral dormer windows at these points.

Plate XXXIII. gives a perspective view of this mansion, taken in a north-east direction.

It will be necessary to enter into some details respecting the interior arrangements and the system of construction adopted.

We give first, figure 7, a section of the building containing the dining-hall (a section on the line *a b* of figure 5) with the passage for the servants. The entresol passage A serves for a linen-room, and is thus in close proximity to all the communications. As regards the gallery B on the first story it gives issue from the apartments destined for the daily use of the family. The grand staircase, as also the servants' stairs, reach as far as the attics, which are arranged for apartments of the second rank, as stated above. Beneath the roofing of the outbuildings there are rooms for the out-servants,—grooms, coachmen, kitchen attendants, etc.

Thanks to the way in which the several parts of the main building counterthrust and support each other, considering the short lengths of the outer walls in proportion to the surface covered, that main building would not entail very considerable expense. Although some of the floorings are very wide—that of the central drawing-room on the ground-floor, for example—the walls that carry them are so grouped and tied together as to offer very firm supports, without its being necessary to have recourse to extremely massive masonry.

Besides, in many parts, and in consequence of the use of iron supports which we shall have to notice in connection with the construction of houses, we should realise considerable savings if we reckon by the system now generally adopted in buildings of this kind,—a system which is somewhat obsolete, and little in harmony with the resources furnished by our manufacturing appliances.

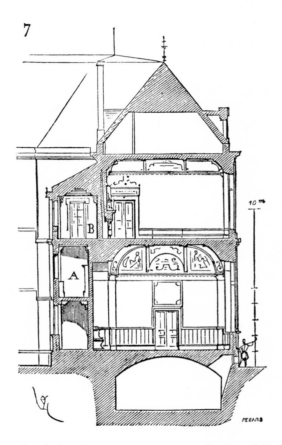

FIG. 7.—Design for a Modern French Town Mansion.—Section through the Dining-room.

For our architects, not satisfied with imitating merely the exteriors of former centuries, copy also their method of construction, which presents no advantage, and does not harmonise with the complicated requirements that have to be complied with.

Perhaps it may be desirable to give a brief summary of the cost of such buildings as I have described.

The surface covered by the main building, comprising the vestibule which has only a ground-floor, is 1060 square yards (in round numbers).

Reckoning the cost of building at £37 per square yard, as the building has only one floor of cellars, a ground-floor and a first story below the attics, we should be outside this mark. The principal building therefore would require a sum of about . . . £39,200

The outbuildings cover a surface of 800 square yards. These buildings allow of cellars under one part only, a ground-floor and one story in the roofing. They would cost on the average at most £14 per square yard, which gives about 11,200

For drains, paving, water, lighting, and awning say 10,000

Total for buildings, ... £60,400

The whole of the ground, comprising the garden, would be about 6570 square yards. Reckoning the land at £16, 16s. per square yard, we have about £110,000

General total, ... £170,400

The plan of the mansion given in figures 2 and 3 presents an extent of 1925 square yards, and for the outbuildings of 790 square yards. Taking into account their elaborate fronts, the main buildings of a town mansion on the ordinary plan, even leaving out of consideration the very expensive decorations of the interiors, would not cost less to build than those whose details we have been discussing.

The cost of the main buildings would therefore be £70,840

The outbuildings, supposing them built in the way just suggested, would entail an outlay of 10,560

Adding the sum assigned above for accessory works, 10,000

We get a total of £91,400

It seems therefore that the grouping of the several parts of a dwelling around a centre, besides greatly facilitating the domestic arrangements, tends to a better utilisation of the ground occupied, and therefore to a real saving. Observation will show that reception-rooms forming a series are very inconvenient, render the proper performance of servants' duties impossible, and cannot be made to accord with the custom, prevalent in our time, of receiving a large concourse of people. The grouping of the various buildings also facilitates warming by *calorifères*.

Further argument in its favour is needless; an examination of the plans drawn according to this method of grouping will show the advantages that can be derived from its application in the building of mansions, large or small. It would seem also possible to make a general application in buildings of this kind, of oblique or polygonal plans; not confining ourselves, when we have a free space at our disposal, to square plans which present parts in such positions as render them difficult to light and arrange, except by sacrificing space.

Without offering the preceding designs as a model to be followed,—presenting them only as an application of a system that accords with modern requirements,—it will be easily seen that this method allows us to gain numerous openings for light in every aspect, and leaves no places unoccupied. When all buildings were only one room deep, returns at right angles offered no inconvenience, because it was always easy to make openings at least on one side, to light angle apartments; but this facility no longer exists if we have buildings of double thickness. A geometrical sketch will put this difficulty in a clear light. Let A, figure 8, be a building one room deep. If the apartment a cannot get windows in the interior angle b, it may be lighted from the side c of the projecting angle; but if a building B, two rooms deep, has a square return, it will be difficult to light the surface f. This apartment f, therefore, in order to have windows, must encroach upon the outside walls of the interior angle; that is, must have its limit at g or h. Even then, the surface f will be but imperfectly ventilated or lighted. But if we adopt the geometrical plan C, the three apartments i K l will be all perfectly lighted. Polygonal plans therefore, with oblique sections, may be very useful in the construction of buildings two rooms deep, and we may well ask ourselves why they are not more frequently employed. Corner *pavillons* (as in D) may also be adopted, as presenting advantages of which the architects of the seventeenth century knew well how to take advantage.

These *pavillons*, forming a projection within the interior angle, also give rise to happy architectural effects. And they are very convenient for stairs, lobbies, or accessory apartments. In building town mansions of moderate dimensions, we generally have no great extent of ground at our disposal; the architect is limited to a comparatively narrow space, shut in by neighbouring properties. We have to build against the walls of the next house, though—if we suppose a garden—we must leave the space necessary for passing from the court to this garden. In this case an angle vestibule and staircase offer the most advantageous arrangements.

Supposing a site with a frontage of 80 to 100 feet, which allows only a narrow space for a mansion, it would be absurd to

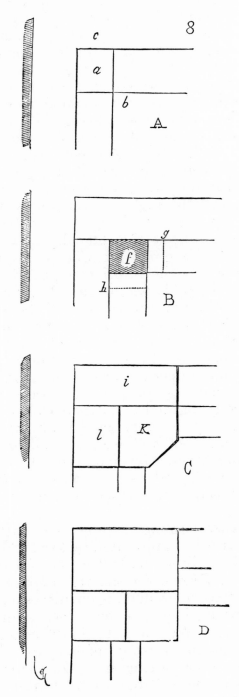

FIG. 8.—Arrangement of Angle Rooms.

think of making central entrances or grand symmetrical arrangements. We shall have to build on the party wall. The
most convenient arrangement therefore is that presented by
the plan, figure 9. As a kitchen courtyard independent of
the court reserved for the family is essential, it would be
well to place the carriage entrance at the side, at A, to
facilitate the passage of vehicles to the carriage porch B.
Carriages may find exit through the passage C, across the
servants' court D. The vestibule at E in the interior angle

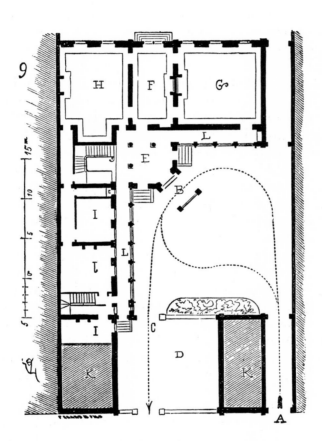

FIG. 9.—Plan for a Small French Town Mansion

gives admission to the saloons F and G. The grand staircase
opens under this vestibule. The dining-room will be at H,
near the pantries I, and the kitchens J. The coach-houses,
stables, and porter's lodge flank the servants' court at K. The
servants easily get to every point from the vestibule along the
glazed porticoes or galleries L. These porticoes do not occupy
the whole height of the ground-floor, because it is desirable
to furnish air and direct illumination above their roof for the
servants' rooms on this wing. The habit of building low por-

ticoes of this kind which are so convenient for communication in private houses has been lost. I do not know why. Probably they are not considered monumental enough ; for we are fond of sacrificing to monumental grandeur. But in mansions, down to the middle of the seventeenth century, they were deemed useful, and were always erected when convenience required them. Under the influence of traditions which in certain respects are much to be respected, but which in many points do not harmonise with our habits, we deprive ourselves of many appliances in our domestic architecture which we might find in methods which those traditions do not sanction, but especially in the suggestions of our own common sense. At every step difficulties have to be encountered in our mansions, and even in houses of less pretensions, which result from that want of agreement between those traditions and our daily wants. Subterfuges are consequently had recourse to, architecture is by no means the gainer, and the inmates thus lose many advantages of which they might avail themselves. The mania for symmetry, at any rate, and the wish to recall the style of the two last centuries, compel us to pervert the arrangements dictated by modern customs. If we examine our modern houses in detail we plainly perceive the efforts, often fruitless in their results, to which architects are compelled to resort with a view to make the arrangements of modern buildings accord with architectural forms that have originated in requirements, or customs, or tastes, other than those of our times. The extreme complexity of modern requirements should however leave its mark on buildings specially devoted to the satisfaction of those requirements. To clothe the complex organism of a modern building in an architectural form originated with a view to satisfy wants comparatively simple, is to commit an anachronism and to produce results against which good sense and therefore good taste protests.

Considering the instructions given us at the *École des Beaux Arts,* and our long cherished and deplorable habit of not reasoning, but doing what a predecessor or a neighbour has done, we shall not succeed all at once in adopting an architecture suitable to the present phase of civilisation ; nevertheless we ought to make a beginning. The present juncture is propitious, since the old social state is breaking up into fragments which no one seems anxious to pick up, so thoroughly worm-eaten do they appear. And amidst this imbroglio shall architects be the last to find the best way out of it ? If they do not or cannot perform this task, engineers,—who are less shackled by traditions and are more anxious to follow a train of reasoning to its consequences,—or building contractors, will accomplish it, and architects will be degraded to the rank of mere decorators; and we might not stop there! We have long had this result in prospect, and circumstances are daily tending to render it more imminent.

While architects are as unwilling as they have been in times past to study and endeavour to solve questions of detail which are continually presenting themselves to constructors; while they continue to make a certain monumental display the supreme consideration,—a display which is of very doubtful character, even in point of taste, but which is patronised by half a dozen individuals, who carry all before them in the school, and who are unwilling that anything should be taught of which they are ignorant; while they continue to express an inexplicable contempt for serious examination or criticism, and a respect quite as inexplicable for works which will bear neither examination nor serious criticism,—behind these architects there is being formed a body of young engineers, who will have no great difficulty in convincing the public, and even administrative boards, however much enslaved they may now be to routine, of the insufficiency of the old methods, and of the waste of the public money that is taking place under the plea of works of art. Then the name of architect will run a very close risk of ceasing to designate a practical artist,—a scientific constructor anxious to promote the interests confided to his charge.

I should anticipate no inconvenience to the public from the disappearance of the name, if the business itself passes into other hands; and it matters little to that public whether a wise and well-founded system of architecture,—the expression of our requirements and industrial appliances,—is carried out by persons bearing the name of engineers or architects, provided it is really carried out by some one. But possibly some of our brethren would not look on such a substitution with an indifferent eye; they would therefore do well, instead of spending their leisure in inveighing against the aggressive spirit of engineers, to give their pupils serious and practical instruction, and to develop their judgment by the habit of reasoning on all the questions that affect the practice of our art.

Would it not be desirable to employ ourselves in improving many of those modes of procedure in building which are vicious, or at least obsolete? Are there not difficult problems daily calling for solution in the structure of our houses, the solving of which is of far more importance than the question of the preference that should be awarded to the architectural styles of the period of Louis XIV., of Louis XV., or even Louis XVI. ?

The method of building in the case of dwellings destined to satisfy the requirements of modern comfort, and of that demand for economy which is becoming more and more imperious, is destined to undergo important modifications. Iron floors of great width and fitted to support partitions have still to be invented; the methods at present in use are simply barbarous. The floorings are intolerably sonorous, and their hold in the walls is clumsily contrived. Slight partitions of great breadth are made in a manner equally barbarous with the floors. Our systems of warming and ventilation are poor in conception, and are still more wretchedly carried out; they are a mere after-thought, the most indispensable preparations for them not having been made during the building. Our method of closing windows is defective, especially for wide and lofty ones. In our interiors architectural ornamentation is put up, like a piece of tapestry, having no relation to the structure, in fact concealing it instead of conforming to it. Iron, which is such a useful appli-ance, affording such stability and security, and enabling us to economise both in material and space,—is had recourse to only as a kind of subterfuge of which we are ashamed. It is concealed or disguised; it is placed under casings whose character is the very opposite of those properties which render it so useful. Wood for joinery-work is becoming scarcer and scarcer; it can no longer be procured seasoned, and soon it will fail altogether. Do archi-tects pay any regard to this fact? On the contrary, they are more than ever bent on adopting combinations of joinery-work that are wasteful of wood, as if it existed in abundance,—to imitate the woodwork of a period during which, by the way, it was by no means well contrived. Yet now would be the oppor-tunity for replacing wood by iron, in many circumstances. But then it would be necessary to inquire and to study; to do something different from what we have been accustomed to do, and from what other people are doing; a struggle must be undertaken against the narrow and timid spirit of our clients, and the attachment to routine among builders. We prefer to keep to the old rut.

It is not the less certain, however, that driving in the ruts may cause an upset.

The ignorance and the infatuation which is its direct con-sequence, that have prevailed among those who undertook to guide the country, and to whose hands the country had com-mitted all authority, have precipitated us into a series of miseries and humiliations, of which we cannot even now get a glimpse of the end. Shall our noble French art, which was so well grounded in reason, so true and original, which bore so clearly the imprint of our manners and customs, and of our genius, also perish in the hands of incapables? Have we not the energy to struggle before the moment of ruin comes, against the tyranny of impotent routine ? Must we see our national honour, our influence in Europe, our military status, our preponderance in the domain of intellect, perish inch by inch, because we have not the sense to abandon in time the apathy into which the long-established habit of ceasing to reason, and of believing that mere feeling or sentiment can be a substitute for study and observation, has plunged us ?

We have a sentimental architecture, as we have had a sentimental public policy and a sentimental war. . . . It is high time we thought of giving sober reason, practical common sense, to the requirements of the times, the improvements furnished by manufacturing skill, and economical arrangements and hygienic and sanitary considerations the importance they justly claim.

Most of the arrangements for warming our dwellings, and those for water-supply and gas-lighting, are an after-thought,— they are contemplated only when the house is already built. Pipes are introduced as they best may be through walls and floorings. The *fumistes* who make the heat-flues for the *calorifères* pierce holes and cut grooves without any great regard for the stability of the structure. Then come the plumbers and gas-fitters, who manage as well as they can. So indifferent are we to the ventilation of state saloons in Paris, that we are half stifled on reception days amid an atmosphere vitiated by the warm air from the *calorifères*, the lights, the absorption of oxygen and the formation of carbonic acid gas. Yet it is of much greater importance to consider these points than to paint ceilings in a style of doubtful taste, and to set up chimney-pieces and panels copied more or less successfully from those of Marie Antoinette's boudoirs.

Since our customs oblige us to crowd into drawing-rooms more people than they can reasonably hold, it should be a main consideration with us to give them air to breathe. In former times, rooms were very spacious, not closely shut up, and not brilliantly lighted ; warming by heating apparatus (*calorifères*) had not been adopted, and comparatively few persons were received at the same time. Our forefathers did not like routs ; *we* have conceived a passion for this mode of passing our evenings ; and it is not for architects to effect a change in such customs ; on the contrary, they must plan their arrangements to suit them.

Hitherto the only method of ventilation adopted in these reception-rooms has consisted in opening the windows, or part of the windows (*i.e.* swing-casements),—a capital way to give people inflammation of the lungs, or at least colds. On ladies' shoulders and men's bald heads there come down douches of cold air, while only two paces off one is plunged in a mephitic vapour-bath at a temperature of 85°. I know that compensation is made—or at least sought—for the mischief thus caused to the constitution, by going to the sea or to watering-places ; but would it not be more natural and reasonable to prevent such mischief altogether ?

Fashionable life, then, consists in poisoning one's-self during three months in the winter for the sake of giving one's-self the satisfaction of going to take an antidote in the summer. It certainly is not thus that a race physically and consequently morally robust can be produced.

The ventilation of reception-rooms in our mansions is therefore a problem of serious importance ; and as it has been made a subject of considerable thought, and systems greatly differing from each other have been suggested, architects should give somewhat greater attention to it than they have hitherto done. If, after having studied such essential matters, they still have time on hand, they may employ it in reproducing such or such a style as may please them or their clients.

The prime condition is air enough to render breathing easy ; for people who are being stifled are little alive to the charms of the most exquisite wainscoting or of a transparent sky painted on the ceiling ; a few cubic yards of fresh air would be far more to their taste.

Our rented houses are, as compared with the mansions we have been discussing, more in advance of their predecessors of recent centuries. More salubrious, better arranged, better built, and tolerably appropriate to present requirements, they exhibit the results of the pressure of necessity. Interest is a powerful stimulus ; and the proprietor of a well-planned house has such an advantage over him who has an inconvenient one, that a maximum of suitability has been secured, which, if it does not reach perfection, evidently comes near to it. But should we decide that nothing more remains to be tried or done ? Certainly not. Before going further in the discussion, we will give proofs of a fact, which, to Paris at least, is of the gravest importance, since it affects one aspect of its prosperity.

The opening of new thoroughfares across the capital, which took place on such an enormous scale under the recent Empire, excessively stimulated speculation in rented houses. The speculators who took advantage of the first and most desirable openings, such as the *Rue de Rivoli* and the *Boulevard de Sébastopol* realised considerable profits ; but in those central thoroughfares which traverse populous and briskly trading quarters, however dear the ground might be, the speculators might boldly proceed to build houses for the tenants of these districts who could not go elsewhere, and who, confident of making a profit by their business, could pay comparatively high rents, and who were inclined to leases at long terms. In these thoroughfares commerce would sometimes invade even the highest stories; and in a city like Paris commerce is represented by that part of the community which can pay the highest rents, since a high rent is one of the essential conditions of high profits. A dealer, *e.g.* gets £200 per month by paying £960 rent per annum, whereas he would only get £40 per month by paying only £240 rent. It is a matter of position,—quarter of the city,—commercial centrality. But when the opening of new streets was extended to points of the city which did not present these commercial advantages,—when new boulevards were opened in the west for example,—the conditions the speculator had to meet were quite different. The ground was no cheaper, and the cost of building was at any rate not less than in the populous quarters. Not being able to get rents for the ground-floor at a very high figure as compared with the surface occupied, he had to reckon on letting handsome apartments on the lower stories. At first this succeeded very well. The district in question is attractive, —near to the Champs Elysées, the Tuileries, and the Bois de Boulogne. These sumptuous apartments were soon let and occupied. But rich as the inhabitants of Paris may be, there are not many who can afford £960 a year for a suite of rooms, and when those who can had been accommodated, there were no tenants for those which speculation was still continuing to provide. Besides, many people thought better to have a small mansion of their own, which, including the site, would cost £20,000, than to pay the interest of that sum without possessing the capital. And it was at this date that a great number of small mansions were built in the outskirts of Paris; and the districts formerly not built on, at Chaillot, la Muette, Neuilly, Passy, Auteuil, etc., occupied. The possession of a mansion or a villa of their own has thus become gradually more habitual with men of moderate fortune. All who had capital at their disposal preferred investing it in a house of their own rather than spending the interest in the rents of a suite of apartments in a hired house.

Thus, the more houses were built by speculators for which they must have high rents,—since the site and the building cost them at least on an average £50 per yard,—the fewer tenants they found inclined to occupy these dwellings; first, because all who could afford from £240 to £960 per annum rent were already accommodated; secondly, because many, considering the sums demanded for rent, preferred to be their own landlords,— that is, to invest money in building a dwelling which would continue to belong to them, and for which they could at any time realise what they paid for it.

The situation of our country, and of Paris in particular, since the disastrous war of 1870-71, is not such as to improve the position of speculators in rented houses in aristocratic quarters. Henceforth we may consider property of this kind as likely to undergo considerable depreciation, and we can scarcely foresee what will become of the numerous buildings which are unoccupied, or are let eventually to foreigners in Paris and our other large cities.

These considerations are pertinent to our subject, and they bring us to this conclusion,—that Parisian customs in regard to the class of habitations occupied are being modified, and that they are probably tending to be modified more and more as time advances.

Individuals and families will more and more wish to isolate themselves. Except in commercial quarters,—in business centres,—large rented houses will be no more in demand, because tenants will become fewer and fewer. He who has formed the habit of living in a house of his own, with no rent to pay at the quarter's end, and without having to fear a notice to quit or a rise in the rent, without having to put up with troublesome neighbours, or a surly porter (as is sometimes the case), will be unwilling to re-enter a hired dwelling. He will prefer to go beyond the limits of Paris, and live in one of the towns in the environs, though business requires him to come into the capital every day.

Thus the abuses that have been caused by the opening of thoroughfares destined to render Paris more habitable, healthy, and attractive, will have as their result a modification in Parisian habits, and will bring it about that some quarters of the city, which have been recently built at great expense, will remain uninhabited, or at least that they will be only occasionally occupied. Consequently those quarters in which there are still many sites on which there are no buildings will suffer a considerable depreciation of the factitious value they had acquired; and when their cost is reduced low enough to be within reach of moderate fortunes, it will not be stone houses five stories high that will be built there, but small dwellings sufficient for one or two families.

The future we are contemplating seems not very distant, unless this great city suffers a decline. It is a desirable consummation; our morals will be improved by it, and Parisian life will be the better for it. A model—a perfect social state would be one in which the great majority of its members were their own landlords, and had an attachment to a home of their own;

which would result in warmer family affections, a disposition to work, a more judicious selection of friends, and the abandonment of vain or unwholesome distractions.

We have here then a new and very desirable programme, which architects will probably be soon called on to satisfy. Attempts have already been made in this direction; some charming houses of simple and modest appearance might be referred to, which, built in remote quarters to the west of Paris, are inhabited by persons of moderate fortune,—quiet families who have bid a long farewell to theatres and routs, and are occupied with the education of their children; where regular work maintains tranquillity and good-humour. But this new programme has still to be developed.

Such houses cannot be mansions in miniature; they will have to be modelled according to the habits referred to, which are not yet fully formed, but will soon be so—at least such is our hope. For it is a remarkable fact that our middle classes, which are the vital force of modern society, have not in France any fashions or customs of their own. They are not the *bourgeoisie* of former times; they have striven latterly to imitate to the best of their ability the external features of an aristocracy of wealth, and have sacrificed to vanity rather than considered the comfort of their homes; we see a good many small dwellings in quarters far removed from the west end of Paris, whose plans are a copy in miniature of magnificent mansions.

Nothing of the kind is to be found in England or Germany, where houses for families whose habits are unpretentious in consequence of the modest extent of their incomes are really adapted to the social position of their owners. Of course architects cannot bring considerations of a moral order to bear on the case when a client comes and asks them to build a dwelling for his own use; yet on many occasions their judgment and sensible representations would exercise a certain influence over such clients. Without setting up for moral reformers, which would be ridiculous in the extreme, an architect may present the results of his observations on such or such arrangements in an attractive manner; but he must have such observations stored up in his mind, he must have discretion and intelligence enough to bring them forward opportunely, and he must regard himself not as a submissive instrument ready to yield to all the caprices of his client, but as a counsellor and guide who should prevent him from falling into errors prejudicial to his own interests. Architects have unfortunately long entertained a different conception of the part they should play; and we cannot wonder at this, while examples of independence and dignity of character were not to be looked for in high quarters,—far from it. There is no hope in fact of our being able to change such habits among those with whom they are inveterate. Servitude leaves an indelible trace in men's minds; it is therefore to the generation that is now rising,—to our youth—that these observations are addressed. It is for them to revive correctness of judgment and firmness of character,—that true function of the architect which consists in enlightening his clients, not in following their most trifling caprices.

LECTURE XVIII.

DOMESTIC ARCHITECTURE—continued.

THE change that is taking place in the habits of large cities, and especially in Paris, in consequence of the excessive amount of rents and the more and more decided inclination of the inhabitants for houses of their own, should be an inducement to architects to seek the most appropriate means for satisfying that inclination.

Economy in the method of building is evidently one of the most essential conditions dictated by this novel programme. And we are accustomed in France generally to build in a too expensive fashion. The division of inherited patrimonial estates and the rapid change of customs, have brought it about that private houses are not required to be built in a way that will enable them to last for many centuries. A hundred years is a comparatively long period of duration; for within the limits of a century a dwelling-house is destined to change occupants five or six times, and at the end of this period the internal arrangements can scarcely suit new generations without undergoing important modifications, which are often equivalent to entire reconstruction.

The object architects should have in view is to build houses at rentals of from £160 to £480 per annum, representing a capital of £3200 to £9600. Considering the cost of sites in our large towns, the problem is a difficult one. It is therefore not in the populous and trading quarters that such buildings can be erected, but on the outskirts of our great cities. When the ill-starred ramparts of Paris shall be condemned to demolition,—a day not far distant we hope,—there will be found sites well adapted for this most desirable purpose, because they must be sold for moderate amounts. Something like 240 square yards would be sufficient for the site of a house of moderate dimensions for one family, with a court or small garden; and if the ground costs £1, 13s. 4d. per yard, the capital invested in buying the site will be only £400. And for £2400 or £2800 at most, a house suitable for the accommodation of a large family may be built. In fact, 120 square yards of building at £20 per yard, gives £2400; and for the sum of £20 per square yard it would not be difficult to build a house with cellars, ground-floor, two stories below the roofing and one in it, if we confine ourselves within the limits of a reasonable economy and do not sacrifice to vanity.

Yet there are few families that can spare from £120 to £160 a year in rent, or have a capital of £2000 or £3000 to apply to building purposes. Recourse must therefore be had in their case to speculative builders who, on sufficiently extensive sites, erect buildings that could be divided, and each section of which, from roof to floor, would be allotted to a single family, paying for it either in a single sum or by redemption within a fixed term. In London this method is adopted, on the principle of long leases; *i.e.* the ground on which houses are built is granted on a ninety-nine years' lease, for a single payment or on consideration of a ground-rent. We have not adopted these usages, which is so much the more to be wondered at, as France is that country of Europe in which fortunes as well as institutions are least secure. We like perpetuity in theory at least, but practically we have no faith in it. Among us, when the father of a family has secured a dwelling for his children and grandchildren that shall be theirs for a hundred years, he may rest content. Taking this into consideration, something might be attempted on the ground which will probably be at our disposal on the line of the fortifications of Paris, and those which, in considerable quantity, have not been encroached on by building since the annexation of the outlying districts.

Intelligent observers have suggested, and with some plausibility, that the aspect of dwellings exerts an influence on the morals of the inmates. If this observation is just, it must be confessed that nothing is more likely to demoralise a people than those great rented houses in which the personality of the individual is lost,—where the love of hearth and home is scarcely possible, and where consequently the advantages that flow from it are absent. Each tenant of these houses, uniform in aspect and in their successive stories, is a temporary visitor, who cannot become attached to these walls in which he will live only a few months or years, which will have seen other occupants before him and will see others after him. How could one attach one's-self to walls which may be tenanted by any one—to these interiors which bear no traces of the taste of the occupant? A private house, on the contrary, however modest its pretensions, always bears the impress of the habits of the owner. Though, as in London, such houses may present a uniform aspect outside, their internal arrangements are modified according to the individual tastes and habits of those who possess them and dwell in them. And it is a characteristic of human nature to become attached to objects which reflect something of one's personality. People always conceive an affection for what they have made for themselves; and such affection, when it is attached to hearth and home, is a salutary one. We cannot, therefore, I think, too warmly encourage the tendency of a considerable portion of the public to relinquish houses let out in flats for private houses; and to a certain degree architects have the opportunity of aiding this change in our habits by studying the most economical means of construction, such as will enable persons of moderate fortune to live in houses of their own.

A considerable number of manufacturers in France have built dwellings for the workmen they employ. These dwellings, separated into allotments, may become the property of the workmen by redemption. The result is that habits of regularity, order, and honesty are rapidly diffused in colonies of this kind; and rarely do these industrial communities give themselves up to the excesses which are so frequently met with in manufacturing districts where this system has not been adopted.

And that which is morally commendable in this system for the working classes is equally desirable for those classes whose education or means, or the character of their occupations, is of a higher grade.

The attachment to hearth and home produces the love of diligent work, order, and a wise economy. We should therefore endeavour to promote that attachment, to render it possible for as large a number as possible, and do our utmost to solve the problem involved in its furtherance. And architects could not engage in a more honourable endeavour. It is one of greater difficulty in France than in England or Germany, because we have been long accustomed to the display of a false luxury, and many worthy people do not consider themselves respectably lodged—crowding being no consideration with them—except within stone walls decorated with gewgaws, and unless the little parlour they occupy is covered with gilding.

Our houses in flats do not permit of making special arrangements, since the rooms of which they consist must suit all persons equally,—that is, nobody in particular. Consequently the apartments they contain are invariably an antechamber, a drawing-room, a dining-room, a kitchen and pantry, and bed-rooms with or without dressing-rooms. Studies or work-rooms are never thought of. All these habitations seem destined for persons who pass their day away from home in bureaux or offices whose business requires their whole time. If a man of business, a barrister, a medical man, a lawyer, a banker, an architect, a civil engineer, or an artificer, takes one of these suites of apartments, he is obliged to turn one or several of the rooms we have just mentioned into the study or consultation room or the workshop with the appurtenances which his occupations require. There is no arrangement for these offices, and they generally find their place in the very midst of the rooms assigned to the family. Thence arise daily annoyances and inconveniences which often render home life intolerable; and thus the heads of families make it the chief object of their life to escape from these inconveniences and annoyances as often as possible. If such dwellings were arranged according to the requirements of the inmates, they would find it more agreeable to stay at home. But such special arrangements can only be made in buildings adapted to this object, and houses in flats, as we have described them, cannot lend themselves to any such special arrangements.

If a person who was entirely unacquainted with our customs were introduced to such houses, he would very naturally inquire where and when the inmates of these habitations worked. And in fact no provision is made in these dwellings for the exigencies of work, notwithstanding that for most persons they are in some form or other prime considerations.

The uniformity and regularity of our new thoroughfares have occasioned a uniformity in the houses, and consequently a uniformity in the interior arrangements; and when it is necessary to find a habitation in which a study or office-room can be contrived, it is still only in the older houses that we have a chance of getting what we require.

Much has been done recently for our citizens in their capacity of promenaders and business men, but a home has been rendered almost impossible to them. In their dwellings they are uncomfortably crowded, and not being able to devote themselves to any occupation, they become disgusted with home life, and pass the time which is not absorbed by business in company or at the *café.*

By rendering separate houses possible for persons of moderate fortunes, architects would solve one of the questions suggested by the necessities of the time, which are continually raising questions whose gravity is more and more apparent to thinking minds, but which official teaching seems to look on with increasing contempt.

Though complying with the municipal regulations for not projecting beyond the line (regulations concerning which moreover we shall have a good deal to say),—which is possible in the case of a private house, since it may be built some distance in rear of the thoroughfare,—the architect can avail himself of features very advantageous to the interior accommodation, such as corbellings, overhanging roofs, and projections. I am aware that arrangements of this kind are not generally thought consistent with strict economy; but whatever truth there may be in this idea it arises from the faultiness of the system of building generally adopted,—a system which, by its very principle, is a too costly one, as it proposes to give buildings a durability which is by no means in keeping with our habits and the social conditions under which we live.

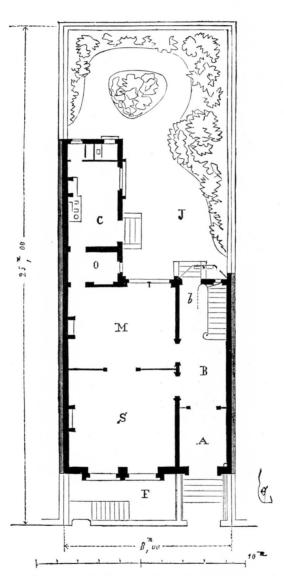

Fig. 1.—Design for a French Private Street House.—Ground-plan.

The judicious use of iron, cast and wrought, would not unfrequently enable us to build very economically, and with an assured prospect of stability for a certain period,—a hundred years, *e.g.*, which is quite sufficient.

We remarked above that it is possible to build a house in

Paris sufficient to accommodate a numerous family for £3200 or less, the cost of site included. Let us examine the matter in detail. Let figure 1 represent a site 80 feet deep by 27 broad, *i.e.* 240 square yards. The house occupies a space of 100 square yards, and there will be a lean-to for the kitchen, covering 18 square yards.

The house will consist of a basement, a ground-floor, a first and second story, and a story in the roofing. Such a building designed in the way we are going to show will cost in Paris

	£	s.	d.
£16, 16s. per square yard at most, . . .	£1680	0	0
The kitchen lean-to, ...	60	0	0
The enclosure walls, palisades, area wall in front, flights of steps, garden, etc., . . .	140	0	0
Total, .	£1880	0	0
Supposing the ground to cost £1, 13s. 4d. per square yard,—240 square yards, . .	400	0	0
Total, .	£2280	0	0

Which at 5 per cent., gives a rent of £114.

On the ground-floor this house (figure 1) contains—a vestibule A, an antechamber B, with a stair leading to the upper stories, and a passage *b* leading to the small garden B, and kitchen C; a drawing-room S, and a dining-room with pantry O. Between the public thoroughfare and the house is a sunk area F, with steps for taking in provisions, removing rubbish, etc. On the first story (figure 2), we have an office-room with library *t* and a large bed-room G, with the dressing-room *g*. The second story contains two large bedrooms with dressing-rooms. In the roofing are two bedrooms for the family, two small rooms for servants, and a linen-room. In the basement story, provision cellars, a warming apparatus (*calorifère*), and a bath-room are lighted from the area in front. It need not be observed that there is a stair down to the basement, below the upper stair. The front wall on the entrance side is built of stone and brick, as we shall show, and is only one foot two inches thick at the piers. Those overlooking the garden are of stone and brick, and at some points are only nine inches thick, fig. 2. A partition[1] of iron fram-

[1] One of the most remarkable examples of the influence of administrative routine among us is presented in the regulations respecting the thickness of outside walls of houses in Paris. Formerly when walls were generally built of rubble-work, the thickness was fixed at nearly 20 inches ; the reason being that it is not possible to build a substantial wall of rubble-work of any height if the thickness is less, *i.e.* if it is not constructed with a double rank of stones. Now as these stones, to form a substantial wall, must have from eight inches to a foot of tail, overlapping they would give about 20 inches. When it was determined that there should be walls of free-stone facing the thoroughfares, the same figure, 20 inches, was prescribed, though a stone wall 16 inches thick is at least as substantial as one in rubble-work of 20. But the most absurd regulation of all is that the requirement in the case of stone was not insisted on for bricks, and while no stone wall is allowed less than 20 inches thick, a brick wall of nine inches is tolerated. In our regulations for street building even more ridiculous anomalies might be cited.

ing filled in with brick separates the vestibule from the large
rooms, and bears the floorings that rest on the party walls. The
flooring joists are of iron and the roofing of wood.

But we will give a detailed explanation of the method of
construction suggested, and which, though the materials are
comparatively costly, allows us to build at a considerably less
expense than if we adopted the usual methods. Plate XXXIV.
gives the elevation of such a house facing the street, and the
section along the front wall; Plate XXXV. the elevation on
the garden, and the section along the side wall. It will be
observed that the lower slope of the roof overhangs the outer

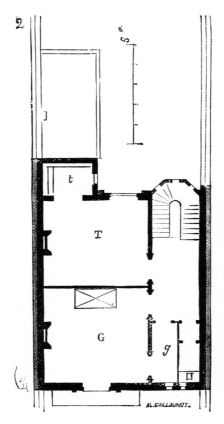

Fig. 2.—Design for a French Private Street House—first-floor plan.

walls, and is supported by means of a system of wood brackets
which form a projecting cornice, and which perfectly shelter
the walls. This system has also the advantage of giving a
square story in the roofing, whose surface is equal to that of the
lower stories.

I have mentioned iron floorings and partitions. The price of
iron floorings in Paris is now very nearly the same as that of
wooden ones; and certain improvements which the manufacture

of iron and the attentive study of architects promise to introduce, would still further diminish the price. We may expect the same reduction in iron-framed partitioning; and this would cost less than wooden studding,[1] for while floors must present over their whole surface an equal resistance to a variable load, it is not the same with wood or iron-framed partitions; the weights they have directly to sustain are invariable, and consequently the resisting points are appreciable beforehand, and these alone will have to be strongly constructed; all other parts consist merely of filling-in, and this can be done in the most economical manner.

Many other questions relating to the structure of our houses deserve study, if our architects would but give them serious attention, and not adhere to obsolete methods. Wooden stairs are also destined to make way for iron ones, which are already manufactured in the most economical way, and which are not liable to be burned nor to settle in consequence of the drying of the timbers, as often happens to our modern stairs made as they are with unseasoned wood,—and none other is now to be obtained. Is there, in fact, anything more defective in principle than those notched circular stairstrings which are held together by oblique bolts and hoop-iron, in contravention of the nature of the wood and its properties, as the bolts in question hold these *crémaillères* or string boards in the direction of the grain, and so tend to split the wood ?

Outside window-blind arrangements deserve special attention, and in houses for single families they are still more important than can be the case in those built in flats. Outside window-blinds in wood (*persiennes*), which are so inconvenient and fragile, requiring frequent repairs and producing such an unsightly effect on fronts, have had their day. For some years sheet-iron *persiennes*, folding back in leaves in the thickness of the window-jambs have been adopted; but unless the walls are thick, the space occupied by these leaves obliges us to set back the window frames almost flush with the inside of the walls, which is very inconvenient, leaving no room for curtains; or there has been a return to venetian blinds with iron laths instead of wooden ones; but venetian blinds do not make a firm screen. But ingenuity has already invented venetian blinds which can be made rigid by a very simple arrangement.[2] Their laths are rolled on a cylinder at the top of the window-bay. Why should not a place for such rollers be provided

[1] See a work on this subject by M. Liger, architect: *Dictionnaire historique et pratique de la voirie de la police municipale, de la construction et de la contiguité,* " *Pans de bois et pans de fer,*" 1867.

[2] At the Paris Exhibition of 1867, English exhibitors produced blinds of this kind, so managed that when let down they had the rigidity of a homogeneous plate of metal.

in the construction ? And as regards windows on the ground floor, which ought to be well protected in houses for single families, why should not a system of closing be adopted similar to that in use for shop-fronts? In this case, again, we have an example of hybrid arrangements, which have the inconvenience of attempting to reconcile ancient forms with habits and customs with which they no longer accord. That eternal window of the Roman palaces, which is reproduced in our fronts to satiety, no more corresponds with the requirements of the modern house window, than the great chimney-piece with its wide fireplace and high mantel, with our present modes for heating. The modern window ought to be a complete arrangement, comprising the glazed part, the provisions for security or for protection against the sun, and to be duly provided for in an opening in the outer wall, properly constructed to receive it, just as we now arrange our chimney-pieces to receive the fire-grate. When the arrangements for window protection are contrived as they ought to be, so as exactly to fulfil their purpose, the openings will be disposed accordingly; but to proceed in an inverse fashion is violating common sense; it is setting ourselves an insoluble problem. Let us then begin by constructing a proper arrangement for closing and screening our windows without troubling ourselves as to whether it can find a place in a window-case copied from a Roman palace of the sixteenth century.

Even down to the seventeenth century windows were very narrow, or if wide, they were divided by a fixed mullion. There was but one leaf with shutters inside for each compartment; this was a reasonable plan; the wooden casement was only a glazed frame set into rebate whose uprights carried their shutters. But when, at the close of the sixteenth century, builders began to introduce in the front walls of houses and palaces wide and lofty window openings without fixed mullions, they adopted two-leaved casements, with a shutter arrangement attached to the middle. Then they applied shutters on the inside independent of the glazed frames; then, for protection against the sun's rays outside, venetian blinds copied from Spanish and Italian houses; and lastly, outside window-blinds projecting on the exterior. The window-cases in use by no means harmonised with this system of blinds; but it did not occur to any architect to modify the classic form in adaptation to the new method of blinds. When the masonry was finished, holes were pierced in the window-cases to suspend the sun-blinds, and the frames of the casements were attached as well as they could be with stay-nails. This was a barbarous method, the result of a series of mere trials and expedients; study and deduction have no part in it. The window-opening ought to be constructed with a view to the system of blinds. It is time that we tried to invent reasonable methods and ceased to have recourse to mere expedients. We should make it our chief endeavour to proceed methodically and logically, if we would inaugurate an architecture proper to our times. We must endeavour to enfranchise our minds from those traditional forms which cannot be reconciled with our requirements. If we cannot at once discover forms that shall satisfy the eye, let us rest assured that when practical requirements have been properly satisfied, a pleasing form will naturally follow.

I was saying that for windows on the ground-floor a system of metal-plate blinds similar to those used in our shops would be, to meet the present requirements of the case, at least very satisfactory, inasmuch as they would be secure, and would not oblige us to open the windows to close the blinds. But to make this system complete, the glazed part and the protecting screen must be combined, and capable of being placed in the opening all in a piece, and even during the building, if thought desirable. Our modern appliances can furnish all the iron-work required, and if a few architects began to adopt a tolerably complete system, manufacturers would soon make arrangements for supplying contractors at moderate prices.

We regard it as certain that wooden windows, like wooden outside blinds, have had their day, and must be relinquished; that they must be replaced by iron, and that these after some trials will be produced at the same cost as those of wood,[1] being, it may be remarked, very superior to their rivals in durability and strength, and admitting more light. The frame of the casement which would also serve as the frame for the blinds, whether in one or in several plates, should be strong enough to sustain the lintels or flat arches of the window openings, and should furnish a substitute for the iron, which is usually sunk in below these flat arches or lintels to the detriment of their strength; these iron frames might even form ties if they were built in as the walls were raised; in slight constructions they would be rigid enough to allow a diminution of thickness in the piers; they would in fact form the skeleton of the front walls; which might then be pierced with openings very near to one another if this should seem needful.

Thus the window-casing would resume its function,—the function it had in primitive constructions; it would afford supports of greater strength than the rest of the wall, which would thus become mere filling-in. The iron, although combined with

---

[1] This has already been attempted, and iron windows have been successfully manufactured, at prices very little exceeding those of wooden ones, by M. Maury, one of the exhibitors at the *Exposition Universelle* of 1867.

FIG. 3.—Design for a French Street Villa. Garden Elevation.

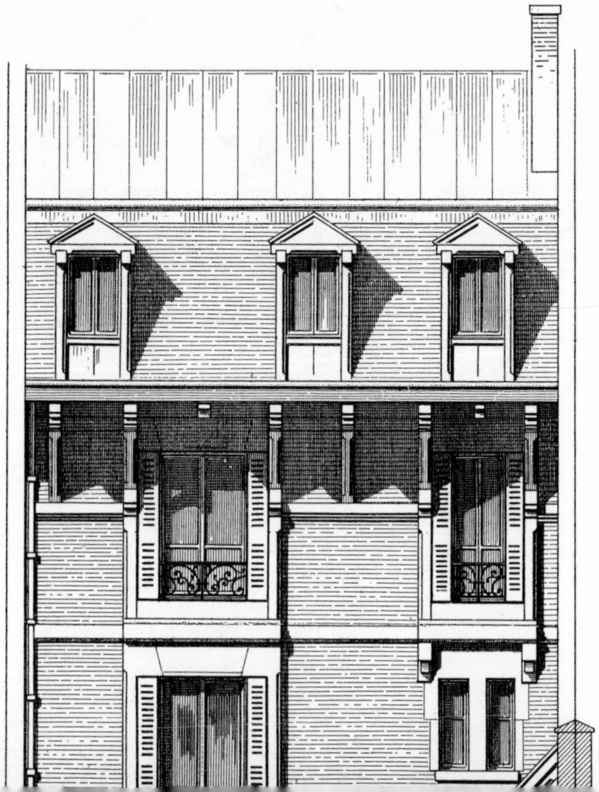

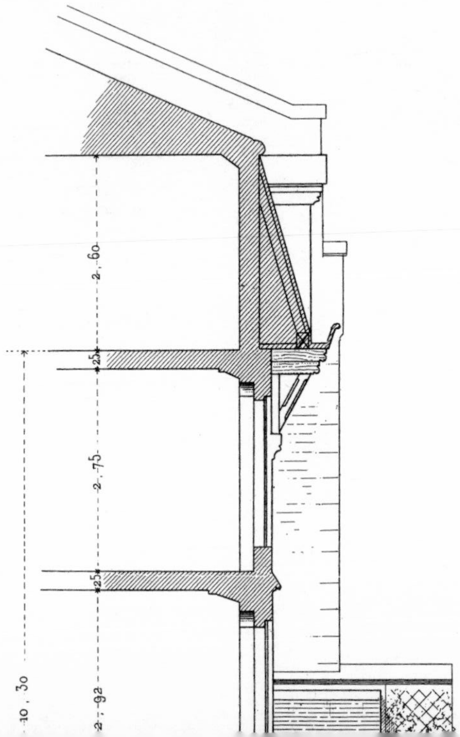

COURS D'ARCHITECTURE

2ᵐ 92

2ᵐ 60

25

2ᵐ 75

25

10ᵐ 30

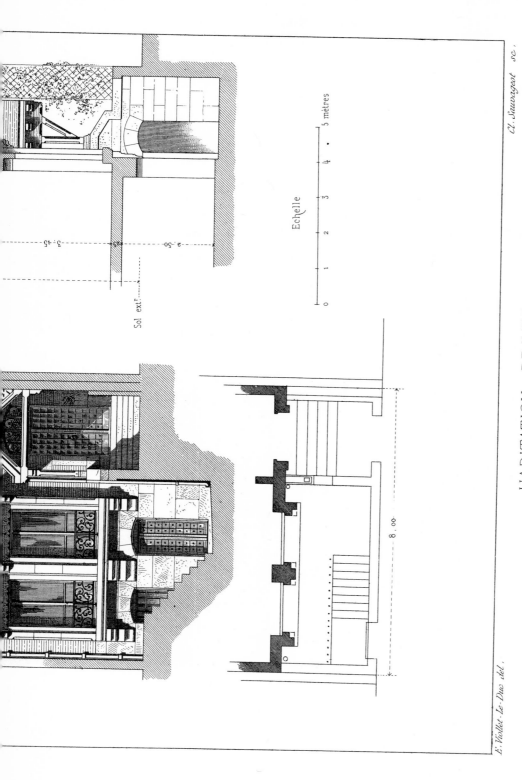

Echelle

0 1 2 3 4 • 5 mètres

Sol extᶠ

3·45

·25

2·50

8·00

HABITATION PRIVÉE

FAÇADE — CÔTE DE LA VOIE PUBLIQUE

COURS D'ARCHITECTURE

COUPE SUR C. D.

FAÇADE SUR A. B.

2. 90   2. 75   2. 60

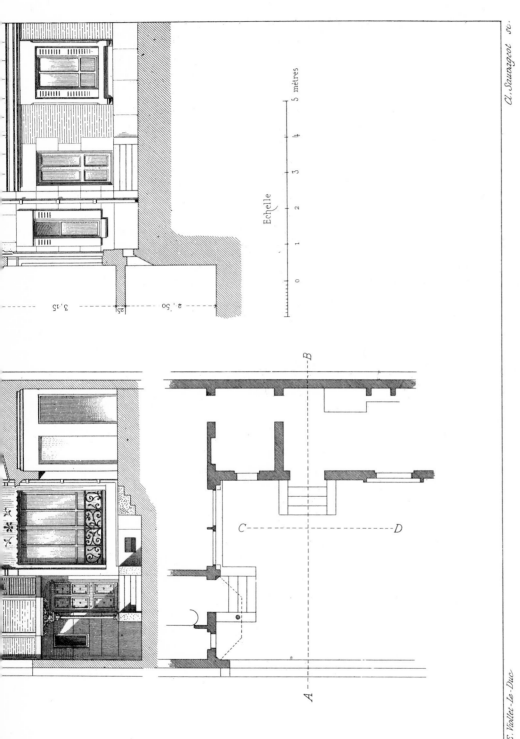

E. Viollet-le-Duc

Vᵉ A. MOREL et Cⁱᵉ Éditeurs.

HABITATION PRIVÉE

FAÇADE — COTE DU JARDIN

A. Sauvageot. sc.

Imp. Lemercier et Cⁱᵉ Paris

Echelle

0   1   2   3   4   5 mètres

the masonry, would preserve its independent function, and would not injure the masonry by the oxidation of the fastenings.

Let us examine in detail the various parts of the small building represented in figs. 1 and 2, and Plates XXXIV. and XXXV.[1] The polygonal part of the staircase is supported by a cast-iron pillar, and projects beyond the line of the ground-floor, as shown in the perspective sketch, figure 3.

On this pillar, or rather on its cap, which supports one side of the polygon, is placed a bearer of angle-iron, to which are secured, by means of corner-couplings, the angle supports (also of iron) of the staircase, to which are fastened the braces of the windows, and the plate-iron strings inside, which receive the risers of the steps. The intervals are filled with brick. This part of the staircase, therefore, is entirely constructed of iron and brick, and may be no more than $4\frac{1}{2}$ inches thick. The projecting roof covers its top as seen in Plate XXXV. and figure 3.

As regards the arrangements for window protection, before speaking of the particular case presented here, let us see how it can be applied in ordinary buildings.

We suppose an outer wall of the usual strength, *i.e.* 20 inches thick in stone or rubble work. Let us take first the window of the ground-floor, which should be securely shuttered-up during the night, fig. 4. The jambs are of stone, forming two exterior projections A, receiving the iron-box which contains the mechanical appliances (an endless screw or chains) for raising and lowering the plates of sheet-iron which are wound up behind the metal valance B. Behind this valance is a stone lintel C, only 7 inches thick; it is a single slab on edge, and bearing on the iron lintel of the window-frame, which is connected with the iron tie-rods. The remaining space of 13 inches is covered by a brick arch D, which bears the joists of the flooring, if these are supported by the front wall. This arch is shown in dotted lines in the elevation. The projection of the jambs A, in the height of the lintel, is increased by corbels bearing the stone capping F, which gives complete protection to the metal valance and the moveable plates. But it would be well for the whole system which constitutes the shuttering to be combined, as remarked above, and that the casements, the reveals, and the mechanical apparatus with the valance should be of cast and sheet-iron, which would tend to give great solidity to the building, and would allow the piers between the bays to be recessed,—thereby affording useful

[1] It has seemed desirable to take a very unpretentious building as a type. In architectural problems it appears advantageous to proceed from the simple to the composite, and it is more difficult to build a small house, with due regard to economy, while rendering it perfectly adapted to its purpose, than to erect a great public building on which vast sums and every kind of luxury, good and bad, are lavished.

FIG. 4.—Design for a French Street Villa.—Details of the Windows.

spaces for furniture. Let figure 5 be an outer wall of an apartment with two windows; the arrangement of window-jambs thus strengthened would enable us to leave very commodious recesses between the windows, which, like the windows themselves, might be arched. The real supports for the front walls would thus be the window-jambs,—a reasonable arrangement, as the walls would not be less strong, but would require less material, and would therefore be lighter. We suppose, of course, that the walls and the jambs are kept at a thickness of 20 inches. The back of these recesses in the piers may be built with bricks, 9 inches thick. The recesses between the

5

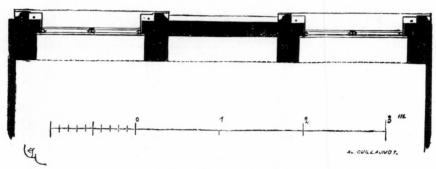

FIG. 5.—Plan illustrating Iron Windows.

windows would therefore be 11 inches deep,—a very useful space, where every inch is of value. It might perhaps be objected that outer walls thus reduced in thickness in the piers would not offer a sufficient cohesion; but to this we reply that these windows, well stayed by the arches and the balustrade bars (whose function would thus be useful to the structure), well tied longitudinally at the height of the casement lintels, composing a homogeneous whole, inasmuch as the thrusting and pulling forces act simultaneously and neutralise each other, would give an absolute rigidity to the vertical surfaces; while these outer walls, thus lightened, could be built on less costly foundations, and would not require such expensive substructure in the case of compressible soils.

Reverting to figure 4, we see how the metal *persiennes* are lodged outside and folded back even with the projecting jambs H, in the space reserved outside the window reveals at L. In plan, these windows exhibit the section A, figure 6; in elevation, the sketch B on the outside and D on the inside; in section, the sketch E. We suppose these metal *persiennes* to be hung not to the arris of the stone reveals, but to the metal reveals forming a frame for the casements, and also for the *persiennes*. This window arrangement may therefore be fixed all complete, and the lintels of the casements be connected with the ends of the tie-rods passing through the piers. These tie-rods are thus

FIG. 6.—Details of Iron Windows.

quite in their place, since they are carried through at the height of the springing of the relieving arches. The stone lintels are no longer weakened, and only form a facing. The string course connects them with the interior relieving arches. The ends of the iron joists of the flooring may therefore safely rest on these relieving arches. As regards the opening of the double window in figure 3, in the ground-floor overlooking the garden, as it is much wider than the window-openings of the upper stories, it is divided by an iron mullion which supports the two relieving arches, and serves to carry the casements of this window. This mullion does not go beyond the external vertical plane of the arches, so that room is left for the metal-plate shutters.

It does not seem necessary, however, to dwell longer on this unpretending building, which has given us an opportunity for suggesting some details applicable to the most modest private dwellings. It is clear, however, that mixed constructions of the kind referred to, in which iron constitutes an important element, can be executed at moderate prices only in large towns, until our great metallurgic establishments can freely supply iron work suitable for such building appliances at very reduced prices, and in great quantity,—a state of things which, we hope, will soon be realised.

As respects the arrangements of great city houses containing apartments in flats, they do not lend themselves to very important changes. The substitution of iron for wooden partitions, and a greater degree of freedom in the form of the windows, will not give these houses a decided character, as their local position and our municipal regulations present obstacles to all manifestations of originality in their architecture.

It is clear, however, that if these regulations were less rigorous, it would be possible for the architects of large cities, Paris especially, to introduce certain improvements into rented houses,—certain convenient arrangements not attainable now. Thus, for instance, though it may be desirable to forbid projections, corbellings, and covered loggias which would intercept air and sunshine in thoroughfares 40 feet wide and under, such restrictions are unreasonable in the case of those whose breadth is more than 65 or 70. Independently of the advantages and pleasure accruing to the tenants from features of this kind projecting on corbellings, the aspect of these streets would be improved; for nothing can be more monotonous than our great boulevards; in vain do our architects tax their ingenuity to decorate their façades with pilasters and ornaments of every description: at a distance these houses look just alike, and do not attract the eye to any particular point. Those whose fronts have been the subject of careful study in their details, do not produce any better effect than those whose exterior walls are decorated in defiance of common sense. The masses themselves, the arrangement of the windows, the height of the stories and the projections being the same for all, these details, whether good or bad, are lost sight of, and interest no one. Since municipal regulations have, however, without sufficient reason, fixed the thickness of freestone walls at about 20 inches (19·69), projecting loggias and corbellings might well have been allowed in the wider thoroughfares, since that thickness of wall allows such features to be constructed with perfect safety. And such projections alone could obviate the tiresome monotony of long lines of uniform frontages.

There is little hope of inducing the administrations of our country to retrace their steps in regard to measures which were excellent perhaps at the time they were adopted, but which have become obsolete as the result of changed conditions; but we should never, as the adage has it, "throw the helve after the hatchet" by refusing to seek for improvements on the pretext that they will be rejected. It is in consequence of such a policy that in France we fall under the tyranny of a routine which is perpetuated because it is deemed hopeless to oppose it. The more intelligent lose their interest, and dull minds conceal their indolence and incompetence beneath a sceptical exterior, which simulates deep insight; the wild and visionary alone rush into the arena and soon by their extravagance justify routine, which does not fail to make the most of its easy triumph by shutting the gates against investigation and judicious criticism.

The innovations which builders venture upon in our city houses are not very extensive. For some time past architects have thought proper to substitute round towers for the truncated cones presented at the corners of our great thoroughfares; the mode has been caught up immediately, and a hundred houses, forming angles in this position, have been terminated by a round tower. This is not an innovation, as might be supposed, but the revival of an arrangement which in certain cases has its advantages, but which has also its inconveniences. A circular apartment is not exactly adapted for furniture. Though such a form may be suitable for boudoirs, or small private apartments, it is not convenient for reception-rooms; whereas in our modern houses it is the drawing-room that occupies this privileged place —that is, it is the apartment destined for receiving company in large numbers. A circular drawing-room is adopted as the fashionable one in a certain clique, just as an inconvenient toilet, which all the world wears, is submitted to. It is a thing of fashion.

I can understand how a municipal administration should be justified in taxing the permission to build projecting structures even in very wide thoroughfares, as they do that of erecting a balcony. "You have the enjoyment of a space taken from the public street: pay for it." That is but just; but if it occasions no inconvenience to the passers along this street, why should it be absolutely forbidden? And why should the administration deprive itself of this source of revenue?

Will it be alleged that these projecting structures are dangerous? It is easy to show that this anxiety is not well founded; besides, has not the municipal body inspectors who can point out faults in construction, and put a veto on objectionable erections? Is it not strange that, with the appliances now at our disposal, which allow of, and even incite to, so many innovations, we should continue to build exactly as we did in the last century? That we should continue to erect heavy piers such as were erected when iron floors had not come into vogue, and heap up piles of stones for the fronts of houses, while walls of the same height and supporting the same weights are built, overlooking courts, in thicknesses less by half, without any accident resulting? It would seem, in fact, as if the houses of Paris, and of the great towns built in imitation of Paris, were erected, not for those who live in them, but with a view to present certain monumental aspects to passers-by, who, be it observed, pay little attention to them; that they are built for show, in preference to other considerations. We thus exhibit to ourselves and to strangers palatial fronts which conceal narrow and unhealthy apartments. Splendour outside, discomfort within; is not this the plan on which most of our great rented houses are constructed? And is not this the material expression of moral infirmities which are conducting us to a rapid decline? Little sterling worth, great vanity and desire to make a show, and as the result of this a social condition in which envy becomes the prime mover; that is, an incessant and immoderate desire to seem grander people than we really are, and a secret hatred for all that is produced superior to what we can exhibit.

Let us suppose that our municipal regulations have been revised, corrected, and brought into harmony with our habits and requirements, and the novel facilities furnished by our appliances for building; that these regulations take account to some extent of questions of art,—of variety of aspect according with the tastes of the inhabitants of a great city; that they give up the attempt to make our dwellings a kind of phalansterium in which each member is supposed to have the same aptitudes, the same occupations, the same tastes, the same desires, the same number of children, the same income, and—the same ennui. Let us suppose that those who have been for some time intrusted with municipal authority, and who say they have been the enemies of Communism, should cease the work of paving the road (by the strangest of contradictions) for the most abject Communism; let us suppose that our administrative body becomes

the opponent of the system of making regulations for everything
and *à propos* of everything; and that its measures tend to protect the initiative of private persons as far as this does not run
counter to the public good, and to further mental independence.
Let us suppose that it no longer meets with a frown, but rather
welcomes with a smile, every innovation, every effort to quit the
beaten path, every attempt to get rid of prejudice, and of the
tyranny of such or such corporate bodies, calling themselves
official or administrative.

Let us suppose that it appreciates the value of time, and perceives that it is very indifferent economy, even in its own
interest,—which we must believe is that of the country,—to
make a tax-payer lose a day's returns worth sixteen shillings to
him in order to make him pay sevenpence halfpenny to the
exchequer. Let us suppose that it considers it its duty to
facilitate and to simplify instead of shackling and embarrassing; let us suppose in fine that it ceases to consider itself
infallible and immutable, and that it recognises the necessity,
in an age when everything changes so rapidly, of anticipating
changes, and not waiting for them to be called for by the public
year after year, and submitting at last with a bad grace and
with reservations. Then perhaps we shall be allowed to add
projecting structures to houses whose fronts open on our wide
thoroughfares. The day when this state of things is realised we
shall be able to assure ourselves that the country is entering on
a new era, and that the French are ceasing to be a flock of sheep,
—docile or *enragés* as the case may be,—absolutely submissive
to the crook, or throwing themselves one after another madly
into the sea as in the episode of Panurge.

In a single morning we change our Government, and pass
through a revolution. We exchange a monarchy for a republic
or a republic for a monarchy in the twinkling of an eye. But it
takes longer to alter a municipal regulation or abolish obsolete
customs which are inexplicable in the new state of things.

What administration will have the daring to recognise the
fact that it is useless to build freestone front walls nearly twenty
inches thick for private houses? Who will dare to give permission to build at a less costly rate by giving these walls no
more strength than they really need? Or, to go further: Who
will grant toleration for corbelled projections? I do not know.
Let us nevertheless endeavour to show the advantages that
would accrue from such toleration and these alterations in the
state of things.

And first let us examine our modern buildings, and note their
defects. Thirty years ago houses were still being built in Paris
of stone, rubble-work, and timber. In this style of construction

there was the disadvantage that stone was laid on wooden brest-summers, for as the latter inevitably decayed beneath the walls, however good the condition of the latter, underpinning was necessary after some years; an operation which is often hazardous, and always very troublesome to the occupants. All the floors were of wood, with trimmers and trimming joists, stirrups, etc. This was not a very good plan, but no other means were at disposal, and very thick walls were necessary to give holding to the thick joists used; besides, thick courses had to be laid on the wooden brest-summers, and they had to be well supported on their surface, which could not be less than 20 inches wide; because, for greater security, it was necessary to make the brest-summers with two pieces coupled together and give each piece a thickness of 8 or 10 inches. But when iron brest-summers took the place of wooden ones, not only was it unnecessary to give them such a thickness, but that the system might be perfectly resisting without an excessive use of iron, the pieces coupled together could be only 12 to 15 inches apart. A wall of 20 inches thick therefore went beyond the brest-summer destined to carry it, and this excess was rather detrimental than useful.

As respects iron floorings, since there was nothing to be feared from fire, and as each joist only has a bearing edgeways of $1\frac{1}{2}$ to 2 inches, and they are placed 28 inches apart, they might be built into the walls without any fear of weakening the latter; so that thenceforth there was no need to maintain the walls at their former thickness. But while the conditions of construction were being changed, the regulations remained the same, and appeared not to recognise these modifications. Builders therefore did not carry out these first essays to their natural consequences. Not long ago, however, many of them drew this simple inference: "Since iron flooring is being used instead of wooden flooring, why should not iron be used instead of wood for the framework of partitions?" Bold though the suggestion was, it had some results, and several iron-framed partitions were constructed at Paris. But timorous people and carpenters asserted that this would be ruinous; though the cost is nearly the same, and it would be diminished as regards iron if this system were generally adopted. It would seem possible to extend this reasoning: "If front-walls were formerly made of wooden framing which served the purpose very well, except that it entailed the great inconvenience of propagating fires from one side of the street to the other, by falling in burning masses on the thoroughfares, and if on this account it was justly prohibited, whereas iron framing cannot burn, there would be no reason for forbidding its use for outer walls, and therefore its use should be allowed. Besides, as iron framing is stronger than timber framing, feats of construction might be achieved with iron which would be impossible with wood!" We see wooden corbellings on stone ground-floors two or three centuries old, and which are still standing; why then should we not erect similar corbellings of iron on stone ground-floors in the present day! Because, *first,* Municipal regulations would not allow it; *secondly,* Because we have lost the habit of well-considered and reasonable systems of construction, and do nothing but reproduce forms to an indefinite extent, which may be classical, but which are certainly little in accord with our requirements, and which are repulsively monotonous.

Iron construction is costly, it will be objected. But in the first place this assertion is questionable. Iron construction is dear when people do not know how to use that material, and lavish it uselessly, as has been done in more than one public building which I could mention; it is dear because architects disdain to study the question, and there is not one in ten who is acquainted with the properties of iron as bearing on the methods of using it. This sort of thing is not taught at the *École des Beaux Arts;* or, if it is taught there, the students, intent as they are on producing pretty drawings to be exhibited at the too numerous competitions, derive little advantage from the teaching. Already, even as things are, it is possible to employ iron largely in building, without exceeding the usual limits of expense. But if its use became general, and if architects would give their serious attention to the question, and put themselves in a position to solve it by earnest study, our manufacturers would soon make arrangements that would enable us to obtain iron wrought under better conditions than exist at present. The supply is in proportion to the demand, and a quality of iron is now supplied at ordinary prices which twenty years ago could only be obtained at an exceptional cost. The more the makers are required to produce, the more copious will be the supply at moderate prices of iron in shapes which are now considered to require special machinery and appliances. It is not for manufacturers to anticipate the demand or to foresee the various kinds of iron-work which ingenious and scientific builders will require: it is for these to study the matter, and to indicate what is necessary for the realisation of their projects. If each waits till the other begins; if builders, to excuse themselves from trying anything new, fall back on the insufficiency of manufactured appliances, and if, on the other hand, the manufacturers delay production till they receive orders, the present state of things may long continue. It must unhappily be confessed that hitherto it is not architects who have called forth the production of iron-work suitable for building, but civil engineers, and a few builders of special classes.   Thus T-irons, angle-irons, rib-irons, those of a U form, sheets of large dimensions and great thickness, have been produced; and though architects have taken advantage of these products, it must be confessed that they have done so with little discernment and still less economy.

Have we not seen iron shaped by planing used in public buildings for windows, and thus four times the cost incurred as compared with what it would have been if the article had been made and put together with rolled iron?   Does it not seem monstrous to treat iron as if it were joiner's wood, especially to those who have to bear the expense of the process?   But architects who profess to be the pillars of their noble art do not as yet *recognise* iron : they employ it, but they dissemble its use, —they do not grant it the right of appearing what it really is ; this is only a left-handed alliance.   And it is the tax-payers and the employers who pay for these architectural crotchets.   If a mere civil engineer or an architect, not admitted into the caste of the great pillars of the art, has invented a system of con- struction which is economical, rational, and consequently most suitable to the purpose and to the material employed, do not suppose that this system will be adopted in the buildings intrusted to the members of the said caste !   Among many examples of this systematic rejection, I may mention that of iron lathing.

It is natural when we have begun to make iron roof fram- ing to avoid the use of wood to support its covering.   To construct the framework of a roof with iron, and then to put rafters and battens of wood on this iron framework to fasten the slates, somewhat shocks common sense, and it is a neglect of the advantage of incombustibility attaching to iron.   We have had a melancholy proof of this in the wing of the Tuileries on the river side and the Pavillon de Flore, all whose roofing was destroyed by the fire which was propagated from batten to batten, from rafter to rafter, above the iron framework, which would not have occurred if iron laths had taken their place ; which might have been done, as the method had been invented and had been recommended to the architect before the roof was constructed.   But this method had the formidable drawback of having been employed with complete success in a building which had not been erected under the superintendence of an architect belonging to the classical caste ; and this is the reason why the tax-payers will have to pay for the restoration of the roofs as well as for the consequences of their destruction.   We shall return to the subject of iron roofing and the system of covering they require.

Let us first see how iron framing might be utilised for outer walls, and the purposes to which corbelling might be turned, supposing the authorities would allow of it in wide thorough-fares.

Though the convenience of trade is incompatible with porticos, and our shopkeepers wish to be close on the street in Paris and other large towns, it is not equally hostile to awnings,—a proof of which is that permission to put them up is solicited and obtained for a consideration from the municipal authorities, with a view to the convenience of customers and for protection to goods against the sun. Besides, many tradesmen rent along with the ground-floor an entresol to give additional storehouse room, or for habitation. And as dealers wish to have their shops as widely open as possible they greatly dislike those great stone piers which occupy so much space; and therefore endeavour to lessen their number as far as possible in building plans. It would appear that if we were to build front walls of no more than adequate thickness, whether in brick, stone, or even iron framing, those great stone piers might be entirely suppressed, except for corners and party-walls. Those intermediate stone piers suppressed between the party-walls, would be replaced, as is already not unfrequently the case, by cast-iron columns. These cast-iron columns necessarily carry iron brest-summers which are now laid very disadvantageously on stone piers which they tend to weaken, and which would be much better secured if they rested only on capitals properly arranged to receive them. If these brest-summers bear the joists of the first floor, those joists may project beyond the exterior face of the brest-summers, and receive at their extremity, on bracketing, the iron framing of a front, just as the wooden joists in ancient houses carried projecting walls of timber framing. But these old wooden houses were not generally very lofty. Their timber-framed fronts were therefore not very heavy. It would be otherwise with our iron-framed front walls on our wide thoroughfares, five stories high, that is 65 feet from the level of the causeway to the cornice.

In this case we must suppose the bracketing to be very strong. On the other hand, if, *e.g.*, we did not erect a single stone pier on a front 65 feet long, and if between the party-walls we placed as supports only cast-iron columns or plate-iron tubes, the perpendicularity of these columns must be secured; they must be prevented from inclining either towards the outside or the inside. Bracketing would give us facilities for obviating this danger, and, while obviating it, the means of giving all the strength necessary for the projection on which the overhanging front wall would rest.

Nothing shows more clearly the empirical character of the

modern methods of building, than those shop-fronts which are contrived for as an after-thought, without any account being taken of the stone piers or cast-iron columns left in the clear. Nothing proves more evidently the influence of routine among us than this continuance of two structures in juxtaposition without any attempt to combine or unite them. Why not make use of these iron columns, which are necessary supports, as uprights for the shop-fronts in question? Why should these shop-fronts be extraneous contrivances instead of being made to contribute themselves to the stability of the ground-floor? The municipal authorities require that front walls should be some 20 inches thick, and consequently that the piers of the ground-floor should be of the same dimension, but it does not forbid those shop-fronts being part and parcel of the construction or the combination of those supporting columns with them, instead of presenting inconvenient and ungraceful independent uprights. Foundries can just as well cast columns of rectangular as of circular section. Nothing prevents these columns from bearing the grooves and shoulders necessary for the iron or wooden frames of the shop fronts. But for this purpose they must be flush with the perpendicular of the exterior face, which is scarcely possible with walls 20 inches thick. Let us therefore abandon these traditions, which have originated not in any structural principles, but in a succession of contrivances gradually adopted without any energetic endeavour once for all to seek a natural and simple solution harmonising with novel requirements. Let us suppose, I say, once more, that our municipal authorities have made a clear sweep of regulations accumulated without reference to present needs and modern industrial appliances. Let us suppose that private enterprise is fostered among builders as well as among those who employ them. A few trials will soon convince us that cast-iron in the shape of supports occasions inconveniences and difficulties when it has to be combined with laminated iron, and that plate-iron intelligently used is much more reliable, and permits of much stronger combinations. This first step taken, we will examine how the programme of requirements just suggested might be carried out with this material.

What is required in most of our large city houses is a ground-floor free, as far as possible, from solid masses, piers or walls : this is what business demands. Shops such as our times call for should present a surface entirely free, separated from the street only by glazed partitions admitting as much light as possible. It is not by half-measures that such a programme can be satisfactorily carried out even to a moderate extent, since piers must be erected supporting front walls as well as those destined to support partition walls. And these partition walls are necessary with a view to receiving the floorings and fireplaces of the upper stories, which at the present day are divided into a number of small apartments, as every one knows. The principle

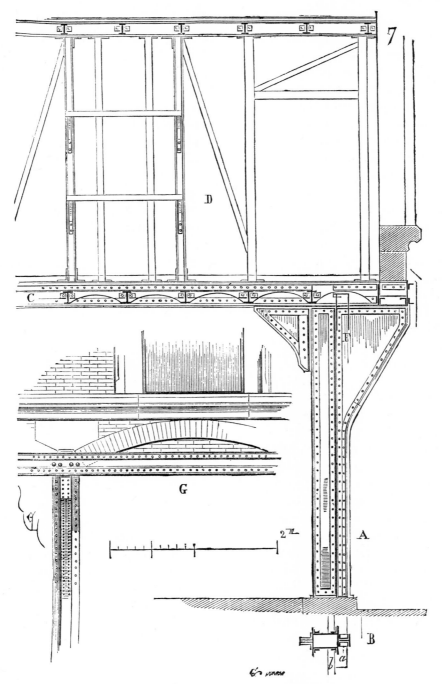

Fig. 7.—Example of Iron-framed Street House.—Details of Construction.

therefore to be observed is,—no divisions on the ground-floor, many divisions in the upper stories.

On the other hand, it is hard to be obliged to cover a good part of the surface with walls, necessarily taken out of the space purchased,—when it is paid for at the rate of something like £4 per square foot, *e.g.*; for it must be observed that our partition walls will have to be nearly 20 inches thick. Each wall, therefore, with a mean depth of building of 40 feet occupies nearly 65 square feet, whereas an iron-framed partition wall $4\frac{3}{4}$ inches thick would only occupy a space of $15\frac{1}{2}$ square feet. But how could chimney-flues be carried up these thin iron-framed partitions? We shall examine this point directly, and show that these flues would require not more than $3\frac{1}{2}$ superficial feet in each story.

We shall begin with the ground-floor, which should be left free from thick supports inside, and open as widely as possible on the thoroughfare.

Fig. 7 shows one of the supports repeated at intervals of about ten feet, between the party-walls of the front of a house. At A this support, consisting of a rectangular tube of plate-iron, is shown in profile; at B in horizontal section below the corbel bracket. These tubes of plate-iron receive the girders C, consisting of plate and angle-iron carrying the double T-iron joists of the floor.

These girders, relieved in their bearing from one front wall to the other by cast-iron columns, also receive the iron framed partition D. The projection of the corbel bracket carries the brest-summers, on which may be placed the front wall, 14 inches thick, in brick, or even stone, or a thinner wall of iron framing.

If these front walls are of brick or stone they rest on brick arches between the two plates of the brest-summers, as shown in a portion of the front G. The shop-fronts are fixed at *b* (see section B), and the boxes for shutter apparatus at *a*. The valance receiving the plates of these shutters is drawn at F.

This is a general view of the method; but in nice constructions of this kind the study of detail—of the mode of fastening the iron-work—is the main point. Let us therefore examine the construction of the various parts of this system, figure 8.

At A is drawn the horizontal section of the support, below the corbel brackets, at *a* the place for the box containing the shutter apparatus. We see at B how the brackets C are fastened between the angle-irons D, and how the plates F, which form the posterior part of the shutter awnings, are fastened to the angle-irons G. The front parts of this valance are fixed at H, and contribute to give firmness to the system,—to prevent the tubes from losing their perpendicularity parallel to the front wall. The two cheeks of plate-iron E prolonged above the top edge of the tube, receive the clips K of the girder, whose anterior extremity L rests on the end I of the bracket. At N are seen the corner-couplings of the front plate forming brest-summer with the other back plate M and the soffit P. A springer R resting on the end T of the girder and on the soffit P

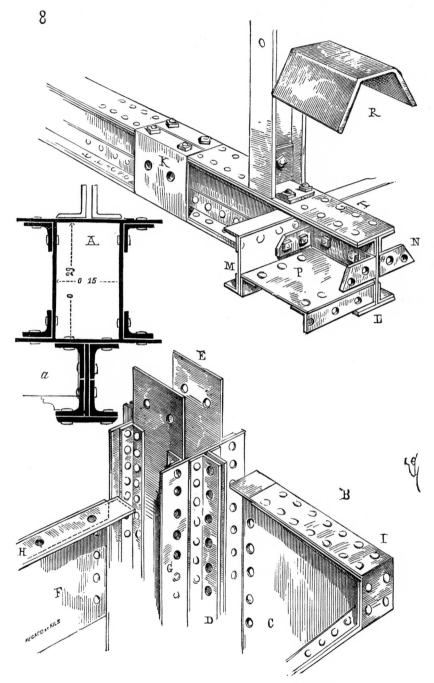

FIG. 8.—Example of Iron-framed Street House.—Details of Construction.

gives the skewback of the brick arches indicated at G in figure 7. An upright of the iron-framed partition is drawn at O. We have mentioned flues for fireplaces that will require to be carried up these iron-framed partitions, as it is understood that in buildings of this construction division-walls of thick masonry may be dispensed with. We consider flues arranged for each fireplace, with special ventiducts for each, to be obsolete and barbarous methods : a single ventilator may serve for all the fireplaces put back to back and one above the other, taking air from below, that is in the best way possible. A single smoke-flue may likewise serve for an unlimited number of chimneys placed back to back and superposed, on the condition that this flue is of sufficiently large section for the number of fireplaces.

The Mousseron system, carefully applied, and with an exact calculation of the sections of the flues, has solved the problem. The results of experiments with it have proved satisfactory.

For each fireplace of average size a flue of 6 inches square, *i.e.* a section of 36 *square inches,* would be quite enough. Supposing ten flues therefore, that is two fireplaces back to back, for five stories we should require a section of 360 square inches, occupying a parallelogram of about 1 foot by 2 ft. 6 in. The same would apply to the supply of air.

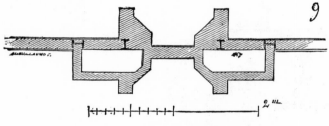

Fig. 9.—Fireplaces and Flues.

Thus against an iron-framed partition the fireplaces may be drawn as in figure 9. One of the shafts is intended to take the smoke of all the fireplaces, the other to supply air to them. It will be understood that if we wish to divide the flues—that is, to have the necessary passages for smoke and ventilation only for a series of chimneys one above another, and not back to back—half the sectional surface given here will suffice. Fig. 10 shows how the shafts may be carried against the iron-framed partition with the help of iron bands A attached by means of angle-plates and supported by struts to the upright B.[1]

We have shown that front walls of stone or brick might be borne on the projections of the corbel brackets. But there is no reason for not carrying out the principle to its ultimate consequences, and with a construction of this kind it would seem more logical to adopt iron framing for the outer walls also. This

[1] See for the general arrangement of these bands, figure 7, D.

iron framing however could not be thicker than 7 inches, and a wall of 7 inches would be scarcely a protection against cold or heat.[1]

A thickness of about 1 foot would be required for healthy habitation. The iron framing of the walls might moreover be connected with the window-cases, which under these conditions

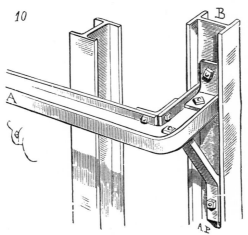

Fig. 10.—Mode of supporting the Fireplaces.

would also have to be of iron. This is the way therefore in which the problem might be solved. We may imagine an external facing of terra-cotta, glazed or moulded according to the taste of the builder, and which would be about 2 inches in thickness. The brick wall behind this facing would be 9 inches thick; and adding $\frac{3}{4}$ of an inch for the joints and interior

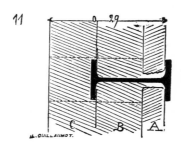

Fig. 11.—Outer Walls of Iron-framed House.

plastering, we have about $11\frac{3}{4}$ inches. The iron framing, fig. 11, would therefore be no thicker than that facing, *i.e.* 2 inches, and a breadth of brick $4\frac{1}{2}$ inches, say $6\frac{1}{2}$ inches between the flanges, or rather more than 7 inches in all. Thus between the flanges we have the facing A and the width of a brick, and we have the width of a second brick as an interior lining. This structure will of course be bonded by bricks laid crosswise. Now let us

[1] This was the usual thickness of the ancient timber-framed walls.

examine the system which would be applicable in this case as regards the window-frames, figure 12. The exterior is at x. At A is drawn the horizontal section of one of the two jambs of these windows; a double L-iron forms one of the uprights of the iron wall-framing. The window-cases project on the outside and form a metal reveal, to which the casement frame is attached.

The section of the sill is given at c, and that of the lintel at B. G is an arch whose slight rise is given by the flanges of the double L-iron fastened to the upright a by means of the

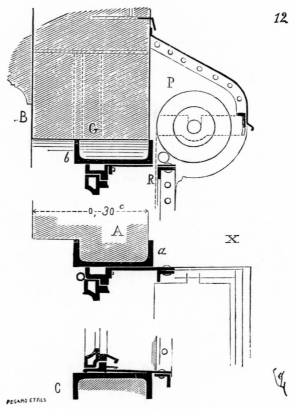

FIG. 12.—Details of the Windows.

metal reveal itself. For this serves the purpose of angle plates, and should be fixed at the same time as the uprights, sill and lintel of the window frame. To the vertical plates of the window-reveal is fastened, by means of small angle-irons, the awning P, which is intended to receive the roller of the metal blinds, whose plates come down through the groove R. Thus all holds together; each part contributes to the stability of the whole in this system of iron framing, and the window-cases participate in the structure. Plate XXXVI. presents the external appearance of this kind of structure. The balconies are supported by plate-iron brackets attached to the awning of the windows and fixed by angle-irons to the uprights of the iron framing.

The inconvenience attaching to thin walls of brick or stone is chiefly that they rapidly communicate the cold or heat of the external temperature to the interior. The iron uprights, if they pass right through, have the same temperature inside as out. An outer wall of framed iron therefore, if not lined inside, would present along each member, during severe cold, lines of condensation of vapour which would produce intolerable deposits even through plaster, and which would mark out the iron structure on the paper-hangings or painting of the rooms. In the outer walls indicated here, a lining is therefore provided, as shown in figure 11. Experience moreover has shown that external facings having damp-resisting, smooth polished, or even varnished surfaces, prevent heat or cold from being communicated to the material behind. And this is the reason why it seems desirable that the fillings-in of the iron framing should be faced outside with glazed tiles.

A propos of these I may be allowed a digression. During the last ten years, England, perceiving the advantage that might accrue from the use of terra-cotta in building, has greatly extended the fabrication of this form of material. Germany, again, has established manufactories on a large scale for the supply of terra-cotta to builders. In both these countries builders have done their best to discover the conditions favourable to the employment of this useful material, and in both very important results have already been secured. At the recent Exhibitions it was manifest to what a degree of perfection Germany and England in particular had brought the fabrication of terra-cotta and moulded and glazed tiles. Our own manufacturers have also endeavoured to raise this branch of production to the level attained by our neighbours. They have made considerable efforts and sacrifices; many have already obtained satisfactory results; but persevering efforts and sacrifices find themselves in this instance, as is always the case in France, confronted by inexorable routine, and, with some exceptions, our builders have treated them with neglect, and rarely employ the products thus offered them.[1] Stone is still readily supplied; they built with freestone yesterday, and that is a sufficient reason for their building with freestone to-morrow. Enormous blocks are accumulated, of which a quarter at least will be lost in the dressing; and that to build an unsatisfactory dwelling, destined only to last a century;

---

[1] The factory building just erected on the Marne by M. Saulnier, architect, of framed iron and glazed bricks, should however be specially noticed. This remarkable construction, of which the *Encyclopédie d'Architecture* will soon give a description, shows that though we are slow in France to free ourselves from routine, we can at least soon come up with our rivals when we are once on the road.

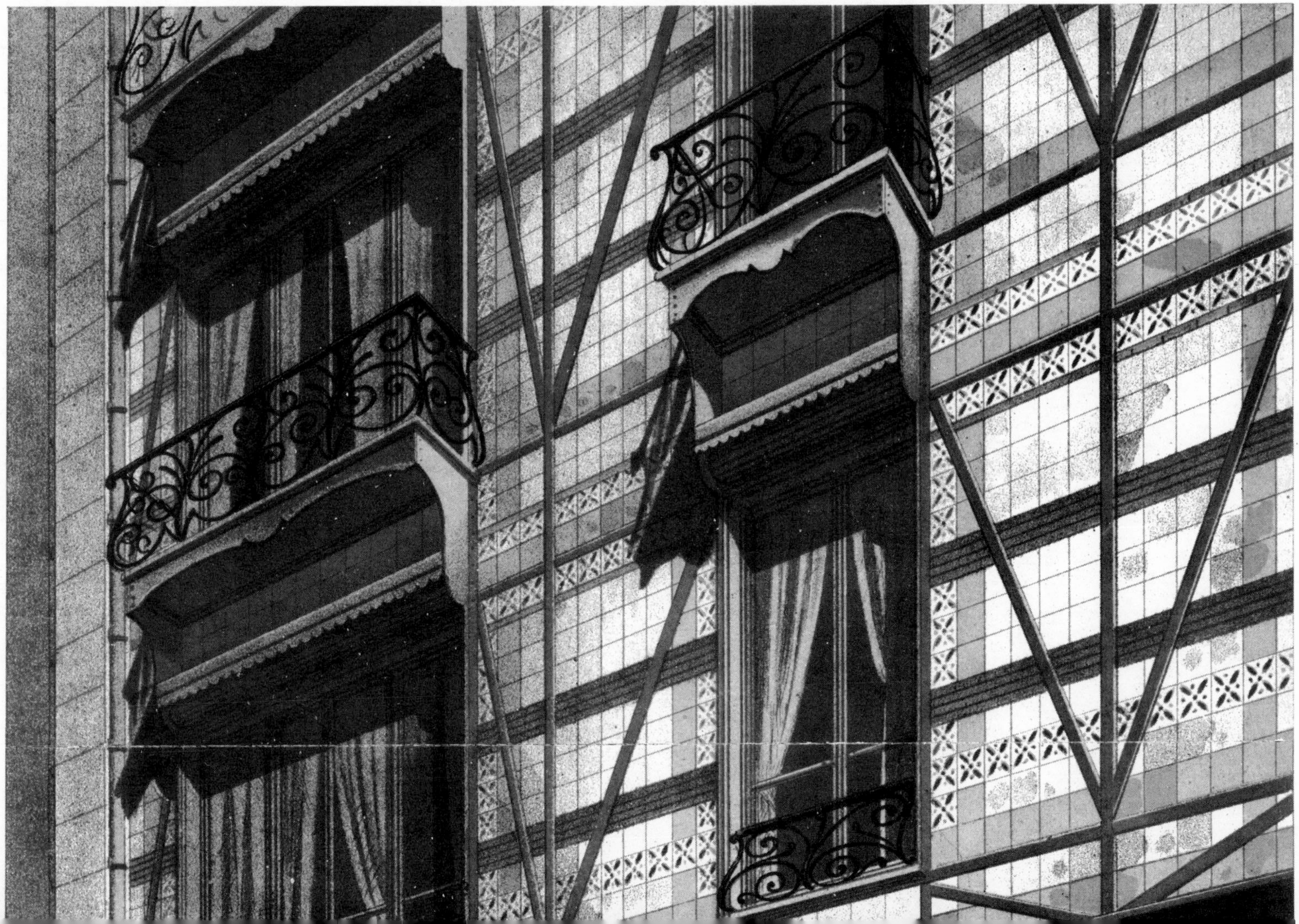

E. Viollet Le Duc, del.

Regamey, Lithog.

PANS-DE-FER DE FACE EN ENCORBELLEMENT AVEC REVÊTEMENT DE FAYENCE.

Imp. Lemercier & Cie Paris.

Vve A. MOREL & Cie Éditeurs.

valuable materials, whose supply is not inexhaustible, are lavished to obtain results which are inconsiderable in every respect, simply that we may have the satisfaction of studying "the orders" decorating façades which rest on voids occupied by shops on the ground-floor.

Confronted by this mania for stone, our French manufacturers who have had the courage to believe in the good sense of architects and their employers, and who have supposed that their efforts and sacrifices would place in the hands of builders materials that are useful in many circumstances, most desirable and easily manipulated,—these manufacturers, I say, have some difficulty, for the most part, in keeping up their works, and what they supply to order is a trifle compared with what they might have expected to supply. We are fain to believe that an International Exhibition will open great outlets for our manufactures connected with building. Nothing of the kind,—for this is what really occurs. In prospect of an *Exposition,* some French manufacturers make considerable efforts and incur great expense to supply new products suited for practical purposes. The Exhibition Commissioners award them a medal. Foreigners study these productions and take advantage of them. As for ourselves, does any one suppose that these productions are any more thought of the day after the Exhibition is closed, or that any attempt is made to utilise them? By no means. We return to the routine that prevailed before the Exhibition commenced; while foreigners profit by our attempts, study and improve upon them, and then some time afterwards we go and buy from them the very products which we have not had the common sense to encourage at home. The *Exposition Universelle* of 1867 furnished a hundred examples of such facts. From this ill-starred Exhibition, in which the manufacturing genius of France so honourably distinguished itself, all have derived benefit but ourselves. All found there inventions which they immediately adopted. Among ourselves routine resumed its empire as before. Satisfied to have gained distinction for the moment, we have taken no care to follow up the great efforts put forth. But I am wrong: this noteworthy Exhibition produced not simply negative results: we displayed before envious, rapacious, and pedantic neighbours our wealth, our resources, and our productive genius; and three years afterwards these neighbours came down upon that wealth to take it away, and endeavoured to crush that intelligence, which, more than our wealth, excited their envy and dissembled rancour.

We cannot prevent our neighbours from indulging sentiments resulting from a long-cherished hatred; but we should be destitute of common sense, and deserving of the insults that have been heaped on us, if we persisted as formerly in not being the first to carry out the endeavours commenced by our own inventive and versatile genius.

It is absurd to refrain from making use of these efforts to our own profit, and besides we are thus destroying sources of wealth. How many branches of industry could I mention which would have increased the riches of our country if we had taken the pains to become acquainted with them,—to know the nature of their products ; and which have been lost to us for want of encouragement at home, while our English and German neighbours were making use of them and making us pay for the results of them ! We have thus become tributary in respect of a great number of manufacturing appliances, whose invention is due to France ; and in this respect those who build, the State itself, and our architects, are blameworthy ; for they thus discourage our manufacturers and occasion a considerable loss of wealth to the country.

Let us now return to our unpretentious habitation. This house, of which Plate XXXVI. shows a part, consists of a ground-floor constructed according to the previous suggestions.

Externally the outlines of the iron framing remain apparent. The filling of brick is faced with tiles of glazed terra-cotta, with some horizontal courses of brick to aid the flanges of iron in holding these tiles to the building. The overhanging stories, resting on corbels, give shelter to the shop-fronts entirely unobstructed along the whole breadth of the front, between the party-walls, which alone are built of freestone.

I do not presume to offer this fragment as a model for rented houses hereafter to be built,—as the *architecture of the future,* but simply as a study, without reminiscences to fall back upon, of the appliances which modern manufactures offer us for building, so as to satisfy the requirements of our times. I am quite aware that it bears no resemblance to the palaces of Rome or Florence, or a mansion of the Renaissance or of the times of Louis XVI. But it will be allowed that here at anyrate the use of iron is not dissembled—that it is frankly displayed.

Let each try his skill in this way, and we shall soon have succeeded in discovering the most suitable and pleasing forms. These facings of enamelled terra-cotta, besides the advantages noticed above, may be left in good condition for an indefinite time by simple sponge-washing, without any necessity for the proceeding in vogue for the last ten years, of putting up scaffolding in front of houses to scrape them to the quick, or to steam them with a view to clean them, to the great annoyance of passers-by and the shopkeepers.

It is evident that constructions of this kind require to be

designed and completely executed in the workshop, before being put up,—a consideration of no trifling importance. At present when a house is being built, the thoroughfare is encumbered, during a whole season at least, with cart drays and scaffolding. Enormous masses have to be hoisted with great trouble and expense; and when the stones are in place—laid almost in the rough—a host of workers and dressers must cover it, who scatter dust, stone, and plaster over the whole neighbourhood. For the neighbours, the building of a house is a calamity; to tradesmen close at hand, a disaster; to passers-by, it is at least an annoyance and a hindrance, and often a cause of serious accidents.

Though it is sometimes asserted that we are the most difficult people in the world to govern, I do not know of any civilised nation more inclined than ours to accept the tyranny of routine with philosophic calmness. In France, people would rather run the risk of being crushed by a stone-cart or old plaster, than seek for the means of avoiding such annoyances. This has been the case hitherto, and so we may expect it to be in the future.

Our builders find it convenient thus to possess themselves of a part of the highway for eight months or a year, to annoy the whole neighbourhood, to encumber the streets with rubbish and building materials, and to sprinkle all who pass by with stone scrapings; this method will serve the purpose. But to construct a house in the workshop, the woodyard, and the factory, and to bring it ready-made like a piece of furniture, only requiring to be put up, —that would necessitate fitting everything beforehand, foreseeing everything, arranging everything according to its destination as to place and time—that would require reflection, study, and pre-vision. It is much simpler to adopt the hand-to-mouth plan, to put up house-fronts in the rough, and cut the stones on the spot, to erect the shell, and then spend two or three months in piercing openings and holes in it in every direction,—for the windows, the doors, the heating-apparatus pipes, those for gas and water, for the shop-fronts, the sign-boards, the iron balconies, etc. etc.

Do not our administrative boards set us the example of such methods of proceeding? A street is cut, and is paved; people pass along it and suppose it finished; but no, they unpave it to make a drain; then they pave it again, and they *re-unpave* it to make branch sewers or conduits for water. Sometimes a com-plaint is made of this method of procedure, but to such complaints the officials answer: "These various branches of highway manage-ment belong to different boards; they each proceed according to their convenience or their means." And all rest content with this irrefutable reason. And the building of our houses is conducted after the same fashion. We make to remake, because the mason and the superintendent of the flue arrangements, the locksmith and the joiner, come each in their turn to the building and give themselves little concern about the requirements of their confrères. It is the business of the architect to introduce order and a combined purpose; but the architect himself follows routine, and has his masonry erected before arranging for what is to be connected with it.

Structures designed according to a system similar to that of which we offer here a specimen, as a simple study, would therefore have these advantages; they would be quite finished in builders' yards, the factories and workshops, before being put up, and consequently they would be erected very quickly, without mishaps, obstruction, or great annoyance to the neighbourhood. But, I observe once more, all must be provided for in advance, and to this our architects are not accustomed.

We are apt to rely a little too much on our facility in getting out of difficulties. This, it would be well to remember, has cost us, and is still costing us, very dear.

Among the serious objections (I do not care to mention others) that may be brought against these proposals, for radical innovations in the construction of our great city houses, might be the expense. Structures of this kind would be costly, it would be alleged. I allow that, as things now are, they would be pretty costly, because we are not provided with the necessary appliances, because things of a novel kind require processes to which we are not accustomed; because the spirit of method and foresight does not exist; because each is waiting for his neighbour to take the initiative; because our great manufactories are waiting for orders before they supply productions involving novel conditions of fabrication, while architects are waiting for these new products in order to employ them; because our workmen have lost the traditions of good execution, and the claims they urge are in direct proportion to their incompetence; because we prefer half measures and compromises, and resolutely adopt reforms only in our talk, never in our deeds, except in the way of overthrowing everything, without having anything to put in the place of what had been established; because everybody blames, and abuses, but no one has the courage to take the bull by the horns; because we have not persistency and tenacity, and from the top to the bottom of the social scale have become averse to patient study.

Yet, in spite of all this, it cannot be doubted that a structure designed completely beforehand, and all whose parts ordered *seriatim* were prepared in the workshop or the foundry, so as only to require putting up, even if the materials to be employed were dear;—it cannot be doubted, I say, that such a structure would be erected at a comparatively moderate cost.

Have we estimated the amount of useless, unproductive

expense in the building of our houses, which at their maximum height at Paris, cost from £30 to £40 per metre? Do we know how much money is squandered on those heaps of stones, of which a fourth is cut away in working and dressing, in the continual alteration of what had been done wrong; and in the successive re-handling of the works by the different orders of workmen, who follow each other without a common understanding? I think I am not exaggerating when I say that in this way a fifth of what is expended is unproductive. A structure contrived beforehand in all its parts, each of which could be brought and placed in due position and at the right time, without the necessity of altering anything that had been done, would, on this consideration alone, make up this fifth, otherwise lost. In fact it would be something worth doing if we only procured a greater amount of space in proportion to the solids. But supposing the first structures thus contrived and prepared before putting in place were to be costly, is it not certain that metal, terra-cotta works, etc., would soon furnish products at less and less cost in proportion to the extent of the demand?

In 1840 the working carpenters took it into their heads to strike: it was a terrible strike. Not a carpenter could be had. Till then iron flooring had been used only in some public buildings, and these were made of very complicated iron-work, at a very high price, in consequence of the nature of the manufacture. The necessity of doing without carpenters decided builders to substitute iron for wood in the floors; they set their wits to work; they first laid iron plates on edge with bridging, and filled in with plaster, or plaster and pottery. Then some works manufactured double T-irons, and the problem of iron flooring was solved at once. Dearer at first than wooden floorings, they were soon reduced to the same price at Paris through the saving in certain parts of the masonry, and the rapidity with which they were laid; for time may certainly be reckoned money. And now all floorings in Paris are made of iron. The honour of the initiative in this case belongs to the carpenters. It were to be wished that an equally imperious necessity compelled us to renounce most of our building processes as now carried on. Wood still occupies too important a place in our public and private buildings; and yet wood for timber and joinery-work will fail long before the iron ore spread over the face of the globe will have been exhausted. One of the inevitable consequences of civilisation in every country is the disappearance of forests, those great stores of useful materials. All the countries that have been occupied by peoples whose culture has been long-lived and distinguished have lost their forests. Asia Minor, Greece, Italy, and the southern part of Gaul, no longer possess wood suitable for building. The north of France is seeing its forests diminished day by day; in another century this part of our country will no longer possess oak forests; this inevitable consummation must be kept in view, and we must not waste such precious materials. About thirty years ago Champagne produced most of our joinery wood; it has ceased to do so, and we have to buy this material from the foreigner. And supposing even that severe and persistent legislation and an intelligent foresight should protect the remains of our oak forests, and that our rural population itself should really feel the necessity for preserving them; the force of circumstances will inevitably cause the diminution of these products of the soil; and we may remark, *en passant*, that forests cannot be restored: to make them flourish a primitive state of the country is necessary, if I may so term it, and which a highly civilised state cannot bring back without renouncing those very advantages which that primitive virgin condition presents. When morasses have been rendered salubrious, water-courses restricted to regular channels, and the lower strata of a district have been drained— a state of things which is the necessary result of an advanced civilisation and skilful culture of the ground,—the conditions necessary to the flourishing of forests are proportionately diminished; and when these conditions have been suppressed it is beyond the power of man to re-establish them, for that disorder and neglect which in long periods of calamity may destroy those improvements in the soil which have been introduced by civilisation, never restore a state of nature. To those who have travelled in the south of France, not following the great roads, this phenomenon is painfully evident. Countries which were formerly covered with forests that have been destroyed through the improvidence of the inhabitants, districts that have long been neglected, do not see their ancient clothing of verdure reappear. Underwood and coarse grass have permanently replaced the forests; Nature, struck to the heart, cannot replace what human improvidence has destroyed.

The Cevennes, the Montagne Noire, a good part of the Carcassonne district, and of Roussillon and Ardèche, were still covered with oak forests in no very remote times. This species of tree, subject to destruction during the thirteenth and fourteenth centuries, has almost entirely disappeared from these regions, and the scanty remains of those ancient forests consist only of clusters of stunted growths and briers fit for nothing but fagots.

We should therefore save our few oak forests for indispensable uses, employ them carefully for purposes for which such materials are absolutely necessary,—for our navy and for manufacturing uses. However little scope we allow to anticipation or however little we may care for the future prosperity of our country, we cannot but see with deep regret the employment for purposes of no serious utility, perhaps for very trifling ones, woods which no human power or wealth can restore when lost.

Similar remarks do not apply to iron : iron mines are inexhaustible ; at any rate they will furnish the human race with materials as long as, in all probability, it will exist on the planet. Besides, while the destruction of forests ruins a country, the manufacture of iron enriches it, for it requires an industrial development and an amount of labour which is the equivalent of wealth. When a tree is cut down there is an absolute loss, for it will probably never be replaced by a similar one. But the manufacture of a bar of iron has caused no loss to the soil, and has no value except in virtue of the labour which its production has necessitated. What it is sold for is the product of labour paid for, that is to say, it represents a portion of the wealth of the country. The more such bars are demanded, the more the prosperity of the country which supplies them is increased. The more timber is cut down in a forest the greater risk we run of destroying a species of wealth which we should not expend except in cases of absolute necessity ; for it is not in the power of man to restore it. In whichever way we consider it, the use of iron in buildings is henceforth obligatory. It is dictated by the necessity, more and more imperative, of preserving our oak, and by considerations of real economy, if we thoroughly study the advantages of iron in point of hardness, durability, and incombustibility.

Without assuming that all the problems in reference to it have been solved, we have shown how iron could be more frequently and more rationally used in private architecture. We must finish our remarks. While in the present day, in the great towns of France, and especially in Paris, floorings of iron are constructed, this material has not been so generally adopted for roofing. Thanks to double T-irons it is very easy to lay an iron floor. The construction of roofs requires a little more care and study. Is this the reason why iron roofing is comparatively rare ? I am inclined to think so. We have not found, as in the case of flooring, a commodious and simple formula, —a practical appliance which can be adopted in all cases. Trials have been made and recourse has been had to all sorts of expedients ; in particular, wood is constantly combined with iron, if only for the raftering, in the roofing of private houses, and even of public buildings. I remarked above that an excellent, practical, and economical plan,—that of using iron laths suitable for carrying tiles or slates fastened with hooks had been adopted some eight years since, but that, through considerations of no creditable kind, this system had not been employed for the roofing of some public buildings erected since that date, and that this strange prejudice on the part of some *official* architects against using appliances discovered or applied by brethren of the craft, less official in their estimation, contributed to the destruction of a part of the wing of the Louvre on the Quay of the Seine. It is to be presumed that this prejudice still continues, and that the same architects will reconstruct this roofing by mingling as before rafters and battens of wood with the main framing of iron; though they risk seeing fire spreading from building to building through the presence of combustible materials which might be so easily dispensed with. But they think it proper to say " Perish all the public edifices of Paris, and the treasures they contain, rather than admit the value of a method of construction that has been invented and applied outside the sanctum of the true guardians of the sublime art."

Not only does it seem probable that iron lathing[1] is destined to replace wooden raftering and battens, but it would introduce novel combinations in iron-framing. In fact this system has the advantage of giving perfect rigidity and cohesion to roofing surfaces and thus greatly contributing to their stability. Thanks to the use of this lathing, the weight of the principal parts may be lessened; and though it costs more than ordinary battens, it allows, if intelligently used, of a compensation in virtue of the diminished weight of the main pieces. In the systems now employed, whether of wood framing or mixed wood and iron, the raftering is a dead weight which does not contribute to the stability of the work, which is laid in fact only to bear the metal, slate, or tile covering, and the lath and plaster ceilings of the stories just beneath the roofing. The timbers enclosed in this plaster, and subjected to the great heat caused by the sun's action, and to the dampness of the atmosphere, decays very soon, and afford only a precarious closing; so that beneath such roofing one is stifled with heat in summer and frozen in winter. Roofing of mingled iron and wood usually requires a complicated system of fastening, which must be managed to a great extent on the spot, thus requiring a long time. After the blacksmith's work comes that of the carpenter and the slater. To fasten the wooden rafters to this iron framing very insufficient expedients are often adopted, and mishaps are unavoidable.

If, on the contrary, we adopt a system studied beforehand, applicable to every case, and which can be completely arranged in the workshop, more regular workmanship is secured, and a great saving of time in the work to be done in the building itself. The following specimens of arrangements tend to exemplify

---

[1] The patent of this lathing—a very remarkable specimen of which, and whose merits were rewarded with a medal, was exhibited in 1867—belongs to M. Lachambre, contractor for blacksmith's work.

this :—Let figure 13 be a portion of roofing A B, at an angle of 45° on a building 40 feet wide. The front walls having been built, and the division walls or ironframed partitions arranged to receive the parts of the flooring and fireplaces, being, according to the custom at Paris, about 20 feet apart. The length A B may be accurately ascertained beforehand, as also that of the ridges.

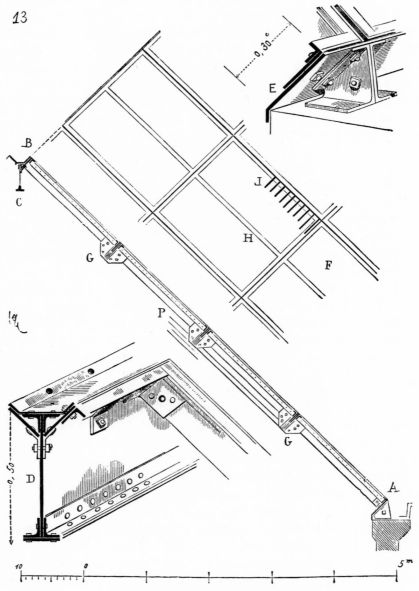

Fig. 13.—Construction of Iron Roofing.

Nothing more is needed than to fix in place the ridge-piece of plate and angle-iron (see the detail D) crowning the cross-walls. At the workshop are prepared frames about $6\frac{1}{2}$ ft. long, each with a breadth of 5 ft. 10 in. at least, or $6\frac{1}{2}$ feet at most.

These frames receive each their lathing. Their sides are formed of plate-iron from 7 to 8 inches wide, with a thickness of $\frac{1}{4}$ of an inch, and an L-iron inside on the upper edge (see detail E). These portions are joined by means of angle-plates projecting below, figured at G; plates whose functions we shall point out. The frames in question brought to the building are joined with bolts in fours, for the length of the roof slope, and offer a rigid surface which may be hoisted with a pair of shears. The first row of frames fixed, the second is placed, which is bolted to the first (see the drawing F). Each of these frames has a rafter H in the centre, consisting of a single T-iron, the flanges uppermost. The lathing I is fixed to these flanges and to the L-irons of the frames. This combination of four frames forming one piece rests at A on the gutter, as the detail E shows, and is bolted at B, under the ridge, as indicated in detail D. As the two parts prop each other, they might in strictness do without the ridge, which is only put there to facilitate the laying, and to obviate the tendency to spreading, and consequently to the thrust which might be produced between one division wall and another.

Let us examine the method according to which these frames are combined, a method which renders them absolutely conjoined with each other, and makes a portion of roofing as large as we choose to imagine one single piece rigid in all directions.

Figure 14 shows at A the fastening of the angles of the frame in elevation, and at B the fastening of the intermediate rafters with the plates of the transverse partitions of these frames. The angle-plates C consist of pieces of iron $\frac{3}{8}$ths of an inch thick, bent as shown in the perspective detail G, which figures in separation the four frames which have to be joined by these angle-irons. That the locking up, on which the solidity of the whole system depends, may be complete, the heads of the rivets must not render it imperfect by resting on each other. The joinings are therefore isolated as indicated at a, the interval being furnished in the direction of the length with plates or cushions b, and in the transverse direction with the two cushions c. Moreover, below the L-iron small wedges are placed, as seen at A, to secure the tight fitting of the upper part. That the fitting may be absolutely tight, especially at the extremity of the angle-plates, it is desirable to wrap the cushions in coarse paper thoroughly coated with white or red lead putty. The rigidity of the whole system depends, in fact, on the complete locking up of the bolts at the angle of the frames. Some bolts (two on the sides, and two at the angle-irons of the rafters) should also contribute to the firmness of the frames. A portion of the roofing thus prepared in the workshop may be very quickly fixed in place, and the slaters will immediately follow the black-

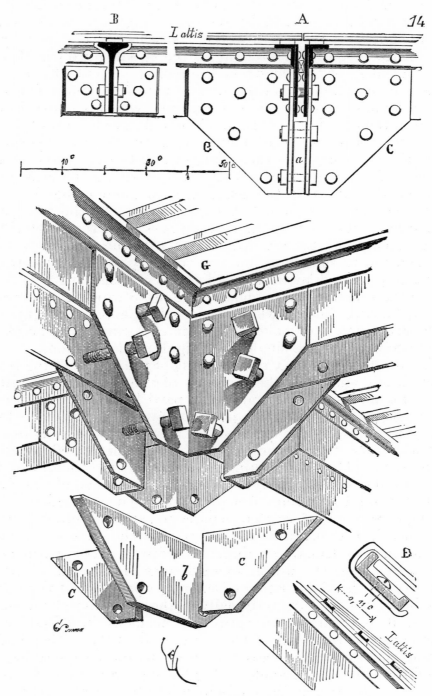

FIG. 14.—Details of Iron Roofing.

smith's work; for as the frames bear their lathing, and are all of equal dimensions in the same piece of roofing, the lathing will fit end to end without trouble. The section of these iron laths is drawn at E half size; and they are placed full 4 inches apart (the length of the slating lap); they are furnished with two flanges, the upper one higher than the other by $\frac{1}{6}$th of an inch, to lodge the head of the slates, each kept in place by a copper hook. This system of slating, which has been tried for fifteen years, has proved very satisfactory: the slates laid in this way resist the most violent gusts; their laying and removal in parts or as a whole is easily and quickly accomplished, and to replace one or more broken slates no nails or new hooks are necessary, and any workman can execute repairs at once. The laths being each 3 feet or 3 feet 3 inches in bearing, do not bend even under the weight of a man, and serve as ladder-rounds for the slaters. These laths are fastened by screws to the L-irons and intermediate rafters; the head of these screws is clear of the slates in consequence of the projection of the lower flange. It should be understood that wedges $\frac{3}{16}$ths of an inch in thickness isolate these laths from the L-irons and rafters, to leave room for the copper hooks. If we wish to ceil the roof inside, it will suffice to place bars of flat-iron edgeways instead of the longitudinal cushions b, for all the part of the roofing that has to be ceiled, as marked at P, figure 13; to join these bars by iron braces and cramps, and to fill in this under framework with plaster.

While this system of frames can be applied to straight roofs, it is still better adapted for polygonal roofs, as the frames thus form a kind of arch, fig. 15. The drawing A gives a section of half a polygonal roof, covering a building 40 feet wide; the sketch B its exterior front with the dormer windows, skylights, and lathing. It will be readily understood how these dormer windows C, of thin plate-iron, can be fastened on the roof frames so as not to require any additional labour or loss of time in putting in place. And similarly as regards the skylight D. The coupling plates F and G may clip the floor joists if thought desirable, which will then form tie-beams. But for the flooring at the level F it is evidently more advantageous to bed the floor joists in the walls or iron iron-framed cross partitions. It does not seem necessary to insist further on this method of roofing, which will be found very advantageous; for though its preparation in the workshop requires care and considerable time, the work is straightforward, all the parts being alike; and there is a great saving of labour in the building itself, since the whole can be quickly raised into place, and there is no need for fitting or retouching many of the parts, as is the case with the present methods. At a is seen the section of the underceiling, which leaves the roofing independent.

While it is necessary for our architects to make themselves quickly acquainted with the methods of construction which the progress of manufacturing industry facilitates, there is another point that should not be neglected : the judicious use of these appliances as influenced by conditions of climate and provincial usages.

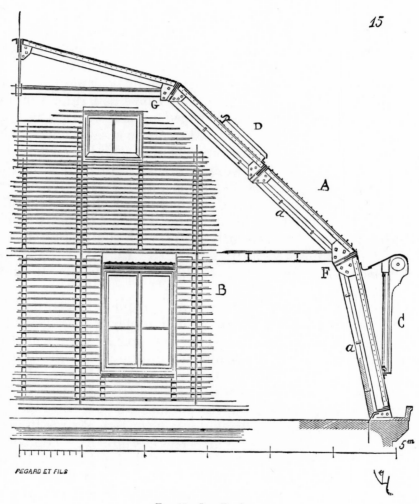

Fig. 15.—Iron Roofing.

From the moment when building at Paris began to exhibit a somewhat factitious development,—the notion of an entire reconstruction having got into people's heads,—all the chief towns of the Departments fancied themselves bound to follow its example. In all our great cities nothing has been thought of for the last fifteen years, but the opening of new streets and boulevards, and (taking the great rented house of Paris as their type) builders have begun to erect, in the North and South alike, structures just like those we have seen raised along our thoroughfares. At Marseilles, in the neighbourhood of the port La Joliette, speculators have built Parisian houses which are uninhabitable, and, in fact, uninhabited. But what suits one climate is certainly unsuitable to another. For three-fourths of the year in Paris the days are hazy and the temperature moderate. Violent winds are rare, and so is excessive heat. In such conditions of climate numerous and large windows are required, and walls adapted to resist damp and moderate atmospheric disturbances. It is otherwise at Marseilles, Toulon, and our southern cities generally. There high winds are frequent, and terrible in their strength ; the heat of the sun is such that special precautions are needed for protection against it ; and pure and vivid light has an intensity such that a very small opening is sufficient to light an apartment. Efficient shelter, streets comparatively narrow, powerful means of ventilation on occasion, good closings for the windows to protect the inhabitants from the mistral, and walls which neither the sun's rays nor the damp of the sea-winds can penetrate, shade and tranquil air, are the chief desiderata. It is evident that a Parisian house by no means fulfils these requirements. Yet even in Algiers buildings are erected like those of our Rue de Rivoli. It would be difficult to push to a more ridiculous extent the mania for imitation in the teeth of conditions of climate. The poorest Algerine house is more suitable as a habitation for that locality than are these Parisian importations, in which there is no efficient protection against wind or sun, or dust or damp, or cold, which is sometimes pretty sharp on the northern coast of Africa.

But who cares to direct the attention of our young architects to questions of this kind ?

France is not the only European country that has abandoned the methods which a due consideration of the locality suggests. Italy, Spain, and even Germany,—which presumes that it can reason better than any other ; and which, like the ancient people of Israel, possesses an illumination and Deity of its own,— and Switzerland, have all on many occasions laid aside traditions established by a lengthened observation of conditions of climate, to adopt an architecture which is in every case inconvenient and false on principle, though Classic, as is alleged. England perhaps alone has escaped this infatuation for certain common-place classic forms in domestic architecture. But the English are and will always continue to be a people eminently practical ; and if they do not make pretensions to carry the art of reasoning as far as the Germans, they proceed instinctively after a practical

16

FIG. 16.—Sheltered Fronts of Old Houses in Geneva.

and correct method. Good sense takes the lead among them, and the pedantry of the Germans is unknown. London houses are not generally handsome, but their plainness is not associated with pretentiousness. Their interiors are convenient, and perfectly well arranged in respect of the needs of their occupants and the conditions of the climate. It is not so with the houses in Berlin; even in the private houses of the capital of the German Empire, we find certain concessions made to pseudo-classical taste which satisfies neither the requirements of art nor local usages, nor the exigencies of a rigorous climate. There is pedantry in the buildings of Germany, whether public or private, as there invariably is in the productions of the Northern Germanic peoples, and in those sterling qualities for which they take full credit, and which no one just at this moment is in a position to dispute.

Virtues which assert themselves backed by twelve hundred thousand men, and artillery in proportion, and by conflagrations of towns and villages, cannot be disputed, unless those who challenge them have twelve hundred and fifty thousand ready to sustain the controversy.

The city of Geneva once possessed houses admirably adapted to the particular climate of the country. At Geneva the extremes of temperature succeed each other: the cold is often very sharp and rigorous there during several months; the summer is generally very hot; the storms of wind are frequent and severe; the snow driven by violent gusts accumulates in that city sometimes to more than a yard in depth.

The ancient houses I refer to, and of which some two or three remain,—if they were not destroyed by the last fire,—consist of a kind of wooden scaffolding fronting a wall in masonry.

This scaffolding, figure 16, forms a portico rising as high as the roof, which it supports. The shops and the different stories of the house are thus completely sheltered from the violent gusts of wind, and from the sun, and the front walls can be kept dry; the sleet can never beat against the window panes. The thoroughfare is not obstructed, and, thanks to the height of the portico, air and light are never wanting. This singular style of structure continues the traditions of the mountain dwelling, with its external timber-work affording galleries at each story, and forming a shelter. But such an arrangement must evidently be limited to a country where fir-wood is abundant. In the present day Geneva builds houses like those they build at Lyons, which are like those of Paris. Since the seventeenth century those primitive arrangements which had been adopted in most of the cities of France and Europe, in conformity with the climate and local customs, have been gradually disappearing.

Has Art gained anything by this uniformity ? or would not an epoch in which so much is said about " distinctive nationality" and " autonomy," be the time for each country to resume those architectural forms which suit its habits and climate ? And would not this also be the time for architects to betake themselves to the study of those local conditions, and conform their plans to them, forgetting for a while Vignole, Palladio, and the palaces of Rome, which for the most part have never been inhabited or habitable ; and, as regards ancient art, to give their attention to the good sense which directed the builders, whether public or private buildings were in question, rather than to the external forms ?   To these questions I know that no answer will be attempted : our architects will content themselves with invoking " high art," and " æsthetics ;" but we shall not thereby be better or more wholesomely housed, unless the public in this, as it has done in many other matters, takes the thing in hand, and concerns itself with a question in which it has a real interest.

LECTURE XIX.

DOMESTIC ARCHITECTURE.—COUNTRY HOUSES.

THOUGH the pyramidal principle may be suitable for some kind of buildings, it is inapplicable to ordinary habitations, as also to various buildings for the use of the public, such as market-halls, assembly-rooms, etc.

That which is essentially requisite for a dwelling is a space amply protected by the most efficacious and simple means.

The principle of construction in a dwelling-house in a northern climate is comprised in this form, fig. 1,—four walls and a roof with double slope.

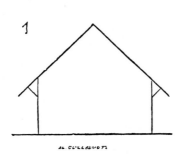

Fig. 1.—Overhanging Roof.　　　Fig. 2.—Retreating Roof.

The adoption within the last half-century, in our large towns, of an arrangement such that the highest story is thrown back from the line of the front walls, fig. 2, may perhaps be justified by the necessity of allowing sun and air to reach the ground in comparatively narrow streets; but it is clear that this retreating story is the occasion of the roofs not sheltering the front walls, and of damage to the stories below from rain and snow; for wide thoroughfares it is not less manifest that the arrangement presented in figure 3 would be much more desirable.

We spoke in the preceding Lecture of the advantages that might be derived from adopting corbelled projections in the case of houses bordering very wide thoroughfares, and we shall not return to the subject.

But while these advantages, which are evident even in reference to town dwellings, cannot be secured in all cases,

FIG. 3.—The Dwelling—Elementary Principles.

particularly where the admission of air and light into streets, narrow as compared with the height of the houses is in question, there is nothing to prevent our availing ourselves of them to the full in houses built in the country.

No one can doubt that a dwelling presenting the outline A, fig. 4, will resist atmospheric effects and shelter the inmates more effectually than one whose outline is such as is shown in B.

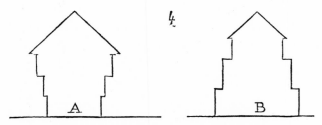

FIG. 4.—The Dwelling—Elementary Principles.

There are climates presenting conditions so adverse to the security of habitations that man is obliged to adopt special means of protection against them. Thus, for instance, in the higher valleys of the Alps, where during four or five months of the year the snow is more than a yard deep, the inhabitants have been obliged to take extraordinary precautions to defend themselves and their household stores against its invasions. We therefore see *chalets* raised on four blocks of stone more than a yard high, thus raising the doorsteps above the level of the snows, and allowing the latter to melt without penetrating the dwelling; or perhaps consisting of a ground-floor in solid masonry, on which the inhabited story is built, projecting beyond the basement, and consisting of a timber construction, or rather of trunks of trees placed one above the other in courses and dove-tailed together at the angles. Centuries pass away, but the style of these buildings undergoes no alteration, because in the districts in question the dictates of climate are much more imperious than the prejudices of the schools could be. We may reasonably suppose that in passing the *cols* of the Alps Hannibal saw *chalets* similar to those which are still built in the passes of those mountains. There, at any rate, the villa of the environs of Paris or the English suburban cottage will never penetrate, as they have managed to do in less inclement regions, though in defiance of local conditions. For do we not see "suburban cottages" at Cannes, "pavilions" with slate-roofed turrets in the country round Marseilles, chalets (constructed of planks, it is true, attached to rubble-built walls) in the environs of Paris? The good people who live in these . . . "follies" are, it is true, very indifferently lodged there; they are baked in the summer or frozen in the autumn, and have to pay heavy bills for repairs every spring, while they have no other compensation than the pleasure of having transported a house from the banks of the Seine to Marseilles, one from the environs of London to Cannes, or one from Switzerland to Paris. We are bound in courtesy to suppose that the satisfaction really compensates them for the want of a good salubrious and comfortable dwelling.

And while these are certain conditions of climate which it is desirable to take account of in towns, such conditions are still more imperative in the country, where isolated buildings are particularly exposed to the inclemency of the weather; where it is difficult to have repairing done, or at any rate where it must often be delayed, and where, if a dwelling becomes uninhabitable, the last resort—a furnished lodging—is out of the question. Yet it would seem as if during the last few years, the indispensable requisites of a habitation in the country had been in many cases quite disregarded.

One would suppose on seeing some of these dwellings, that their sole object was to adorn the landscape, and gratify tourists, like those pasteboard villages which the courtiers of the Empress Catherine had stuck up during her journey through the steppes of Russia. When the sun shines without being too oppressive, when the nights are mild and tranquil, when there is neither rain nor wind, the plank-built chalets on the shores of the Channel, the pasteboard châteaux on the shore of the Mediterranean, and the "cottages" of Arcachon, are fairly habitable dwellings; but when heat, tempest, mistral, or fog supervenes, we long to be back in the little inn of the neighbouring town, though that was no palace.

It must be understood that I am speaking here exclusively

of ordinary houses in the country, not of good substantial manor-houses or châteaux whose inmates are agreeably housed. It is ordinary country-houses that I have specially in view, because these are numerous, and the taste for buildings of this kind has been very widely diffused within the last half-century. Yet such is the disorder prevailing in the architectural domain, and such are the odd or puerile fancies of those who build houses, that it is only a very few buildings which fully satisfy the requirements of a country dwelling of moderate dimensions.

There are two different ways of meeting these requirements, one of which I shall call the English, and the other the French method.

The English method consists in uniting small blocks of buildings, each containing one or two apartments, according to the taste or convenience of the owner—often with a ground-floor only, without any regard to symmetry; each of these blocks being of such a height as suits the apartment it contains, with windows according to the aspect preferred, and communications more or less advantageously contrived. In such a plan as this for a dwelling in the country we see the impress of that practical good sense which distinguishes the English.

The French method consists in building a pavilion, that is, a concrete symmetrical block, in which the various services, instead of being scattered as on the English plan, are united in a succession of stories, under the same roof. This is an old traditional method in France, and which has its advantages. The genuine French country-house is the French *château de plaisance* of the sixteenth century in miniature, as the English "cottage" is the English manor-house of the middle ages in miniature, with its blocks of buildings variously placed according to the convenience of the inhabitant. Some French proprietors have indeed endeavoured to introduce the English style, but I do not think that these dislocated arrangements accord with our habits, unless these should change, which is hardly to be expected. The English method preserves, even amidst relations of close intimacy, a kind of independence,—a personal isolation which is very rarely to be found among ourselves. When Frenchmen find in each other grounds of an intimate friendship, or fancy they do, they seem disposed to have all things in common, and to make an absolute sacrifice of their individualities; though when intimacies too hastily formed give rise to disagreements, the quarrels that result are violent enough. This however is not our worst fault, as it has its good side. But when a family, or even when real friends, assemble, it would seem desirable that their life in common should be as concentrated as possible. The more strictly observed the community of habitation the better.

For a Frenchman therefore a country-house is a kind of common tent, whose inmates all observe the same daily custom. Among ourselves, life in a country-house is regarded as lively and agreeable only when all are within reach of each other's voices, when the rooms closely adjoin, and conversation can be carried on through partitions or floorings. It will therefore be very difficult to persuade Frenchmen enjoying a retreat in the country that the best means of keeping up a cordial understanding with each other is none other than the avoidance of this enforced contact at all hours of the day, and the preservation of a fair amount of independence. Of course I do not include exceptional cases. It is the result of our habits of life that the type of a French country-house of modest pretensions, hitherto at any rate, has been, and continues to be, what is called a *pavillon.* It is for the architect to conform to the established custom, doing his best under the circumstances, without falling into vulgar obsequiousness, and while studying carefully the real conditions of the programme as well as those which are concerned with the salubrity and the thorough and easily available means of preserving the dwelling.

With very few exceptions, the ground-floors of houses in the country are sure to be affected by the dampness of the soil; the most scrupulous precautions must therefore be adopted to avoid the inconvenience. And there is another remark regarding health in reference to this matter, to which I would call attention.

We observe cottages and houses occupied by peasants, the ground-floor of which is on a level with or even below the ground outside, and with no cellars, yet whose inmates live to a great age without being even troubled with rheumatism. But if a townsman lives and sleeps in them for a week, he will suffer in every joint. The inconvenience is certainly unfelt by persons who have been born and bred in this humid environment; but it is quite otherwise with those who have been accustomed to the very dry apartments of large towns, and who are only temporarily subjected to the conditions in question. Now, as houses in the country are destined to be inhabited for only part of the year by persons who pass the rest of their time in large towns, and who were born there, they must not be exposed to this dangerous change. While seeking in the country for a purer air than that of the cities, they must not encounter those humid emanations to which they have been in no degree accustomed. It cannot be doubted that a considerable part of those rheumatic affections by which many of the dwellers in our cities are afflicted arises from the too often insalubrious state of the country-houses in which they sojourn in the summer. Although the bedrooms are generally not on the ground-floor, the parlours,—the apartments where the day, and especially the evening, is spent,—are little raised above the level of the ground outside. The walls of these rooms often throw out saltpetre more than a yard above the floor, and the painting has to be renewed every spring. Who has not observed ground-floors in which funguses spring up in a night in some corner or other? Besides, the walls, which are often thin and wretchedly built, are poorly or not at all protected from rainy winds, and these walls are imbued with a dampness which they never lose, and which they throw out in the interior during the nights that follow warm days. In fact we should be better lodged in a tent.

With a view to avoid these inconvenient and even dangerous contingencies, the walls on the side exposed to rainy winds are in certain Northern countries covered with shingles or slates. But the best protection—and that which requires least repairing—is roofing projecting sufficiently to prevent the rain from dashing on the walls, and the sun from shining too powerfully over the whole of their surface; for a freestone wall even sixteen or twenty inches thick, which has been greatly heated by the sun, if a storm of rain supervenes, will be very deeply penetrated by the water. The outside of the moistened stone evaporates rapidly, but that part of the humidity which has reached the middle of the wall makes its way into the interior. Three or four days after a violent storm, I have often seen walls which outside had become perfectly dry and dusty again, but whose inner side was so damp that the papering was moistened.

We must also take account of the nature of the materials employed. In the case of stone, the coarse-grained limestones are after all the best; those which, on account of their very porosity, dry most rapidly to a great depth. Sandstone, on the contrary, even when the walls are thick, retains a considerable quantity of water, which is constantly transuding into the interior. Very compact materials, *e.g.* limestone of the kind called ' cold ' (*froides*) offer serious disadvantages; stone of this kind is colder and damper on the inside, the warmer the external temperature is. Brick is in fact one of the best materials that can be employed, especially if the walls are thick enough for the bricks not to pass through the wall at any point. As regards coatings, mortars stand the weather much better than plaster, but they conduct the damp with much greater rapidity. Mortar coatings ought to be well sheltered; only on this condition will they be well preserved, and if they have been suitably treated they are the better for age.

In the country, thick oak, or even deal framing, and showing, when duly sheltered and with a filling up of brick, forms an excellent protection against cold, damp and heat, especially if care is taken to cover the external facings, particularly those of the horizontal pieces, with shingles or slate, or even battens placed one over the other; for it is only the horizontal pieces that retain the damp which is arrested by their fibres.

For roof covering, tiles are always preferable to slates, unless the latter are pretty thick. I say nothing of zinc, which in the country is the worst of all coverings, since it is liable to be damaged by wind, is difficult to repair, and does not preserve the roof from the effects of cold or heat.

The result of these considerations is that, to place a house in the country in the best condition as regards health and durability, it is necessary to secure a dry and equal temperature, whatever be the state of the atmosphere externally. To secure this result the essential point is to isolate the house as far as possible from the external soil; the second, to give the walls as much protection as possible, by giving them a sufficient thickness and choosing the materials for their construction with due regard to climate and aspect.

The conditions to be observed in regard to windows are different in the city from what they are in the country. In a city we can rarely secure direct horizontal lights; the houses are fronted by others on the opposite side of the thoroughfare; consequently the openings receive the light at an angle whose mean is 45°; it is therefore necessary to have windows large in proportion to the size of the apartments, and whose sashes shall obstruct the light as little as possible.

Besides, the wind rarely has a powerful effect on the fastenings; the houses serve as a screen to each other; the air has not the penetrating sharpness of that which is breathed in the country. The sashes of the windows may therefore be of large dimensions in the houses of a city. If they suffer damage they can be readily repaired. It is otherwise in the country: skilful and prompt workmen are not to be had; wide glazed surfaces are therefore undesirable; it would be better for them to be small, and numerous as occasion may require. The English have quite understood this necessity in reference to their suburban dwellings, and their windows are very conveniently arranged. Even in the glazed projections in front of their houses, they take care to have numerous frames, so as to be able to open them partially or all at once as may seem desirable. There were many similar arrangements in French habitations down to the seventeenth century; but at that epoch the rage for the grandiose caused those window frames to be adopted with two leaves only, which are so inconvenient to shut and open; and which, if on a somewhat large scale, are especially liable to be warped under the action of heat and moisture and get out of order. When wind and heat prevail, if they are opened for the sake of air, it is impossible to stay in the room for the gusts, while if they remain shut, one is half stifled. Small sashes are imperatively required in country dwellings. They should each have a shutter inside as a protection against severe weather and an external protection (sun-blinds) to shelter them from the sun's rays and to prevent violent gusts from driving hail or snow against the panes.

Warming apparatuses (*calorifères*) are necessary in country-houses to keep their interiors dry in the winter, and to prevent the exhalations caused by thaw; but this should be their only use. Good fireplaces should be provided in all the apartments; for even in summer a fire is often necessary, and is a great restorative after the fatigues of the field, and to ward off the dangers of excessive perspiration. The fireplaces should be wide, high, and arranged for getting bright fires quickly lighted. They ought to be furnished with fire-boards, so that in winter the moisture of the atmosphere may not get into the rooms through the flues.

In the country still more than the city, the sonorousness of floors should be avoided. In the city the incessant noises of the street prevent the ear from distinguishing sounds in the house itself: it is otherwise in the country, to which we repair to find quiet, and where the least sound is audible. If the floor is on iron joists, between the filling in of these and the boarded floor an interval should be left to isolate one from the other. If the flooring is of wood, besides the spaces between the joists, there should be a space contrived by means of secondary joists, filled in with seaweed or rushes rendered incombustible by immersion in plaster-water. But there is a method which will be sufficient of itself to check the sonorousness of the floors almost entirely. Nothing more is needed than to attach bands of the coarse felting—sold at a very low price to cover temporary buildings—with strong glue to the joists before nailing down the floor. This can scarcely be done, indeed, in the case of herring-bone flooring, but there is no difficulty with those laid in the English style; that is in long boards. But I think it necessary to give some details respecting the construction of floorings in country-dwellings. Except in the neighbourhood of great metal-works, iron floorings have hitherto been too costly in country districts; besides, it is impossible to find workmen there who are able to lay them properly; it would be necessary to get them from Paris or other great centres: forges would have to be built for the special purpose; and all this would involve expense. If a piece should be wanting, there would be delay in getting it. There are few dis-

tricts in France where there is oak suitable for flooring.   In the
southern provinces, and in the west, and part of the centre, deal
only is available.   This kind of wood is moreover very useful
for the purpose, if the wood is not enclosed in coatings of plaster
or mortar, and if mortises are avoided, which are not sufficiently
secure in deal.   I have seen timber-work in deal planking three
or four centuries old which was still in excellent condition; but
the wood had been left exposed.   Deal flooring can be made
very durable by means of certain arrangements which it is worth
while to mention, and whose value has been confirmed by

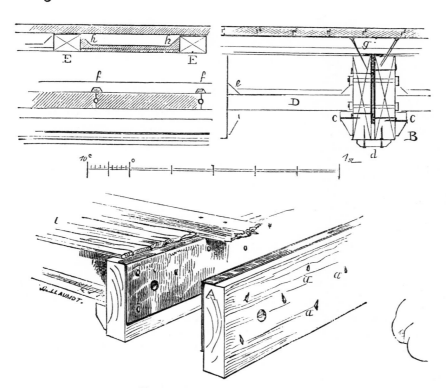

FIG. 5.—Floorings of thin Deal Joists.

experience.   Deal in large pieces is liable to deep splits, which
are often even dangerous.   It is therefore desirable to use it in
thin pieces.   With joists of this wood two inches, or even an
inch and three quarters thick, floors of the greatest solidity can
be constructed.   To secure this result, figure 5, we need only
nail strips of sheet-iron (one twenty-fifth of an inch thick at
most) on one side of each joist, taking care to fold back these
strips of sheet-iron one inch wide on the edge above, as shown
in the perspective drawing at A.   These strips should only reach
to within an inch and a half of the lower edge.   They may be

readily pierced by a brad-awl to nail them to the joists. The nails should be two and three-quarters of an inch in length, leaving three-quarters of an inch for clenching on the other side, as shown in the figure at *a*. As the strips are not always as long as the bearings, the pieces must be nailed together, with an overlap of nearly four inches. Joists thus furnished are coupled together with bolts, the strips of iron inside (see the figure drawn to scale, section B). Strips of wood C are nailed on the sides and another *d* beneath. These joists, with a space between their centres of sixteen inches and a bearing of nearly twenty-four feet, can bear the heaviest weights a house flooring is likely to be required to sustain. On the side strips are placed slabs of plaster D from an inch and a half to two inches thick, or of terracotta or even clay well beaten, if other materials are not at our disposal. These slabs are fixed with plaster by fillets *e* and *f*. On the joists are placed E thin secondary joists nailed obliquely with good wrought nails, as seen at *g*. Moreover, from one joist L to another are laid thin boards *i*, or reeds, and a thickness of plaster or clay with fillets *h* along the sides. Then the parquet is nailed on these secondary joists, the precaution mentioned above being used against the sonorousness of the floor.[1] But for the floorings of rooms it will be necessary to arrange trimmings for the passage of chimneys, or for crossing the vacant spaces of windows. In such cases, when using deal, tenons and mortises should be avoided, and their place supplied by a very simple and substantial system of stirrups, figure 6. These stirrups are formed of strips of iron one-third of an inch thick and about two inches wide. For joists of the size referred to here each strip of iron should be three feet and a half long (see A). They should be forged into all the foldings indicated at *a*, so that these strips may take the form drawn in perspective at B, and in elevation at C. The notch *e* made in each joist receives the foot of the stirrup. Nails are driven in at the side and above (see B). The small triangles *g* (see A) form cramps. When the wood strips *l* have been nailed beneath, a small triangular piece is driven in at *e* to close the void. Stirrups of this kind, which are easy to make, since they are of very thin iron, are much more substantial than tenons and mortises, for they grasp the wood in its whole depth and force it to support itself against the trimmer or the trimmer joist. This plan may also be adopted as a substitute for notching in bearers along walls, unless these are placed underneath the ends of the joists, which is always better.

We observe, figure 5, that ceilings thus constructed leave

[1] Deal planks an inch and a half thick, strengthened with cheeks of sheet-iron, strips thus nailed on the inside, at distances of fifteen inches, with a simple flooring an inch and a half thick, and with a bearing of twenty-six feet, have sustained enormous weights of corn unequally divided.

the wood visible on the lower side, which suffices to secure it from dry rot. The squares of plaster which form the inter-joists may be moulded and the terra-cotta glazed, if we wish to obtain a very brilliant and rich effect.

The best preservative against damp on the inside of walls is wainscoting. It entails expense, but very simple and (where wood is abundant) cheap wainscoting may be put up. In default of wainscoting, canvas stretched on frames, with a

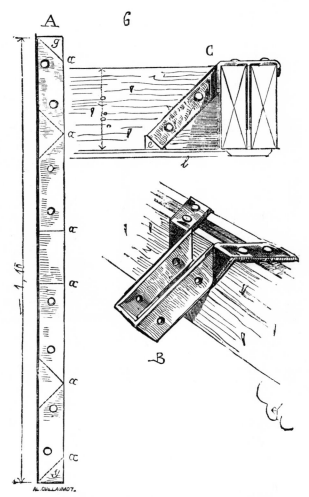

Fig. 6.— System of Trimming Joists.

coating of clear plaster laid on with a brush on the wall-side, is a good protection against damp. These canvases may be painted or papered.

If the flooring is of wood, too much care cannot be taken to prevent the decay of the bearings of the joists in the walls. The most effectual means is to avoid fitting these bearings into outer walls, unless the latter are of timber framing. But if this is unavoidable, it is desirable to cover the end of each joist with a thin sheet of lead or zinc, forming a return, like a half-box, and to take particular care to leave a space between the end of the joist thus protected and the masonry; allowing a communication between this void and the spaces left between the main joists and the secondary joists. It is well ascertained that the bearing of a joist passing right through a strong wall, and exposed to the air outside, decays much less rapidly than one that is enclosed; the great point therefore is to allow the air to reach them freely.[1]

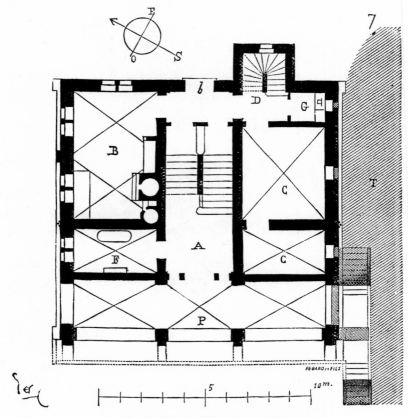

Fig. 7.—Country Villa. Basement Story.

In houses built in the country the chimneys and the flues are frequently too little considered. It would seem as if they were regarded as a matter of secondary importance, and few architects study it attentively. A skilful arrangement of the chimney-stacks so that the flow of rain-water shall not be impeded, nor their outlets too much exposed to the wind, so that

---

[1] I have frequently observed, in peasants' houses at least a century old, bearings left thus exposed along the outside of front walls, and which had suffered no decay, whereas we constantly see joists that have not been laid twenty years, whose bearings built in the walls are thoroughly rotten.

the smoke may not be beaten back into the house by the rebound of the air from a higher roof, securing for the flues a section sufficiently large in proportion to the fireplaces, and putting them in such position as to prevent the house being set on fire: these, and similar considerations, demand serious attention.

It will perhaps be thought that I am entering too minutely into details respecting the building of houses in the country, but my reason for treating them so largely is, that most of these buildings, as they are now constructed, are even more faulty in respect of such details than in their general arrangements, which usually reflect the tastes and requirements of the owners. The architect cannot always be blamed for the method of carrying out a plan which his client has dictated, and whose suitability he is not permitted to discuss; as it is natural after all for the proprietor to claim the right of arranging his dwelling according to his own ideas. But in executing the several parts of the plan, the architect is, or ought to be, free to act; for example, he cannot be excused for arranging a chimney-flue in such a way as that the floorings near the fireplace are likely to take fire. In such a case he must interpose his veto or renounce his responsibility, for if the house is burned, those faults of construction which caused the accident will be justly laid to his charge.

In accordance with what we have said, it would seem that the conditions of a dwelling in the country on a modest scale, and not affecting to be a château, might be thus summarised: the ground-floor, which generally contains the apartments where the family assemble, should be protected from the dampness of the soil; the walls should be effectually sheltered by the roofing; the apartments should be so disposed that a small staff of servants may suffice for them; the most salubrious and agreeable aspects should be selected; complicated construction should be avoided, especially in the roofing, which as far as possible should be built without valleys and intersections, and without complicated gutterings; the simplest arrangements, which will be easiest to keep in repair, should be adopted for the exteriors, for instance as regards chimney-stacks. The following plans have been drawn according to the conditions thus summarised. Figure 7 gives the plan of the ground-floor, which is in fact only a basement story nine feet high beneath the vaulting. At P is a low porch leading to a hall A, at the end of which is the principal stairs. At B is the cooking-kitchen with its back-door *b*. Cellars and storage places at C; a bath-room at F. The servants' stairs at D. All these apartments are vaulted with light materials, such as brick or tufa. We suppose the ground to rise at T, so that the vault C and servants' closet G are half underground. The first story (which is only a ground floor **9 ft. 10 in.** above the level of the ground outside, figure 8) consists of a drawing-room A, dining-room C, and pantry D; a billiard-room B, and a smoking-room or study F. A balcony *b* runs all along the front wall by the drawing-room and billiard-room, and terminates in two flights of steps leading down to the elevated part of the ground near it. All the basement story is in stone masonry: the side walls of the story, figure 8, are of timber-framing projecting two-thirds of its thickness beyond the corresponding walls of the basement. The second story

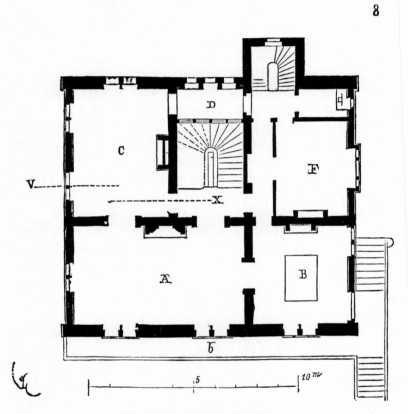

Fig. 8.—Country Villa. First Story.

contains the bedrooms for the family, and the attic story those for the servants, the linen-rooms, and an upper drying room, the middle of which left open lights the stairs, and serves to ventilate the central part of the building, so that a section along V X in the plan, figure 8, gives the drawing A, figure 9. Half the figure B presents the gable front of the building, figure 10 the side front. It will be seen that the chimney-shafts are grouped around the upper part of the staircase which forms a drying-room and a reservoir of dry air. The roofing has a continuous slope, without valleys or intersections; gutters placed at c (see figure 9) collect the water from these slopes, and discharge it on the ground by two lateral downpipes.

We may be sure that a country-house thus constructed requires no great amount of repairs, since all parts of the building are sheltered by roofing constructed in the simplest way; that it is perfectly healthy, as all the rooms for the family are protected against the dampness of the soil and of the atmosphere;

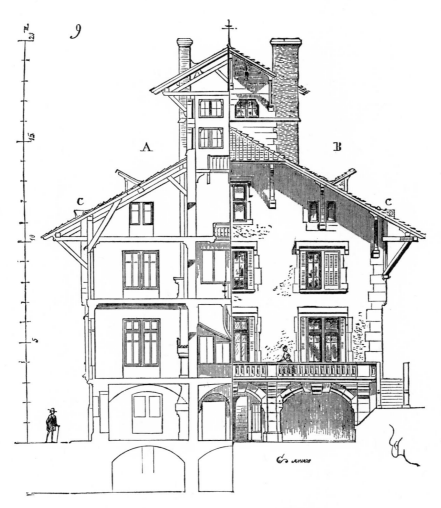

FIG. 9.—Country Villa.   Elevation and Section.

that the servants' work is facilitated by its arrangements, since these apartments are grouped around a central flight of stairs; and that the erection of such a house does not require exceptionally expensive appliances, or such as are difficult to get executed at a distance from large towns. Built on a moderate scale, this dwelling is after all only a villa suitable for a family passing the summer in the country. But there is a kind of country-house which architects are rarely called on to build, but which nevertheless deserves their study. I refer to dwellings adapted to the requirements of persons who pass the greater part of their time out of doors, either because their tastes and favourite pursuits are of a rural character, or because they have interests in the country that require their surveillance, or agricultural labours to direct.

Fig. 10.—Country Villa. Side Elevation.

In our fertile plains of Languedoc and the district around Agen, there are many houses of this kind which merit the attention of architects, inasmuch as they completely accord with the requirements, although their appearance is very unpretentious, and everything in them is sacrificed to the due satisfaction of those requirements. These districts have retained certain local traditions, which have not suffered those changes which are too often met with in many other French provinces, resulting from a passion for vulgar luxury and the desire to make a show. But while those who are curious in architectural details may find nothing of interest in these country abodes, the circumstance that they are built in conformity with the requirements of their owners gives them a character of their own, a style proper to them we may say, and one which admirably harmonises with the natural features that surround them.

While great mansions and châteaux with their complicated roofing covered with dormer-windows, their turrets with sharply pointed summits, add to the effect of an imposing natural environment and beautiful parks adorned with venerable trees, the miniature imitations of these abodes, surrounded by paltry gardens, excite a smile, and remind us somewhat of the fable of the Frog and the Ox. Yet how many of these microscopic châteaux have been built in our country districts looking like toys, with turrets which would scarcely accommodate a dog, with battlements made for cats to crawl about on, and architectural details in plaster or terra-cotta, and zinc vanes and crestings. Silly, uninhabitable, pretentious dwellings, whose only merit is the brevity of their duration, and the fact that they make simple and genuine forms seem more estimable still to persons of sense.

The country-houses of our southern districts, which are both villas and farm-houses, offer one of those frankly devised dwellings which, dictated by the kind of life led by the inmates, who are true *campagnards*, exhibit in their features a stamp of comfort, convenience, and stability, which contrasts with the paltry and tasteless appearance of most of our suburban houses. The plan is simple, as is the case with all our old habitations. The main object is security against inclemency and heat ; the aspect is generally carefully selected. In the districts in question the north-west winds are the most to be dreaded, as they bring rain and bitter cold ; an angle, therefore, not a front, should be opposed to this quarter of the horizon. During half the year a direct south aspect would be very undesirable ; the most agreeable aspects would then be the north, east, and south-east. Contrary to the customs in England and North Germany, it is desirable to unite all the apartments under a single roof, and to build thick walls, but to allow the apartments to be readily ventilated towards evening by a central current of air. An open portico or vestibule is necessary ; it should be low and deep, and a second direct vestibule should run parallel with it. In houses of this kind the kitchen must be very spacious. It is in the kitchen or the room next to it that the peasants of the neighbourhood would be received. It should have ample appendages in the shape of pantry and store-rooms. The dining-room should be near it, though not so as to allow cooking odours to reach it. The parlour, or rather *hall*, is an apartment at a distance from the entrance, and opening into the dining-room. Lastly, a very extensive shed should be provided close to the buildings of the house, which will contain the stables, coach-

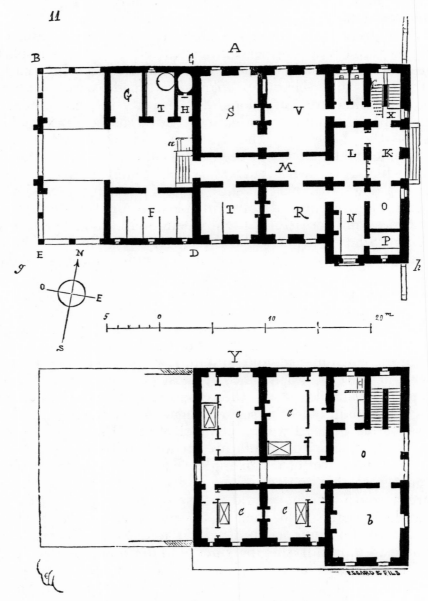

FIG. 11.—Southern French Rural Dwelling.   Ground and First-floor Plans.

house, bake-house, wood-piles, and wide spaces to shelter wagons, washing and drying arrangements, etc.

On the first story, besides the living-rooms, an apartment near the stairs must be provided for the master of the house:

a parlour or study in which matters of business may be transacted. A house of this kind greatly resembles a little Gallo-Roman *villa,* and we may reasonably suppose that it has retained the traditions of the latter. Many such country-houses in the plains of Toulouse and the Agen district have seemed to us so completely to realise the programme of a rural abode, that we think it desirable to exhibit here a kind of type or résumé, figure 11 ; especially as this type in question is in itself a striking criticism of those meaningless architectural toys which we have been accustomed for some years to regard as typical country residences.

At A is the plan of the ground-floor, built partly on cellars of no great height, to which the steps *a* descend. The whole space B C D E is a very extensive pent-house, containing stables at F, coach-house at G, bake-house at H, and wash-house at I. The dwelling-house against which this pent-house leans consisted of a porch K, closed only during the night by a *grille* or gate of wood palings ; a vestibule L, leading to a corridor M, which runs through the building ; a cooking-kitchen N, near the entrance, with a receiving room O, to take in provisions ; lavatory P, and servants' pantry, R. The room marked T serves purposes of various kinds ; a bath-room, or apartment for ironing, or a linen-room. At S is the hall, and at V the dining-room. The stairs X lead to the first story opening on a chamber, O (see Y). At *b* is the master's apartment, and at *c* are chambers for the family, with their closets. The second story contains one or two bed-rooms, and those for the servants. Houses of this kind are generally built of unburnt brick in the upper parts, and burnt brick for the ground-floors ; the timber-work is of fir. Genoese cornices with projecting rafters completely shelter the thick walls. Constructions of unburnt brick—the genuine pisé—have the advantage, when the walls are thick enough, of preserving the interiors from excessive heat and cold ; well made, they will last for centuries. Care is always taken to build the angles and the jambs of the windows with burnt bricks.

Figure 12 gives the side elevation of the house in question along *g h*. Lofty elms generally shelter these little *villæ* from the too powerful rays of the sun ; close to them are the ploughed fields, kitchen-gardens, and orchards.

Figure 13 presents the front elevation, overlooking the path or highway, and which has scarcely any windows. It is only from the logias that the inmates can see who is coming. This is another traditional feature which imparts a characteristic appearance to the front of these houses.

In the ancient Languedoc château we also find this typical arrangement of a central corridor passing right through the building, admitting to apartments on the right and left. Near

Castelnaudary there still exists a château, dating from the commencement of the seventeenth century, which certainly affords one of the most interesting specimens of a manorial abode of that epoch, and which is designed throughout in accordance with the requirements suggested by the habits of the district and the

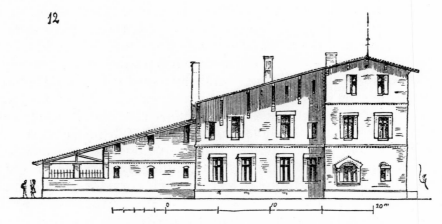

Fig. 12.—Southern French Rural Dwelling. Front Elevation.

customs of the time.   It is the château de Ferrals, the residence of a rural landholder of noble family, a captain in the army; it presents the double character of a fortress and an agricultural *villa*.   Built at the time when the noblesse of Languedoc, who were to a great extent Protestants, were endeavouring to secure

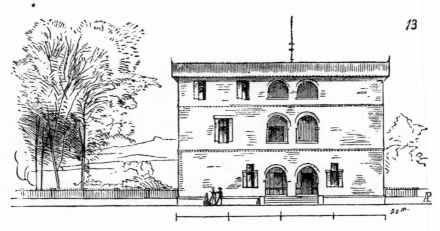

Fig. 13.—Southern French Rural Dwelling. Side Elevation.

their position against the Catholic royal power, its construction must have been interrupted after the taking of Montauban by Louis XIII.   In fact the roofings have remained unfinished, and provisional coverings have sheltered the stories of the building from that time down to the present.   Figure 14 gives a drawing

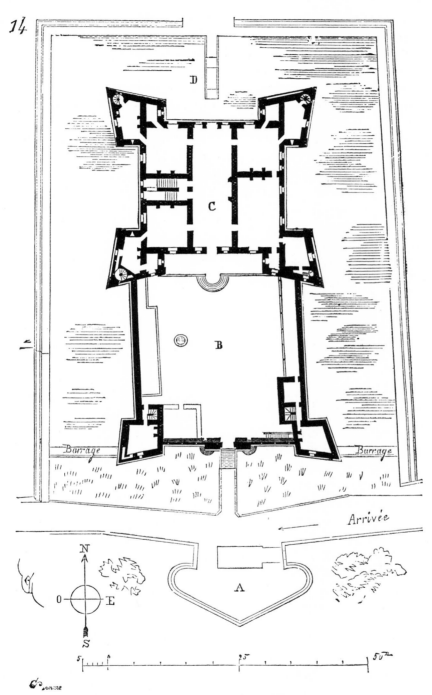

Fig. 14.- Château de Ferrals.

of the whole of the château with its demi-lune at A; its fore-court at B, and its main buildings at C. This main building, as shown in the plan, consists of a large hall which traverses its whole length and gives access to apartments communicating with rooms placed in the flanking turrets in the form of bastions, and which besides their windows are furnished with embrasures for cannon. A wide moat with its drawbridge at D, communicating with the gardens which are well laid out, completely surrounds the château. A basement story is lighted by windows opening on the fosse, and there is a first story over the ground-floor. Above the first story there must have been a rampart walk of which only the traces are visible; behind which the roof-story surmounted the entire main building. The two turrets (bastions of the fore court) are connected with the main building by lofty curtain walls, against which are built covered passages. The masonry, of hewn stone and massive quoins, has an appearance of sturdy strength which perfectly harmonises with the wildly picturesque features of the country it overlooks, bounded on the horizon by the Pyrenees.

However alien to the present age this huge building may seem, it is nevertheless one of the most genuine representatives of the rural mansion of the south of France; and if rendered habitable it would be a residence as salubrious as conformable to the customs of the country. The great central hall, open only at its two extremities, is as well lighted as could be wished, owing to the brilliance of the light in that district. This is the place of assembling for the family, but where conversations apart would be possible, though all were in the same room. The rooms occupying the turrets are reached from the central apartments and the great hall itself; but this arrangement, which even in our times is not reckoned inconvenient in the country, where intercourse between the inmates is much more free than in the city, is customary in southern habitations, and is so much the less objectionable in the case in question, as at the château de Ferrals private stairs place these rooms in communication with the lower stories, and the servants can reach them without passing through the great hall. The first story presented the same arrangements, except that the apartments flanking the great hall served as bed-chambers, and communication with those of the turrets was facilitated by private outlets opening on the two extremities of the great hall.

Such a block of buildings grouped under one roof is the best means of protection against the heat and those northerly winds which are so annoying in the south of France; the arrangement in question therefore should always be retained in designing country dwellings in that district. Scattered buildings, such as we find in the rural dwellings of England, would be intolerable in a southern climate, as they would not be sufficiently protected against the heat, the winds from the north, and those charged with humidity coming from the Mediterranean; nor against the dust or that excess of light which brings insects of all kinds into the interiors. Architects, therefore, should pay much more regard to these conditions of climate than to certain features adopted in the neighbourhood of Paris or London, and which it is the fashion to import from the English Channel to the Pyrenees, or from the Atlantic to the Rhine. But I would ask, Are the suburban dwellings around Paris constructed with a due consideration of the exigencies of the climate and the wants of the occupants? This may well be doubted, and even if we say nothing about those castles of cards we mentioned just now, do those turrets, exposed to all the four winds, those roofs with pendent eaves, those narrow apartments, and windows all of the same size, notwithstanding the difference in the amount of surface of the rooms they have to light, does this constitute a rural architecture appropriate to its objects? Are not such arrangements rather the result of a want of study and sound reasoning, and of certain order of routine that has become inveterate in the public? In the suburban abodes of Paris the aspect and variety of prospects is scarcely taken account of at all; the chief aim is to give a showy appearance to the fronts rather than to satisfy the daily needs of the inhabitants.

In this respect the English country-houses are better suited to their purpose. Should they therefore be copied among ourselves? Certainly not; the climate of England and the habits of the English differ from ours, as we have already pointed out. Besides, even in England, the plan of irregularly grouped buildings has not always been adopted. Some of its manorial residences exhibit a symmetrical grouping. Among others, we may mention Warkworth Castle in Northumberland, whose plan presents a large square with canted angles, and a polygonal projection in the centre of each front. Thus each story contains eight apartments surrounding a central nucleus surmounted by a watch-tower.

It must be acknowledged that English country-houses have a considerable advantage as compared with our own; the architecture adopted in them is certainly one suited to dwellings in which the comfort of the inmates is made the first consideration. The English have had the good sense to preserve certain traditions of the Middle Ages which sanction irregularities of plan,— arrangements in details adopted to suit special requirements. In France, when any one intending to build is possessed with the idea of having a house erected according to what he imagines the "style" of the Middle Ages, his architect straightway sets to work to stick upon a front—which might really belong to another style—ornaments borrowed from some manor-house of the fifteenth century!—to introduce symmetrically along the front windows more or less "Gothic,"—to put up high-pitched gables, and to make "pointed arches" here and there. This generally produces a very inconvenient and always a ridiculous design. It is not windows of a certain form, mouldings, or even high-pitched gables, that constitute mediæval houses, but perfect freedom in the management of the plan, and ingenious arrangements fitted to make the dwelling harmonise with the habits of its inmates. The only advantage that can be derived from models left us by the Middle Ages is our learning from them to give an artistic form to every requirement in an architectural programme, and never to pervert the architecture by forcing certain conventional forms into combination with requirements that are alien to them.

When the unfortunate idea took possession of our countrymen of adopting the architecture (called Classical), which was in a certain measure an offspring of Italian art, and which was in fact not unsuited to very large dwellings; and when, in an ill-advised spirit of imitation, they proceeded to adapt its forms to habitations of an inferior order, the traditions of local art, which were in fact but the result of lengthened experience, were lost. The true and simple forms dictated by custom and time-honoured practice were sacrificed to an outward show which was quite at variance with the requirements. For example, absolutely symmetrical arrangements were imposed on parts of a plan which require unlimited variety in the dimension and the distribution of the apartments, in the method of lighting them, connecting them in the economy of the house, and of protecting them against the sun's heat or the cold.

Of those who build country houses, and of architects themselves, very few understand the true spirit of our mediæval architecture. To most persons, the domestic architecture of the Middle Ages seems a mere affair of taste—a peculiar style of decoration—something like the wearing of an old-fashioned dress. This being the case, we can readily understand how those who wish to hold that middle course which commends itself to intelligent persons—who in fact do not wish to be conspicuous—should shrink from appearing in public in such obsolete, pretentious, and inconvenient attire. If it had been our habit to study such matters seriously—and I wish we were inclined to form such a habit,—our architects would have soon discovered that mediæval art, applied to domestic as well as to every other kind of architecture, is not an affair of mouldings,

or of the few commonplace forms with which antiquarian collections are occupied, but that it involves first and foremost a
principle of freedom in the means of execution which can adapt
itself quite as well to the requirements of mankind in the
fourteenth century as in the nineteenth. It is true that in
architecture, as in politics, though we talk much of liberty and
inscribe the word on our public buildings, we have but little
comprehension of what it really implies. There are, for instance,
many architects who would not adopt a " Gothic " arrangement
because they would not wish to be thought to sympathise with
the *parti clérical!* To them " Gothic," " dominant Church,"
" feudalism," " glebe-lands," " tithes," and " serfdom," are all
contained in the same cask, so that if one of them is turned out,
all the others must necessarily come out too. It is of no use to
tell these good people that the lay art of the Middle Ages,
which was essentially free in its principles, ways of proceeding,
and expression, has no connection with the bishops, feudal lords,
monks, and barons of the Middle Ages, or with the " Holy
Inquisition;" they will stop their ears, and rather than run the
risk of raising these ghosts will remain enslaved by academic
doctrines, which are much more tyrannical and narrow than ever
were the mediæval schools of art, which were perfectly independent of all influences foreign to their development.

The English, however, who are more practical than we can
contrive to be, have preserved those elements of their ancient
domestic architecture which are available in the present day :
viz., the spirit of liberty and individuality. Yet they are not
on that account the prey of the *cléricaux.* They have considered it desirable to make use of appliances which have been
recognised as good and which have been consecrated by long
usage ; though they reserve to themselves the liberty of improving them rather than hastily throwing them aside and adopting
forms absolutely foreign to their habits and climate, and torturing
themselves and their families by living in houses whose style is
pronounced orthodox by a coterie. They have discovered that
the uncompromisingly symmetrical style applied to their dwellings involves useless constraint, or at least inconvenience, and
they have rejected it. They are convinced that well-chosen
aspects, openings for light and air contrived with a view to the
requirements and the comfort of the house, are preferable to
those uniform fronts with windows all of equal size (sometimes
stopped up), and with equal spaces between them, which we
build in the country as well as in the city ; and they have continued to take account of the aspect and the requirements of the
interior in arranging and lighting the various apartments. They
have also maintained that in the mode of construction applied

by their ancestors to houses in the country there were simple
means, easy and evident in execution, and a great variety of
features accommodated to all the requirements of a dwelling;
and they have continued to adopt these means without the
slightest suspicion that their civil liberty might be compromised
by their thus respecting an advantage which had been secured
to them by gradual acquisition. This is how our neighbours on
the other side of the Straits of Dover understand the exercise of
liberty. We take a very different view of things. If we have
drunk at a despot's table, as soon as he is dethroned we break
the glass, but, whether we are the better for it or not, this does
not prevent another despot from coming who makes us pay very
dear for the glass we have broken.

15

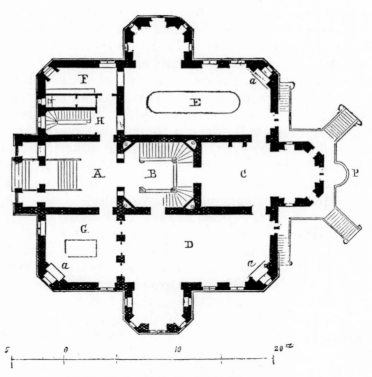

FIG. 15.—Warkworth Castle. Ground-plan.

Warkworth Castle may supply the type of an excellent
arrangement for a country-house of considerable dimensions.
And this arrangement would be quite as desirable in France
as in England. We will try to show how the principles it
exemplifies may be made available.

Figure 15 gives the ground-floor: at A is a vestibule which
is entered by a porch covering a flight of steps. From this
vestibule we reach the great staircase B, which also serves

as a hall, and thence we pass into a first saloon C and the great drawing-room D. The dining-hall is at E, with pantry at F. At G is a billiard-room directly communicating with the great drawing-room, and with the vestibule A. At H is the servants' staircase leading down to the kitchens and up to the attics. From the saloon C there is a direct descent to the garden by flights of steps P, which forms a balcony and affords an entrance from the outside not only into the saloon C, but also into the dining-hall and great drawing-room D. The deep bays projecting at the axis of the building form annexes to the dining-hall E and the drawing-room D. This annex greatly facilitates the service of the dining-hall, being close to the pantry, and it supplies a very convenient retiring place from the great drawing-room; the chimney-pieces are at a in the truncated angles in front of the windows.

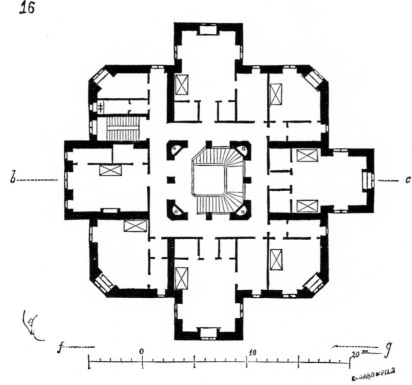

16

FIG. 16.—Warkworth Castle. First-floor plan.

The great staircase ascends only to the first story, figure 16. It is surrounded by a gallery which leads to seven suites of rooms, each consisting of a bedroom with small sitting-rooms and dressing-rooms.

The principal staircase (see the section along $b\ c$, fig. 17 A) forms a central turret, lighted lantern-fashion on the four sides. Around this turret are arranged wide gutters draining the roofs in four down-pipes of easy access, contrived in the angles of the staircase (see the plans).   These down-spouts communicate with a collecting drain.   They can be kept warm in winter by the central heating apparatus, to avoid the inconvenience generally experienced from the freezing of the spouts ; moreover, as they pass the galleries connected with the suites of bedrooms, they receive the slops from the dressing-rooms, while the pretty spacious shafts which enclose them also contain the pipes for water supply.   It may be remarked that these pipe-shafts are wide enough to allow of a man's getting into them to repair the pipes when required.

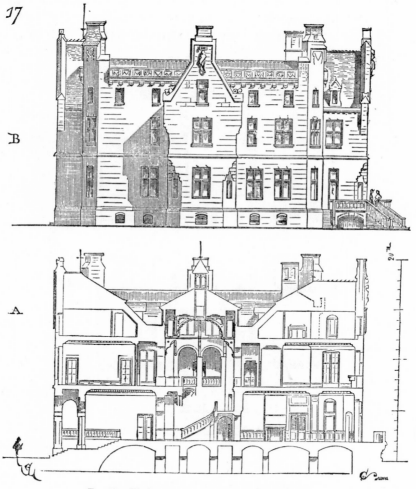

FIG. 17.—Warkworth Castle.   Elevation and Section.

At B, fig. 17 is given the elevation of front *f g*.   The roofs of the projecting bays are terminated by gables on the outside and are hipped on the inner side.

Owing to this arrangement of the central staircase, which is well lighted and ventilated, the different services may be grouped around it without leaving any room dark. Views are obtained towards all points of the horizon, which greatly adds to the charm of a habitation in the country. The construction of so compact a building, in which the front walls as compared with the surface occupied are not very extensive, is less expensive than that of a building of the usual thickness with wings. In fact this great agglomeration of rooms occupies not less than 6800 square feet, while the linear extent of the frontage walls at the base is only 370 feet.

While there is an advantage in point of economy as regards building in adopting this compactly grouped arrangement, communication is undeniably more easy, and keeping the mansion in repair less expensive. The spouting in consequence of the simplicity of the method cannot occasion any of the inconveniences that so frequently occur in houses in the country, which are more exposed to the inclemency of the weather than those in the towns. The accumulation of snow in the four central gutters cannot do any damage, as these gutters have a very rapid fall, and the down-pipes can be kept at a temperature that will always leave their upper orifice free. Moreover a leakage in these down-pipes, isolated as they are in wide shafts, cannot occasion any disaster.

These interior roofs are sheltered from the wind and consequently are rarely exposed to dilapidation. The chimneys which are for the most part placed on the outer walls and crowning gables are firmly built, and rise high enough to prevent the draught being obstructed. The roofing can be readily inspected, and without danger.

We may therefore derive instruction from some of these mediæval designs and adapt them to our modern western requirements, better than we could those adopted in certain châteaux of majestic exterior, built during the seventeenth century, or in Italian villas, such as Palladio's for example, which were for the most part only temporarily occupied for festive purposes. From the fact that many of our châteaux or large country houses of the seventeenth and even of the eighteenth century are by no means comfortably arranged, it has been concluded that the further we go back into the past, the more conspicuous will the inconveniences become. But such is not the case. It is from the middle of the seventeenth century that we must date a passion for symmetry and " the majestic," which can scarcely be said to have possessed preceding periods. In those remote times the first consideration was the convenience of the inmates of a dwelling, however large ; and the forms adopted in their architecture were deduced from what that convenience required. It would seem that so practical an age as ours ought to favour this wise and natural principle ;

and that we should be inclined to abandon those prejudices of the school to which the public even more than architects themselves remain attached, and make it a point to conform to the rules of good common sense before all things.

Some wealthy individuals, struck by the comfortable arrangements displayed in most English country-houses, have made the experiment of employing English architects for châteaux or smaller houses. This attempt has not been successful. Whether it is because their builders have not preserved freedom in their work away from home, or that their employers have endeavoured to make them adopt architectural forms other than those to which they were accustomed, or that they have not taken the trouble to become acquainted with our methods of building, these dwellings neither exhibit the advantages of those which are regarded as models in England, nor have they the charm of our own. Ill-built and gloomy, they possess no other merit than that of presenting tolerably convenient minor arrangements and generally well-devised dependencies. But it is not in this quarter that we should look for models.

We possess in France itself, in our ancient architecture (if we will take the trouble to look about us), a much more extensive variety of methods of construction than England offers ; a fact which, apart from our more versatile genius, may be explained by the difference of climate in different parts of our country, and the diverse nature of the materials suitable for building. That we should not attempt servilely to copy these so numerous examples may be all very well ; but that we should take no notice of them,—that we should not take advantage of the results obtained,—cannot be justified by any sound reason, especially as the features which are conspicuous in the various modes of construction formerly adopted are, great freedom, and an abundance of resources for conquering all the difficulties presented by the requirements of the case. Why then should we deprive ourselves of the advantages already provided for our use ?

The limits to which these Lectures are restricted will hardly allow of my mentioning many of those ancient building methods which are now disdained, but which could be so easily adopted and even improved upon in our day. It seems desirable, however, to mention some which are exemplified in the last example we have presented.

Thus we see in this country mansion that the central bays, all polygonal in plan on the ground-floor (to allow of oblique views and to clear the angles), are square on the first story,— a form preferable for bedrooms.

This arrangement, which is but seldom adopted in the present day—I do not know why,—was formerly very common, and the problem was solved in a very simple manner, as shown in figure 18.

The oblique face on the ground-floor (see A in the plan) is 6 ft. 7 in. wide. The rectangular walls are 2 ft. 1½ in. and the oblique walls 2 ft. 4 in. in thickness. On the oblique face is a window 3 ft. 3. in. broad. Two corbels of two courses each prolong the face of the walls at a right angle, as far as the point where they meet above the lintel of the window on these corbels; two other courses *a b* form a corbelling and bear the angle of the story *c*. There remains a small horizontal triangular soffit at *e*. The elevation B sufficiently explains this construction, which is so simple and in many cases so advantageous.

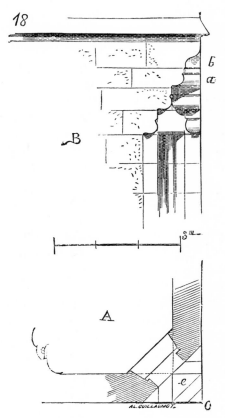

FIG. 18. Warkworth Castle. Canted angles of the bays.

Let us now examine the structural system of the ceiling of the central lantern which crowns the staircase of the country mansion, a general view of which was given in figures 15, 16, 17. Skylights in the roof, on which the rain pours directly, are not without their disadvantages in towns; but in country districts where repairs cannot be executed directly, the inconvenience is much more serious; if a violent hailstorm occurs, the glass is broken and the interior is deluged, the mischief cannot be remedied immediately; while, if it snows, the interior is darkened; and driving rains invariably penetrate through these glazed roofs, however well constructed. We should consequently avoid them. And so we observe in the section, figure 17, that the central lantern has vertical lights, well sheltered and double, with room for passing between to allow of cleaning and necessary repairs. Figure 19 shows the construction of one quarter of this lantern in its interior. The quarter of the plan A is taken at the level of the openings; it shows at a one of the shafts containing the down-pipes. Four strut-trusses P are placed in the direction of the two axes, the lantern being square; eight brackets H are fixed at the corners of the skew faces of the shafts. Each pair of these eight brackets is united at their head. The strut-trusses are framed as shown in the section, at B. They consist of an upright placed against the internal face of the wall, and resting on a corbel; of an inclined piece C, two couples D, a headpiece F, a second inclined piece G, halved into the first, a second post I, bearing on a beam L. The diagonal trusses, whose elevation is drawn at M, rest on feet supported on the brackets H. The ends of these eight trusses support the octagonal frame O. Glazed casements are placed at N in the stone windows; a second set of casements of iron, also glazed, are placed at E. A passage K thus remains which can be reached from the roofs. The outer windows N, pierced much higher than those marked E, allow the light to penetrate into the staircase in the most desirable manner. The truss timbers are from 4 in. to $4\frac{1}{2}$ in. square. They are cased with boarding on the two faces, as our drawing shows, and which may be cut to a curve and be moulded as may seem suitable; this nailed boarding adds greatly to the strength of these trusses; and they may be perforated as seen at J. Moreover, if care has been taken to fill in between the ends of each pair of boards with a piece of deal cut to the same section as those ends, each truss will thus have the appearance of a homogeneous rib. Of course these casings of boarding can be decorated as richly as may be deemed desirable with carving or painting.

On the eight trusses (4 along the axes and 4 diagonal), wooden ceilings will be placed at s according to any design that may be chosen. At T, there will be a ventilation valve. The internal glazed frames v comprise therefore all the space left between the eight trusses and give as much light as possible.

We can easily see that such a construction could be erected at very little expense. Being perfectly well roofed and sheltered it can be decorated with painting without any fear of injury from damp. The trusses are cramped at x; but there is no fear of

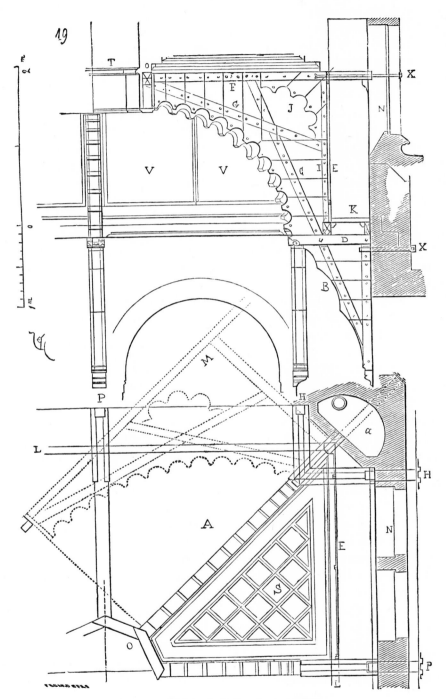

Fɪɢ. 19.—Warkworth Castle.   Lantern ceiling.

their giving, as they are supported against the octagonal frame, which cannot be put out of shape, being equally pressed at its eight angles.

It is always desirable in building in the country to avoid as far as possible the direct contact of the wood with the masonry, —as remarked above—as also excessively large window-sashes and doors of unnecessary height; for the effects of damp and of sudden changes of temperature are more to be feared in the country than in the city. On this account the plan of dividing the windows by fixed mullions is especially applicable in dwellings in the country, because though large windows are secured, the sashes can be divided and they are of no great extent of surface. The only difficulty it presents would arise in attempting to put up external sun-blinds.

But as the walls of dwellings in the country built of masonry must always be pretty thick, there would be no difficulty in putting metal jalousies in the window jambs folded back in leaves eight inches broad at least, for the lower lights. As regards the upper lights above the stone transoms, they cannot be closed by means of jalousies, as it would be impossible to open or shut them from the inside without a ladder. For these upper parts of mullioned windows therefore, another method must be adopted. Mechanical contrivances have the disadvantage, especially for houses in the country, of getting out of order, or tending to get rusty in the inclement part of the year, and so not working. The great point therefore is to discover a simple method that does not require constant keeping up. And the simplest arrangement for closing in the higher parts of windows constructed with mullions and transoms would certainly be inside shutters fixed by hinges to the frame itself of the glazed casement. These shutters may be perforated if thought desirable, or even made of metal plates. It would be easy to open and close them from below, by means of a latch and cord, or a very slight iron rod.

But we shall have occasion to enter more fully into all these details in a special work now in preparation on "Town and Country Houses in the Nineteenth Century" (*L'habitation urbaine et des campagnes au XIXe siècle*); a work in which specimens of buildings executed according to inexpensive plans, and suited to incomes which are tending and will tend more and more in our day to a moderate average, will have particular attention.

Though our requirements are perfectly definite and our appliances for building are very considerable in extent and excellent in character, we have not been able to constitute a Domestic Architecture any more than to establish a Public Architecture. We are hesitating undecidedly between traditions which are still vigorous and associations which are more or less influential, and the necessity of satisfying new requirements which are out of harmony with most of those influences and traditions. Thence has arisen a strange compromise which but very imperfectly satisfies the demands of our times and the requirements of art. In fact a new phase of genuine art does not spring forth suddenly from an architect's brain; such a form can only be the result of a series of logical deductions inseparably connected.

The public and the architectural world itself is, I think, too much engrossed with questions of the form of art proper to our time. This will make its appearance gradually if the public, and the architects likewise, regard it as their chief object when building to satisfy the purely local exigencies or those which result from the needs to be satisfied. If this method of proceeding does not immediately furnish those harmonious and complete forms which constitute art, it conduces to their discovery. Besides, there is no other way of securing them. All civilisations that have possessed an art have been obliged to commence in this way. It is thus that the traditions or influences which must have accompanied them at starting were transformed to such a degree as to be recognisable only by archæologists.

This phenomenon is observable among the Greek civilisations, whose architecture, beautiful and complete as it is in its various expressions, was evolved by degrees—by the due satisfaction of requirements resulting from a state of society in process of formation—from those Asiatic elements which surround its cradle. It was produced in the West among ourselves, when a lay art arose in the Middle Ages, which took as its starting-point the Gallo-Roman traditions and the transformations to which the religious orders had subjected those traditions during the period from the eighth to the thirteenth century. If we subject to analysis the first attempts of those masters who formed our French mediæval art, we perceive that the new forms which arise and evolve themselves by degree from the Romanesque style are due to an attentive appreciation of the needs that arise and their more and more perfect satisfaction. To seek for new forms outside this natural development is to rush at hazard into the way of imitation and to attain no other result but compilations of data without ever creating forms capable of improvement; since forms are capable of improvement only through their having been suggested by the exact appreciation of the properties of the materials to be employed and of the method in which they are employed. No one will deny in theory that the various properties of the materials ought to be considered in the form given to them when employed in building. Stone, marble, wood, cast or wrought iron, and the various forms of baked clay, have widely different properties: in view of this variety and even opposition of character in the several materials, the form which suits one of them cannot suit another. This being regarded as indisputable, it must, I think, be granted that many forms habitually adopted in our edifices take no account of the properties of the materials, and can only be referred to certain traditions which show a want of accurate knowledge of those properties.

We might seem justified in supposing that since modern science has carried the knowledge of the various properties of the material employed to a high degree of perfection, our builders would take advantage of its researches to give to the materials forms bearing a due relation to those properties : but it has not been so ; or at any rate the attempts made in this direction have been but timid, and exhibit a constant anxiety to introduce no alteration into the traditional forms bequeathed by anterior phases of art. Civil engineers themselves, who had been among the foremost to extend the domain of science in that direction, were less than others perhaps, disposed to make the forms which they gave to the material harmonise with its properties. This has arisen from the false direction given to the teaching of art,—a teaching which only gives examples borrowed from former civilisations, without ever explaining the reason why the forms and the materials in which they were produced were originally adopted.

The teaching of architecture, as carried on in France, instead of allying itself intimately with science and criticism, seems inclined to look askance at both of them, encouraging them only on the condition of their not encroaching on what it is pleased to call the traditions of "high art;" as if the chief condition of art in architecture as well as in every other department was not conformity to truth in adopting forms suggested by the harmonious concurrence of all knowledge relating to the department in question. And so we hear it maintained in the present day, as it was formerly, that iron cannot be employed in our edifices without dissembling its use, because this material is not suited to monumental forms. It would be more consistent with truth and reason to say that the monumental forms adopted, having resulted from the use of materials possessing qualities other than those of iron, cannot be adapted to this latter material. The logical inference is that we should not continue to employ those forms, but should try to discover others which harmonise with the properties of iron.

But I would say once more : the body into whose hands instruction in architecture has fallen is averse to reasoning. It regards reasoning as a heresy ; its claims are rejected and authority is brought in to oppose it. But this is not the way to enter on the path of Progress.

LECTURE XX.

THE STATE OF ARCHITECTURE IN EUROPE—THE POSITION OF ARCHITECTS IN
FRANCE—COMPETITIVE ARRANGEMENTS—CONTRACTS—BOOK-KEEPING IN
CONNECTION WITH BUILDING-YARDS, AND THE SUPERINTENDENCE OF THE
LATTER.

As regards the arts in particular, we are in neither a worse
nor a better position than we were before the late war ; and
the victories of Germany have not, any more than the incendiary
practices that have marked the invasion, advanced it a single
step in the path of civilisation generally, or of the arts in special.
It will perhaps erect a few more public buildings at Berlin with
our money.   But will they be more beautiful than those which
it built before ?   That may be doubted.

I shall not be accused of taking a too favourable view of our
institutions for promoting art any more than of the method of
official instruction which they continue to pursue, and in which
with a certain narrowness of view they have adopted some retro-
gressive measures to avenge themselves for the decree of the
13th November 1863, under favour of the absorption of public
interest in other matters and the complaisance of a director of
the *Beaux Arts* and member of the Institute.   These circumstances are, in fact, of little importance during the prevalence
of a public opinion, which, unfavourable to such petty intrigues
of coteries, insists on everything being brought to light.   If
however we calmly examine our art institutions, especially if
we take account of the progress of opinion among artists and
the public at large—the element in which our art productions
originate—and compare the position of artists as determined by
it, with that which is assigned them in the other countries of
Europe, the balance will still incline in our favour.

Thus, for example, public attention has been directed to the
efforts made by our neighbours the English to develop æsthetic
studies and tastes ; and for some years past neither money nor
encouragement of any kind has been wanting.   But with what

results ? There has been a marked improvement in the workmanship,—the material execution. But as regards critical discernment and selection—taste, in fact—no very great success has followed. The fact is, an art cannot be improvised. An æsthetic discipline is the outcome of a long course of tradition handed down from age to age. To produce artists they must be placed in a contagious medium, so to speak ; a proof of which is exhibited in the case of the very skilful artists and craftsmen who have left France for some years, and have then returned to it ; what they produced after this exile had lost all its charm, all piquancy, and whatever efforts they made they could not succeed in recovering that clear and delicate execution which they possessed, without being conscious of it, while they were living in a favourable medium.

Art in France enjoys a vigorous vitality,—it grows in open ground and free air ; in fact it must be so or it would not have survived the artificial cultivation which has been imposed upon it during the last two centuries. While the hot-houses thus produce a great number of uniform and feebly-tinted flowers, Nature from time to time resumes her supremacy, and one of these plants, more vivacious than the rest, breaks through the glazing that is stifling it, expands its blossoms all brilliant with their native tints, and, in spite of the gardener, flings on the winds the seeds which will spring up far and wide. They become wild plants once more, to the great delight of all those who prefer the vivifying odours of the fields to the sickly perfumes of the hot-house.

The soil of France has always been propitious to the development of the arts ; what we ask is that no attempt should be made to impose a factitious culture upon them, but only the means of growing and blossoming be supplied to them. This, however, we have not yet been able to secure ; for we are possessed with the strange mania of making everything an object of administration and regulation ; while the political revolutions which upset so many things among us, but especially our ways of thinking, and our sense of right and justice, have not yet introduced the exercise of liberty into our conduct, or the sense of independence and individual dignity into our minds.

The State thinks itself bound to teach the arts ; it recognises their importance and consequently regards it as its duty to watch over their development. And nothing would be more desirable if this solicitude were limited to securing freedom for the development of art in its various forms. But this is not what is really done ; the State—I have often said it, and I repeat it—is only the secular arm of a *mandarinate*; and if among those whom different governments have placed at the head of the administration of the arts, some have been found who have had a sense of justice and an independence of character sufficient to induce them to enter on liberal courses, they have soon been forced to abandon this thankless position; artists themselves being generally the first to refuse the liberty offered them. Nevertheless French architecture still occupies the first place in Europe — such vitality has this art among us. Besides, it must be remarked that other countries have not understood the advantages attached to liberty better than we have. In England, for example, if architects are not, like those of our own country, subject to an administration which is only the instrument of a corporate body of artists, and which in the natural course of things can never be anything else, they are subject to the rigorous yoke of the speculative builders. Yet there is such an amount of private enterprise on the other side of the Channel, and a practical good sense so fully developed, that young architects succeed in getting their education in spite of superannuated institutions. In England the ancient guilds still exist, though these rich corporations are now scarcely anything more than associations for charitable purposes.

If a young Englishman wishes to become an architect, his father articles him to a master who is more or less worthy of the title, and for a hundred guineas a year this master engages * * * probably to teach him what he knows himself. The pupil on beginning his studies is bound by written agreement to be at the office every day from half-past nine till five o'clock,—on Saturdays only till half-past two,—to give his master all his time, not to divulge the *secrets* of the craft, nor to do anything that might be detrimental to the interests of his principal; to conduct himself with due respect in his daily relations with the principal, and not to " commit matrimony " without his consent.

For two years the pupil is occupied with tracing and making fair copies of architectural drawings and details of execution which are in many cases begun by him and finished by a fellow-pupil. If he wishes to visit the building-yards he can do so only during his leisure hours—and it is obvious that these are not many—or in the absence of the principal.

Nevertheless, such a pupil, being engaged in the practical work of his profession at the very outset, pretty soon acquires familiarity with building methods; he becomes acquainted with the difficulties of execution and of superintendence, and, if he is intelligent and a worker—the English are generally such — this stage in his career is of use in training him for his profession. He has been learning during this time the methods followed by his master, and his way of dealing with contractors and workmen. Some share of the responsibility has fallen to him, for if in the details intrusted to him,—in the combinations involved in a building—he has left anything to chance, if he has not anticipated all contingencies and furnished sufficient explanations; if, as the consequence, the wrong thing is done,—he, the pupil, will be blamed, and in this case he risks his prospects for the future. This course furnishes an education which may not be of a high character, but which produces men of practical ability, and who make a really serious business of their profession.

In recent times the students of architecture in England have felt the insufficiency of this ancient method, which is a tradition of the mediæval guilds, but they have not yet gone and asked their Government to take charge of their interests; they have simply formed a society which has nearly six hundred members paying an annual subscription of ten shillings. Its meetings and classes are held during the winter. They assemble once a fortnight, in the evening, to discuss questions suggested by the members. These discussions generally relate to the working out of conditions very minutely detailed.

The classes are occupied with, first, elementary design, that is, an executive sketch of a given programme; the president criticises the drawings which are brought before him again at the next meeting with details of construction, ornamentation, etc. Secondly, developed design, *i.e.* comprising plans of larger extent or more difficult execution. Thirdly, construction properly so called, with explanatory memoranda, and details and diagrams on the black-board in presence of the class.

During the summer the members of the association visit the building-yards in small parties and undertake courses of practical trigonometry, and sketch from nature. They read works on architecture together and comment on them, or discuss suggestions that may be offered. Prizes are given in each of the classes, which are publicly distributed at the beginning of the year. There is a library to which the members have access.

This is evidently a more intelligent and useful institution than the *charges d'ateliers* in vogue among ourselves, the convivialities and the *oaths* exacted from the new pupils.

In Germany the position of architects is a more or less independent one, according to the usages of different localities. There is every reason to believe that Prussia will amalgamate the system of regulations under which their body also will be allowed to practise their art. But Germany is subject to frigidly passionate impulses which are little propitious to the regular development of the arts. Sometimes it will incline towards the Middle Ages, sometimes towards ancient Greek art, not as the result of logical deduction, but as what in France we call a *fashion;* and among the Germans fashions are tenacious and intolerant. It had suggested itself to an intelligent man, the old King Louis of Bavaria, about forty years ago, to erect in his good city of Munich buildings imitating more or less closely the Greek, Roman, Byzantine, Mediæval, Italian, and Northern architecture respectively. He was thus giving his subjects a specimen of all the architectural products of art that could be made available as models, and seemed to say to them : "Now choose." The object contemplated was little understood at Munich ; for the German mind is by no means eclectic, and King Louis's buildings, which moreover were erected according to methods whose economical aspect was in many cases little in accordance with the style of architecture which they profess to reproduce, are in fact only a kind of "Exhibition" of works of art a little more durable than ordinary displays of the kind.

Although Germany has for some years been deeply smitten with a taste for the products of Greek art, and has made some pretensions to be the continuator of the illustrious age of Greece, —considering itself the last scion of the Aryan stock, and the only genuine one, and consequently summoned to govern the whole world still more by its understanding and genius than by its arms ; it is none the less imbued to the very marrow with the traditions of the Middle Ages, and will find some difficulty in securing that place in Europe which Athens occupied in the ancient world.

Hellenizers are to be found in Germany, and will continue to be found there ; but though its genius may be to a certain extent compared with that of the Macedonians, and though the sovereigns of Prussia have some points in common with the kings of Macedonia, it would be mistaken if it supposed itself capable of taking the first place in the domain of the arts. The instinct of intellectual independence is wanting in Germany, and no development of art is possible without it. The *Teutonic* architecture of the Middle Ages, though sometimes displaying great skill, is defective on the score of dryness and monotony, though with great pretension to effect. This architecture, moreover, is essentially only an imitation of our ancient French art of the commencement of the thirteenth century, executed by those who do not understand its dominant principles ; the proof of which is, that they do not follow these principles, but commit themselves to scientific formulas, endeavouring thus to provide a substitute for that artistic instinct which they do not possess.

The German architect therefore finds himself placed in disadvantageous conditions, as being not destitute of method or science, but subjected to the fluctuations of intolerant and exclusive fashions, without having for his guidance a system established on logical principles and deductions. He is destitute of critical and analytic intelligence; or, if this intelligence is possessed by him individually,—as often happens,—he cannot make it penetrate the refractory medium in which he is placed, and which is passionately devoted to changing abstractions.

A philosophical system may be modified from day to day; but this cannot be the case with an art which is practically useful, and which is intimately connected with habits and manners—such as that of architecture.

A style of architecture can only be the result of a long series of traditions, which have bound together the individuals of a nation in a community of national interests and feelings; Germany does not yet present these conditions; and supposing that the amalgamation of the German nationalities should be accomplished—which the philosophy of history scarcely allows us to anticipate,—the Germans will have to wait at least two or three centuries before they can possess an architecture that will be the original expression of their civilisation. This gives us some respite. But at this date it need not be supposed that Germany will be superior to us in the power, sovereignty, and originality of its arts,—at any rate not of its architecture.

But while, strictly speaking, a German architecture does not now exist, we find in the countries which are comprised in Germany, local developments whose merit is indisputable. Bavaria offers excellent examples of domestic architecture. The same may be said of Hanover and of Würtemberg. The buildings in these countries which do not aspire to be monumental accurately reflect the local customs and needs of the inhabitants. The houses, and the smaller public buildings, such as schools, markets, and railway stations, are always economical in plan, and are executed with care, and with a practical feeling bordering on a certain amount of grace which is somewhat severe, but is not without its charm. The same may be said of private houses in the rural districts. Rarely pretentious, these buildings are abodes in which nothing has been sacrificed to luxury or display, but in which the domestic life of the inmates has left a lively and original impress. They are generally very simply, but very well built. Of all German localities, Vienna is certainly the most notable traditional centre of art. Vienna has its academy and its official school; but it is not these to which its artists owe their excellence. This is owing to a sufficiently extended education, the result of a profound study of foreign works,—those of Italy, France, and North-western Germany. And though the education thus relatively extended, which is enjoyed by the architects of Vienna, has not yet produced the style proper to the nineteenth century, and to Southern Germany, it has at least enabled them to erect buildings perfectly suited to their object, sensibly designed, quickly and very well executed, and of very pleasing aspect. The Opera at Vienna, among other buildings that might be mentioned, took less than eight years to build, and cost only £320,000. This vast erection is the best and most complete of its kind in Europe.

But in point of unity and originality of style, Russia will probably have secured its position before Germany. Russia has long found itself in the favourable condition resulting from unity; and at the present time it is making efforts of which we in France (in consequence of our habitual indifference to all that occurs in foreign countries) have little conception, but which are nevertheless very earnest. Russia, before the fashion (dating from Peter I.) was introduced among its architects of imitating the arts of the West, had an art of its own, an art which was coarse and unformed, but which had a local character and originality, or if we choose so to call it, an autonomy. It is a mixture of Oriental, Byzantine, Tartar, and even Hindoo elements, and which had not reached its complete development when the Russian noblesse were smitten with a passion for the pseudo-Roman of the seventeenth century. In the present day there is an endeavour to recover the elements of that ancient architecture, and with the aid of modern criticism to bring them back to those natural combinations which would produce their complete development. This is a noble idea, and the higher class of minds in Russia recognise its importance; they are consequently setting themselves to work. Already schools are being formed, and a system of instruction is being organised; and all this without great display, but with that slow tenacity which characterises the Russians, and which ultimately triumphs over all obstacles. Russia is seeking within its own resources for the elements favourable to the production of an autonomous art; and this is a fruitful conception, which, however, does not prevent it from carefully studying what is done in other countries.

Italy, imbued though it is with local traditions of undeniable power, does not abstain from efforts to free itself from them, as far as they hinder the development of the novel conditions imposed on the architect. It is restoring ancient buildings with a highly developed critical intelligence; and this is a step towards the application of the same spirit of criticism to novel conceptions.

Carefully to restore buildings erected under conditions different from those amid which we ourselves are placed, is to compel our minds to pass through the different phases which have produced a certain development of art; it is to oblige our reason to draw logical deductions which are applicable as well to the present as to the past; for there is only one method of reasoning. This work of conscientious restoration to which Italy is giving itself cannot therefore fail to produce good results; especially as the Italians have the good sense not to separate their architects into two classes,—the restorers of ancient buildings and the constructors of those adapted to novel requirements. They seem to judge that an artist who is capable of appreciating an ancient style of art, and placing himself by a course of reasoning in the circumstances which existed three or four centuries ago, is quite as fitted as any other,—if not more so,—for understanding the needs of the present day and conforming his conceptions to them. It must also be taken into account that the Italians have never allowed certain constructive methods employed by them during the Middle Ages to be entirely abandoned, and that they do not repudiate those methods, as is affected to be done among ourselves.

A decided artistic movement may also be recognised in the northern countries of Europe; Belgium, Holland, the Danes and the Swedes, are seeking by means of the study of local traditions, and by appropriating to themselves the resources which they are capable of furnishing, to trace art down to the present time. It must therefore be acknowledged that, some devious movements excepted, there is a marked tendency in Europe to discover an autonomous art for each variety of civilisation. The principle of nationalities which is destined to effect revolutions in the midst of this old Europe, or rather to produce political developments of which our children probably will not see the issue, is manifesting itself even in the domain of art. Ethnological and historical studies have given the impulse to this movement, whose significance as regards the development of civilisation may be disputed, but whose importance cannot be ignored. France has been among the first to induce the nationalities of Europe thus to assert themselves. It has contributed to the reconstitution of Greece and Belgium, and has platonically defended the independence of Poland, and by arms and policy has aided Italy to secure its position in Europe.

Nothing is more dangerous than to maintain a principle, and then refuse to admit all its consequences. Has France acted rightly or wrongly, as far as its own interests are concerned, in maintaining the principle of nationality in Europe? Of course I shall not discuss the question, foreign as it is to the subject in hand; I merely state a fact,—and this fact admitted, it is impossible to ignore its importance. It seems more desirable to make the best of the only advantages that may still accrue to us from it, rather than to lament over it. And the real cause of these advantages is the facility with which France can re-assert an autonomy which has been established by length of time, the conformity of races, tastes, customs, and one of the most favourable of geographical situations that can be conceived. In presence of so many instances in which nationalities that had been obscured by political intrigues and a long period of neglect have vindicated themselves, France ought to give, and can give to its own, a power sufficient to protect it against neighbouring nationalities. To obtain the result, it must very accurately appreciate the nature of its genius and the resources it can furnish. This is what Germany has been doing for the last sixty-six years, under conditions much more embarrassing than we have been subject to; and the result has been a success of a very conspicuous character, if not established on solid foundations. How has Prussia attained this result? By developing patriotic sentiment, I allow; by organising within its domain, methodically and economically, the vital forces of the country: this I also recognise. But the main cause of this success has been the establishment in Germany of a kind of systematic inquiry into all that is being done in foreign lands, both in the political sphere, and in the arts of peace and of war, and in the several branches of science. By comparison, and by incessant friction against neighbouring communities, it has gradually assimilated to itself that which suited its temperament, which it corroborated by ascertaining the weak and defective points of those communities. If such a work has been possible in a body politic so heterogeneous as is that of Germany, what might not be effected in this direction in a country like our own, all whose elements are so firmly united by a long course of ages? And to come back to the art which is engaging our attention,— what is that strange assumption which induces us to recognise in it only a cosmopolitan character, independent of surroundings, nationality, and climate? I fully allow that we should study all the forms of art that have been produced in ancient and modern times under the influence of certain media favourable to their development; but that we can draw from these studies, indis-criminately and without critical investigation, the elements adapted to constitute a national art, is not admissible from any point of view. I am quite content that art should not be regarded as limited to one country; but each expression of art should have its own, and it is not worthy to be considered an art except on this condition.

The frivolity with which our neighbours are accustomed to tax us, and not without some reason, is nevertheless more at the surface than at the bottom of our national character. Our fault is much less that of being frivolous than of allowing frivolity *carte blanche* among us, and appearing to take seriously deeds and talk which we know have no real significance. Trifles which make us smile, but against which we do not protest, and which sometimes amuse us,—are taken beyond the frontier for the expression of our character. We thus endorse eccentricities which really attach only to some obtrusive individuals, entirely wrapt up in themselves, and who make our indifference or complaisance a pedestal on which to display themselves. It is only in France that we see in the arts, in literature, and even in what is called politics, certain notorieties gaining distinction by scandalous or shameless conduct.

There is no country in which boasting on every occasion, pronouncing judgments at random, talking incessantly of one's-self, one's achievements and alleged merits, succeeds so well as it does in France among the numerous brotherhood of idlers. But the thirty-eight millions who compose the French nation are certainly not all members of that fraternity. There is a substratum of good sense and right feeling,—I was going to say of honesty,—in our country, which revolts against playing the part of either the dupers or the duped. The great body of the public pass the mountebank stage of the former and the gaping wonderment of the latter with utter indifference. They simply shrug their shoulders. But this is not enough : to keep aloof and withdraw into the background in presence of what is evil, impertinent, or foolish, is to make ourselves its accomplices, and must incur the penalties which wickedness, folly, and impertinence bring with them. We are only too keenly experiencing the results of this complicity just at this moment. Indifferent to what has been going on, or really duped by it, we have to pay for the follies we have allowed to be committed without protesting against them, or which through ignorance or indolent simplicity we have approved. If this is always to be the case, we must despair of the future of our country, and the small minority of those who protest against such a state of things will have no resource but exile, that they may be no longer the accomplices or the witnesses of this moral decadence.

The disasters we have experienced have deprived us of our prestige in Europe except in one point,—the productions of art. This is a trifling advantage certainly, and a great nation should feel some repugnance at being no longer anything more than the amusers of the civilised world. But even this advantage will be soon snatched from us if we do not exert the greatest energy possible, and bring the greatest liberality of mind to bear on the teaching of this branch of intellectual productivity. All the manifestations of the life of a nation are interdependent, and intellectual distinction goes hand in hand with superiority of every kind. It was in association with political development, profoundly patriotic sentiment, moral energy, philosophy, commerce, and industrial energy, that the arts reached a high degree of excellence in ancient Greece and Rome, and during the Mediæval and Renaissance period in the West; and we cannot hope to see the arts continue to flourish among us when France is reduced to the lowest grade among civilised nations. Although it would be rash to infer the future of our country from what has taken place since the end of the war of invasion and the civil war, and though we must leave the country sufficient time to recover itself after such crises, it would nevertheless be wrong not to point out those tendencies which are fatal to the re-establishment of that normal state of things which is favourable to progress.

We have a republic . . . but the name is of no consequence to the practical bearings : we should prefer the reality without the name to the name without the reality. An oligarchic or a democratic republic may be very favourable to the development of intellectual efforts, and therefore of art. If it is a democratic republic that is established—and ours can have no other form,—the conditions appertaining to this form of government must be supposed, viz., absolute respect for the laws of the country; the strength of the government firmly based on these laws; the non-existence of privileges; the constant control of all over every department of State action, and responsibility to the full extent of the functions devolving on each; labour, supervision, and, that such labour may be earnest, persevering, and consequently advantageous to the commonwealth,—the inviolability of the fruits of labour. I do not think there are ten intelligent persons who would not most heartily subscribe to these requirements; but their realisation must be absolutely secured, since any doubt respecting their fulfilment would render abortive the good promised by such a social condition. Doubt paralyses the good-will of individuals, whereas it is only by their co-operation, without any *arrière pensée*, that such a social condition could be established. And who are they who should inspire the greatest confidence? Certainly those intrusted with the executive. It is therefore to the accomplishment of these requirements that their acts should conspire,—those most insignificant in appearance as well as the most obviously important. But if the Executive or their agents proceed in certain circumstances in such a way that their intentions may be supposed hostile, or even indifferent to the accomplishment of those requirements, doubt arises in the minds of even the best disposed,

and, as the result, discouragement paralyses the most determined volition, and frustrates the best efforts for the restoration
of public prosperity.

Under the last Empire considerable importance seemed to
be attached to the progress of art; it was asserted in official
discourses that this progress was one of the sources of national
wealth; much "encouragement" was given to artists, *i.e.* considerable sums were expended in supporting mediocre talent, to
which this assistance was indispensable, and what was entitled
the *Direction des Beaux-Arts* was a Board of Relief. Many
edifices were erected, and with a view to satisfying as large a
number of applicants as possible, they were loaded with sculptures outside, and decorated within on a scale of luxury unheard
of till then. The Empire seemed to wish to have an art that
should mark its date, so that at some future time people might
say, "The style of the Second Empire," as we say, "the style
of Francis I.,—of Louis XIV." Has this result been secured? I
think not. Was such a result obtainable? Perhaps. But it
could not be secured by the quantity or the sumptuousness of
the buildings erected, and most assuredly not by spending so
much money in "encouraging" mendicity. The amount of money
expended is nothing to the purpose. The great point is to
spend money,—whether little or much,—only on what is good.
The difficulty lies in knowing what really is so. If those in
power presume to be judges in matters of such delicacy, and
with which they are not well acquainted, the chances are that
they will be deceived, and their mistake brings them into
discredit, and it is fatal to the free and regular development of art; if they delegate the authority they possess to a
corporate body, it is to be feared that this body will be only a
coterie much more anxious to assert its own ideas, and especially
its own interests, than to protect the interests of the community
at large, and the free expression of the public taste. The last
Empire veered about between the two systems; sometimes
endeavouring to foster a school of art emanating from the Court,
as had been done under Louis XIV., and sometimes having
recourse to the guidance of a body which assumes to be the
highest expression of intellect in France, and the guardian of
certain dogmas which it declares incontrovertible. In fact the
Empire satisfied no party; it provoked the ill-will of the Institute by not allowing it unlimited authority, while the time
had gone by when the Court was able to exercise any influence
whatever over intellectual enterprise. It issued the decree of
the 13th of November 1863, relating to the re-organisation of
the *École des Beaux-Arts*, which was a feeble measure, and dared
not even put this in execution as far as its real intention was

concerned in presence of the hostility of the Institute ; so that it disorganised the old machine, while it did not feel itself capable of constructing a new one. To disinterested persons it seemed as if the State was endeavouring to become the sole and uncontrolled possessor of a power which it declared the Institute to have administered ill. And such disinterested persons could not see that the State was more capable of directing the teaching of art than a body consisting of persons competent in point of art itself.

The Empire, which even at this late date possessed considerable power, had only one means of breaking with an injurious system, viz., liberating the arts from its own protection as well as from the predominance arrogated to itself by the Institute. In a word, it needed nothing more than to proclaim absolute liberty in the teaching of the arts, reserving to itself the right of choosing among and protecting the novel developments which such liberty could not fail to originate.

The Empire having fallen, those who had combated the liberal ideas timidly advanced by it in 1863, and who for seven years had succeeded in utterly defeating their effects,—thus rendering them rather injurious than otherwise, by effecting the most complete disorganisation,—were sure to take advantage of this disorganisation which they had persistently furthered, to try to bring about a kind of restoration of the older system.

Circumstances have favoured them. Who would take the trouble at such a time of national misfortune to inquire whether it is advantageous to the arts for the Institute to be or not to be the supreme arbiter of the instruction and the interests of artists ? Things of a widely different nature are absorbing our attention. And so a Government which is called republican is taking, or allowing to be taken, a retrograde step, and is showing itself less liberal than the Empire.

If it is possible for privileged bodies to exist under an absolute monarchy without great harm accruing to the commonwealth, because these bodies then find a counterpoise in the power of the sovereign, and are in a certain degree subject to it, it is not so in a republic; for those corporations or fraternities constitute an irresponsible invulnerable power, against which there is no counterpoise, and against whose abuses there is no remedy. We have an *imperium in imperio*, an oligarchical republic in the midst of a democratic republic. And if, as is the case with the *Académie des Beaux-Arts*, such a fraternity selects its own members, its standard soon becomes debased,—*i.e.* it seeks to recruit itself only among mediocrities who could not alter its fixed habits or propose useful reforms. Besides, it soon becomes the tool of some crafty ambitious spirit, which finds no difficulty in guiding it in favour of its own ambitions and aims.　When this is achieved nothing more is needed that that one of its delegates should be introduced into the administration, to make it, secretly or openly, absolute mistress of the situation, in spite of the heads of the State and other recognised authorities, and in spite of public opinion and the protests of the few independent minds that offer resistance to this clandestine tyranny.

This, at the present moment, March 1872, is the position of artists and of the arts in France, in spite of, or rather under the sanction of, our republican form of government.　For my own part, I feel no embarrassment in discussing the question, as I ask nothing, hope for nothing, and desire nothing, except the re-establishment of the prosperity of my country, and of its moral dignity and influence on the civilised world.　I shall not wait for my neighbour to speak before opening my mouth, or to put his thoughts on paper before offering mine.　I say distinctly therefore, and without any feeling of hostility towards individuals—for most of the members of the *Académie des Beaux-Arts* are my friends, and for whom individually I have the highest esteem,—the arts in France are rapidly hastening towards their decline under the predominance which, through weakness or indifference, the Academy has been allowed to take in teaching and administration.　This irresponsible power stifles all independent initiative, all individuality; it is the natural enemy of independence of character and of critical investigation.　By its very nature it is led to foster the conventional, and to favour complaisant mediocrity.　It ostracises at its pleasure those who do not recognise its authority, but presume to act independently, because it has its connections everywhere.　Irresponsible and invulnerable, as I have remarked, it never discusses a question, it never gives a direct reply to strictures, but pursues its object by means of every description; for what an individual would consider himself disgraced by doing, an irresponsible body may essay without a sense of shame; each of its members, as an isolated individual, having always the right to regard himself as no party to a decision adopted by the whole,—a decision which he perhaps reprobates in the secrecy of his conscience, but to which his personality and name have yet brought their contingent of support.

This state of things is now becoming more detrimental than ever, and it is high time for those who have the future of their country and its prosperity at heart to give it their serious attention.

I can understand how statesmen should refrain from discussing questions of art; it is not their business, and it would be as ridiculous as out of place for them to do so.　But I maintain that it is the duty of those who are at the head of a republic not to leave its citizens, even were they in a minority, to the discretion of an irresponsible fraternity, even if it consisted exclusively of the highest intellects. I think it the duty of those high functionaries to protect independence of character in as far as that independence does not encroach on the respect due to the laws. I think that admitting the arts to be a power in the State, it is through the independence of the artist that they advance and rise, and not through a blind submission to a kind of secret authority. I believe, moreover, that the moral enfeeblement which is the great cause of our misfortunes, results in great measure from the carelessness of former Governments as regards respecting, protecting, and honouring that individual independence which is the parent of civil virtues. That such independence should be regarded as troublesome under an absolute government may be easily imagined, but that a republic should not make a point of fostering it, should treat it, or allow a corporate body to treat it as a pariah, is scarcely conceivable.

As respects architects in particular, some people suppose that it is enough to institute a "Central Society," or some other aggregate more or less numerous, to form a corporate body. This is a mistake; a body, to deserve the name, must consist of independent individualities. Now, it is that very independence of character which distinguishes the *individual* that is wanting in the architects of our day. We speak of the body of physicians, barristers, or engineers, because these bodies are in fact formed only by the union of men who have each a sense of their own claims and worth; who in no circumstance or under any pretext would be disposed to allow the independence of their convictions or character to be infringed. But is it so with our architects?

Under the last Empire we saw the Prefect of the Seine setting to work to *organise* into a corps the architects of the city of Paris, —a step prejudicial to the public works and the finances of the city as well as to the interests of the architects themselves. The illustrious Prefect of the Seine of that day had a weakness for organisation. He would say to any who were willing to listen to him: "Architecture is nothing else but administration" . . . that he, though occupied with such various cases, was as much an architect as you or I, and that he by no means granted what was claimed by architects, viz., that if they erected a public building, they created a work personal to themselves; that the *edifice* was the work of all, but particularly of him who ordered it and paid for it. This way of looking at things, which is harmless enough in the case of the townsman who has a country box built at Asnières for himself and his family, has produced disastrous effects in the architecture of our times, and it certainly carried the Prefect of the Seine farther than he would have wished.

The *service d'architecture* of the city of Paris was therefore organised very much like our military staffs. There was a marshal; there were generals of division and of brigade, colonels, commanders, majors, and captains. To-day you, General A., have to command such or such a brigade; that is, build such or such an edifice. The convenience of the Government, or simply the need of displaying authority, calls you elsewhere; you leave your brigade here—I mean the building you have commenced—and General B. is called on to finish it. . . . That an administrative intellect should form such a notion of things is natural enough; but that it should find architects willing to lend themselves to this extraordinary *constructive* procedure is really wonderful, for with such an arrangement what becomes of the responsibility of the artist, or even of the legal responsibility? Which of the two is it that guarantees the work?—the one who begins it, or the one who finishes it?

The Prefect of the Seine to whom I refer had a truly superior mind, and could appreciate things very fairly; so that if when this administrative suggestion came into his mind, a man of sense, courage, talent, and of an independent spirit had pointed out to him the injurious results of this system, he would have conceded the justice of the representation and have yielded to it. . . . But no one said a word. Such a remonstrant did not present himself; all, though certainly dissatisfied with it, submitted to this monstrous arrangement; yet the Director of the architectural staff for the Department of the Seine was careful to choose his assistants and *employés*—for we cannot give the name of architects to these *embrigadés*—among the laureates of the *École des Beaux-Arts*, where administration is perhaps not taught, but where great stress is laid on submission to Academic authority.

And while that arrangement was by no means favourable to individual enterprise or the development of original talent, and while it was little in harmony with that independence of character which the artist ought, above all men, to preserve intact, it was not adapted to protect the financial interests of the city of Paris. For in building, the interests of the client can be guarded only by the independence of the architect he employs. The following is a proof of this:—

On the 20th of January 1864, the Architects of the Section (*Sectionnaires*)—for this was their title—received an intimation whose purport was: "that the requirements of primary education necessitated the establishment in Paris of more than fifty schools; that consequently Mr. ——, architect of the section, was requested to assist in his department in providing the accommodation required.

"The Prefect," adds the circular, "does not wish to *buy* or to erect these school-buildings at the expense of the city, but commissions Mr. —————— 1*st*, to look for buildings already erected, combining the conditions required for a school; 2*d*, to prepare the stipulations of agreements to be made with persons who would undertake to erect buildings suitable for the purpose in question."

These school-buildings were to be taken on leases of not less than twenty years, power being secured to the city to buy such premises during the period of the lease. The city would *keep the buildings in repair*, and pay for furniture and other expenses. An annual rent of five per cent. was to be given on the value of the ground occupied, and six per cent. on the value of the buildings prepared by the architects of the city.

If the city should think proper to avail itself of the power to buy, the amount offered would be in the one case a sum equal to twenty times the rent of the ground, and in the other case sufficient to refund the cost of construction.

On receiving such imperfect instructions, and which left loopholes for abuses which it would be superfluous to specify, architects not so well trained to obedience as those of the city of Paris, and who regarded themselves as counsellors rather than clerks, would certainly have pointed out to their chief objections of no inconsiderable weight. They would, among other things, have drawn attention to the fact that to "refund" the sum spent on a building erected in anticipation of a twenty years' lease, and to be kept in repair by a tenant who becomes the purchaser—a sum moreover whose proportion would not be exactly known, since the buildings in each case were to be paid for by the persons in question, and since when bought they would not be purchased at a valuation, which is considered the equitable plan—was anything but a good bargain for the city, for it would be safe to wager a hundred to one that that "refunding" would be the payment of a sum considerably greater than the real value of the article, and was in fact only a bounty offered to speculators to induce them by the offer of extraordinary advantages—since they would receive at once more than five per cent. clear on the capital expended, or supposed to be expended, to construct the school-buildings in question. In fact, it is one of the plans adopted by people who are in difficulties, and who are obliged to borrow at high interest. I am not aware that any architect of the city protested against this usurious style of borrowing, or refused his co-operation. Yet if they could not protest individually they might have done so in a body, with all the consideration required in so delicate a matter. But the *Société Centrale*, which had manifested no disquietude when its members were formed into *regiments,* or in presence of the extraordinary system adopted by the Prefectoral administration, was not likely to trouble itself about the consequences of the state of things thus established. The *Société Centrale* deems it enough to write reports on the *prospectuses* which contractors or manufacturers send to it, or to find fault with those among its members who show a disposition to have things reformed. It is a mere antechamber of the architectural section of the *Académie des Beaux-Arts,* but it is not in itself a corporate body.

Or did the *Société Centrale* concern itself when, under the Empire, the architects of the departments were made absolutely dependent on the Prefects, under pretext of decentralisation?

Was not this the very moment for expostulating with the Government, and showing that this was a measure which by depriving the architect of all independence in regard to the Prefect might occasion the most disastrous abuses? Formerly, indeed, the nomination of the departmental architects, or their recall by the Prefect, had to be submitted to the Minister of the Interior. This was a guarantee given to an architect who should conscientiously fulfil his duties, and which enabled him even to refuse his co-operation if he thought that there was an intention to oblige him to act in a way contrary to the interests of the department. The architect was thus attached to the departmental administration, and not subjected to the caprices of a Prefect. This was found embarrassing, so that, under cover of *decentralisation,* an independent agent commissioned with the administration of part of the affairs of the department was replaced by an agent of the Prefect. And thus this agent had to comply with all the requirements of that exalted functionary on pain of dismissal,—such as clearing of credits, substitutions of expenses, etc. If architects had formed a body united by sentiments of personal independence and dignity such a state of things could not have supervened.

But to constitute one of those bodies of which I was speaking, which are able to insure the dignity, the independence, and the interests of their members, each of those members must acquire independence in his own person, beginning by renouncing his allegiance to that narrow and exclusive domination which the academic fraternity exercises; shaking off that continual fear of displeasing it, and of acting apart from its dictation; the submission to the caprices of clients and administrative bodies; that tyranny which mediocrity attempts to enforce in the school on the intellects of all, by prescribing them a limited path in which they will have to move under pain of ostracism. Every one is in his conscience well convinced that he ought to free himself from this yoke; but, as in all other cases in our unhappy country, where of all virtues civic courage is certainly the rarest, each waits for his neighbour to begin, though ready to follow when he has received the first fire, and if he has not fallen under it.

Competitions.

There has been much discussion recently respecting competitions. This question, which was first raised in connection with the rebuilding of the Hôtel-de-Ville of Paris, has assumed a comprehensive aspect. Some have declared themselves partisans of competition in all such cases. Others, without denying its value, would limit it to certain special cases.

I would not suggest a doubt respecting the sincerity of the partisans of either opinion ; but this question somewhat resembles that concerning compulsory education. It is not enough to decree compulsory instruction,—it is desirable at the outset to know whether, when the law is promulgated, schools and masters will be immediately forthcoming in numbers sufficient to make legislation practically efficient.

It is desirable to establish competition as a principle in the case of all new architectural works. But that such competition shall give useful results, we must suppose competitors ; and that the competitors may be worthy and in earnest we require a jury of arbitrators such as can give these competitors every security for impartiality, and, which is of greater importance, for capacity.

Before establishing competition as a principle, therefore, we must think about finding competitors. And to find competitors we must find judges.

We are quite disposed to allow that in France a decree of the Legislature is quite sufficient to establish a new order of things. And yet our Official Report of Laws is crammed with decrees that have never been put in execution, because they found themselves in presence of a void.

Among the recent reports and documents that have been published in reference to competitions generally, and the competition relating to the rebuilding of the Hôtel-de-Ville in particular, one of the arguments advanced by those who were opposed to competitions was this : " There will be no competitors among architects of real ability ; these will not be willing to risk losing half a year's labour and compromising their reputation to some extent should they fail in a public trial." The argument is a reasonable one, considering the precedents and the actual state of things. But it would perhaps fall to the ground if we broke with those precedents and altered the state of things.

We may observe in the first place that competitions in the case of buildings of a rank deemed secondary, either in importance or situation, have generally yielded excellent results ; but that it has not been so in the case of competitions which, from their exceptional importance, specially attracted the attention of the public, and which would immediately place the successful candidate in a position of unparalleled distinction.

For the former it is easy to find an impartial jury uninfluenced by any consideration foreign to the matter in hand ; but for the latter this is much more difficult.   In the latter case the juries resemble those " conclaves " in which all the judges have a secret understanding that such or such a one shall not be the winner, to whom the name of the victor is of little importance, provided it be neither a Barberini, nor a Doria, nor a Chigi.   Such is human nature, and we shall not be able to change it by establishing a republic.   And the more distinguished and capable the judges are, the more firmly do they hold to their own ideas ; and their conscience is so entirely guided by their passions that they think they act for the best, not by giving the palm to the most meritorious, but by preventing such or such a one from obtaining a great advantage.   In a question of art they honestly fancy that they ought to make the chief consideration that which they regard as a matter of principle.   It is of trifling importance to them that N., who is quite unknown to fame, and whose capacity is questionable, secures the prize, provided M. does not get it : for if M. were successful the whole world would in their view be subverted, or at least the whole future of the great art—the art they love—would be compromised ; the remainder of their existence would be full of bitterness.   I have had the good fortune to be present at one of these famous judgments, and I must say that never in my life have I seen a more interesting comedy, or one in which the human heart was more clearly revealed in spite of the endeavour of each to hide from his fellows, and perhaps from his own conscience, the real character of his thoughts.   Here, as in all such cases, the chief aim was to prevent the success of those competitors whom the *vox populi* in the simplicity of its judgments expected to conquer.   And when, as always happens, a name was pronounced which the public little expected, and for which the jury themselves were as little prepared before the decision, the joy manifested on a good many countenances was a flash of light that penetrated to the inmost thoughts of each, and laid it bare.

In competitions for very important buildings where are we to look for judges ?   In the first instance, and this is natural enough, among the members of the Institute.   But these gentlemen, though sometimes they are not very sympathetic with each other, are certainly agreed on one point, viz., to put out of court every competitor who is in no way affiliated to their body.

There arises this dilemma, therefore : they would not prefer to vote for one of their equals, supposing there were one among the competitors. And they would never vote—this is a matter of principle—for a competitor who had opposed their doctrines,—if the name "doctrine" can be applied to the ostracism which condemns all individual independence. And since we can hardly expect to find great capacity except among the members themselves of that body, or among those who evidently ignore their influence, the chances are that they will vote for some obscure mediocrity whom they will thus suddenly raise to distinction. Such fraternities by their very nature incline to discover an unknown talent rather than recognise one already acknowledged, and in which they have a rival. And should this unrecognised talent be a mere nonentity, so much the better ; it will owe its distinction to the selection that has brought it to light. It is an example of "prevenient grace," and corporate bodies like nothing so much as to play the part assigned by some to Providence.

The public which does not, and cannot, peep behind the scenes, is generally amazed at these awards ; but, good-natured French public as it is, and long since habituated to consider all that emanates from any authority as for the best, it applauds the blunders of the laureate, for which it will certainly have to pay very dear.

In the second place, for very shame, and that they may make some show of impartiality before that same public, the administrative boards which adopt a competition in the case of some very important affair, and often with a view to cover their own responsibility, add the names of architects who are not members of the architectural section of the Institute to the best of those who are. Generally these are a minority ; but even if they formed a majority, the vote would be most frequently in accordance with that of the members of the fraternity, and it would be given the more readily as there would be aspirants to the Academic chair among those whose names were thus added. I have myself been a witness of the facts I state here without any concealment (this will certainly be allowed) ; so that on several occasions having satisfied myself of the isolated position of the independent additions to the members of the fraternity, and those aspirants to its membership who join their vote with it, I have thought it preferable to hold myself aloof.

This is the way in which juries have been selected for important competitions in the past. Will the same course be pursued in future? If so, we must expect to find no candidates among architects of eminence ; we shall have nothing but mere *school* competitions. Something unquestionably may probably come of them, but we may well doubt it. In any case it is evident that architects whose position is established will not go and benevolently thrust themselves into such a wasps' nest, knowing as they do that their acknowledged capacity and acquired experience, and the scrupulous attention they will pay to the interpretation of the programme, the carefulness of their estimates, and the exact accordance of their plans with such estimates, far from giving them a chance of success, will be a reason for excluding them ; for the more decided proof they give of their capacity, the less likely are their plans to be approved, for the very reason that the fraternity is opposed to competitions. Dominating over the Administration, it considers it unseemly that the Government should not select the architect for a great work among its members ; it therefore takes care, and always will take care,—its interest impels it to do so,—that competitions shall be abortive, either in point of art or from an administrative and financial point of view.

The safest plan in the world in which we live is never to expect from people, and especially from bodies that have no individual responsibility to incur, efforts of disinterestedness or heroism—shall I call it,—which are never other than exceptional. And to ask of artists who have a just or an exaggerated sense of their own talent, who have obtained from their equals the highest post of distinction, and who cherish the very laudable ambition of attaching their name to some work of public importance,—who during their whole lives have entertained the hope of finding a favourable occasion for showing what their abilities are, or what they conceive them to be,—who have the passions attaching to a school or a coterie, their antipathies and rivalries, —that they should see without a certain degree of bitter feeling this so much coveted opportunity slipping from their grasp ; that they should even themselves aid in its being granted to another more capable, or equally capable, is to require of human nature more than it can give ; it is to tempt virtue, a course always undesirable and dangerous.

What then is to be done ? How can we compose a jury if we decide positively that in the case of every new public building competition should be allowed ?

But we must ask, in the first place, whether the plan of competition is really the best, and whether it should be always adopted. Good or bad, this is the plan now favoured, and it will be difficult not to adopt it cordially. It may be granted that in a case of resumption of work once commenced, or of adaptation of existing structures, or of the restoration of old buildings, competition would be superfluous,—would serve no purpose,—and that in this case the most reasonable plan would be to choose a man of recognised ability.   It would seem to follow, as indeed in the case above referred to—the restoration of the Hôtel-de-Ville —that competition in such a case would be inapplicable.   But if a building entirely new has to be erected, a country whose whole political system is based on universal suffrage can find no sound reasons for refusing to adopt the plan of competition, not only in designs for architectural works of the usual order, but in Government works generally,—in military constructions, etc.

If we adopt competition, however, we imply competitors and judges ; and the existence of competitors presupposes instruction. If we would have a worthy competition, we must have capable competitors ; we require a thorough course of instruction.

In the present state of things the instruction which the State gives, or which it is supposed to give, to young architects,—an instruction whose direction it has just replaced in the hands of the Institute, after having made a timid and unsuccessful attempt to withdraw it from the direct influence of that body,—this instruction, I say, is not of a sound and thorough character ; it is not in accordance with our social organisation, nor with the methods of construction introduced by the manufacturing skill of the day, nor with the requirements of economy and administrative rigour, nor with those methods of reasoning by which civilised countries must be unceasingly guided if they would not forfeit their position.

We have reached in France that critical state of affairs in which every question that is raised, raises in its turn a thousand others.   Our old machine used to go "after a sort," thanks specially to the fact that no one dared open the case that concealed its works, to examine the state of them.   Or if any one chanced to lift a panel of the casing, all shut their eyes, crying, "Anathema." . . . But the old turnspit has been violently dislocated, it must be repaired. . . . But no ! we must make up our minds to the sacrifice whether we will or not ; the turnspit cannot be mended ; another must be made, and that in all haste, for—the meat is burning !

The question of "*compulsory education*" is being raised.   It seems a very simple matter to enforce the attendance of all children at school !   But the question immediately arises, as I was just saying, of school-buildings that have to be erected, and schoolmasters who are not yet forthcoming ; of the financial means for erecting those buildings and paying those masters ; the question of normal schools for training them ; whether the teaching shall be in the hands of laymen exclusively, or lay and clerical according to the wish of parents ; the question which necessarily follows, of the separation of Church and State ; the question of children's labour in factories or in the fields ; and that which is connected with it, of the obligation to indemnify parents who may be old or infirm, or very poor, or whose families are very large, and who are consequently dependent on their children's labour. But I leave these considerations.

If the principles of taxation are discussed, immediately a hundred other vital questions present themselves. It is the same with everything we chance to touch. In fact we have before us an old worm-eaten world; we no sooner lay a finger on one point to repair a damage, than the part restored obliges us to renew everything around it to make it hold; it cannot be fixed in decay.

But to return to the subject of competitions: We might reasonably say to those who take charge of the teaching of architecture in France: "Begin by training men for us who are able to present something better in the way of competition than mere exhibitions of pictures; for what is required is not sending young men to Italy at the expense of the Government, but providing buildings that shall be useful, that shall supply a felt want; for which we pay, and which we therefore wish to have well constructed, and in every sense reasonable." We might say to those who are appointed judges in these competitions, or who are chosen to watch the building of public edifices as superintendents, "Consider that while such a nation as France ought to possess monumental structures indicating its greatness, the nation has to pay for them; that it is therefore of the first importance not to spend its money uselessly,—not to ruin it under the pretext of honouring it, and not with a view to do an ill turn to the advocates of competitions to choose that competitor who offers the fewest substantial guarantees of ability, and who will compromise the affair."

Must we then, in view of these difficulties that accumulate around every question that is raised, resign ourselves to inactivity and yield to discouragement? Certainly not. "Sufficient unto the day is the evil thereof," and in the case of every undertaking, however difficult it may appear, if we would accomplish it we must make a beginning somewhere.

Let us then use the elements we possess, but so as to derive from them a maximum of advantage.

To secure really strenuous and productive competitions, in which undoubted talent will be displayed, and that we may not give ourselves up to mere hazardous results under colour of such competitions, we must therefore offer attractions to talent; but we cannot attract talent unless guarantees are presented that time and reputation shall not be sacrificed to rancour, rivalry, perhaps to mere imbecility of judgment or volition.

If the Institute had not the complete control of instruction, and of all the important positions, through the pressure it can bring to bear on the administration, the plan of having the jury nominated by the candidates themselves would offer sufficient guarantees. But in the present state of things this plan would not secure to competitors not connected with the fraternity a jury whose impartiality would be beyond question.

And as the majority of the candidates would be evidently in the rank of mediocrity, it would nominate a jury favourable to that mediocrity.

It must be noticed that for the erection of a new building it is of the greatest importance to choose a capable man, not to please such or such a school or coterie. But such a capable person might chance to be completely isolated, unconnected with any body of the kind.

We cannot reckon therefore upon any such body choosing such a man, whereas the juries nominated by artists themselves, in the case of a competition, always contain a majority belonging to a coterie, whether from among the members of the Institute or outside it ; and impartiality of judgment would none the less be compromised. The formation of a jury by lot from a list of persons distinguished in the arts would be preferable to the system of election ; but even with this method the chances are many that an isolated candidate—one with no connections—though perhaps the most talented, and in all respects the most capable, would not be chosen. It might be supposed that competitions —I have in view only those which have great notoriety, and are likely to excite lofty ambitions—would generally bring into notice talent which had been " ignored," which had grown up in obscurity, but which possessed remarkable power and originality. But this is not the case, for the reasons sufficiently discussed above. Celebrated competitions sometimes place an obscure individual on a pedestal, but not because he shows in the works he exhibits proofs of high capacity, so much as because he is a kind of neutral ground on which the rival powers of which the jury consists can in any case come to an understanding with a view of avoiding what they dread before all things,—the selection of a distinguished name,—a man of real ability. And yet a jury consisting of men of real eminence, whatever passions may animate them when examining the works exhibited, will generally bring to the discussion sound reason and just appreciation : for among those who practise the same art or the same calling there are questions respecting which those whose opinions are the most opposed agree. And in architecture in particular, which involves not only an art, but positive science, practitioners can scarcely avoid agreeing in some important points. In decisions of this kind, therefore, we observe juries apparently yielding to the soundest reasons, admitting certain incontestable qualities, and agreeing as to certain equally obvious faults on the part of such or such candidates, yet voting in a direction absolutely opposed to the judgments, favourable or unfavourable, which that discussion seemed to have elicited, and which seemed certain to direct the opinion of the judges. As a practical man or an artist, the juror submits to evidence and to the sound reasoning advanced in one direction or the other; but as a man he votes according to his passions.

In order that the merits of the candidates might be appreciated as equitably as possible, a discussion should be held in presence of their works, between professional men of acknowledged capacity, and able to exhibit the reasons for their preference or censure; and this discussion should be listened to by a jury commissioned to give its votes in favour of the candidate whose merits that examination had established.

What can we suppose would be the fate of defendants in our Courts of Assize if they were to be tried by the counsel,—the Attorney-General and the barristers engaged on the trial? Yet this is the very position in which architects are placed in the competitions in question.

It would be safe to wager, *a priori*, that before examining the plans, each juror has made up his mind, and has said within himself, that, whatever happens, he will not vote in favour of so-and-so.

The fiction according to which the judges are supposed not to know who are the competitors on such an occasion, especially when the decision is an important one, is puerile. There is not a member of the jury summoned to decide competitions of this kind who does not know the name of the artist which the motto is presumed to conceal.

It would therefore be desirable to abandon this hypocritical custom, which only lends a veil of impartiality to the passions which determine the judgment. This puerile fiction being discontinued, and the candidates being no longer supposed to be thus concealed, it would be reasonable that they should be called on to explain these plans themselves, and the means of execution they propose to adopt. There is nothing impracticable in this.

Of a considerable number of plans exhibited there will be at least three-fourths which, from their manifest inferiority, are put out of the discussion and will not bear examination.

A very limited number of plans will remain, which will give occasion to the warmest debate, and among which it will be difficult to choose the best from all points of view. And at this stage—even supposing in the case of the juror an impartiality equal to his capacity—an incomplete or unattractive presentation, or an arrangement not clearly understood by the judges, will set aside a design which nevertheless from the practical side has very commendable characteristics.

Besides, it must be observed that the more capable an architect is, the more clearly does he perceive the difficulties accumulated in a programme of requirements and the means of execution to be employed, and the greater is his embarrassment in explaining the solutions which he proposes; whereas a mediocre artist, who has no doubt about anything—and there are cases in point—has no difficulty in displaying his limited appliances. He does not seek to solve difficulties which he does not even foresee, and his design on paper is marked by the confidence he feels in his own strength. The judges are but men, and they generally resemble other men in not liking to take too much trouble. If a certain part of a design exhibited does not seem to them perfectly clear, they conclude that the author's intention was not clear to himself. Many of the judges, even if capable men, do not represent to themselves the effects which will result in the execution, but merely look at the design as drawn. Many do not trouble themselves to inquire whether the plans, sections, and elevations are in perfect agreement. Others take no account of the means of execution; and no one examines the estimates carefully to see whether they exactly tally with the designs as drawn.

If the competitors were severally called to explain their designs, and to state the reasons which led them to adopt such or such an arrangement, to state the means of execution they intended to adopt, and the relation of the estimates to the drawings, an entirely new light would be thrown on the matter, and it might happen that a plan which met with disdain at first sight would be put in the first rank.

Still, the examiners ought not to vote; the verdict should be given by a jury of persons of repute, who have not been architectural practitioners at all, or who have ceased for some time to be so, and who would be present at the discussions of the artists respecting the designs submitted, and the examinations to which they would subject the candidates respecting their own plans.

We will not affirm that this mode of proceeding would be perfect,—unfortunately, human judgments are rarely irreproachable; but this method would at least give sufficient guarantees to attract capable artists, and it would certainly hinder a great many inefficient candidates from competing. Judgment given with closed doors in the case of such competitions is to be deprecated from all points of view: it makes the judges irresponsible; it opens the door for certain scandalous proceedings, and the results generally surprise the public, not without cause.

If the plan here proposed were adopted, it would suffice that a single member of the jury,—or rather, I should say, the board of examiners, for that would be their proper name,—should call attention to the merits of a plan by the way in which he would explain it, and by the questions he would address to the candidates. The reasons given and the answers to the questions put would evidently make an impression on the real jury, in spite of the preconceived or erroneous opinions of the majority of the board of examiners. Thus worthy competitors would no longer have to fear "falling between two stools" as the result of the judgment of a majority given with closed doors.

It may indeed be objected that this jury, consisting as it would of persons who are not architects, or who have ceased to be so, would be incapable of duly appreciating the discussion carried on between the examiners, or the answers given to the questions by the competitors. This objection is not tenable.

Architecture is not one of those branches of knowledge which are full of mysteries, which bristle with technical terms and formulæ incomprehensible to the bulk of intelligent people. There is no problem in architecture, difficult as it may be, that cannot be understood by educated persons, though strangers to the practical side of the profession, if it be clearly explained to them, with a reliance on that common sense which is essential to the appreciation of everything. We may even affirm that the very necessity imposed on the architect-examiners—I shall refer to them in future by this name—of explaining the reasons that induce them to reject or adopt such a design, would not be unaccompanied by great advantages; for we have sometimes seen judges adopting or rejecting a design without explaining the reasons that led them to do so, or influenced by motives which they certainly would not avow before an independent jury.

There are certain reasons which would not be given, and which could only produce an impression with closed doors. But what would prevent our nominating on such juries—commissioned not to discuss themselves, but only to listen and give their verdict, after having heard the debate between the examiners and the answers of the candidates—engineers of the "*Ponts et Chaussées*," civil engineers, members of administrative boards who are not unfamiliar with public works, or functionaries of the higher class, independent by character and position? Such persons would be quite capable of giving a judgment on plans, if not at first sight, yet certainly after the discussions and the examination I have suggested.

With such a jury there would be no reason for fearing those prejudiced decisions which many among us have witnessed,— those Reports which I will not absolutely call untrustworthy, but which have been quite opposite in tenor to the direction which a discussion in certain cases had taken.

In conclusion then, if the plan of competitions is adopted for all new architectural works, we must make the composition of the juries the chief consideration; for as long as the system hitherto adopted prevails, it is certain that many, if not all, capable artists will refrain from being candidates.

The present state of Contracts.

The question of Competition naturally leads us to speak of Contracts. Every one is acquainted with the law relating to contracts.

The Legislature, sensible of the inconveniences and abuses which the usages of private contracts might occasion between the Administration and the contractors for public works, has determined that there should be a public competition between these contractors, on a basis of schedules, plans, estimates, and conditions of charges determined beforehand and submitted to the competitors, who send sealed tenders stating the abatement they will allow on those prices for work or materials. The contractor who offers the largest discount is accepted as contractor by law, if when he has sent in his tender he has given the security required and furnished the necessary certificates of ability to supply the work or materials in question.

Can any law be clearer, or seem better suited to protect the interests of the State and the municipal bodies?

Let us examine how it works.

In the first place, for a contract to be sound and valid, the two contracting parties must be both in a position to fulfil their engagements, unless prevented by force; they must each act independently, and under their own responsibility. But this law, which appears so simple, clear, and equitable, is among those which present the greatest difficulties, and give occasion to the most frequent contests and litigation.

There are two forms of procedure when buildings are to be contracted for: either these works are intrusted to a general contractor, commissioned to get works of all kinds done which building requires, on his own responsibility; or recourse is had to contractors of the several trades, who carry on their work simultaneously or successively, according to the architect's orders.

In the former case it is evident that the general contractor who has agreed to an abatement in the lump on all the works, —masonry, timber, locksmith's work, roofing, plumber's work, joinery, etc. etc.,—has not individually either the knowledge required for directing all these labours, nor workshops suitable for their execution. He therefore has recourse to sub-contractors, and he will certainly not sub-contract except at lower prices than those allowed him by his contract; for instance, if he has allowed 5 per cent. discount, he sub-contracts with the carpenter for 6 per cent., and so with the rest. Either the State and the municipal bodies might therefore have the advantage of this larger discount, if they treated directly with these sub-contractors, or the work furnished is paid for at a higher price than it is worth. But this is of little importance if the contractor is a capable and honourable man, and if he has sufficient capital at command. By his intelligence and energy he exactly performs his engagements while making a higher profit on the work than he is supposed to make. If he gets one or two or three per cent. more than his supposed profits from the sub-contractors, on the other hand he has to advance capital, and in fact only recovers the interest of his money. He spares the administrative boards complications of accounts, and by taking the entire responsibility on his own shoulders he offers a more substantial guarantee than divided responsibilities could do. But very few contractors have the ability, intelligence, and energy necessary for completing a comprehensive undertaking. And in fact, many who are the really responsible persons take refuge behind their sub-contractors if the work of the latter is unsatisfactory, and try to shift that responsibility on them. Indeed, the architect who directs the works is always obliged, even when a general contractor is engaged, to enter into direct relations with each of the sub-contractors. He cannot explain to that general contractor, who is perhaps a mason, how the plumber's work ought to be done, so that it is absolutely necessary for him to give his orders direct to the plumber, the slater, the carpenter, and the locksmith. So that if there is any bad work, the general contractor has no longer a direct responsibility, but may say to the architect: " I have put my locksmith or plumber at your disposal; you give him your orders directly, and he does or ought to do what you require; do not therefore complain to me of such or such bad work, which it was for you to obviate by your acquaintance with the matter, and the direct surveillance you exercise over my sub-contractor without my intervention." It is clear that though the general contractor continues to be

responsible, this responsibility is practically illusory. And here
I am supposing that contractor to be an honourable man. But
if he is not so,—if he has induced his sub-contractors to make
exorbitant abatements, and if he has an understanding with them
to get an unlawful profit on the materials and workmanship,— what
will be the position of the architect? He applies to the sub-
contractor, and reproaches him with bad work; the latter replies
that he has received his orders from the general contractor.
The architect goes to the general contractor, but he replies that
his sub-contractor knows his business; that as for himself, he,
the general contractor, has no acquaintance with plumber's and
locksmith's work; that the architect has given the sub-contractor
direct orders, and that he himself has nothing to do with the
matter. Thence arise interminable disputes; the matter has to be
investigated before the Board, which does not like such complications, and puts off its decision. If the facts are too grave to be
ignored, it is necessary to require the cancelling of the contract;
but that is a serious matter; the works are suspended, or they
are carried on independently of the contract; but there are law-
suits, claims, appraisements, surveyors' reports, and so on. And
if the contractor becomes bankrupt (as sometimes happens),
there is nothing to fall back upon but the securities or deposits,
which are not always sufficient to make up for the loss resulting
from the bad work, the loss of time, and expenses incurred. In
such circumstances the position of the architect is at least a
delicate one, and often a false and compromising one. He
cannot demand the cancelling of the contract unless the facts are
serious enough to call for it: but then the mischief he ought to
have prevented is done, and a strict Board of administration
may in any case thus remonstrate with him: "It was your duty
to prevent the bad work which you have pointed out, and which
is perhaps irremediable."

If the other mode of contract is adopted,—that is, if the contract for building-works is made with the trades separately,—
other difficulties arise. These trades must work either simultaneously or successively. If one of the contractors fails to
perform his engagements, or performs them badly, he hinders the
work of the others, and these latter may throw the blame of the
imperfection or delay with which they are charged, and sometimes justly, on the first. This second mode of contract is however preferable to the other, inasmuch as each representative of
the several trades is directly responsible, not only before the law,
but practically; and a skilful architect well acquainted with
building ought to know to which of the contractors who are
working together a piece of bad work ought to be attributed.
This method of contract necessarily involves some delays, and

on this account a general contract is preferred in circumstances which require a very rapid execution. In fact, it will be readily understood that, while in certain cases the several trades have to work simultaneously, some will have much to do while the others have a comparatively small share of the labour; the former have to keep their men constantly at work, whereas the latter have only to act occasionally; and it would be unreasonable to require the constant presence of a staff of workmen at the building, who for three-fourths of the day would be doing nothing. It is the architect's duty therefore to foresee the precise moment at which the latter ought to be ready to help; and this precise moment is often difficult to ascertain. The work may go on faster or slower than was anticipated; this will occasion delays, as we cannot wait to call the men wanted till the instant when their presence is required, and the mere transmission of orders takes time. When the contractors are what they should be, when they are duly paid, and so devote themselves to the work, each feels an interest and pride in satisfying the requirements of the enterprise; but if, as only too often happens in the case of contracts, excessive abatements have been consented to, the contractors are anything but hearty in the matter, and naturally seek for pretexts to make objections of all kinds. Certain of gaining nothing, or even of losing money in the undertaking, they evade orders which seem to require a sacrifice of time and money to be executed with due celerity. This is the really sinister aspect of our method of public contracts, and which prevents the most capable and conscientious contractors from being willing to undertake works of very great importance.

The administrative Board possesses the data necessary for determining schedules of prices. It knows as well as the contractors the cost of materials and of labour at any given moment. In fact, these prices are no mystery to any one. A computation is made therefore by adding the usual profits and incidental expenses. These profits and expenses are calculated to amount to fifteen per cent. It advertises for tenders; and a contractor comes and offers an abatement of twenty per cent. It follows either that the Board has been greatly mistaken in its estimates, or that the contractor consents to be ruined; or that he reckons on being able to cheat the Board. The first of these suppositions is a very unlikely one, the two others imply grave immorality.

Why, however, does this so frequently occur? Because there is a whole class of contractors whose sole object is to get hold of money to cover previous embarrassments, and who therefore borrow at usurious rates. They know very well that the bargain will be a losing one for them; generally they have neither the wish nor the power to cheat their employers, but money they must have, come what may, either to pay off arrears, or to keep their business going, or—which is the chief reason— to maintain their credit. Thus, adding to their liabilities, they hasten more and more rapidly to bankruptcy. They hope for some unforeseen chance; they will get up a complete system of demurrers; the result of which is delaying the settlement of their affairs, which will enable them to hold out such hopes to their creditors as will induce them to be patient. Though they are already half bankrupt, they put off the catastrophe as long as possible. When he has to do with contractors of this class, the position of the architect is as embarrassing as it well can be : if he has some knowledge and experience in such matters, he knows perfectly well that every day is adding to the contractor's difficulties. He is incessantly in fear of being cheated; while he hesitates about demanding from a man who is evidently ruining himself those sacrifices which are often necessary either for hastening on the work or to insure its perfection. Sometimes bankruptcy supervenes before the undertaking is completed, and then the embarrassments, delays, and difficulties of all kinds that arise render its success problematical.

It may also happen that the architects who have to do with speculators who have entered on those ruinous contracts are inexperienced. And if such contractors are cunning, they find means of evasion. On grounds which may or may not be valid, but which they always contrive to represent as such, they obtain from the architect the permission to substitute one class of material for another. They pretend, for instance, that those specified in the list of prices (stones, for example) are no longer to be had—that the quarries are exhausted; in fact, they succeed in getting him to allow the use of bad materials.

Then they pretend to be overwhelmed with regret, exclaim against the dishonesty of the purveyors of the materials, and propose to accompany the architect to the quarries to examine the beds themselves. They go there in fact, and make the architect, who knows little enough about stones in a quarry —for how could he have learned it?—believe anything they choose.

Then it is decided to employ other materials than those mentioned in the estimate and lists.

The law respecting such contracts has provided for this contingency; it is stipulated, "that the materials not specified in the lists shall be estimated by comparison" (*par analogie*). All therefore goes on quietly enough till the accounts come to be settled. Then the contractor objects to the estimate adopted by the auditor, and there is no end of protests and litigation.

This is quite in the interest of the contractor, since as long as the matter is unsettled he hopes to maintain his credit. In such circumstances it rarely happens that the Government or the municipal bodies are not obliged to sacrifice a good part of the money they thought to economise by excessive abatements.

But I leave these and similar rogueries. The moral to be inferred is, that the best way to prevent ourselves from being cheated or duped is never to put people into such a position as that they shall be induced to dupe or cheat in order to get out of a difficulty.

I am not sure that our system of contracts, when public works are concerned, enables us to economise to any extent ; but I am sure that in its working it is immoral and hazardous, in nine cases out of ten, and that it gives to a whole class of " shaky " contractors the means of carrying on business after their fashion, and to usurers of a certain stamp an opportunity of making a profit out of those contractors in a most scandalous manner.

How then do matters proceed? One of the contractors, always on the verge of bankruptcy, has to meet his engagements at a certain date ; he wants—say £1600—to pay his bills to tradesmen and his workmen's wages. It will be a month before he will be able to draw on his employers. He therefore makes an assignment to one of those money-lenders on whom every such " shaky " contractor is dependent. He receives £1600, and gives an acknowledgment for £1800, and interest at 8 per cent.

This assignment empowers the lender to receive £1600 at the end of the month, and he enters £200 and the accumulated interest, to the debit of the contractor.

But the latter has soon to pay again, and the lender becomes more urgent as the work advances ; so that, besides the reductions which swallow up all his profits and more, the unfortunate contractor sees the gulf of debt daily widening.

Above the class of " shaky " contractors who make disadvantageous bargains with the sole object of having money at their disposal and a factitious credit, there is a class of incompetent contractors who consent to ruinous abatements, because they have no clear understanding of what they are doing, and because out of three or four undertakings which they are carrying on at the same time, they do not know how to distinguish those which will give them a profit from those by which they will lose, because in fact they do not know how to strike a balance between them. As they keep no regular accounts, and never duly take stock of their affairs, they are not aware of their position till the moment when their debts so greatly exceed their assets that they are obliged to declare themselves bankrupt.

Among such contractors are many who were formerly fore-men, and who having amassed a little capital by industry and skill have thought proper to commence business on their own account.

Having seen contractors by whom they were employed realising a very respectable profit on undertakings in which they allowed discounts of 10 per cent., they reason thus: "If my employer made 10 or 12 per cent., I, who shall be satisfied with a profit of 5 per cent. in a similar undertaking, may very well consent to an abatement of 15 or 17 per cent." But this is a delusion, as they soon find out. In fact a skilful and prudent contractor, whose credit is firmly established, who is not obliged to borrow in order to complete his contracts, or who can at any rate borrow at 5 per cent. on property of his own, and who can therefore make advantageous bargains for materials, who can even avail himself of chances of buying largely on favourable terms, is in a condition to be able to consent to very consider-able abatements, and yet secure handsome profits. Besides, his books are well kept, his stock-takings are regular and *bona fide;* he always knows what his position is. It is not so with the worthy man who, finding himself possessed of a little capital of £2000, determines to contract for an important under-taking. The security he has to give, the materials required, and the expenses at the commencement that have to be met at a short date, or with ready money, soon exhaust his £2000. The payments he gets on account come in but slowly. The irregular way in which his books are kept prevents him from knowing his exact position; and having already exhausted his capital, he is quite surprised to see that, even making the best of the situation, it is not an enviable one.

Then he has recourse to loans, and as he cannot offer any other security than the moneys that will be due to him on account of the works he has undertaken, he falls a prey to the usurers. Then to the 15 per cent. reductions must be added 15 per cent. on the capital he has borrowed. It is easy to see that this cannot last long. And it need not be added that he becomes the enemy of "Capital," and finds our social organisation a most objec-tionable one. All who quit the building-yards in which they were foremen to engage in business on their own account do not indeed experience this unhappy fate. There are some who are better informed and more prudent, who begin cautiously, do not run the risk of large contracts, learn to keep their books, and advance gradually as their resources increase. These become very reliable contractors, well trained to their calling, men of integrity and knowing how to manage their building-yards well; accurate, and of thorough practical ability. The best provincial contractors are of this stamp; their work is very thorough, and deserves the highest commendation. For whereas the contractors who have large capital in our great towns are not always unexceptionable, they are at any rate experienced men, they are fertile in expedients, and can save the directors of the works, and consequently the boards of management, considerable trouble; but it is not the same in the provinces, where most of the contractors, being mere business men or capitalists rather than builders, have not any professional skill, and in fact only supply the funds, caring little about the quality of the work provided they get their profits. Being generally indifferent accountants, as far as building matters are concerned, they are scarcely acquainted with book-keeping except by double entry, according to the usual method, which is far from sufficient in public or private works of the kind.

There is one thing to be set against this inconvenience that has just been pointed out, resulting from our methods of public contract. A contractor can only be accepted (if his tender should offer the most favourable terms) on the stipulation that he shall furnish a certificate of capacity, etc., signed by two Government architects or engineers (*des Ponts et Chaussées*), and countersigned by the architect commissioned to superintend the building in question. If these certificates were always *bonâ fide*, and never given merely in the way of complaisance, or if the architect intrusted with the execution of the work to be contracted for always refused his *visa* when he had not full confidence in the contractor, nothing more would be needed to prevent incapable or unscrupulous contractors from applying. But it is evident how delicate a matter it is to refuse certificates, and especially a *visa*, except for very grave and manifest reasons; so that contractors of both orders, good and bad, succeed in obtaining them. Such a *veto* is therefore all but illusory.

Book-keeping and Superintendence in Building-yards.

According to present arrangements, both in public and private undertakings, the contractor keeps regular accounts of his own, and the architect likewise; but there have been, and are, cases in which neither does so, or at least only in a very imperfect fashion.

The contractor's books ought to be so kept as to show the exact position of matters from day to day. Scrupulous accuracy should be observed, so that should disputes arise there may be incontestable proof of honest management.

As remarked above, book-keeping by double entry, though offering great advantages in the way of checking accounts, is insufficient, and even impracticable, in building, on account of the variety of details involved. The contractor's accounts are at once industrial and commercial; they ought to combine these two characters, and should be so connected as to allow of their being efficiently and clearly checked.

Commercial book-keeping, as ordinarily conducted, is sufficient; except that certain redundancies, practically useless, might be suppressed; the general accounts might be restricted to five to avoid confusion, though at need accessory accounts might be opened. Such a method of accounts gives a very simple *résumé* enabling the contractor by a few minutes' examination to find the details he may want to ascertain. Besides, repeated copyings would thus be avoided.

Accounts ought to be preceded by a full and correct inventory, and this is the most irksome part of the business. A contractor's inventory is necessarily extensive, because of the multiplicity of items of which his stock consists,—the quantity of materials of which an exact statement has to be made. It is evident, however, that it is only this first inventory that requires lengthened and minute specification; the subsequent ones, if orderly notes are kept, may be prepared easily and quickly.

The inventory therefore is the starting-point.

For the works in course of execution a current statement of expenses incurred constitutes the chief account-book. This book, in which a daily account is kept, is a record of the expenses connected with each undertaking. These expenses are arranged under three heads: *materials, labour,* and *incidental charges.* The contractor can thus see from time to time what has been supplied, and how it has been employed,—what had been done by his workmen; and by comparing it with work of the same kind, he can ascertain whether they are losing time, and whether a proportionally large amount of money is going out in wages: he has a record of the various expenses, cost of carriage, and other disbursements, fees, interest of moneys borrowed, and depreciation of the value of materials; and lastly, the profit or loss on each transaction, as calculated from the difference between the net cost and the returns of the business. The transfer of materials should be recorded in a special account, referred to a separate *folio,* and checked by their entry in other building accounts in the column stating where the materials came from.

The following is a specimen of the folio of current entries, fairly copied out :—

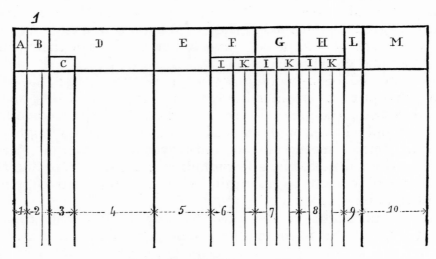

FIG. 1.—Form of Building-account Book.

Column 1 is allotted to the numbers of the order-tickets, to enable the contractor to check the accounts of materials and goods supplied. In some undertakings, especially if they are at a distance from his residence, such a means of check is necessary.

Column 2 is for dates.

Column 3 registers quantities, whether in length, surface, volume, weight, or price and number.

Column 4 records all the materials brought to the ground, all the work daily executed, without omissions or abbreviations ; items for carriage, and disbursements of all kinds.

Column 5 shows the places from which materials have come, or the names of those who supplied them, according to the indications furnished by the estimates or the price list, or the architect, so that if any item is disputed, the invoice or ticket may be shown by its date to correspond with that of the second column, and thus justify the contractor's claims.

Columns 6, 7, and 8 show the net prices and the sums allotted to each article in the current statements of items. In this table of items only the prices and amounts of articles employed in the work, or articles reckoned at their money value, are entered. Against articles whose quantity has to be measured, there will be blank entries until the measurement can be taken.

Column 9 gives the name of such or such a foreman or workman or architect who is to be referred to if information respecting any particular matter is required.

Column 10 is for the architect's remarks, or diagrams that seem needed to accompany a written instruction.

Heading of the Columns.

At A : Nos. of tickets.

At B : Dates.
At C : Quantities.

At D : Designation of works.

At E : Where material come from.

At F : Materials.
At G : Wages of Labour.
At H : Incidental expenses.
At I : Prices.
At K : Amounts.

At L : Name of the workman or foreman superintending the works.
At M : Remarks.

These folios of items, fairly copied out, should be without erasures, intercalations, interlineations, or notes in the margin. Any error or incorrect entry is put in parenthesis and corrected elsewhere.

As the articles that have to be measured have blank entries in the columns of prices, F, G, H, it will be impossible, when this account is drawn up, for an article to be entered twice, or for anything to be forgotten, as these articles are recorded day by day.

These folios of items, which form a book, are submitted to the inspection of the architect or the employer as often as either wishes to see them. Both may verify the details on the spot as often as they choose. And as the accounts are only extracts from this book, all whose articles they have had the opportunity of checking, it is clear that the contractor cannot be subjected to arbitrary reductions, and that in case any dispute or litigation arises, this book is an unexceptionable witness to his probity before the Courts, or before those who may be called on to make valuations. Moreover, the responsibility of the architect as regards the control of the works and their value is greatly lightened, since he and his clerks have nothing else to do but to verify the correctness of the record of the book of items daily entered in a fair copy.

Thus the main point in the book-keeping required by a contractor, in the industrial side of his business, is keeping a book of entries.

This book should be kept in two forms: current entries and a fair copy.

Such a book, after any particular undertaking has been completed, will furnish the contractor with much information which will be very useful to him in regard to future contracts of the same kind. But its chief utility is the daily account it supplies of the causes of his profits and losses, thus furnishing him with the means of increasing the former and diminishing the latter.

If kept in an orderly way, the total result of the book entries, even in the case of important undertakings, will only fill a line in the ledger, without any need for a number of accounts.

The book of entries, which is sufficient for most building undertakings of an ordinary kind, may, in certain exceptional cases, require the keeping of additional books. But this would imply no change in the general system explained above.

Architects would find it of great advantage to be able to consult the contractors' books of entries, as they would in this way readily gain an exact acquaintance with the state of things, and know whether they may reckon on an excess or a diminution of estimated expense as the work goes on. These books, examined and signed by the architect during the progress of the building of private houses, *e.g.*, would obviate the necessity of his keeping an entry of details, which must always be incomplete, since neither he nor his clerks, in the case of private houses, can be always at the works, and certain details will escape his attention and that of the clerks in question.

During the last five-and-twenty years various methods of book-keeping have been adopted for public architectural works undertaken by the government of the city of Paris, and the simplest system has been that which experience has proved most desirable.

The multiplicity of the entries that have been made in the execution of these commissions only tends to confusion, and what seems to promise to be a means of checking accounts only occasions the disguising of irregularities,—disorder in fact, under the appearance of perfect order and regularity.

The architect and his clerks have a twofold function to perform in the construction of important public buildings. They have, first, to give all the graphic details and the instructions necessary for explaining them, and carefully to superintend the different sets of workmen during the execution of the work; secondly, to ascertain the nature and amount of the work, so as to be able to estimate its value correctly in reference to the several contracts.

These functions are therefore very extensive and diverse. Yet few architects' assistants, most of them having come from the *École des Beaux-Arts*, are capable, even after they have spent five years in Italy or Greece, of fully discharging their duty; the boards of administration therefore, if the affair is of importance, employ accountants to help them, who have to get the information required to make fair copies of the entries and procure the data required for verifying the accounts. These accountants are rarely men acquainted with building; and it is not their province to superintend the building operations. They must rely on the statements or accounts furnished by the inspectors, who, having either too much to occupy them, or being little versed in a kind of work that requires long experience, only supply these accountants with the information they themselves receive from the contractor's clerks. Although it is said that there should be two copies of entries,—one kept by the contractor and the other by the clerk of works,—it often happens that the clerk only takes notes, and does nothing more than look over and copy the entries furnished by the contractor.

The great point is not so much to have two entries (which is of no use if one is only a copy of the other) as to have entries exactly in accordance with the truth, *i.e.* the actual performance of work. Daily note-books have therefore been adopted, which, kept by the clerks of the contractor and clerks of the architect, are intended to check each other. But in very large undertakings, where so great a number of small details of all kinds has to be considered, it is often difficult, if not impossible, to enter them all; though, numerous as they are, they affect the sum-total of the accounts. This occasions disputes, which are generally settled by a compromise, which is not the absolute truth.

The contractor has only one object in view—to get a profit. The administration, on the other hand, thinks only, and ought only to think, of paying according to the stipulations and conditions of the contract. If the contractor perceives that he is making no profit, he seeks by every means he can to increase the apparent value of the work; if the architect perceives that his anticipations are exceeded, he endeavours to bring the stipulations respecting prices to bear upon reducing the amount of the sums to be paid, as far as he can. The truth, or rather the real value of the work, lies generally between these two extremes. And the important point is to ascertain this value exactly. Only duly kept entries can determine it. The system indicated above is, in fact, a complete and satisfactory one only as regards the contractor. Those current entries, if fairly copied, even suppose they are regularly kept, do indeed record the expenses incurred by the contractor for materials, labour, and incidentals, but they do not prove that such amounts are lawfully due.

Let us take an example: A contractor for mason-work buys stone for a building and has it brought to the site. There can be no doubt, according to his entries, which only mention the deliveries of materials, that he has really got and paid for so many cubic yards of stone, mentioned in the books of entries aforesaid; but if he has a competent stone-dresser, the waste in preparing it for the work will be only one-tenth; whereas if the dresser is incompetent or careless, the waste may amount even to one-fifth. Now, what the architect ought to reckon for is the stone as most economically used. The account ought to be for this maximum of waste only; therefore, although the contractor's entries prove to the architect that he has really spent the amount entered, it does not prove that this amount is due to him, or that there is a fixed proportion to be deducted from this sum, which only represents a material in the rough. The architect's account is therefore distinct from the contractor's entry, and mentions only what is recognised by the clerks as actually used. The accounts from the architect's point of view are calculated from the entries he has made by his clerks, and which ought to be checked and examined by the contractor, so that no discussion may be raised when the accounts presented are scrutinised. And whereas the books of entries are easily kept, when weights, numbers, surfaces, and lengths are concerned, they require long and often difficult calculations when volumes are in question, that is to say, freestone actually used, and whose forms are complicated, very variable, and on which an allowance for waste is granted, which the contractor is naturally interested to represent as considerable.

There is a very simple method of avoiding these difficulties respecting the volumes to be charged as actually used, viz., that the architect should himself furnish dimensions for the dressed stone.

But generally he is occupied with questions of another kind, and when he gives a detail, he does not foresee in what way the stone-dressers will arrange the beds, joints, and sections of the stone which is to be used in this detail. Without speaking of

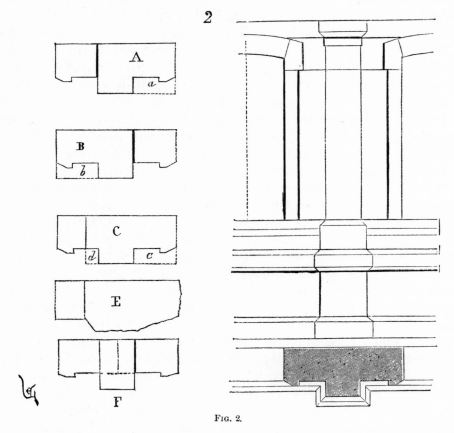

FIG. 2.

the inconveniences, both in regard to art and construction which result from such disdain on the part of architects for this matter of dressing, an opportunity is given in its management for the most scandalous abuses and useless expenses. And it is on negligence or carelessness respecting it on the part of architects in charge of great public works, that unprincipled contractors reckon for getting handsome profits, whose legitimacy it is impossible to contest.

Thus, supposing (figure 2) a detail given by the architect to

the stone-dresser, without indicating the section of the joints—
I select here one of the simplest examples. The stone-dresser
who understands and consults the interests of his employer will
take care not to arrange the joints of the pier as indicated at A
for one course, and at B for that above; he will place the joints
as marked at C. For both as regards the piece A and that marked
B, only the volumes *a* and *b* are allowed as waste on the stone
dressing, whereas volumes *c* and *d* are allowed for the piece C.
Now, supposing the stone-dresser to understand his business, he
will look out for a stone in the rough, E, canted or sloping at the
corners, and paid for to the person who supplies the stone at the
rate of its real volume, whereas the architect will reckon as waste
triangles that never existed, and will on his part pay the contractor for this piece so used as if it were a much larger volume
than it really was; and as the contractor is paid not only the
value of the stone supposed to be cut down to the form in
question, but also an allowance for labour in cutting it down,
the result is that he is credited with one amount for which no
equivalent has been received in materials, and with a second
amount for work that has not been done. The Renaissance
architects who were economical in regard to materials, would
have jointed these piers with pilasters as represented at F. They
would have built one course with the pilaster forming a header,
and the course above with an axis joint and a pilaster block,
following the dotted lines. In this way they would have avoided
waste of stone altogether.

In the above example the loss is trifling; but when architectural details are complex, when the square returns are
numerous, when the projections are very decided, the indifference which most official architects manifest respecting the
mode of jointing the stone, results in useless expense of considerable amount.

If, on the other hand, architects took the precaution, as was
done in the "barbarous" mediæval times, to give the dimensions
of the stones to be used and to indicate the jointing, they would
be able to avoid those needless expenses, and from their data
extract reliable entries, which would be a saving of time to the
clerks and insure good execution.

It is indeed true that for giving these data for stone-dressing
the architects must take account of the nature of the materials
(*i.e.* stone) supplied for the building.

Formerly the courses of hard stone used in Paris were of
inconsiderable width; Bagneux rock was not more than 20 inches
between the beds, and lias 10 to 12 inches. In our days hard
stone is brought from the quarries of Eastern France and Burgundy 24 to 32 inches high. It would be reasonable to subor-

dinate the members of the architecture to these dimensions,—within certain limits,—as the "barbarous" masters of the Middle Ages and those of the Renaissance subordinated the members of their architecture to the heights of courses at their disposal.

Our architects do not seem to pay any attention, for the most part, to such questions, and we have to bear the cost of their carelessness in this respect. Thus any one may see in public buildings recently erected stylobates (figure 3), whose beds are placed at J instead of at A. The consequence is that, as we said above, the stone that occupied the space of the sinkings at *a* and *c*, and the work of cutting it down, have been paid for, instead of only the chamfering *bb*. If this is repeated in lines of building extending for a length of five or ten furlongs, and several times in the height of the elevations, these needless expenses reach a considerable figure.

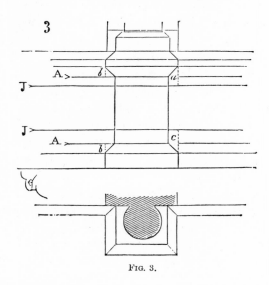

FIG. 3.

Our Boards of Works are generally very indifferent to considerations of this kind; what they look for are statements of accounts in good form, and duly balanced, so as to be perfectly regular in appearance.

What they are chiefly concerned with is to comply with the tastes of an all-powerful corporate body which has favours and places to dispose of. The employment of simple, reasonable, and economical methods has little interest for them.

And what has just been said respecting stone is applicable to all parts of the construction also. The superfluous weight of iron employed in most of our public buildings is more than any one could imagine, because architects will not calculate the strength which is absolutely necessary, and generally rely on the contractors, who are not likely to find fault with the excessive use of such materials. As iron is paid for by weight, and as the workmanship which constitutes a great part of the value of the result is not proportioned to the weight, it is always to the interest of the contractor to supply heavy pieces; and if the architect is not in a position to determine the maximum of weight necessary for a given part, if he has not become perfectly acquainted with the strains and pressures,—he will be disposed, for fear of compromising his own responsibility, to give ear to the representations of the contractor, who in his own interest is always inclined to exaggerate the weight required. And I would ask whether it is at Rome or Athens that architects are likely to gain the experience required for deciding in such a case?

When building is well managed, the entries will follow almost word for word the orders and details given. And if the boards of management were careful to protect the interests intrusted to them, rather than willing to submit to the dominant coterie or school; if, instead of meddling with questions of art with which they are not conversant, and which they are not capable of discussing, they would concern themselves with the interests with which alone they have to do, their attention would be chiefly occupied with an attentive examination of these details of building transactions.

They would then soon become aware of the amount of useless expense which they suffer to be incurred, though the books are kept with perfect regularity. They would perceive that the great point is, not to avoid paying for more than is done, but to prevent so much from being done,—paying for what is unnecessary; not to allow ignorance, indifference, or caprice to swell the budget of charges with items by which no good result is secured, and which scandalise sensible persons, without any advantage on the score of architecture, whose first law is to proportion the outlay to the object contemplated.

As soon as a board of management presiding over architectural operations, instead of being a mere registry-office for the laureates of the Institute (who are more and more completely alienated from those studies which our times require for producing good builders), and for the associates of the dominant body,—shall determine to take the place assigned it in the commonwealth, it will interest itself in the management of building works in a far different fashion from that which consists in making regulations which do not invariably harmonise with practical requirements. It will insist on knowing how the architects it employs deal with the contractors, and how their orders are given; if there are any who endeavour to simplify methods and appliances, it will take care to distinguish them; for it may be remarked that in case their artistic merit is always allied with a capability of directing the works, initiative power, a clear understanding between them and their subordinates, simplification of the methods adopted, and regularity in keeping accounts.

There is one more question of prime importance, which ought to have the serious attention of the boards of management on whom the direction of public works devolves, viz., that relating to the determination of a scale of prices.

Hitherto the administration of the city of Paris, as is the case with others, has been accustomed to fix a scale of prices for the current year. I do not doubt the care exercised in fixing these prices, but the proverb, " He who reckons without his host has to reckon twice," is applicable to the case in question. It is very strange that administrative bodies, however enlightened, should undertake to determine *unaided* the bases of their bargains with contractors. This method, which is none other than that of the *maximum* imposed on commerce, has been long and justly condemned by political economists. The materials supplied and worked up by a contractor are, in fact, a kind of commodity, quite as much as a loaf of sugar or a coat. It is now proposed to ask contractors to co-operate in determining price-lists in future; this is a step in advance. But would it not be more just to allow full liberty in such arrangements, and to fix price-lists not for the works to be undertaken during the whole year, but for each undertaking in particular? This would oblige architects to concern themselves with these important questions to which they pay no attention now; to inquire for themselves into the prices which such or such circumstances or class of work would reasonably suggest; and perhaps the obligation to study this matter would oblige them to modify plans to the advantage of their clients, which, for the most part, are prepared with a very imperfect knowledge of the means adapted to realise them.

An architect cannot see to everything himself: he must have an extraordinary faculty if he can; but he ought to be aware of all that is being done, and must have the various details present to his mind, so that he may give a clear answer to the questions that are continually being put to him.

Each of his clerks, if he employs several,—and he has generally more than is needful, because the board makes a point of providing as many posts as possible,—would have a definite part of the work intrusted to his supervision, and consequently a share in the responsibility. Each of the clerks, I say, would give a daily account of his section of the work, of the delays occasioned, and the difficulties that may have occurred, as also of the cases of faulty work, if any such have to be reported; and these observations should be consigned by him to a register kept for the purpose. The architect, if he observes at all, will soon have recognised the special aptitudes of each of these clerks, and he will employ them accordingly. The architect himself should be quite free in the choice of his clerks, for if he assumes a responsibility, the very least he can require is the liberty to choose the staff he thinks suitable. Instead of nominating those employed in such agencies, the administration should simply grant the architect such or such a sum in proportion to the extent and importance of the undertaking, leaving it to him to allot it in such a way as he thinks fit to the clerks he chooses. But it is clear to all that we have not advanced far enough for this, and that we should have to make many changes in our administrative régime before we can attain such a correct appreciation of responsibility in public works.

The clerks of works, of whom the number employed is too great, as remarked above—clerks who are insufficiently paid, because there are too many of them—do but little, and that little without much order or method. Consequently, it is often difficult to verify statements of accounts, and there are contests and disputed claims without end, as also an insufficient superintendence of the works. The clerks visit them in the afternoon, at nearly the same hour. The foremen are not long in observing this, and if they have any defective materials to smuggle in, or if they have any interest in neglecting a part of the work, they take care to manage it between six in the morning and noon.

The indifference, incapacity, and want of care and exactness which have been so fatal to us lately, and which have all but ruined us, have long been characteristic of our building operations. Is it to obviate the consequences of such a state of things that architects are accustomed to employ in the public buildings they erect, half as much more of materials than are needed? Is it to prevent the catastrophes which that want of supervision and precision might sometimes occasion, that they have recourse to this excess of strength? However this may be, there is room for reform. But to secure reform, the very first requirement is that we put aside questions of persons; whereas hitherto, both under a monarchical and a republican form of government, French administration makes questions of persons the chief consideration.

The management of building operations requires certain abilities which are not universally met with, and to which perhaps it would be well to call attention in that part of a course of instruction which should treat of administrative questions. It can be proved that architect's clerks employed in works adopt more or less the master's ways of doing things, because this stage in their course is almost the only training of the kind they get; as the

École des Beaux-Arts does not consider it necessary to indicate any rules of conduct in such matters. If the master is a man of sense, orderly, exact, and skilful, the clerks subject to his orders become habituated to such modes of being and acting, and derive advantage from them. But if that master is a blunderer, uncertain and unskilful in his relations with the contractors and the workmen, his staff of clerks soon fall into the same undesirable ways, having had no previous training to prevent them from doing so. And thus we see deplorable methods propagated from generation to generation.

Besides merit as an artist, an architect ought to possess qualifications of other kinds which are required in his relations with boards of management or clients, and with his subordinates. Although such qualifications pertain to general character, they may nevertheless be developed to a certain extent by education, in the case of those who do not originally possess them. I say by *education.* Along with the theoretical instruction which young architects require, certain rules of conduct should be taught them which are now left for experience, time, and circumstances to teach them, often at a considerable cost to themselves, or to the detriment of their clients. If architects formed a body, it would be the duty of this body to determine such rules of conduct; but we have explained above why the constitution of such an association is impossible under present circumstances: the elements being wanting, and our architects not being generally convinced of the necessity of maintaining independence of character before all things in presence of those influences with which they come in contact. We are so little accustomed to such independence that many confound that mental characteristic with an odious fault,—viz., the being constantly in a state of revolt against, or systematic opposition to, authority. And yet, if we would reflect and observe a little, we should see that really independent characters are those which give to such authority, whatever it may be, the surest guarantees; for the very reason, that having accepted a contract, a commission, a function, a charge quite freely, they have no other desire than that of acquitting themselves, with the greatest credit, of engagements to which they have freely consented, without any other thought than that of furthering the object they have to promote.

It is the weak point of arbitrary power that in a short time it has to fall back upon those who have no settled conviction,—however submissive they may be,—who have no independent opinion or individual energy,—and who cannot therefore be reckoned upon at a critical moment. When that power becomes enfeebled, the servility which is called devotion, abandons, if it does not even turn against it.

A building-yard is a government on a small scale; and we soon perceive, from the way in which its affairs are administered, and from the results produced, whether he who directs it is equal to his work or not. To know how to inspire all with the sentiment of duty by being himself the most energetic in performing it, is the chief obligation imposed on the architect. To do everything simply and without "fuss," but exactly at the right moment; to anticipate the course of things, and not to adopt any decision before having maturely reflected on it and listened to the criticisms of all who are interested in it—though having once adopted it, to maintain it unchangeably firmly and consistently,—such is the line of conduct whose prudence and wisdom will enable us to avoid grievous miscalculations. Always to be on good terms with subordinates, without lapsing into familiarity; to listen patiently to all remonstrances, but to examine everything one's-self; to be perfectly equitable in all cases of dispute; to take on one's-self the responsibility of agents directly subject to the orders of the chief, reprimanding them, however, in private with due severity, if they have committed an error; never to trust to mere affirmation, but to verify it by personal examination; to have a clear idea of one's plans, and to explain them intelligibly, and to remain true to one's word, will secure deference, respect, and confidence among employés, and attach men of good principle to one's interests—the only persons whose devotion is worth having; for it must not be supposed that in building-yards devotedness based on the esteem and respect felt for the principal can be dispensed with. Neither the satisfaction of material interests nor high salaries can take the place of support of this kind, which is necessary to the success of undertakings; the attachment which we think we secure by giving mere material advantages is as transient as these favours themselves can be. He who has pocketed his profit or his salary, has put into his purse, along with his money, the attachment he had shown, and it is ready to pass into other hands. But attachment to an equitable, firm, and benevolent character,—to one who knows how to appreciate and recognise the service that has been rendered, and to sustain those who have aided him in the accomplishment of a duty,—attachment of this kind may be permanently relied on; and though few men are capable of offering it and maintaining it, you may at least be assured that it will never fail you. Good discipline in a building-yard can be established only on the respect felt for the principal and his abilities and character. On the other hand, want of discipline results in imperfect execution and needless expenses, if in nothing worse; and it occasions embarrassments without end. Yet do our boards of administration seriously concern themselves with these conditions?

We have all observed architects whose habit it is never to give clear instructions; who are constantly agitated; who are out of temper with everybody and *à propos* of everything; rude to their inferiors, and obliging them to begin again and again a detail for whose execution they have not given a single precise order; who think they impose respect by blustering and the often groundless outbreaks of their imperious anger; who are incapable of examining and correcting a diagram, and who resent criticism because they are unable to discuss its validity,—assuming to determine everything by their own arbitrary will. . . . But see these very persons, who fancy that they inspire respect or fear in their subordinates by this ridiculous attitude, but whom the latter deceive as often as they can,—which by the by is not very difficult,—see these men in presence of the directors of administrative boards. They are supple as gloves, fair-spoken, and full of the most obsequious deference; promising everything, affirming everything which it is wished they should affirm, and saying *no* to everything for which a negative is desired. . . . And so they are looked upon with a favourable eye, and are sure to obtain advantages of all kinds. Other types among this favoured class of architects might be noticed. . . . But why should we enlarge? It is more to the purpose to remark, in conclusion, that to make an architect we must get in the first place what was formerly called "an honest man;" and we may safely assert that in nine cases out of ten such a character is associated with true talent, knowledge, and experience.

CONCLUSION.

THIS work makes no pretension to offer a complete course of theoretical or practical Architecture,—to give architects who are entering on the profession, or the public at large, a *résumé* of the knowledge requisite for those who devote themselves to the art of building. Written at intervals, these Lectures are only a kind of landmarks whose object it is to show the direction which architectural studies should take, if the question should ever come to be seriously discussed.

Owing to various circumstances an interval of more than twelve years has elapsed between the day when the first of these Lectures appeared and the issue of the last. But sentiments foreign to the art whose cause I have endeavoured, and shall, I trust, always endeavour, to defend, have never influenced my thoughts.

Begun in a spirit of perfect independence, this work is concluded in the same disposition of mind, and with the deepest conviction that art can be developed and maintained at a superior level only by liberty united with an incessant study of the novel conditions which science is from time to time imposing on our civilisation.

During the interval referred to, some inadequate endeavours have been made to restore to architectural studies a more serious and liberal direction; and painful events have subjected our country to the severest trials. All are convinced that most strenuous efforts are necessary to replace France in the position it ought to occupy in Europe, if only in the interest of civilisation,—to say nothing of its own advantage. Hitherto we are not *able* to say whether the salutary reaction in favour of studies whose extreme importance is recognised by all will become a practical as well as a theoretical one; and in fact as scarcely a year has elapsed since the terrible shocks to which the country has been subjected, we can scarcely expect it to have already regained its *sang-froid* and tranquil deportment. But it is for men of principle to endeavour to make some advance every day, and to restore intellectual as well as material order. It is something to have recognised numerous defects in our system of instruction, but this does not amount to the attainment of a satisfactory system; and from the desire to possess to actual possession there is a considerable step. It is this step which we should take without delay. Still, it is well to know what this really imports.

Our temperament, as Frenchmen, inclines us to pass rapidly from one extreme to the other; and just as we were disposed under the late régime to regard everything as for the best in the intellectual domain of France; just as we gave way to an infatuation which the wisest did not succeed in shaking off, so now we are disposed to an excessive disparagement of our advantages, knowledge, and social condition. But let us endeavour to be just to ourselves, and not discourage minds which are only too easily disheartened, by exaggerating the amount of effort we have to make. We thought too much of ourselves formerly, there is no doubt; but there would be quite as much danger to the future of our country in the contrary extreme. Our misfortunes have not deprived us of our intellectual and moral advantages; they have only discovered to ourselves defects which our country alone of all European nations was unwilling to recognise.

The last word of Septimus Severus when dying is in all men's mouths,—"*Laboremus.*" It is a noble word; let us proceed to translate it into action.

But there are two methods of working: there is methodical work,—that which supposes persistency, examination, and observation; and there is also work of a diffuse, impulsive, unproductive order, and which can be compared with nothing so well as the motion of a squirrel in a rotating cage. The agitation in which the country has been plunged has moreover prevented it from distinguishing that kind of labour which could alone deliver it from its depression, and promise it a better future.

If the terrible shock which France has just experienced did not serve as a warning; if the country believed—whatever form of government it may give itself—that it could continue to live as it had done, its part among European States would be already played out.

Many persons, while regretting our departed prosperity and diminished glory, fondly imagine that to restore our prosperity and recover our time-honoured reputation, it would suffice to replace the label "Empire" or "Monarchy" on our country's front. . . . Grievous delusion! . . . No such inscription can conceal that of which we have been the witnesses, or deliver us from those millions of enemies whom a crafty and fore-sighted policy has long been arousing against French intellect and its influence.

Only one way of deliverance remains to us,—only one method of inflicting that retaliation which some think so easy, viz., a calm, persevering, sustained, and orderly effort, organised by individual enterprise in all departments,—politics, manufactures, commerce, agriculture, finances, war, science, arts, and literature.

We must yield to the conviction that our means of instruction are insufficient, since they have allowed us to be surpassed by those envious neighbours, with their slow though crafty intelligence, whom, in our simplicity, we formerly regarded only as rivals.

Patriotic sentiment is enfeebled among us—let us hope that it is not extinct; education alone can develop it once more, as it did among our neighbours on the other side the Rhine, after the wars at the beginning of the century. Not that I think it commendable to make the diffusion of knowledge among a people the means of exciting hateful passions against those neighbours by falsifying history or the circumstances of our own time. Sooner or later such a course is injurious to those who adopt it; moreover, I do not think it can even temporarily succeed among a people whose discernment is naturally acute; on the contrary, I believe that in everything honesty is the best policy,—in statesmanship as well as in the ordinary affairs of life; considering that it is not necessary to be either a dupe or an ignoramus in order to be honest. An education, liberal in the most comprehensive sense, would remove a great many prejudices which now divide us. And I do not intend by this merely primary education, but the higher teaching, which among ourselves has remained narrow and exclusive, and tends rather to limit men's intellects than to widen their views in every direction. In architecture, for example, the *École des Beaux-Arts* gives expression only to limited formulas, and has ceased to hold even beliefs; its influence over the minds of its pupils is derived simply from the prizes it offers and the places for which it bids them hope as the result of gaining those prizes. Far from seeking to develop *individuality*, it suppresses it as far as possible, and declares open war against *originality*. Independence and the spirit of inquiry are its dread.

The *Académie des Beaux-Arts* assumes infallibility like the Church of Rome, and excommunicates those who refuse to admit it. And,—which is a matter of serious moment,—the Government makes itself the executor of its decrees, through indifference quite as much as weakness.

There is in my view only one means of conquering this *vis inertiæ* and eliciting a real development of æsthetic studies; and that is the cessation of State interference with matters of art, and the limiting of its patronage to the recompence of results;

to the exclusion of the plan of holding forth hopes of place and preferment.

Artists, it will be objected, are incapable of providing themselves with a government, and consequently of providing the means of instruction. They are certainly incapable of doing so, but it is because for the last three centuries there has been an assumption on the part of others of the right to govern them. But should we endeavour to abandon this régime? In the present state of things, and in consequence of that long tutelage, every artist looks at the interest of his fellow-artists through the medium of his own. As for the interest of art itself, or of that which pertains to it, and its development and glory, each one regards it as bound up with his individuality as an artist. Cease to undertake to arbitrate between these novel interests, whether of individuals or coteries; do not cherish the vain hope of gaining any advantage from commissions, committees, and associations; abandon a system of protection which only protects mediocrity.

When the first agitation has passed away, and when the minds of our countrymen, disturbed by such violent shocks, are somewhat tranquillised, we shall see the level restored. Honourable and elevated intellects,—by their very nature disposed to hold aloof from partisan considerations, and the wearisome commonplaces of studios,—compelled to quit their position of neutrality, will ultimately disentangle what is true and important in art from that chaos which protection only serves to prolong.

Leaving aside personal considerations, whatever the school to which they belong, artists of real worth will take their stand by wide and liberal ideas.

Those among them who love their art will be willing to sacrifice questions of secondary importance in order to save its interests.

I do not indeed flatter myself that among those exalted personages whose position is secured, and who, through a natural instinct of self-preservation, are little disposed to hold the ladder on which rising talent may ascend, there will be many such conversions. I have never put much faith in "*Nights of the Fourth of August.*"[1] But our younger men will be roused to energy when the enervating allurements of prizes, the gaining of which they are led to believe will insure their fortune, shall have been removed; when they are convinced that nothing but persistent study and labour will secure them a distinction which cannot be purchased by those chamber triumphs which are too often obtained by methods with which art has no concern. "Do

[1] The 4th of August 1789, when in the National Assembly the Viscount de Noailles, the Duke de Châtelet, and others of the nobility, proposed the abolition of privileges.— *Tr.*

not abandon artists to their own guidance," say those exalted personages who are honestly convinced that art cannot dispense with the guardianship of the State. "They are incapable of directing the interests of art; it would be the ruin of the French School!" But surely we must suppose art in our days to have a very frail existence if we can suppose it crushed by the abolition, for example, of the *Direction des Beaux-Arts*. What! art in France? in the nineteenth century?—that art whose vitality appears everywhere, which is displayed in our manufactures, our habits and customs, our dwellings, our dress—that art which has become an unconscious need, so to speak, of the inhabitants of our towns,—can this art be dependent on a *bureau?* Abolish that . . . and art in France ceases to exist, and we suddenly fall back into barbarism!

No; such is not the real order of cause and effect, and it is high time we referred such matters to a higher source. Art is our own; it depends on ourselves, and is not at the mercy of a *mandarinate* or a board of administration. I am inclined to think that, on the contrary, art would be the gainer if artists were responsible for consulting their own interests—if necessity obliged them to occupy themselves with their own affairs, and if they had a feeling of collective obligation. At all times there have been short-sighted persons who have insisted on the existence of precipices in every domain extending beyond their own sphere of vision. The exercise of liberty and individual enterprise necessitates results which no human prudence can foresee.

The duty of the State as regards the teaching of the arts in general, and of architecture in particular, is to open museums and galleries of art, arranged so as to promote study, and libraries; to endow courses of lectures of a superior order; and to facilitate instruction by all available means.

The encouragement it gives should be limited to selecting the best among the productions offered, paying well for them, and exhibiting them as models to be copied; and making the designs of public buildings to be erected subjects of competition, obliging the competitors to give a real proof of their powers, which should be submitted to a jury, as impartial as possible,— as remarked above.

With these exceptions, let it leave the care of forming capable men to private enterprise, and select from among the latter as the result of trial, not choosing the favourites of a coterie, or those who have passed tedious hours in the ante-chambers of board-rooms.

Above all, let the State not attempt to discriminate between high and inferior art. That is not its concern; it is no more capable of deciding in such matters than of ascertaining whether its citizens are more or less profoundly devout, or whether they are devout at all. If the State requires a public functionary, it seeks for, or ought to seek for, an honest and capable man; it does not ask him whether he has performed his religious duties; and in the same way, if it wants an architect it should not take upon itself the responsibility of educating, instructing, and providing for him up to the moment when it thinks it will be ready to employ him; for if in spite of all this the artist is an incompetent man, it has only itself to blame for such incompetency on the part of one whom it has, so to speak, fashioned for itself.

The duty of the State consists in choosing capable men; it is not its business to train them. If it should chance to indulge this ambition, it establishes *mandarinates*,—a corps of official talent,—and deprives itself of the services of the highest intellects, which in art, as in science, are developed by a long series of individual efforts, and by the exploring of untried paths.

Intellects of the highest order are produced and matured only by liberty. To secure their position they require neither *organisation* nor *direction*, for it is they themselves that organise and direct.

To place no obstacle in the way of their development,—to give them all the elements that constitute an education, while leaving it to them to choose what they can best assimilate,—is the duty of the State. To go further than this is to insure the predominance of mediocrity. History sufficiently indicates the conditions favourable to the development of architecture, as of other branches of art. But history does not exhibit the development of the arts as at any epoch a result of State intervention or official regulation. It teaches us, on the contrary, that art has never reached an elevated position except as the result of the most absolute freedom for those who cultivated it. It shows us moreover that the arts, and architecture in particular, have culminated during periods of scientific development. Architecture is the sister of Science; the former undergoes modifications and advances hand in hand with the latter, and reaches its point of greatest splendour when Science itself has just passed a glorious stage in its career. But we must make this distinction between Science and Art; Science suffers no eclipses. What it has acquired by means of observation, analysis, and logical deductions, is a permanent gain, and is, as it were, incorruptible. It is not so with that art which is nearest of kin to science, viz. architecture. Architecture, whose principles are based more directly than any other art on Science, may disregard this support to such a degree as to be entirely unconscious of its value, and so decline. And it can only recover itself by immersion in the vivifying fount of science. Facts prove the correctness of this remark. Without going further back than the Hellenic epoch, we see that the Parthenon, that singularly noble specimen of Doric architecture, was built in accordance with arithmetical laws very delicately applied.[1] Though I never enjoyed the privilege of conversing with the architect of the Parthenon, I am sure that he would have been much surprised if he heard it asserted that architecture can dispense with scientific laws. He would have replied by simply producing the plans and elevations of his own *chef-d'œuvre*, the Parthenon, where all the members present a mutual correspondence, which is certainly not the result of chance or mere fancy. And it is not less certain that although arithmetic and geometry were not neglected by the successors of Ictinus, the buildings they erected were inferior to his. Ictinus possessed the power of completely applying the knowledge he had acquired to the art he professed; and it cannot be maintained that without the knowledge thus acquired he would have been able to produce the work which we still so much admire, and which so completely satisfies the eye by the perfect harmony of the whole.

Roman art, on the other hand, exhibits remarkable grandeur through the exact application of the knowledge then acquired to architecture. The knowledge in question was of a practical order, and due rather to the observation of facts than to the theoretical speculations in which the Greeks indulged; the genuine Roman erections are therefore strongly impressed with practical discernment, and the attentive observation of material laws of stability and cohesion. It is to the exactness of such observations that Roman architecture owes its chief merits; the profound impression it produces is due to this, and not to those borrowed decorative features which often exhibit a very vulgar character, especially in comparison with Greek work. We have then an independent architecture in that of the Romans,—one which deserves the name of art because it also is based on a certain phase in the development of positive science. The knowledge acquired was not absolutely lost, even under the later Emperors; though architecture allowed those principles to be neglected which had raised it to such a pitch of grandeur during the first century of our era.

Then came the long period of barbarism which followed the extinction of the Empire of the West. It is not till the beginning of the twelfth century that we see architecture rising again

[1] Consult on this point the works of MM. Aurès and Choisy, engineers, who have ascertained, with a very high degree of probability, the purely geometrical laws of numbers and forms according to which the architect Ictinus erected this incomparable masterpiece. It reflects somewhat on our profession that these researches and discoveries are due to engineers, while none of those architects who have passed months at Athens in measuring the Parthenon had dreamed of comprehending the laws of its construction, and only brought away more or less faithful pictures of it. This alone shows how essentially defective is the official instruction given to our architects.

and endeavouring to relinquish the last modified reminiscences of Roman traditions. The revival of architecture in the West, towards the middle of the twelfth century, exactly coincides with the great intellectual movement of that period in Literature, Science, and Philosophy.

It was at the beginning of the thirteenth century that attention was turned towards physical and mathematical science; and architecture immediately joined in the movement, and completely altered the traditional forms which it had hitherto retained.

The same phenomenon may be observed in the sixteenth century; it was by taking advantage of the scientific progress of that brilliant epoch that architecture modified the superannuated forms of the period called Gothic.

But few ages can compete with our own in the glory of its scientific achievements. Do our architects, like their predecessors, eagerly avail themselves of this source of æsthetic renovation? No; they prefer to ignore the close connection of science with art, and to give us public buildings of a hybrid style, more or less influenced by the debased architecture of the last two centuries. Well, such being the case,—I say again in conclusion,—if they thus persist in rejecting that light, and in refusing that aid which science would gladly give them, the function of the architect is obsolete; while that of the engineer is commencing,—that of men really devoted to construction, and who will make purely scientific knowledge their starting-point to constitute an art deduced from that knowledge and from the requirements of the times.

THE END.

INDEX.

INDEX.

A.

ABOU Sembil, Egyptian statues at, II. 238.

Académie des Beaux-Arts, II. 140 *et seq.;* the natural exponent of the system of Louis XIV., II. 141.; present tendency of its efforts, II. 144.; exposure of its working, 144.; necessity of its separation from the State, II. 147.; historical sketch of, II. 148.; present position of, in relation to the State, II. 151 *et seq.;* advantages of disconnexion with the State, II. 158, 163, 433.; damping influence of, on students, II. 159.

Æschylus, " Persæ " of, I. 74.

Agen, country-houses of, II. 360.

Agrigentum, an example of careful selection and improvement of natural site by the Greeks, I. 68.; basilica of, *illustrated,* I. 212.; temple of Juno Lucina at, *illustrated,* I. 254.; temple of Concord at, proportions of, *illustrated,* I. 394.

Agrippa, buildings erected by, I. 112.; Rotunda of, *see* Pantheon.

Ajunta, temple of, stone imitation of timber construction, *illustrated,* I. 40.

Albano, villa, I. 168.

Alberti, Leon Batista (1404—1472), I. 239.

Alhambra, the, similarity to Roman construction, I. 432.

Amiens, cathedral of, proportions of, *illustrated,* I. 403.; sculpture in, II. 226, 230.

Amphitheatre, Roman, its Etruscan origin, I. 131.; typical arrangement of, *illustrated,* I. 132 *et seq.*

Ancy-le-Franc, château de, I. 368.

Anet, château d', example of tendency toward antique structure in 17th century, I. 376.

Angles, treatment of, by the Greeks, *illustrated,* I. 291.; treatment of, by secular Gothic school, *illustrated,* I. 294.

Antoninus Pius, temple of (now the custom-house at Rome), example of want of harmony between the structure and the requirements, I. 373.

Apollodorus of Damascus (architect), basilica of, I. 154.; example of magnificence of size and materials, I. 154.

Apophyge, abandonment of, in 12th century, *illustrated,* I. 313.

Appius Claudius, aqueduct of, I. 120.

Arab architecture, resemblance of houses to those of ancient Rome, I. 168.; introduction of Greek art through the Nestorians, I. 193, 227.; geometry in, I. 227.; a Greek modification of Persian art, I. 428. *See also* Persian Architecture.

Arch, Etruscan origin of the Roman, I. 72.; extradossed and not extra-dossed, *illustrated*, I. 186.; under entablature in debased Roman art, *illustrated*, I. 212.; early Byzantine example of, built directly on columns, *illustrated*, I. 212.; at Solomon's temple, date discussed, I. 218.; under lintels, I. 93.; over lintels, I. 226.; iron and masonry, method of counter-thrust, *illustrated*, II. 60, 76. *See also* Ogive, Vaulting.

Arches, triumphal Roman, proportions of, *illustrated*, I. 397 *et seq.;* sculpture in, II. 219.

Archæology, the province of, in architecture, I. 139, 158, 486.

Architect (modern), position of, toward his client, II. 248, 254, 267.; relations toward contractors, II. 412.; necessary practical qualifications of, II. 428.

Areopagus of Athens, ancient mud roof of, I. 36.

Arles, Arena of, example of typical Roman amphitheatre, I. 130.; example of Roman concentric arch, II. 8.

Art, defined, I. 11 *et seq.;* stronger effect on men in primitive form, I. 12.; independent of degree of civilisation, I. 13 *et seq.;* independent of quality of execution, I. 14.; independent of political or scientific state of a nation, I. 14.; contrasted with utilitarian improvement, I. 15.; emotions excited by, analysed, I. 18.; imagination is its source and imitation of nature its means of expression, I. 25.; develops itself when riveted to manners and customs of a nation, and declines when severed from them, I. 30.; creative power in, exhibited by all the early civilisations, I. 30.; gesture in, an index of grade of civilisation, I. 31.; style the substitute for gesture in high state of civilisations, I. 32.; with Greeks is sovereign, I. 76.; with Romans subservient to interest of State, I. 76.; in middle ages is isolated from surrounding circumstances, I. 76.; in middle ages the only refuge of liberty advancing because autonomous, I. 78.; sentiment in, art, I. 82.; archæology and art, I. 139, 158, 486.; danger of sophistry in art, I. 143.; real basis of opinion in art must be something stronger than amateur criticism, I. 144.; statics in, I. 144.; invariable principles of, rather than the forms, should be taught, I. 146.; influence of Christianity on art, I. 171.; absence of invention in art, I. 172; imagination in art, I. 173.; definition of *style* in art, I. 177 *et seq.;* definition of mannerism, I. 188.; influence of geometry on, I. 227.; influence of Reformation on, I. 241.; hybrid nature of modern art, I. 244; alliance between sculpture, painting, and architecture in ancient times, I. 250.; cause of the disruption between them, I. 250.; oriental respect for art, I. 251.; sincerity essential to style in art, I. 282, 304.; Aryan influence

C.

E.

U.

V.

LIST OF WOODCUTS.

Volume I.

Volume II.